D0149130

THE RISE OF THE CONSERVATIVE LEGAL MOVEMENT

PRINCETON STUDIES IN AMERICAN POLITICS:
HISTORICAL, INTERNATIONAL, AND COMPARATIVE PERSPECTIVES

Series Editors
Ira Katznelson, Martin Shefter, Theda Skocpol

THE RISE OF THE CONSERVATIVE LEGAL MOVEMENT

THE BATTLE FOR
CONTROL OF THE LAW

Steven M. Teles

PRINCETON UNIVERSITY PRESS   PRINCETON AND OXFORD

Library of Congress Cataloging-in-Publication Data

Teles, Steven Michael.
The rise of the conservative legal movement : the battle for control of the law / Steven M. Teles.
p.   cm. — (Princeton studies in American politics : historical, international, and comparative perspectives)
Includes bibliographical references and index.
ISBN 978-0-691-12208-3 (cloth : alk. paper)
1. Law—Political aspects—United States. 2. Law—Economic aspects—United States. 3. Justice, Administration of—United States. 4. Conservatism—United States. 5. Liberalism—United States. I. Title.
KF385.T45   2008
340′.11—dc22   2007040836

British Library Cataloging-in-Publication Data is available

This book has been composed in Sabon

Printed on acid-free paper. ∞

press.princeton.edu

Printed in the United States of America

10 9 8 7 6 5 4 3 2

For FSA, whose faith and patience, never wavering, sustained me.

Contents

Acknowledgments

IN WRITING THIS BOOK, I have acquired more than the usual authorial debts. My parents were this book's earliest and most important patrons. They lavishly invested in my human capital and provided a vital in-kind subsidy to the research process—if they lived outside the Washington Beltway, I could not have afforded my many research trips to D.C.

I drafted chapters 3 and 7 while a fellow at Princeton University's James Madison Program, and I owe a special debt to Professor Robert George, an organizational entrepreneur of unusual skill as well as a true intellectual. Yale University provided me a wonderful home for the last year and a half of writing this book. I would like to thank Yale's Alan Gerber, whose Center for the Study of American Politics provided me a fellowship in 2005–6 (which was partially devoted to this project), and Dan Kahan, who as Associate Dean helped arrange for me to teach at the Law School in the fall of 2006. The Achiles and Bodman Foundation provided a very generous—and timely—grant for the 2003–4 academic year that helped fund my nonsabbatical leave, and the Earhart Foundation provided summer and research support for the project. I would never have completed this book without this support.

I also owe a debt to my many sources within the conservative movement. Pride of place goes to Eugene Meyer of the Federalist Society, who provided my first real breakthrough in obtaining internal organizational documents. Gene was under no obligation whatsoever to provide me the remarkable access that he did—I still recall being pointed to the file cabinet, in a cramped closet in the Society's offices, and being told that it was mine to rummage through. Thanks are also due to Steven Calabresi, David McIntosh, Lee Liberman Otis, and Gary Lawson, who subjected themselves to interviews, follow-ups, and reading an early draft of chapter 5. Their willingness to trust someone who was clearly not "on the team" is to be commended.

In the area of public interest law, my debts are even wider. Clint Bolick, Chip Mellor, Terry Pell, Michael Greve, Jim Moody, David Kennedy, and Michael McDonald, among others, shared their time, and, in most cases, were willing to talk to me multiple times and read draft chapters, in order to help me get the complicated stories of the organizations straight. I was repeatedly struck by their candor, even to the point that, more than once, I penned e-mails reminding them that they were on the record. Special recognition must be given to Michael Greve, who replied to dozens of e-mails, and read drafts of the chapters on public interest law and the

Federalist Society. In addition, in one especially important case, his encouragement to look beyond the public record helped me to avoid a particularly spectacular case of historical oversight.

My chapters on law and economics would have been much poorer without the help of numerous scholars in the field. Robert Cooter, Christine Jolls, Robert Ellickson, Steven Shavell, Mitch Polinsky, Roberta Romano, Jerry Mashaw, Todd Zywicki, Michael Graetz, and others read chapters 4 and 6, providing terribly useful suggestions as well as, in some cases, their firsthand recollections. My greatest debt is to Henry Manne, who dug out, from numerous sources, much of the documentary material that chapters 4 and 6 are based upon. Henry also interrupted his otherwise idyllic life in Naples, Florida, for a number of very long interviews, and was willing to respond to dozens of e-mail requests for information. Henry truly went above and beyond the call of duty.

At the Olin Foundation, Jim Piereson and Cary Hemphill were much more cooperative than they had any obligation to be. They provided me uncensored access—at a time when they were busy putting the foundation out of business—to the grant officer reports, grant proposals, and the minutes of the Olin Foundation, a gold mine on the history of the Foundation and the conservative movement overall. The account of the movement's history in these pages would be much the poorer without their willingness to trust a nosy political scientist.

Much of chapter 2 would have been impossible were it not for the Ford Foundation's remarkably open archives, and the help of two wonderful archivists, Idelle Nissila and Jonathan Green. Special thanks go to Thomas Hilbink, who generously gave me access to his remarkable interview with Sanford Jaffe. The story in chapter 2 would not have been the same without it. I was also blessed with Sandy's firsthand recollections during a visit to New Haven.

I am especially indebted to the many scholars who read parts or all of the manuscript. Mike McCann, Robert Gordon, Jacob Hacker, Jack Balkin, Peter Skerry, Reva Siegel, Mark Blyth, Adam Sheingate, Stuart Chinn, Robert Mickey, Chuck Epp, Keith Whittington, Art Ward, Sandy Levinson, Stephen Skowronek, Shep Melnick, Bart Sparrow, David Fontana, Dan Ernst, Ilya Somin, Jack Goldstone, David Bernstein, Mark Tushnet, Brian Glenn, and Ken Kersch all provided incisive comments on the manuscript at various stages. Martha Derthick and Larry Mead are owed special notice. Throughout my career they have read everything I sent them, providing a combination of sharp commentary and credible support. Oliver Houck of Tulane University Law School saved me when I had all but given up on ever finding a copy of the Horowitz Report. Special thanks are due to Paul Pierson, who read a great deal of this book, but even more valuably reminded me constantly that it had to be finished.

One final, largely silent, debt must be acknowledged. This book began as a comparative study of Social Security privatization. Although I eventually switched cases, my original question remained the same: what explained conservative strategies for undermining the modern liberal activist state? Much of my emphasis on organizational entrepreneurship and long-term strategy came out of a series of interviews with the Heritage Foundation's Stuart Butler. I doubt this book would have been possible were it not for Stuart, who taught me so much.

A deep debt of gratitude is owed to the research assistants who did work on the book. At Brandeis, Sam Dewey, Dan Kenney, Melissa Bass, and Sarah Staszak did excellent work for me. I am especially indebted to Melissa, now a professor at the University of Puget Sound, who helped get my writing in shape on criminally short notice. At Yale, my research needs increased considerably, and I was very lucky to have the assistance of the university's remarkable students. Grace Leslie did heroic work on chapter 2, Judy Coleman gets credit for much of the book's readability, Jonathan Dach did a magnificent job with the final copyediting, Sophie Lee scrutinized all the historical chapters and saved me from innumerable errors, and Sarah Egan introduced me to a great deal of work on social movements. The excruciating final revisions of the book were supervised by Judith Miller. It would be impossible to say enough about Judith's intelligence, organization, and sharp editorial skills, but it must suffice to record for posterity that (despite her distaste for sporting metaphors) she dragged me across the finish line.

Finally, Chuck Myers at Princeton University Press was an exceptional editor. In an age in which so many presses simply produce books rather than edit them, Chuck actually read, with great care, the entire manuscript and provided simple, elegant solutions for problems that otherwise would have made this a much less readable and coherent book. I would also like to state my appreciation for the generous and helpful comments of the three reviewers that PUP solicited for the book.

What is good in this volume is due to the candor of those willing to share their memories, their files, and their wisdom. The failures are mine alone.

THE RISE OF THE CONSERVATIVE LEGAL MOVEMENT

Introduction

REFLECTING ON RICHARD NIXON'S sweeping victory over George McGovern in the 1972 presidential election, the young White House aide Patrick Buchanan told the president that, even though liberalism was still dominant in institutions such as the media, "the Supreme Court is another story. The president has all but recaptured the institution from the Left; his four appointments have halted much of its social experimentation; and the next four years should see this second branch of government become an ally and defender of the values and principles in which the President and his constituency believe."[1] Buchanan's hopes, and those of the conservative movement, would soon be proven sorely misplaced, as the Burger Court revealed itself to be the "counter-revolution that wasn't."[2]

Flash forward to 2005. President Bush has nominated one of his closest advisers, Harriet Miers, to replace Sandra Day O'Connor on the Supreme Court. The reaction from the conservative legal establishment is immediate, harsh, and pointed. William Kristol, editor of the *Weekly Standard*, groaned that the nomination left him "disappointed, depressed and demoralized."[3] Todd Zywicki, professor of law at George Mason University Law School, summed up the mood of many in the conservative legal movement when he opined in the *Legal Times* that

> inspired by thinkers such as Scalia, Thomas, Robert Bork, and Richard Posner, and nurtured by groups such as the Federalist Society and the Institute for Justice, the conservative legal movement in America has grown in confidence and competence, building a deep farm team of superbly qualified and talented circuit court judges primed for this moment. The prevailing liberalism of the contemporary legal culture was on the ropes and primed for a knockout—only to have the president let it get off the canvas and survive this round.[4]

Within weeks of Kristol's and Zywicki's laments, Miers's nomination was withdrawn and replaced with that of Samuel Alito, whose connections to the conservative legal movement were so strong that they became a central topic in his confirmation hearings.

The contrast between these two vignettes is telling. The inability of Nixon's four appointees to transform the Supreme Court taught conservatives that electoral success was not enough, in and of itself, to produce legal change: conservatives' failure in the Court reflected a deep imbalance between their forces at the elite level and those of their liberal counterparts. A generation later, the conservative legal elite—a group that did not, in any meaningful sense, exist in the early 1970s—led the charge against the president's nominee and pushed the president to appoint one of their own. This book will explain how the conservative legal movement, outsmarted and undermanned in the 1970s, became the sophisticated and deeply organized network of today.

By the time of Buchanan's memo, conservatives were well on their way to capturing the Republican Party and turning it into a powerful, movement-based vote-getting machine, capable of prevailing in mobilization-heavy contests like the battle over the Equal Rights Amendment.[5] Grassroots liberalism, by contrast, was shrinking, while its forces at the elite level—in the professions, universities, the media, and Washington-based public interest organizations—were surging.[6] These new liberal elites, and the Democratic Party of which they were an increasingly central part, were of little use at election time. Yet conservatives like Buchanan would find themselves repeatedly frustrated by the liberals' success at limiting the impact of conservative electoral power on the law.

Although conventional wisdom holds that the Republican coalition was held together by anticommunism and opposition to taxes, just as important were the specter of "activist judges" and the liberal organizational network that supported them. Businesses hated the courts for legitimizing and accelerating the expansion of the federal regulatory state. Western farmers, ranchers, and extractive industries detested them for limiting their use of federal lands. Southerners continued to resent their part in dismantling segregation. Northern ethnic refugees from the Democratic Party seethed at the "forced busing" mandated by judges like Massachusetts's Arthur Garrity. Religious conservatives were enraged by the Supreme Court's constitutional sanctioning of abortion and its restrictions on school prayer. While their particular grievances differed, the conservative coalition was drawn together by a shared opposition to liberal judges, professors, and public interest lawyers and by a unified call for "strict constructionism" and "judicial restraint."

What conservatives in the early 1970s only dimly recognized was that reversing liberal accomplishments in the law was more strategically problematic than other conservative goals, such as reducing taxes and stiffening the American response to the Soviet Union. While relatively little elite mobilization was necessary to translate electoral victories into policy outcomes in these areas, in the law conservatives faced liberal opponents with a much more impressive set of resources: elite law schools, a large chunk of the organized bar, a vast network of public interest lawyers, and the still-powerful liberal understanding of rights. If they were to have any chance of influencing the development of the law, conservatives would have to compete directly with liberals at the level of organizational, and not simply electoral, mobilization.

Spurred by their overlapping grievances, informed by an increasingly sophisticated knowledge of how to produce legal change, and coordinated by a strategically shrewd group of patrons, conservatives began investing in a broad range of activities designed to reverse their elite-level organizational weaknesses. While similar kinds of organizational development were happening in other domains where conservatives faced liberal entrenchment, in no other area was the process of strategic investment as prolonged, ambitious, complicated, and successful as in the law.[7] This book is an effort to explain the legal regime that conservatives faced, how they responded to it, and what accounts for the timing and relative success of their response.

My explanation for the character of conservative countermobilization in the law combines multiple traditions in the social sciences. From historical institutionalism, I draw a focus on how the choices of social and political movements are decisively influenced by the nature of the regime they seek to dislodge. I borrow insights from organizational theory to explain the *internal* challenges that insurgents face and how these can decisively shape their ability to devise optimal competitive responses to entrenchment. Finally, from the sociology of knowledge and the professions and the political science study of the policy process, I draw lessons on how the status quo is protected by constructions of expertise, conventional wisdom, and prestige.

My choice of these tools does not mean that I ignore the importance of electoral power or the intrinsic merits of ideas. Against the trend in political science studies of law, however, I argue in chapter 1 that changes in the form of political competition over the past half-century, especially the increasing importance of ideas and professional power, have led to a decline in the power of elections to cause comprehensive change, especially in highly entrenched political domains. As a consequence of this shift, the rhythm of large-scale political transformations in highly insulated policy and institutional domains, such as the law, is increasingly determined by nonelectoral mobilization. Change in these domains is generated by the ability of insurgents to develop strategies appropriate to specific forms of entrenchment, and to generate organizations capable of effectively implementing those strategies. The "problem solving" character of countermobilization, therefore, requires combining a structural focus on inherited constraints with close attention to the problem-solving efforts of political agents.

I take seriously the argument that conservatives have found greater success in the law because their ideas—such as the negative side-effects of state planning and regulation—were shown over time to be superior to those of their liberal counterparts. My reconstruction of the history of the conservative legal movement shows, however, that ideas do not develop in a vacuum. Ideas need networks through which they can be shared and nurtured, organizations to connect them to problems and to diffuse them to political actors, and patrons to provide resources for these supporting conditions. Of even greater significance, the market for ideas is one in which incumbents have substantial resources with which to frustrate the challenges of competitors, regardless of how compelling their ideas are. In short, while there is a "market" for ideas, it is one that is institutionally sticky and requires entrepreneurial activity to give it life. For this reason, intellectual history is necessary but not sufficient.

Given my focus on the structural constraints facing countermobilizers, it is essential to place the mobilization of legal conservatives in the context of the regime they opposed. Chapter 2 sets the stage for the examination of conservative mobilization that is to come by tracing out the development of the liberal legal regime, identifying the sources of its strength and durability, and thus the strategic challenges that it presented to conservative countermobilizers. This framing also reveals that legal liberals faced some of the same challenges that their conservative successors confronted a generation later.

Chapters 3 through 7 shift the analysis to the primary subject of the book, the conservative legal movement.[8] Chapters 3 and 4 examine the earliest organizational response to the rise of legal liberalism. The "first generation" of conservative public interest law firms, driven primarily by locally rooted, business-supported firms, was largely unsuccessful, and led the conservative movement to reconsider its approach to legal change. By contrast, the intellectual school known as "law and economics," both at the University of Chicago and in the programs of Henry Manne's Law and Economics Center, was remarkably successful. The differing outcomes of these two efforts at organizational countermobilization demonstrate that the movement's success was not simply determined by the availability of financial resources, the perception of threat, or the opportunities provided by electoral victories, but was critically shaped by the decision-making of organizational entrepreneurs.

Chapters 5 through 7 take the story into the 1980s and 1990s. Chapter 5 examines the Federalist Society, showing how a group of network entrepreneurs built a formidable organization to establish a conservative presence in the nation's law schools and created the social capital upon which the movement's intellectual and political entrepreneurs would draw. In chapter 6, I pick up the story begun in chapter 4, focusing on the Olin Foundation's efforts to institutionalize law and economics in America's elite law schools and Henry Manne's ambitious project to create an entire law school around the field. In chapter 7, we return to the subject of conservative public interest law, with a comparison of the Center for Individual Rights and the Institute for Justice, the quintessential "second generation" conservative public interest law firms. I show how they responded to the organizational design and strategy failures of the first generation, and how they drew upon the conservative support structure's new intellectual and network resources to challenge legal liberalism in the courts.

The core of this book, chapters 3 through 7, is based almost exclusively on interviews and internal organizational papers. Unfortunately, very little of the documentary history of the conservative legal movement has been archived. Almost every document referred to in this book, therefore, was given to me directly by the organizations involved. To acquire these documents, I agreed that, while I would be free to quote from them in any way I thought appropriate, they would be for my exclusive use. I offered this arrangement to my sources because I believed that it was the only way that this material would ever get into the public domain. Because other scholars will not be able to check my arguments against the original documents or interviews, I have erred on the side of longer quotations, and have not strictly limited my presentation of the cases to material with direct bearing on my theoretical arguments. This should allow other scholars to draw different conclusions, and provide a foundation for future scholarship on these subjects.

I have found repeatedly through the writing of this book that the combination of interviews and contemporaneous documents was essential. While interviews are quite important, memory, on its own, is fallible, as most people tend to remember events in such a way that they form a coherent narrative. Memory, however, is often tidier than history. Contemporaneous documents, especially grant proposals—a wonderful and woefully underused source—help to fill in the holes of memory. What is more, they help to correct for the very real problem of survivor bias in the study of organizations, the tendency to focus on projects that worked (and thus were continued) and to ignore the equally interesting ideas that were tried and failed, or were considered and shelved.

Even these sources do not completely convince me that the story told in these pages is definitive. The history of the conservative legal movement is still in its infancy, and, in almost all my cases, I was working more or less from scratch. As a result, this book is only as good as the papers that organizations kept and the candor of my informants. Events on which there was a large documentary base, for example, may loom larger than those that were equally important, but less thoroughly documented and preserved. My hope is that this will be the first of many books on the subject. I look forward to having my errors corrected by those who come after me.

1

Political Competition, Legal Change, and the New American State

> Whether a given state changes or fails to change,
> the form and timing of the change, and the
> governing potential in the change—all of these
> turn on a struggle for political power and
> institutional position, a struggle defined and
> mediated by the organization of the
> preestablished state.
> —Steven Skowronek, *Building a New
> American State*

A Polity Transformed: The Rise of Nonelectoral Party Mobilization

Political competition, as the epigraph of this chapter asserts, is mediated by the structure of the state. Challengers to a dominant regime do not operate in an empty playing field, but are forced to challenge inherited norms and institutions, or to adapt their insurgency to the structure of the regime they seek to dislodge. To understand why the conservative legal movement took the form it did, therefore, we need to begin with an account of the regime created by its opponents and the form of political competition that it produced.

In the process of creating a vast new set of policy commitments—from social insurance and economic regulation to civil rights and environmental protection—liberal reformers also transformed the American political system. This new policy process put a premium on knowledge, expertise, and professional credentials, and developed in tandem with the "legalization" of society, marked by an increasingly dense maze of laws, regulatory agencies, courts, and litigants.[1] In some cases, the national government actively encouraged professionalization in order to generate linkages between levels of government and between the state and society and encourage policy changes that could not be produced directly.[2] As universities expanded, graduate programs increased to sate the demand for professors, credentialed teachers, social workers, public administration professionals, and policy analysts. The higher education sector grew in tandem with the expansion of this new political system, generally accepting its assumptions and supplying cadres of trained individuals sympathetic to its preservation and expansion.

The fraying of separation of powers, federalism, and limits on governmental authority produced a policymaking system with multiple, overlapping programs, paid for and administered by different levels of government and nongovernmental organizations. Responsibility for policy outcomes was hard to affix in this complex system, making mass mobilization difficult and diverting participation into particularistic, piecemeal forms.[3] The diffuse character of government meant that coordination and control of the policymaking system were produced by networks that cut across agencies, levels of government, and the state-society divide, rather than by political parties.[4] Even as the Democratic Party's electoral power waned in the late 1960s, its strength in these policy networks waxed. These networks, built largely through subsidy by third-party funders such as charitable foundations,[5] facilitated policy change by encouraging courts, congressional subcommittees, and bureaucrats to collaborate in a process of low-visibility, incremental policy expansion.[6] These changes in the structure of the policymaking process made elections decreasingly important as sources of large-scale policy change.[7]

The flip side of this institutional transformation was a political system increasingly sensitive to expert opinion, issue framing, and professional networks.[8] Many of liberalism's achievements derived from the skillful use of power by a transformed federal bureaucracy, staffed by actors sympathetic to (or previously involved in) social movements. This system's advent gave liberal Democrats the ability to push their policy agenda even when the presidency was in the hands of Republicans.[9] Shifts in attention, driven by interest groups, the media, intellectual entrepreneurs, and litigators, became important drivers of cycles of policy change, independent of the electoral fortunes of the political parties.[10]

By the 1970s, political scientists became convinced that these changes had permanently displaced parties as significant political actors. We now know that this claim was wrong—or at least incomplete. Rather than destroying parties, this transformed state produced a new form of party competition. Social movements and interest groups that had been organized in opposition to political parties eventually became institutionalized, cemented to the state, and coordinated in a network increasingly connected to the Democratic Party.[11] This activist network, primarily concerned with policy rather than electoral outcomes, became the dominant faction in the Democratic Party. The rise of this faction led to George McGovern's nomination in 1972, as the head of a strange new coalition unlike any the Democrats had ever seen. In short, the new Democratic Party that emerged by the mid-1970s was "new" not just in the sense that new groups were incorporated, but also in how those groups were organized, coordinated, and centered.[12]

The Democrats created this new party system as it incorporated interest groups and social movements that had once defined themselves in opposition to the party. A loosely coordinated network that bridged state and society—what some observers called a "new class"—came into being as these activists moved into the professions, foundations, educational organizations, and the media.[13] At the same time, older American elites who had once thought of themselves as part of a cross-party establishment linked themselves to these new actors, giving them access to institutions with substantial resources, connections, and prestige.[14] While this network of activists, organizations, and elites cut across the two political parties through the 1960s, it became firmly incorporated into the Democratic Party in the early 1970s as the Republicans began to identify themselves with resistance to liberalism.

In contrast to European political systems, which feature a broad array of these kinds of activities and movements formally linked to the parties, the nature of American law (especially the tax code) and the strategic advantages that could be had from avoiding an open partisan coloration forced the relationship between the Democrats and their nonelectoral wing to remain informal. Despite this formal delicacy, an activity is partisan in a behavioral sense because of what it does, not what it is called. Political activity can be said to be "partisan" to the degree that participants operate as a "team" (their behavior is "coordinated") and integrate their activities with a corresponding team of ambitious officeholders (their behavior is "coupled"). Understood this way, "party" is a continuous, rather than a bimodal, variable: organizations are more partisan to the degree that their behavior is coordinated with the party's office-holding side. It is not necessary that every individual in a particular institution, such as a profession or a university, actively conceive of his or her activity as partisan for it to function as a support for a partisan coalition. What matters is whether there is general sympathy with the policy goals of a party, and whether the institution in question helps to coordinate action consistent with those goals and provide services to support them. Understood this way, the broad liberal network that worked closely with the Democrats to develop ideas, coordinate strategies, recruit personnel, and implement policies was now a part of the party system, in effect if not in name.

For a time, Republicans responded to this newly configured Democratic Party only in the electoral dimension, avoiding direct competition at the level of elite organizational mobilization. As a result, they were frustrated in their effort to create change except where a policy venue had a strong electoral lever (as in tax and defense policy), or where their objectives could be achieved by preventing action from occurring.[15] In the new American political system of the 1970s and 1980s, access to specialized knowledge, networks across government and society to diffuse information and strategies, and allies in institutions that trained and recruited future policymakers were increasingly important, and conservative Republicans were at a severe disadvantage in all of these areas. This elite organizational imbalance explains the otherwise puzzling fact that many of the issues that the Republican Party now defines itself in opposition to were passed with almost no organized conservative response or critique.[16] It was only when Republicans developed a parallel set of elite organizations that they could avoid being overwhelmed by the Democrats' advantages in information, organization, networks, and professional power.

Political parties have always reached beyond the small core of office-seekers who carry their label in elections, but in the transformed party system that came into being in the 1970s, these nonelectoral dimensions of party activity have become increasingly important.[17] As the parties became more polarized on ideological lines, the distinction between partisan and ideological activity became blurred.[18] Increasingly enmeshed with political parties, these activists and their institutions have become the subject of fierce ideological competition, testament to which can be found in contemporary arguments over the composition of universities, the media, and even the medical profession.[19]

Parties have gone where the action is in American politics, seeking to control government not just through electoral warrants from the voters but also by coordinating the behavior of actors across society and among the different branches and levels of government. Explaining political competition in the era of electoral displacement does not require that we abandon assumptions of rational, optimizing, competitive behavior. Rather, it demands a recognition of the evolution in the locus of policy change and the effect that this has had on the collective pursuit of American political power. Much of the action in American politics currently resides in the realm of elite organizational mobilization, where the great battles of modern politics are being fought and where the alignment of the political system is increasingly determined. Far from disappearing, parties (rightly understood) are now competing over a much wider terrain than in the past.

The New Political Competition: The Case of the Law

Complex, technical, and professionalized, the politics of American law and courts has proven acutely sensitive to the increasing significance of ideas, information, networks, issue framing, and agenda control in American politics. Despite these changes, political scientists have, if anything, become even more likely to identify shifts in electoral power and public opinion as the motor of large-scale legal change. Electoral stimuli obviously influence legal change through the mechanism of judicial appointment. Purely electoral accounts of legal change are too quick to see continuity in the legal politics of the period up through the New Deal and that of the last fifty years. If the argument up to this point is correct, then explaining conservative countermobilization in the law demands a more capacious tool-belt than electoral theories can provide.

Theories that look to electoral stimuli as the key to understanding legal change are hardly new. Fifty years ago, Robert Dahl gave this argument its classical formulation: "Except for short-lived transitional periods when the old alliance is disintegrating and the new one is struggling to take control of political institutions, the Supreme Court is inevitably a part of the dominant national alliance. As an element in the political leadership of the dominant alliance, the Court of course supports the major policies of the alliance."[20] Subsequent authors have followed Dahl's lead, claiming that the judiciary is too weak to avoid supporting the "dominant alliance,"[21] actively advances the goals of the dominant party,[22] or changes its behavior only in "constitutional moments" produced by realigning elections.[23] Other authors less interested in general theories of constitutional change have argued that the Supreme Court, independent of the composition of its members, appears sensitive to shifts in popular preferences, although this effect is typically somewhat small, and—significantly for our purposes—possibly in decline.[24]

Students of the courts have devoted increasing attention to the conflict between the courts and the other branches of government that Dahl thought limited to "short-lived transitional periods." Because of the long (and growing) length of justices' terms, these periods may be more sustained than scholars in the Dahlian tradition recognized, and therefore of substantial constitutional significance.[25] The nonsimultaneous response of political institutions to external stimuli sets the stage for conflict between the judiciary and the other branches of government. As J. Mitchell Pickerill and Cornell Clayton argue, the Court's attempts to disrupt the agenda of the dominant political alliance "will provoke an institutional response—such as a constitutional amendment, legislation to strip the Court of jurisdiction, or Court packing—to realign the Court's jurisprudence with the priorities of the governing regime."[26] Despite their useful addition of durable interbranch conflict, these arguments are not fundamentally different from others in the Dahlian tradition: it simply takes longer for the legal market to clear (that is, to align with the "dominant political alliance") than earlier supporters of the "political court" theory believed. Entrenchment happens in this theory, but both its source and its remedy are electoral. Courts eventually change when, and only when, the dominant political alliance has sufficient time and power to reshape the composition of the court.

Dahl's successors are clearly right to understand legal change as tightly coupled to larger processes of political competition. However, if the argument of the previous section is correct, neither partisan entrenchment nor disentrenchment can be understood predominantly by reference to electoral stimuli, as partisan conflict ranges well beyond the electorally rooted institutions that analysts of a "political court" usually assume drive long-term judicial change. What is more, theorists in this tradition give relatively short shrift to the declining prevalence or efficacy of institutional devices to align the courts with the dominant political alliance. Finally, modern Dahlians ignore the "thickening" of the American political system produced by the growth of the modern state, which has been shown in other contexts to have weakened the mechanisms of disruptive, electorally inspired change.[27] In short, "partisan entrenchment" occurs not only in courts, but also in the social institutions that feed the courts with ideas, personnel, and cases. In particular, professional associations, the politically motivated parts of the bar, and law schools are all sites for attempting to temporally extend a partisan coalition. Jack Balkin and Sanford Levinson recognize this when they note "one important feature of intellectual paradigm shifts and constitutional revolutions: the takeover of those institutions charged with teaching the young by newcomers imbued with the new learning and inclined to dismiss, often quite rudely, the purported verities of their predecessors."[28] But Balkin and Levinson say nothing about how, if at all, "entrenchment" in law schools occurs, and give us no reason to expect that the process by which law students (and ultimately law faculties) change should resemble that of the courts, for which the political mechanism is at least reasonably clear.

The work of Charles Epp provides a useful frame for understanding the nonelectoral sources of judicial entrenchment. Epp argues that for major legal changes to occur, a shift in the judiciary's character is insufficient.

> Many discussions of the relationship between the Supreme Court and litigants assume that the resources necessary to support litigation are easily generated and that, as a result, litigants of all kinds have always stood ready to bring forward any kind of case that the Court might indicate a willingness to hear or decide. But that presumes a pluralism of litigating interests and an evenness of the litigation playing field that is wholly unjustified. Not every issue is now, nor has been in the past, the subject of extensive litigation in lower courts, due in part to limitations in the availability of resources for legal mobilization.[29]

Hence, in explaining why legal change occurs, we must focus on the supply side (litigants), rather than simply the demand side (courts) that the

Dahlians focus on. Epp's supply side, which he refers to as the "support structure" for legal change, includes not just those bringing cases, but also those who create legal ideas and strategies, such as law professors, litigants, and their patrons.[30] Where the composition of the judiciary is reshuffled without a corresponding shift in the support structure, legal change may fail to occur or, at the least, be substantially limited and poorly coordinated or implemented.

What is it about the law that makes this support structure so important? First and foremost, courts have substantially less agenda control than other political institutions. Because of this, social actors who are mobilized and skilled at organizing litigation campaigns are likely to prevail over their unmobilized and unskilled counterparts.[31] Whether the Court hears a case at all depends upon the ability of litigants to produce enough cases to create a conflict between circuits, and whether the cases produce the outcomes they want depends upon those litigants' ability to effectively shape the fact pattern presented to the courts.[32] This feature of strategic litigation substantially advantages those who control the supply of cases, and disadvantages those who are forced to respond.

Furthermore, for legal ideas to be taken seriously by the courts they cannot be seen as wholly novel or outside the realm of legitimate professional opinion. This is work that first must be done outside the courts. Balkin, for example, has convincingly argued that

> the question of what is "off the wall" and what is "on the wall" in law is tied to a series of social conventions that include which persons in the legal profession are willing to stand up for a particular legal argument. In law, if not in other disciplines of human thought, authority, and particularly institutional authority, counts for a lot. The more powerful and influential the people who are willing to make a legal argument, the more quickly it moves from the positively loony to the positively thinkable, and ultimately to something entirely consistent with "good legal craft."[33]

As a consequence, groups with disproportionate control of the institutions that produce and legitimate legal ideas, groups who have legal "authority," will enjoy a significant advantage in persuading judges and other significant legal actors that their demands are reasonable and appropriate. If, as Owen Fiss has argued, the "disciplining norms" within a legal community constrain the range of legitimate interpretation, then the ideological bias of that community should strongly influence the kinds of arguments that are successful in the courts.[34] Control of the institutions that embody this interpretive community, in particular law schools and the organized bar, is only weakly coupled with the cycles of electoral politics. These institutions not only produce legal ideas, but are also the dominant force in training successive generations of lawyers, influencing their no-tions of the proper function of law in society, of which legal claims are "off the wall," and of how a career in law might be pursued. In short, as gatekeepers to the profession, control of legal education shapes, over time and not without substantial room for error, patterns of recruitment to the profession, and ultimately determines who will be soliciting cases and arguing before the courts.

This support structure is also important because the courts, and the Supreme Court in particular, typically look for cues from other elite institutions. For instance, students of the Supreme Court have found that pro-life advocates in the 1970s were significantly disadvantaged because of the overwhelming support pro-choice activists had from professional organizations,[35] while justices were, in the area of civil rights, especially attentive to the perceived attitudes of national elites.[36] Because Supreme Court judges are, first and foremost, lawyers, they are unusually sensitive to the dominant opinion in the legal community. In addition, judges can reasonably be understood as an "enterprise" that includes their clerks, who are drawn overwhelming from a very small group of elite law schools: in the Rehnquist years, for example, 77 percent of clerks came from just seven law schools.[37] The ideological team best able to influence the conventional wisdom among these professional elites is likely, all other things being equal, to have a substantial advantage in court.

Control of the legal support structure also matters because it has the potential to shape not only the supply side, represented by cases and legal norms and ideas, but also the demand side, represented by the composition of the courts themselves. If both parties were equally possessed of a cadre of talented, trained, experienced, and ideologically motivated potential judges and justices and had a network that allowed those promising individuals to be identified by those in charge of nominations, then the men and women placed on the courts might simply reflect the balance of forces at the time of their nomination. But there is no reason to believe that the nominees in the pool or the network that brings them to the fore are always in rough ideological balance.[38] The side that has the deeper, more readily identifiable, and better-networked supply of potential justices will be able to maximize its influence on the courts by reducing the chance of miscalculating a potential judge's views and by offering presidents enough options that they can act on their narrowly political motivations for judicial selection (which are often quite significant) while also satisfying their longer-term ideological objectives. Legal networks influence both the supply and demand sides of law, determining the scope of electoral opportunity that a political coalition can actually exploit.

While this support structure is critical when groups are on the outside, it is equally important when they are no longer pressing their noses up against the legal glass. Once their major victories are won, the support structure can then insulate these accomplishments from unsympathetic successors. What is insurgent in one generation becomes entrenched in the next. While achieving a legal revolution may require a heroic development of organizational resources, once this support structure is developed, it may be relatively easy to maintain and very difficult to dislodge.

One simple example makes the point. While judicial entrenchment may seem quite impressive, given that the average term on the bench is approximately twenty years, that is just over half of the career of the average law professor. But even this analogy will tend to underestimate the depth of entrenchment in the law schools, since, unlike the courts, law school faculties are almost totally self-reproducing. While Supreme Court justices are chosen by presidents and confirmed by senators who represent contemporary political majorities, law school faculties are chosen by committees staffed by a previous generation of professors. It is a commonplace in the sociology of knowledge that disciplines tend to reproduce themselves, and ideological and disciplinary projects are tightly interwoven in legal academia. As a result, we would expect law faculties to reproduce themselves ideologically, even in the absence of an explicit individual desire to discriminate, by defining alternative ideological research projects as marginal or unimportant.[39] While there may be some important linkages between electoral change and shifts in the character of the institutions that shape legal culture, they are far from direct and probably not first in importance.

If this is true, then we would expect that for a new political coalition to fully translate its electoral power into legal change, it must either substantially weaken the support structure of its older rivals or create a competing support structure of its own. In the terms of the previous section, it must become competitive in the sphere of nonelectoral mobilization. But as that section suggested, control in this sphere is likely to be very sticky and substantially disconnected from electoral change. In short, nonelectoral mobilization follows a logic of its own. To understand the challenges that conservatives faced in developing their own legal support structure, therefore, we must recognize countermobilization as a peculiarly *organizational* problem. It is to the challenges of creating such organizations that we now turn.

The Challenge of Countermobilization

Scholars in the social movement tradition have been especially active in trying to understand the organizational challenge of mobilization, explaining patterns of success and failure by focusing on either "political opportunity" or "resource mobilization." The political process tradition explains the existence and effectiveness of social movements by reference to the "political opportunity structure," which incorporates such factors as the openness of the political system, the tolerance of protest, and the existence of elite allies.[40] Resource mobilization theorists take the opposite tack, beginning with social movement's *internal* resources, such as money, labor, networks, coalitions, organizations, and ideas.[41] Both of these theories, like the arguments in political science and law discussed in the two previous sections, assume that organization is an automatic, agentless response either to opportunity or to resources.

A useful theory of social movement organization needs to pry open this black box of organizational development, to explain where effective organizations come from and how their leaders use them. After accounting for the effects of opportunities and resources, Marshall Ganz has argued, significant variation still remains: "Some leaders see political opportunities where others do not, mobilize resources in ways others do not, and interpret their causes in ways others do not. To the extent that strategy influences the emergence, development and outcomes of social movements, we must ask not only why different leaders devise different strategies, but why some leaders devise more effective strategy than others."[42] My argument places Ganz's insight in historical context, situating political agents in an inherited regime that sets the conditions under which strategic decisions are made. Within those conditions, however, agents have the capacity to make better or worse decisions, decisions that subsequently become part of the context in which future choices are made.[43] Political outcomes are, therefore, the product of this interaction between *inheritance* and *agency*. I begin with the challenges of entrenchment, and then move on to describe the actors who make up the support structure that seeks to overcome them.

The Challenges of Entrenchment

The challenges of countermobilization are more severe when the governance structure of a field is well defended. This is especially the case in professional domains such as the law, where there are clearly defined *barriers to entry*. For example, as described earlier, leadership selection in professional institutions (such as faculty hiring in law schools) is typically controlled by incumbents. This puts members of a countermovement at a substantial disadvantage, either because of active discrimination, through an allocation of positions favoring incumbents' interests and skills, or simply because outsiders lack access to the information that flows through personal and professional networks. A similar phenomenon is often present in the control of federal agencies. Accounts of agencies as diverse as the Social Security Administration, the Environmental Protection Agency, and the Equal Employment Opportunity Commission have shown how they were staffed by personnel sympathetic to, or in some cases drawn from, the social movements that were pressuring them.[44] This tight relationship between agency personnel and outside interests left those who were unsympathetic to their objectives, such as conservatives, out in the cold. Barriers to entry can also come in the form of "rules of the game." Outsider groups that mobilize against, and eventually take effective control over, institutions may also change political processes in a way that durably advantages their resources and tactics. The form of legal politics that legal liberals developed, for example, put a political premium on Washington, D.C.—based organizational presence and connections to legal academia, while disadvantaging the sort of grassroots mass mobilization that conservatives were in the process of perfecting.[45]

Outsiders must respond to normative and cultural, as well as institutional, entrenchment.[46] A regime is most likely to endure when it can make its ideas seem natural, appropriate, and commonsensical, consigning its opponents to the extremes. Gramsci described this phenomenon as *hegemony*: control through direction and consent, instead of dominance and coercion.[47] Given the increasingly fractured character of advanced societies, it is more useful to conceptualize modern societies as characterized by differing spheres, or, in Pierre Bourdieu's term, *fields*.[48] Each field—legal, economic, educational—is governed by its own logic and sensitive to different, incompletely transferable, forms of social, cultural, financial, and human capital. Understood in this way, the concept of hegemony comes close to the role of culture and ideas used by scholars of the public policy process. So, for example, Peter Bachrach and Morton Baratz claimed that the most important form of political power was the ability to mobilize "the dominant values and the political myths, rituals, and institutions which tend to favor the vested interests of one or more groups" in order to keep substantive challenges to the existing regime off the political agenda.[49] A regime that has achieved hegemony makes its principles seem like "good professional practice," "standard operating procedure," "the public interest," or "conventional wisdom." Those who fail to affirm these principles are stigmatized, and their arguments are dismissed. This ideational entrenchment is likely to be especially powerful in professional settings like the law, where opportunities for concealing normative choice in technical garb are widely available.

Operating in a hostile and unfamiliar environment and without clearly analogous precedents upon which to base decision-making, a movement faced with institutional and ideational entrenchment will find it difficult to identify a rational response to its predicament. Put another way, countermobilizers face a condition of profound *uncertainty*.[50] Uncertainty may be compounded by insurgents' inability to recognize their opponents' vulnerabilities,[51] or by their limited repertoire of possible responses.[52] Faced with such challenges, countermobilizers may fall back on existing tools and strategies that require less adaptation of the movement's infrastructure and strategic repertoire but may be highly unsuited to the challenges of political entrenchment.

The Components of an Alternative Governing Coalition

To respond to the challenges of elite entrenchment, countermobilizers must develop what Stephen Skowronek called an "alternative governing coalition," a concept roughly equivalent to Epp's "support structure" for legal change. An alternative governing coalition is composed of *intellectual*, *network*, and *political entrepreneurs*, and the *patrons* that support them. This section describes the role that each part of this alternative governing coalition plays in responding to the challenges of entrenchment, and in the process points to the limits of countermobilization when this coalition is immature or incomplete. As argued earlier, changes in the form of governance have made elite higher education, through its credentialing of expertise and control of the production and legitimation of ideas, an important source of political power. Because cultural capital—the habits, skills, and bearing that allow one to be taken seriously in elite circles[53]—is transmitted through these institutions, an effective challenge to the dominant regime must sink roots in those institutions or produce alternative institutions also capable of producing not only knowledge but also reputations, prestige, and distinction.[54] This points to the importance of *intellectual entrepreneurs* as a part of an alternative governing coalition.

The first function of intellectual entrepreneurs is to "denaturalize" the existing regime, by exposing the hidden normative assumptions embedded in seemingly neutral professional, scientific, or procedural standards and practices, forcing those assumptions to be justified and alternatives to them entertained. The activity of intellectual entrepreneurs signals that a domain is vulnerable to challenge and provides the legitimacy for others to follow up their arguments with action. Intellectual entrepreneurs also provide insurgents with rhetorical formulations, or frames, that give intellectual substance to otherwise silent grievances.[55] These frames, as Erik Bleich has argued, "help actors identify problems and specify and prioritize their interests and goals; they point actors toward causal and normative judgments about effective and appropriate policies in ways that tend to propel policy down a particular path and to reinforce it on that path;

and they can endow actors deemed to have moral authority or expert status with added power in a policy field."[56] These alternative frames support "oppositional consciousness," which "requires ideational resources—ideas available in the culture that can be built upon to create legitimacy, a perception of injustice, righteous anger, solidarity, and the belief in the group's power."[57]

Intellectual entrepreneurs provide countermobilizers with an alternative vision of social order, drawing upon examples from private orderings, foreign examples, logical argument, or the polity's past experiences.[58] Given that, in its early stages, the alternative governing coalition is likely to be composed of widely scattered members, themselves isolated in hostile institutions and lacking substantial organization, these ideas can generate "coordination without a coordinator," providing guidance for action, confidence that risks are worth taking, and reassurance that others will be acting as well.[59] Finally, intellectual entrepreneurs help to create durable relationships between groups with disparate interests, forms of organization, and animating ideas. The idea of the "general strike," for example, helped to fuse previously uncoordinated French socialists, republicans, anarchists, and corporatists in the late nineteenth century into a coherent political Left.[60] The *National Review* played a similar function on the American Right in the 1950s and 1960s, where Frank Meyer's idea of "fusionism" transformed libertarians, business, social conservatives, Cold Warriors, and Southern segregationists into the modern conservative movement.[61] Intellectual entrepreneurs help make coalition partners attentive to areas of overlapping interests and provide the emotional glue that helps coalitions maintain relationships in times of stress.

Given my argument in the first section that party activity is increasingly found in diffuse policy domains characterized by networked forms of organization, intellectual entrepreneurs must be accompanied in an alternative governing coalition by a second category of actor, *network entrepreneurs*. For my purposes, political networks are a form of social capital, a series of connections between persons that reduce the transaction costs of political activity. However, as James Coleman has pointed out, "Because the benefits of actions that bring social capital into being are largely experienced by persons other than the actor, it is often not in his interest to bring it into being."[62] Consequently, an alternative governing coalition needs entrepreneurs willing to invest their time and energy to facilitate these networks.[63] Network entrepreneurs help to build "strong ties" by circulating stories, complaints, and symbols that knit people together, identify a common enemy, and encourage intense bonds to a particular group. They create "weak ties" through the opportunity for repeated interactions and the provision of a ready source of contacts across a wide range of social fields.[64] The association with the network allows individuals to trust one another because membership demonstrates common opinions or prejudices and allows for the development of reputations.[65] Network entrepreneurs facilitate the diffusion of ideas by nurturing linkages among intellectuals, political entrepreneurs, and the rank and file; the rapid transmission of information and lessons across space;[66] and the intense emotional connections and repeated interactions that facilitate intellectual development.[67] These networks are most likely to be dense and effective when their development is the principal concern of specialized actors capable of generating trust across the divides within a political coalition.

Translating the work of intellectual and network entrepreneurs into concrete change is the task of *political entrepreneurs*. The most important functions of political entrepreneurs are to identify and take maximal advantage of political opportunities in the present and make investments that will produce additional opportunities down the line.[68] The need to effectively recognize opportunities means that political entrepreneurs who can effectively serve as a component of an alternative governing coalition are likely to be "insider-outsiders," persons who are products of the regime they seek to dislodge.[69] Experience in and credentials from the existing regime give organizational entrepreneurs the cultural capital to be taken seriously in fields with deeply embedded expectations of participants' experience, knowledge, and cultural competence. Finally, political entrepreneurs need to embed their strategy in organizations capable of maintaining their focus on the long term, given that regime change is likely to unfold slowly, requires actions in multiple stages, and depends on effects that are difficult to trace and thus to claim credit for.[70] They must be effective in persuading actors whose time horizons and ultimate political objectives are different from their own, while simultaneously aligning their sources of organizational maintenance with their strategic goals. This latter factor is likely to be especially important, given the tendency for organizations to become focused primarily on short-term organizational maintenance, rather than long-term strategy.[71]

The extent and quality of organizational infrastructure described above does not emerge spontaneously: to solve the collective action problem inherent in supporting these actors, a final component of the alternative governing coalition is necessary—the *patron*.[72] All of the functions of patrons depend upon their role in providing subsidies for organization, especially during periods of organizational genesis. In this start-up period, information about organizational outcomes may be limited or nonexistent, the costs of determining probable organizational quality high, organizational entrepreneurs' time scarce, and thus the opportunity costs associated with fund-raising significant.[73] Without patrons willing to invest large amounts of money in speculative ventures in their early stages, the scope of organizations able to take advantage of political opportunities will be greatly limited. In order to limit the pressure on entrepreneurs to water down or obfuscate the content and aims of their programming, effective patrons need to share with the groups they fund an underlying strategic vision.[74] In order to obtain otherwise inaccessible information on the quality of agents whose quality may be hard to evaluate from public sources, they must also be embedded in a common network with their objects of support.

Patrons also need a significant degree of strategic sophistication, a coherent overall vision, and the intellectual self-confidence to make investment decisions whose success is uncertain. Spurring the creation of organizations capable of exploiting existing opportunities and creating new ones requires patrons with certain specific characteristics and strategies:

A. Spread betting. Given the uncertainty associated with countermobilization, effective patrons will spread their bets over a wide range of alternative strategies and entrepreneurs rather than focusing their resources on a single approach or individual.

B. Feedback mechanisms. The effectiveness of spread betting depends upon the existence of patron mechanisms for evaluation, learning, and lesson-drawing, so that resources can be withdrawn from low-return investments and diverted to those that have shown more promise.

C. Long time horizons. In addition to spreading their bets, the challenge of countermobilization under conditions of entrenchment demands that patrons extend the time horizon within which they expect results.[75]

D. Willingness to accept and the ability to measure diffuse outcomes. Many of the social and political outcomes in organizational countermobilization are more diffuse than electoral returns. What is more, even those outcomes that can be easily measured may be difficult to trace back to the actors that produced them.

The effectiveness of patrons in pursuing these strategies depends upon a combination of their skill, the absence of internal organizational conflict, and the richness of the networks in which they are embedded. Effective feedback mechanisms, for example, depend on both the ability of patrons to determine the appropriate metric for evaluation, and the reliability of the networks that transmit information about a venture's success.

The most effective patrons are also important coalition actors in their own right, not just sources of funding. When patrons develop permanent, professional staff with substantial continuity over time, their position in the ecology of organizational development can provide an alternative governing coalition with strategic coordination and institutionalized "memory." The information they receive in the feedback process may give patrons a sense of where the movement is weak, allowing them to actively encourage additional programming to fill holes or provide linkages between existing efforts, thereby accelerating the process by which opportunities are recognized and exploited. The institutional memory of patron staff will increase the probability that resources will be funneled away from projects with a low probability of success, while increasing the "hit rate" of new investments. These are critical parts of the strategy of learning-by-doing intrinsic to building an alternative governing coalition under conditions of uncertainty. Patrons are therefore critical coordinating structures, the site in an alternative governing coalition where information is gathered, lessons drawn and disseminated, and slack resources directed.

Developing an alternative governing coalition with the qualities described above is an extraordinarily difficult process, and one that is likely to be characterized by significant mistakes, long periods of learning and lesson-drawing, and significant lags between the emergence of opportunities and their effective exploitation. If the theoretical account presented here is correct, we should expect large-scale political change—especially legal change—to be determined as much or more by the idiosyncratic rhythms of organizational development as by the more visible tides of electoral success and failure. As a result, it should not be surprising to find that the policy and institutional impact of a rising partisan regime should vary dramatically, in relation to the depth of entrenchment and the sophistication of the field's alternative governing coalition.

2

The Rise of the Liberal Legal Network

TO UNDERSTAND THE PROCESS of conservative organizational development examined in chapters 3 through 7, we must begin with what I will refer to as the *liberal legal network* (LLN), the collection of individuals and organizations in the legal profession, law schools, and public interest law groups that formed what Epp called the "support structure" for the rights revolution.[1] The LLN was at least as important, however, in the *entrenchment* and *extension* of the rights revolution as it was in their original *achievement*. The LLN protected and extended liberal accomplishments in the law, even when the electoral coalition that had originally supported them began to wither. It was the LLN's power and its seeming immunity to direct attack that sparked conservative organizational countermobilization. To understand the character of this response, therefore, we need a clear sense of where the LLN came from and why it was such a potent and resilient force for entrenching legal liberalism.

Conservatives studied the liberal legal network to understand what they were up against, and to draw lessons for their own activism. As later chapters will show, they learned that successful legal change requires a beachhead in the legal academy, ideas capable of generating passionate commitment, channels for recruiting lawyers into public interest law, and professional networks to build the movement's social capital. The professional entrenchment of legal liberalism meant however, that there were limits to the lessons conservatives could learn from their liberal counterparts. Chapter 3, in particular, shows why this process of lesson-drawing was so hard, and why there was such serious resistance to it.

This story of the growth of the LLN starts with the New Deal, whose revised constitutional orthodoxy paved the way for an expansion and centralization of government. The New Deal created both the demand for and the supply of new kinds of lawyers, and, in the process, changed the character of the legal profession's elites and ultimately the legal academy. The chapter then traces the development of the proto-support structure of the NAACP Legal Defense Fund and the American Civil Liberties Union, and how they were able to produce legal liberalism's early victories. One of these decisions, *Gideon v. Wainwright*, led to the creation of a network of legal aid organizations under the sponsorship of the Office of Economic Opportunity. The rise of legal aid, along with the maturation of an earlier generation of lawyers raised under the New Deal, led to a dramatic shift in the character of the organized bar, from being a staunchly conservative force to one that actively assisted the LLN. In this same period, law schools began to change as the elite legal professoriate grew steadily more liberal, eventually incorporating a small but growing contingent further to the left. These law professors, in conjunction with an increasingly liberal judiciary, devoted their scholarship to legitimating an assertive role for courts in advancing egalitarian social goals.

Law schools also changed institutionally. While they had once staunchly opposed clinical education, law schools began to create clinics at a rapid pace. This change was propelled by a confluence of factors: a long-standing concern in the profession that legal education was insufficiently practice-oriented, pressure from radical students to make education "relevant" to the pursuit of social justice, an increasingly sympathetic pool of professors, and funding from the Ford Foundation.

These changes created the necessary preconditions for the final element of the LLN, a network of public interest law organizations with interests far beyond those of the ACLU and NAACP LDF. With a ready pool of ideas from a more liberal professoriate, a generation of law students looking for a new way to practice law, the experience of legal aid, and a judiciary willing to remove legal impediments to bringing cases, liberal public interest law exploded in the early 1970s. Despite these permissive environmental conditions, the growth of liberal public interest law depended on a number of highly contingent factors, especially the staff of the Ford Foundation's success in convincing their board of the field's philanthropic propriety and the defeat of the Nixon administration's effort to deny their tax exemptions. Having overcome these obstacles, legal liberals were able to use their superior legal sophistication, the cultural halo of rights, and support in the media and Congress to advance the legal agenda far more effectively than conservatives could further theirs. This success genuinely shocked conservatives, especially those in business, and led them to explore developing a legal infrastructure of their own.

Two themes clearly emerge from the story told in this chapter. The first is the critical role played by the nation's legal and philanthropic establishment in the development of the LLN. From the perspective of the early twenty-first century, it is perplexing why these wealthy, well-positioned, white men—presidents of the American Bar Association, leaders of the nation's largest foundations—put their support behind a project to liberalize the legal profession. Part of the explanation has to do with the times. By the 1960s, liberalism had become the philosophy of the middle ground. Civil rights, criminal procedure reforms, prison reform, women's rights, and environmentalism all came to be associated with progress, modernity, and "good professional practice." It was, for a brief period of time, strangely uncontroversial—a bulwark against something much worse, holding out the promise of order and stability in a world that seemed to be spiraling toward radicalism and polarization. While many of the changes described in this chapter have become controversial over time, only a few were at their inception. My story thus tracks that of John Skrentny, who found that the "minority rights revolution" was made at least as much by elite white men in positions of power as it was by masses of ordinary men and women protesting on the streets.[2]

The second theme of this chapter is that legal liberalism is impossible to understand without appreciating that its most important practitioners saw it as *legal*, as well as *liberal*. This was not a movement populated, for the most part, by people who were cynical about the law, who believed that it was simply "politics by other means." If anything, legal liberals had a more exalted vision of the law than their realist forebears. Older liberals were made uncomfortable by their faith in the federal courts, and future generations of legal realists, the "crits," would claim that legal liberals failed to see that law was always an instrument of power. Legal liberals, however, quite consciously operated under the "spell of the law." The patrons, intellectuals, and political entrepreneurs of this movement believed deeply in law's possibilities, and sought to remake the law to facilitate what they saw as its highest purposes. They were, in that sense, temperamental conservatives, who believed that deep reforms in the profession were necessary in order to keep law "relevant" to rapidly changing times. It was this idea of progress and relevance that underlay a new professional ethos and provided legal liberalism with its most powerful source of legitimacy.

To understand the peculiar character of the regime that conservatives faced in later years, it is critical to appreciate the deep ambiguity built into legal liberalism. While it was encoded with ideological content, this content was subterranean, complicated by the need to reconcile a project of social transformation with the management of institutions that, precisely because they were professional in character, limited how openly and directly it could be pursued. This ambiguity was, in part, legal liberalism's strength, since it forced conservatives to spend time and resources uncovering the ideological character of the modern legal profession. The simultaneously professional and ideological character of legal liberalism forced conservatives to adapt to this changed understanding of professionalism. It would take them decades to do so effectively.

The Birth of the Liberal Legal Network

From the late 1930s to the early 1960s, the liberal legal network passed through its germinal stage. A generation of New Deal lawyers, informed by legal realism and experienced in government, created new kinds of law and new kinds of lawyering, and became in the process an integral part of America's legal elite. At the same time, further from the centers of elite power, the ACLU and NAACP developed a new, politically engaged approach to the law. With it came new linkages between the law, legal education, and legal intellectuals. Law schools began their long march to academic respectability and institutional prosperity in the late 1940s, and, as they grew, their faculties absorbed a large number of ex—New Dealers, Jews, and young lawyers more connected to the New Deal than to the traditional conservatism of the bar. The professional bar, by contrast, was staunchly conservative through much of this period, but some of its leaders began to make hesitant steps in the direction of reform in the middle to late 1950s—steps that would rapidly accelerate in the 1960s.

The New Deal was a watershed moment for the legal profession. FDR's administration brought into positions of power lawyers cut from a very different cloth than the conservative, Republican WASPs who controlled the legal profession. Their service in government, and the experience and contacts that it produced, gave these New Deal lawyers a market value to corporate America that they lacked before the depression, and hence the ability to create their own firms. Perhaps the most important of these new firms, Arnold, Fortas and Porter, included New Dealers with experience in the Antitrust Division of the Justice Department, the Departments of Agriculture and Interior, and the Federal Communications Commission.[3] Even as the Republicans recovered some of their lost political power at the war's end, the New Dealers' networks, understanding of the modern administrative state, and prestige derived from their government service made them indispensable to corporate clients. Peter Irons found that, of the New Deal lawyers he surveyed, "two thirds moved into private practice, most often in large, big-city firms. A substantial number established their own firms in Washington and New York, guiding clients through the maze of federal statutes and regulations they helped to draft, administer, and interpret."[4] Doing well also meant the firm had the wherewithal to do good, as they understood it. For example, when their former friends and colleagues in government were targets of the loyalty campaigns of the 1950s, Arnold, Fortas and Porter put its resources and prestige behind their defense; at times in the 1950s "loyalty cases were consuming between 20 and 50 percent of Arnold, Fortas and Porter's working hours." The firm was able to charge only expenses for these cases because the corporate side of the business was so fantastically lucrative.[5]

The resources, orientation, and ideology of America's law schools changed markedly after World War II. Soon after the war the Association of American Law Schools (AALS) and ABA began to increase their standards for accreditation, requiring the appointment of a full-time dean in 1948, a minimum student-faculty ratio and faculty size in 1952, and gradually restricting admission to students with college degrees.[6] Many law schools went well beyond these minimum requirements by increasing the number of law school professors and ratcheting down their labors, thereby increasing the attractiveness of law teaching to those of intellectual ambitions. The growing quality of state university law schools was especially notable: by the 1950s, Berkeley, Wisconsin, Minnesota, Michigan, Virginia, UCLA, Illinois, Indiana, Iowa, and Texas had become national institutions, with growing resources and faculty.[7] At Michigan, there were twenty-five professorial appointments in the law school between 1946 and 1956, as compared to nine between 1927 and 1946, combined with "an increase in research and writing."[8] In the fifteen years after the end of World War II, Berkeley's law faculty increased 47 percent, the school moved to a new building five times the size of the old one, and its "strong California orientation was diluted by faculty members who were new to the state, brought perspectives from other parts of the country, attended a wider variety of educational institutions, and had different preteaching experiences."[9] Increasing in size, resources, and ambition, these rising law schools were vastly more valuable to social movements than they would have been just a few years earlier.

Encouraging the liberalization of the legal academy was the decline of anti-Semitism. Before the war, the elite law schools accepted a small handful of Jews; in the years after the war, hiring of law professors increased sharply, quotas capping the number of Jewish law faculty gradually fell (lowering constraints on hiring), and the number of Jewish law students exploded (increasing the number of Jews with the credentials to successfully enter the law-teaching market). Meanwhile, constraints on practice in the top law firms remained, so law teaching was an attractive opportunity for many of the best (and overwhelmingly liberal) Jewish lawyers.

At the same time, a sizable portion of the New Deal lawyers who chose not to join the burgeoning government-relations bar in Washington went into law teaching. At the start of the New Deal only Yale had decisively embraced liberalism, supplying Jerome Frank, Thurman Arnold, William O. Douglas, and Walter Hale Hamilton to FDR's administration.[10] At Columbia and Harvard, by contrast, leftward movement was limited to a handful of the faculty, such as Harvard's Felix Frankfurter and James Landis and Columbia's Karl Llewellyn and Adolph Berle. Beyond these elite institutions, most law schools focused primarily on getting their students past bar exams, and for the rest "money was generally short, the faculties miniscule and generally undistinguished, and libraries in most cases modest."[11] By 1948 Yale Law had hired New Deal veterans Boris Bittker (Lend-Lease Administration, law clerk to Jerome Frank), Fleming James (Office of Price Administration), Thomas Emerson (National

Labor Relations Board, National Recovery Administration, Social Security Board, OPA), and Eugene Rostow (Lend-Lease Administration and Department of State).[12] If anything, the hiring of veterans of the New Deal or war service at Harvard Law was even more impressive: nine were hired in quick succession at the end of the war.[13] Of the eighty-two lawyers surveyed in Irons's *The New Deal Lawyers*, a dozen went into law school teaching, and the impact on Harvard was especially striking: two became deans of the school (Landis and Erwin Griswold) and another five became tenured professors (Paul Freund, Stanley Surrey, Louis Jaffe, Henry Hart, and Milton Katz).[14] Two more of Irons's subjects joined the law faculty at Columbia (Milton Handler and Telford Taylor).

At the other end of American legal education's class system, Charles Hamilton Houston was laying the foundations at Howard University for a new group-focused and politically engaged vision of law. Houston believed that the "Negro lawyer must be trained as a social engineer and group interpreter. Due to the Negro's social and political condition . . . the Negro lawyer must be prepared to anticipate, guide and interpret his group advancement."[15] This conviction drove Houston to transform Howard Law from a night school that could barely meet the ABA and AALS's newly stringent rules to "perhaps the first public interest law school, with an institutional focus on the effects of the legal system on the black community."[16] A graduate of Harvard Law, Houston parlayed his connections, especially with Felix Frankfurter, to convince Michigan, Yale, and Columbia to support fellowships designed to build up the quality and prestige of Howard's professors. The faculty and graduates of Howard's law school would play a critical role in the support structure of the civil rights movement.

Houston was put in charge of the NAACP's legal program, and promptly hired his former Howard Law student Thurgood Marshall. Many observers (including many conservatives) have attributed great strategic acuity to the NAACP's focus on education, and its decision to move from equalization suits (which demanded equality within segregation) to a direct attack on the constitutionality of segregation. In truth, while the NAACP's litigation strategy did have a strategic component, its decisions were driven as much by organizational maintenance imperatives (such as the lower cost of directly attacking the constitutionality of segregation, and the availability of foundation patronage) as they were by the disciplined, long-term design that contemporary observers have read back into the past.[17] The NAACP LDF under Houston and Marshall was loosely organized, scattershot, opportunistic, and improvisational, its history littered with "proposals made by planners who were removed from implementation of the plans, the abandonment of those plans in favor of others that reflected the NAACP's internal organizational constraints, decisions altered because of the preferences of the staff, and negotiations over plans with constituencies having diverse interests."[18] Its genuinely critical strategic decision was "to create a central staff concerned with litigation, not any of the particular decisions the staff made."[19] A permanent organization, staffed by very talented lawyers who could leverage and organize the resources of the black community, did not need a clear, multistep strategy because its continuity over time facilitated learning and adaptation, which would not have been possible in a more ad hoc form of organization.[20] By creating a durable organization Houston and Marshall could pass on a legacy to the future development of the liberal legal network: a series of pathbreaking precedents, a template for public interest lawyering, infrastructure that could be adapted to future struggles, and a vision of the role of the lawyer in progressive struggles that was to have a powerful cultural impact on the profession.

Complementing the emergent NAACP LDF was the ACLU, which had initiated an aggressive plan of expansion as early as 1929, when it decided that "the time has come to decentralize our work; to build up local organizations all over the country."[21] By the mid-1940s, an organization that had once been led by labor radicals and socialists had become wholly mainstream: the ACLU's twenty-fifth anniversary was marked by supportive messages from President Truman and New York governor Thomas Dewey.[22] Starting in 1951, the ACLU started to ramp up its membership considerably, growing from 30,000 in 1955 to over 60,000 by 1960 and finally reaching an impressive 275,000 in 1974.[23] The ACLU expanded its staffed affiliates, growing from only four cities with full-time staffed offices at the beginning of the 1950s to chapters throughout the country, including the South, by the end of the decade. By 1964, the ACLU reinforced the ranks of the civil rights movement by adding a very expensive, but necessary, Southern Regional Office in Atlanta, built on the funds that surged into its coffers as the civil rights struggle heated up.[24]

Changes in the mainstream bar in this period were considerably more limited. Until well into the 1950s, the American Bar Association was a rigidly conservative organization. The ABA's president from 1935 to 1936, William Ransom, accused the New Deal of being built from "blue prints borrowed from old world dictatorship."[25] The American Liberty League, the most determined and best-funded enemy of the New Deal, drew substantial support from the ABA's leaders.[26] Through the 1950s, the ABA continued to warn darkly of creeping socialism, which it connected to the destruction of older constitutional norms, and projected itself as a bulwark against government activism. In 1950, the ABA pointed to the need to "reexamine generally all legislation now in effect which has a tendency to involve or promote the socialization of business and to hamper individual initiative and the continued development of the free enterprise system."[27] In the following year the ABA president could not "escape the conviction held by so many of my fellow lawyers that the 'Supreme Law of the Land' has been distorted out of its original pattern."[28] In 1955, the ABA published a report drafted by Fred and Phyllis Schlafly that criticized the Supreme Court for its excessively liberal approach to domestic Communism. "Anticommunist groups across the country distributed copies to the grassroots by the hundreds of thousands."[29] The ABA in the 1950s was, by any measure, an organization of the Right.

This conservative posture alienated many members of the bar, and in 1937, the National Lawyers Guild was founded to provide a forum for dissenting voices. The Guild brought together a number of prominent New Deal lawyers, such as Jerome Frank and Karl Llewellyn, who were connected by "disparate motives and hopes: some were dismayed by the corporate law identity of the ABA; others were distressed by its active involvement in conservative politics; some wanted to rally lawyers to the New Deal; still others (Llewellyn especially) desired an organization committed to the provision of low-cost legal services. They were united only by the conviction that the ABA should no longer be permitted to speak for the legal profession."[30] The Guild would later become the object of furious ABA attacks in the 1950s, explicitly on the basis of its ties to Communists, but implicitly "to undercut guild proposals for public funding of legal services for low-income groups" and to embarrass prominent liberals who had once been members of the organization.[31]

The perceived threat of socialism cut two ways, however. It also pushed the ABA toward a greater concern for the social obligation of lawyers, in order to defend the profession against the attacks from the left and to prevent the "socialization" of the legal profession. The ABA was deeply disturbed by the evidence of government-funded legal aid in the United Kingdom and by "contemporary developments in the medical profession," which together "raised the specter of eventual socialization of the practice of law—a possibility that American lawyers cannot view with complacency."[32] The ABA's fear of socialism was a powerful resource for more liberal members of the bar who wished to push the organization into a more supportive role in the provision of *private* legal aid. In 1951, ABA president Cody Fowler opined that "legal aid is the shield of our profession. It protects the integrity and independence of the bar by blunting the attacks of those who would make us servants of the State. The establishment of legal aid offices through the land will dissolve the only tenable argument advanced by those who argue for socialistic measures to correct present conditions."[33] Despite this rhetorical support, the commitment of the profession to legal aid in this period, compared to what was to come in the 1960s, was shallow.[34] What was important was that the bar had publicly accepted that adequate legal defense was not simply a matter for the market, but was a *social* and *professional* obligation. This would have significant consequences in the years to come.

At the same time that the ABA expanded its interest in legal aid, legal liberalism gained a significant patron in the recently reconstituted Ford Foundation. In 1953, the foundation gave $120,000 to the National Legal Aid Association (NLAA), founded just four years earlier by figures close to the ABA, and $50,000 to support its Committee on Administration of Criminal Justice.[35] These donations would be the first of a steady flow of funds supporting legal reform, including support to the NLAA for civil legal aid as well as criminal legal defense.[36] The Ford Foundation also showed considerable interest in law schools in this period, giving grants to the AALS in 1957 to examine "the problems of lawyer education for public affairs" and for a "study of resources for legal education."[37] These were followed by a quarter-million dollars in 1958 to support fellowships for young law teachers, a million dollars to Notre Dame, Penn, Vanderbilt, and Wisconsin to "help strengthen the research and teaching programs of their law schools in law and contemporary affairs," and large grants to Northwestern, Wisconsin, and Illinois for research into criminal law and corrections.[38] The Ford Foundation's support for the bar's liberalizing trends was, however, just beginning.

By the early 1960s, American law schools were attracting more liberal professors and increasing their resources, the bar was becoming more diverse and supportive of liberal understandings of its social obligations, and the ambitions and capacities of liberal public interest law were increasing. Over the next decade, the LLN would expand much further. Along with the increasingly ambitious Warren Court, a powerful apparatus for legal and social change was taking shape.

Breakthrough: *Gideon*, the ABA, and the Rise of Legal Aid

Starting in 1963, the prospects for public legal aid changed dramatically with the Supreme Court's decision in *Gideon v. Wainwright* and the federal government's commitment to free legal services as part of the War on Poverty. In the process, the concept of legal aid changed from representing individual indigents to encouraging broad-based political and social change. Remarkably, given its furious opposition to the idea in the 1950s, the bar ceased seeing legal aid simply as a "shield" to defend itself from state interference and became a key supporter of this critical part of the expanding LLN. As the bar signaled its movement away from the conservatism of the past, it attracted into its fold a generation of more liberal lawyers who would have previously shunned it.

Two events in March 1963, one prominent and the other obscure, dramatically altered the fortunes of legal aid. In that month the Supreme Court, having appointed Abe Fortas to represent the petitioner, handed down *Gideon v. Wainwright*, declaring that "in our adversary system of criminal justice, any person haled into court, who is too poor to hire a lawyer, cannot be assured a fair trial unless counsel is provided for him."[39] The Court's decision that access to attorneys in criminal trials was a fundamental constitutional right had a powerful impact on the ABA, which immediately set up a committee, headed by Whitney North Seymour (ABA president from 1960 to 1961), to survey the legal aid situation in all fifty states.[40] *Gideon* had an impact beyond its immediate application to criminal defense, elevating the status of access to legal services—both criminal and civil—on the agendas of policymakers and the legal profession.

In a more obscure corner of the world, the Mobilization for Youth, a Ford Foundation—funded program connected to the president's antidelinquency program, made a decision to create a legal program that would provide "1. direct service and referral; 2. legal orientation for MFY staff members who were not lawyers, clients and community leaders; and 3. the achievement of social change primarily through legal research and the persuasion of governmental administrators to change their policies."[41] By September of that year, MFY decided to jointly operate the new legal program with Columbia University, and that it should be headed by a young labor lawyer, Edward Sparer. With funds from the Ford Foundation, and later with assistance from the OEO Legal Services Program, Sparer began to implement an ambitious strategy to use the law to transform the operation of the welfare system, stripping it of what he saw as illegitimate discretion and intrusion into the private lives of the poor.[42]

These two events influenced the creation and the character of the government's Legal Services Program. The LSP was something of an afterthought in the planning for the Great Society. It might not have been included in the president's proposals at all were it not for the internal government lobbying of Jean and Edgar Cahn, who had led an abortive legal services effort in New Haven and whose "The War on Poverty: A Civilian Perspective," became the blueprint for the LSP. The LSP produced a massive expansion in the size and scope of legal aid. "In 1965 the combined budgets of all legal aid societies in the United States totaled $5,375,890 and their combined staffs comprised some 400 full-time lawyers. By 1968 OEO Legal Service had an annual budget of $40 million and had added 2,000 lawyers."[43] The impact of the LSP went far beyond increasing the legal access of the poor, as it rapidly developed into a remarkably effective strategic litigant. Between 1966 and 1974, the LSP submitted 169 cases to the Supreme Court, 73 percent of which were accepted for review (a rate that exceeded that of the Solicitor General).[44] The LSP was especially successful in the area of welfare rights, where (largely under the direction of Edward Sparer) cases like *Shapiro v. Thompson* and *Goldberg v. Kelly* helped transform the administration, and ultimately the politics, of public aid.[45]

The ABA, which had red-baited the National Lawyers Guild only a decade earlier for its support of legal services, suddenly reversed course, and with each succeeding year the ABA's support for the LSP intensified. In 1961, the ABA's Standing Committee on Legal Aid Work observed that "we have been forced into placing greater emphasis on defender systems by recent Supreme Court decisions pointing out that in federal courts every defendant must have counsel unless such is intelligently waived, and that in the state courts the right to have counsel provided for the poor is unquestioned in capital cases."[46] In the wake of *Gideon*, this support became even more intense, and spread into civil as well as criminal legal aid. In 1964, the ABA House of Delegates declared that the legal profession's most important task was to ensure that "adequate provision is made everywhere to insure that competent counsel are provided for indigent defendants in serious criminal cases," and insisted that training lawyers for indigent defense should be a priority for state and local bar associations. OEO-supported legal services was still in its germinal stages at this point, however, and, during the early planning of the Legal Services Program, the ABA was wary and suspicious. Working within OEO, the Cahns recognized the need to get the ABA on board, believing that "the ABA could provide just the muscle needed to persuade OEO to affirmatively promote legal assistance for the poor."[47]

By the following year, the LSP was a reality, and the ABA became its most important supporter. In 1965, ABA president (and future Republican nominee to the Supreme Court) Lewis Powell stated that his first priority had been "an acceleration and broadening of efforts to assure the availability of legal services," and that applying *Gideon* had produced greater demand for such services than expected.[48] Tellingly, Powell observed that

> the resulting expansion of legal services should not affect lawyers adversely. Indeed, to the extent that the poverty program succeeds, the base of potential clients should expand significantly. . . . It is true that most lawyers would have preferred local rather than federal solutions. Certainly this would have been my own choice. But the complexities and demands of modern society, with burdens beyond the will or capacity of states and localities to meet, have resulted in federal assistance in almost every area of social and economic life. [There] is no reason to think that legal services might be excluded from this fundamental trend of the mid-twentieth century.[49]

By 1966, ABA president Edward Kuhn evidenced even greater enthusiasm, declaring that "render[ing] legal services to the indigent within the framework of the plan announced by the Legal Services Division of the Office of Economic Opportunity and in accordance with the high ethical standards of our honored profession" is "the greatest project ever undertaken by the legal profession."[50] Kuhn dismissed the "portent of socialization of the law," stating that the profession was no nearer socialization than it had been a year before, and that the ABA's support for legal services (evidenced by its support before congressional committees for a generous LSP appropriation) "should tend to prove that we have not neglected the interest of the poor or the principle of equal justice."[51] In 1967 Orison Marsden was elected president of the ABA. Marsden had been the most energetic supporter of legal aid in the mainstream bar since the 1950s, and during his presidency the ABA pushed the administration to support the LSP more generously, rather than simply taking the government's lead.[52] By 1970, the ABA's Special Committee on Availability of Legal Services admitted that the association's attitude toward legal aid a decade earlier had been misplaced and that "the experience of the last five years has demonstrated beyond the possibility of serious dispute that maintenance of even a limited Legal Aid program is no longer within the capacity of the legal profession and those civic and governmental agencies who provided the financial support before the advent of OEO."[53] Reflecting an attitude that had become the conventional wisdom of the ABA's leadership, the 1970 president, Bernard Segal, called the bar to "assist in the critical process of curing those afflictions that the gathering of time, population, technology and social movement have visited upon American society" by "combining the principle of preservation with the principle of reform so that American society may move forward again within the confines of its basic institutions."[54] Support for a liberalized legal system had been reframed as an instrument of modernization and as the responsible, establishment alternative to anarchy.

The ABA's commitment to legal aid in the 1960s and 1970s went well beyond rhetoric. Having developed a standing committee on Legal Aid and Indigent Defendants, the ABA went on to add other committees that reinforced the aims of legal liberalism. A Special Committee on Housing and Urban Development Law was created in 1969 with support from foundations (including Ford) and the government, followed the next year by special committees on the environment and correctional facilities and services and a new Division on Individual Rights and Responsibilities, with committees on civil rights and responsibilities, hunger, overpopulation, alcohol and drugs, and the protection of the rights of women and the American Indian.[55] The ABA also developed an increasingly dense network of committees to research, plan, and coordinate the project of legal aid in tandem with the government and lawyers on the ground. The support of the bar gave legal services allies at the highest levels of the legal profession, as well as, through its chapters, presence on the ground in every congressional district in the country.

Especially against the backdrop of the 1950s, the ABA's vigorous support of government-funded legal services seems, at the very least, peculiar. What can explain this shift? First, the ABA was moving in this period from an exclusive to a universal model of membership, and in the process the class basis of its members changed.[56] Second, even though most lawyers continued to work for and sympathize with business, the balance of the profession shifted as the generation of lawyers who were socialized into the profession prior to the depression gradually gave way to those whose attitudes toward government were shaped by the New Deal and World War II. Third, as government grew in the postwar period, increasing numbers of lawyers (and their clients) developed a stance of accommodation with the state, while others went further, seeing legal liberalism as a philosophy of modernization and progress.[57] Finally, important figures in the profession concluded that, in the words of ABA president Kuhn, "if you don't serve the public as it needs to be served the public will force some kind of change in the profession."[58] Government-funded legal services, while not the first choice of many elite lawyers, at least seemed less intrusive on the profession's autonomy than the alternatives.

Throughout this process, the Ford Foundation played a critical role. Its "Gray Areas" project, initiated in 1960 to provide intensely focused services for poor urban areas, provided the early support for the work of Jean and Edward Cahn.[59] In December 1962, three months before *Gideon*, the Ford Foundation approved a five-year, $2.4 million grant to the National Legal Aid and Defender Association to create model defender services, establish new defenders offices in major cities, and provide fellowships and internships "to attract outstanding law graduates" into legal aid work.[60] A year after *Gideon*, the foundation invested an additional $2 million to "take full advantage of the tide of interest in defender services resulting from the Gideon case,"[61] and a year later it provided substantial funding for Sparer's work at Columbia. Reinforcing the increasing ambition of the LSP, in 1966 the Ford Foundation appropriated $1 million "to assist in selecting, coordinating, and financing significant test cases likely to establish fundamental precedents in remedying injustice and advancing the rights and opportunities of the poor."[62] Throughout the 1960s, Ford reinforced the movement for legal aid by providing grants to law schools to increase their curriculum in poverty law and related areas, and provided direct assistance to the ABA as it deepened its support for the movement. At each stage in the growth of legal services, the Ford Foundation's support appeared both before that of the government and the organized bar and rapidly thereafter, increasing the speed and depth of the legal aid movement. While foundation patronage was not, in and of itself, a sufficient condition for the institutionalization of the LSP, it, along with the active support of the national bar, does appear to have been a necessary one.[63]

The Transformation of American Law Schools

On the evening of August 2, 1966, just months into his leadership of the Ford Foundation and against the background of riots in numerous American cities, McGeorge Bundy spoke to the Urban League about his plans for the nation's largest foundation. Bundy's declared, "We believe that full equality for all American Negroes is now the most urgent domestic concern of this country."[64] Pointing to the brave leaders of the civil rights movement, Bundy insisted that "these men and women need to be multiplied. They need reinforcement. We hope that we can help in that objective."[65] The example of the civil rights movement had implications well beyond the rights of black Americans. "Finally, and yet really first of all in the list of things we take for our concern, I put the idea—and the practice—of justice. The legal rights of the Negro are a part of it and so are the legal rights of all who are poor . . . and we see a real chance here that what has been learned in the struggle for Negro rights can be put to the service of other Americans as well."[66] With the fires of Los Angeles and other major cities as a backdrop, Bundy pointed to a future day of reckoning and warned that "if that day ever comes, history will mark it as the white man's fault, and the white man's companies will have to take the losses."[67] Civil rights, including the reform of the law, had become a necessity for the white establishment, represented by the men who made up the Ford Foundation's board.[68]

As Bundy hinted, the reform of the law would be at the core of the foundation's work in the coming years, and that project would reach beyond civil rights. The Ford Foundation had been involved in legal reform for more than a decade, but with Bundy's rise to the foundation's leadership, its work in the area became much more ambitious and far-reaching.[69] For our purposes, the most important examples of this expanded ambition were the foundation's work in legal education and its patronage of the public interest law movement, which will be discussed below (see "The Explosion of Liberal Public Interest Law"). Without its patronage these critical pieces of the liberal legal network would have developed slowly and lacked the strategic coordination that the foundation provided.

Changing Curriculum, Changing Students

No demand of 1960s law students was as prominent as making their education more "relevant" to the cause of social justice, and the clearest example of what relevance looked like was clinical legal education. These clinics have been among the most persistently irritating parts of the LLN for conservatives. In the 1980s, the conservative Washington Legal Foundation published a report attacking legal clinics, and the drumbeat of conservative opposition has continued up to the present day.[70] Conservative author Heather McDonald, for example, has attacked clinics for "engaging in left-wing litigation and political advocacy for 30 years," claiming that they "offer the legal professoriate a way to engage in political activism—almost never of a conservative cast."[71] Most clinics engage in "left wing litigation and political advocacy" only in a strained sense of the term, but there is little question that their caseloads over the past thirty-five years have included little to please modern conservatives, and provided a significant source of free labor, training, and recruitment for the public interest law movement. Like most of the liberal legal network, however, clinics never would have emerged had they simply been, in McDonald's words, the "perfect embodiment of a radical new conception of lawyers and litigation that emerged in the 1960s—the lawyer as social-change agent."[72] Legal clinics emerged out of a peculiar confluence of factors: a long-standing and apolitical movement within the profession to better prepare law students for the real world of legal practice; pressure for law schools to do their part to live up to post-*Gideon* expectations of legal access for the poor; the demands of an increasingly radicalized law student body; and the willingness of the Ford Foundation to invest a remarkable sum of money into overcoming the legal academy's suspicions of clinical education. Clinical legal education never displaced the old law school curriculum, but it did succeed in finding a home for itself in the nation's law schools, becoming in the process one of the most controversial parts of the LLN.

The roots of clinical legal education were far from radical. The earliest foundation support for clinical legal education began in 1959, when the Ford Foundation gave a seven-year grant of $800,000 to the National Legal Aid and Defender Association to support the creation of the Council on Legal Clinics (CLC), chaired by Orison Marsden, then-head of the New York City Bar, with a board composed of ABA, AALS, and NLADA representatives. "The organization's purpose was to improve legal education by getting law students involved in practical experience, including legal services; accordingly, CLC offered grants to finance the introduction of clinical programs into law school curricula."[73] In a sign of the increasing legitimacy of clinical legal education, in 1965 the CLC was taken over by the AALS and became the Council on Education in Professional Responsibility. In 1967, COEPR's leader, Howard Sacks, left to become the dean of the University of Connecticut Law School, and its board (including the future Republican attorney general Edward Levi) sought to accelerate the organization's work and make it independent. The Ford Foundation stepped in to lead the project, renamed the Council on Legal Education for Professional Responsibility, putting up $6 million over the project's first five years ($26.25 million in 2004 dollars), followed by an additional grant of $5 million for its last five years ($17.28 million in 2004 dollars).

Just as important, Ford gave to the project its chief program officer in the area of law and the administration of justice, William Pincus, who believed that America's law schools, and by extension the legal profession, were fundamentally flawed. An official Ford Foundation report recalls that he wondered whether "a professional school which prides itself on the selection of brains and on the excellence of its technical training, whose diploma is bound to be worth large fees or prestigious jobs in combination, [should] also concern itself with other matters—such as the legal and social problems of the poor, the availability of legal services, the economic structure of the profession and criminal justice?"[74] CLEPR had the ambitious mission of injecting clinical education into every law school in the country, and making the idea an institutionalized part of legal education. To do so, CLEPR gave grants to law schools to set up clinical programs, which had to be partially, and increasingly over time, matched by the institutions themselves. This funding was critical to overcoming faculty opposition, as "the programs are expensive, and many older faculty members are skeptical. It is easy for a dean to sell his faculty on a program that is funded from the outside, much harder for him to get approval if the school's own money is required. Similarly, the needed appointments—whether of tenure-ladder teachers or of clinicians brought in outside the usual ladder—were much easier to arrange because they were backed by New York money."[75] This support was essential in helping spread the idea of legal clinics: while only a dozen law schools gave credit for clinical work in 1968, four years later 125 of 147 law schools did.[76] The structure, and not just the extent, of clinical legal education was influenced by CLEPR, since its substantial funding gave it power over law schools lacking in other substantial external funding sources. The foundation concluded that "if there had been no CLEPR, or if CLEPR's requirements had been less strict, the pattern now visible across the country—for-credit programs attached to weak seminar components, with placements in criminal or civil legal aid offices—might be less consistent."[77] By 1972, the foundation had concluded that clinical legal education had been fully institutionalized. "Partly because CLEPR has been administered so well and has been so careful to demand rising contributions from the law schools that have been its grantees, clinical legal education of the sort that CLEPR has supported is almost certainly here to stay, to be carried on with the schools' own money."[78]

The motivations for this extraordinary injection of foundation funds, and law schools' acceptance of them, were complex. The oldest and least controversial motivation was a sense that legal education had become too distant from the actual practice of law, leaving lawyers, in Chief Justice Burger's words, "to learn their craft in the courtroom."[79] A modest injection of clinical education was a way for law schools to deal with these criticisms, without changing the Langdellian core of classroom education. Clinical education was also seen as part of the bar's support for legal aid. At the annual meeting of the ABA in 1960, its Standing Committee on Legal Aid Work noted that the CLC would "advance the cause of legal aid by encouraging law schools to expand their existing clinical programs, including legal aid."[80] Clinical education was seen by the ABA's leaders as a way to train the army of lawyers necessary to make their commitment to greater legal access a reality.[81] Clinical education was law schools' contribution to the War on Poverty and the Court's decisions on access to counsel, as a 1965 report to the Ford Foundation by Professor Ralph Brown of Yale Law School observed.

> We believe that the timing of the program has been especially auspicious. The higher standards which the United States Supreme Court is exacting for the defense of the indigent and for the safeguarding of the rights of individuals have compelled widespread attention to these matters in the bar and in government just as the Administration's War on Poverty has begun the mobilization of resources to meet a wide range of social needs. These developments will call for the services of more lawyers, and it is plain this call must be answered chiefly by recent graduates of the law schools. Those graduates who have participated in the projects sponsored by the program should be among the best qualified for the new professional roles that are emerging.[82]

In order to vindicate these national commitments, the character of law students had to change. This desire to use clinical education for transformative ends existed as early as 1965, when Brown observed that

> the need for direct confrontation [with the legal needs of the poor] is especially important for many students because their professional work will insulate them from these community problems and from the human distress with which most of the projects we have been observing have been concerned. For these lawyers the law school might provide the only occasion in their careers to deal with such matters or to observe them at first hand. We, therefore, believe it a reasonable hypothesis that the lawyer who, as a student, has had the experience that these

projects provide will be more likely to take an active role in civic or professional efforts to minister to the community's social ills.[83]

The staff report to the Ford Foundation Trustees that accompanied CLEPR's initial grant request carried forward this transformational mission, stating that, in addition to improving students' skills, clinical education would "reinforce the social consciousness of certain law students and professors through confrontation with injustice and misery; and to expose others, perhaps less socially motivated, in such a way that they take with them a sensitivity which may be aroused in the course of their later life and professional career."[84] It would be easy, in retrospect, to interpret this as a desire to liberalize the law school curriculum, but at the time encouraging "sensitivity" among young lawyers was seen as a way of keeping the legal profession relevant to a rapidly changing world, in which concern for economic and racial inequality looked like anything but a passing fad.

While the financial support of the Ford Foundation, the moral support of the bar, and pressure for law schools to do their part to increase access to legal services contributed to changes in the law school curriculum, these changes were also driven by intense pressure from law students themselves. In the decade between the early 1960s and the early 1970s, the political attitudes of law students and their reasons for attending law school changed markedly, and at elite schools dramatically. Robert Stevens found that "the 'desire to serve the underprivileged' "

> shows a steady, and, in some cases, dramatic increase over time. At Yale the percentage of those attributing "great" importance to this motive more than quintupled between 1960 and 1970. By 1972 almost half the class indicated that this factor was of "great" importance. Indeed, with the exception of U.S.C., the large majority of entering students in 1960 had regarded service to the underprivileged as being of "no" importance dwindled to a minority by 1970 and almost disappeared by 1972. . . . With respect to working in a legal aid office, the percentages rose between 1960 and 1970 from 11 to 28 at Iowa, 15 to 23 percent at Pennsylvania, zero to 18 percent at U.S.C., and seven to 26 percent at Yale. Most dramatic however, was the increased anticipation of performing "civil rights or civil liberties" work. During the decade, the percentages rose from four to 28 percent at Iowa, from 11 to 27 percent at Pennsylvania; from four to 27 percent at U.S.C; and from 17 to 48 percent at Yale.[85]

Driving these changed goals was the shifting ideological contour of the law student body. Stevens found that law students were more liberal upon entering law school and moved to the left in school as well.[86] The ideological shift was especially rapid at the very top of the law school world: an October 1967 straw poll at Harvard Law showed that 31

percent of the student body identified as Republicans, but a year later the percentage supporting Richard Nixon stood at just 21 percent, and by 1972 those planning on voting for Nixon dropped to a mere 11 percent.[87] Changing demographics as well as the tenor of the times also played their part in this shift. Women and ethnic minorities, whose representation in law schools shot up in this period, reported even greater aversion to traditional corporate law careers and had ideological preferences further to the left. By the early 1970s, the ideological makeup of elite law school students had changed enormously from where it had been just a few years earlier.

The changed ideological character and professional expectations of law students was to have a durable effect on law schools. The persistent demand for "relevance" and the expansion of government led to changes in the curriculum that complemented clinical education. In the view of the Ford Foundation, "The clinical movement has been inseparable from the growth in courses in poverty law (including welfare law, consumer credit law, landlord-tenant law), family law, criminal law, and prison law. Lawyers and students have been more concerned with these fields because of general trends in the society, and because of heavy federal funding for legal services programs that inevitably encouraged activity in these areas."[88] These curricular changes would only accelerate over time.[89] While these forces could generate more elective courses in the law schools, it took the increasingly strident demands of the students, combined with the financial wherewithal of CLEPR, to produce the major institutional shift toward recognizing clinical education. Laura Holland's history of clinical education at Yale found that

> at Yale Law School student discontent with the American legal system and the legal education system manifested itself in symptoms ranging from general malaise and boredom with the traditional law school curriculum, to building a counterculture tent village in the law school courtyard, to a mass demonstration on the New Haven Green. Clinical education was but one battle in a war against the academic law school as an institution. . . . The struggle to reform the curriculum centered on the students' demand that their legal studies bear some relevance to the pressing legal and social issues of poverty and racial equality.[90]

In sharp contrast to students' demands for a role in school governance, support for clinical education was one demand that the faculty was not implacably opposed to, so long as the resources were available.

Had the massive growth of clinics occurred ten, or even five years, earlier, their ideological character might have been different. It was not inevitable that legal clinics would develop caseloads more comforting to liberals than conservatives. The fact that clinics were such a persistent demand of students meant, however, that it was *their* priorities that were stamped

on the caseloads.[91] Also important in shaping the character of clinics was the proliferation of legal services, especially those supported by the OEO. Many of the clinical professors hired by law schools in this period were veterans of legal services, and brought their legal networks and mission of serving the poor with them. In addition, public interest law firms had proliferated by the late 1960s. Clinics and public interest law firms complemented each other, clinics giving public interest law firms substantial free, skilled labor, and the public interest law firms helping to identify and organize cases of interest to students and professors. As a result, much of the caseload in legal clinics came to reflect the political attitudes and preferences of the students who demanded them, the character of contemporary legal services, and the mission of liberal public interest law firms. This set a template for the future development of clinical education that became self-reinforcing, to the point that the more liberal character of the clinical caseload is now seen by many in the academy as part of the definition of clinical education.[92]

Student protesters left their footprint in other ways. They demanded, and with few exceptions received, more aggressive affirmative action in admissions and faculty recruitment. Flowing out of their previous demands for clinical education, when this generation of law students graduated and went into practice, corporate law firms substantially increased their pro bono programs in order to convince graduates that work in a law firm was not inconsistent with the pursuit of social justice.[93] This allowed the fledgling public interest law movement to leverage the substantial resources of private firms, at a time when its budgets were quite modest.

Student protesters did not get, in all but a few cases, meaningful participation in law school governance. By pushing for affirmative action and curricular change, students did help to create the conditions for a change in the demand for professors, a demand that many of these same students, seeking an alternative to corporate law, helped to fill.

A Changing Legal Professoriate

In this period, the law professoriate continued its earlier leftward drift. Even more consequential, however, was that the legal liberalism of law professors changed dramatically in this period. Liberal law professors became much less committed to their New Deal predecessors' deference to the administrative state and the political branches. Inspired by the jurisprudence of the Warren Court and the example of the civil rights movement, they also developed a vision of legal scholarship that eschewed the older realists' insistence on debunking the moral status of law, replacing it with a conviction that law could be grounded on something more than politics.

The period of political ferment on college campuses, and in law schools, coincided with a massive increase in the size of the professoriate. Between 1962 and 1977, the number of full-time professors of law in the United States increased from 1,628 to 3,875, the great bulk of which growth occurred in the five years between 1967 and 1972.[94] The legal professoriate swelled because new law schools were created in response to increasingly strict rules for entering the profession (the number of ABA-accredited schools went from 111 in 1947 to 163 in 1977) while standards for accreditation of law schools, including pressure to hire more full-time faculty, were stiffened.[95] As a consequence, hiring among law schools was especially intense at precisely the time that the law students who would fill those positions were moving decisively to the left. Law teaching was especially attractive for the substantial portion of recent JD's with an ideological aversion to traditional law practice, as well as for aspiring social scientists or historians who noticed the dire shape of the job market in those fields.[96] These two trends also helped pull the ideological attitudes of law professors to the left, and given that academic political attitudes tend to skew to the left as one climbs the ladder of prestige, these general trends were felt especially intensely at the elite schools that disproportionately supplied their graduates to law teaching.[97]

In a 1972 survey of academic attitudes, the Carnegie Commission on Higher Education found that law professors, while substantially to the left of both academic and American public opinion, were still to the right of social sciences and humanities professors. Law professors reported voting for Nixon in 1972 at a much higher rate than social scientists (35 percent compared to 20 percent) and fewer law professors reported being "very liberal" than social scientists.[98] By the 1990s the political attitudes of law professors had converged with their colleagues in arts and sciences, probably the result of generational replacement, as law students from the late 1960s and 1970s moved into the academy and their predecessors retired. John McGinnis found that elite law faculties are now almost exclusively Democratic: at the University of Pennsylvania, Stanford, Yale, Georgetown, Columbia, and Duke, 89 percent or more of law professors who made political donations gave exclusively or predominantly to Democrats, primarily to those on the left side of the party. By contrast, there was not a single elite law school with a majority of Republican donors.[99] Among the elite law faculties that have a disproportionate influence on the character of scholarship, establish the legal conventional wisdom, and help determine professional norms, liberalism and the legal professoriate have become synonymous.

Equally important as changes in law professors' attitudes were transformations in their roles and functions. Two stand out. The first is the growth of the "activist law professor," connected to social movements and liberal

litigants and skeptical of bureaucracy. The earliest example of this trend at the elite level was Yale Law School professor Charles Reich, who in the mid-1960s produced a stream of major articles that marked a decisive break with the New Deal legal tradition.[100] These provided "the scholarly foundation" for welfare rights in the courts.[101] Where the New Deal tradition had emphasized bureaucratic discretion, legal informality, and deference to the elected branches, Reich was gripped by fear of the state New Dealers sought to empower. In language that anticipated (and influenced) the arguments of the public interest law movement, he drew attention to the fact that "Congress and the executive have developed institutional characteristics which . . . disable them from being satisfactory custodians of the constitution" and that bureaucracy had proved itself to be "characterized by its need steadily to increase its own powers; it seems intrinsically incapable of imposing limits, constitutional or otherwise, on itself."[102] The threat of a growing state, empowered by the New Deal's deference to Congress and the executive branch was, for Reich, terribly real. Reich's study of "midnight welfare searches," developed as part of a project for the Field Foundation, drew on meetings with the nascent welfare rights network (including Sparer) and argued that the modern welfare state had become a threat to fundamental constitutional liberties.[103] In his famous article "The New Property," Reich pointed to the reinvigoration of constitutional formalism as a solution to this threat. Reich reached back to the pre—New Deal court in his suspicion of delegated power,[104] and called on the courts to resuscitate the "unconstitutional conditions" doctrine[105] and to insist on a much higher standard of review of administrative decision-making.[106] Reich's work provided a powerful example of how legal academics could be integrated with the mission of progressive social change, offering "a vision of progressive 'law reform' to be promoted through constitutional and statutory rulings favorable to the poor."[107] Reich also helped legitimate the idea that, while a welfare state under Congress and executive branch control was a danger to liberty, expansions of state power directed by or under the supervision of the courts were not.

The role of legal scholar-activist became increasingly well institutionalized in the years after Reich's work. Of special interest in this regard were the LSP's "backup centers," which helped to coordinate appellate strategy for cases emerging from the LSP's ground-level work. The first backup center, for welfare rights work, was Columbia University's Center on Social Welfare Policy and Law (which had received support from the Mobilization for Youth), and once the LSP was established it replicated the Columbia program at UC-Berkeley (housing law), Boston University (consumer law), St. Louis University (juvenile law), Harvard (education law), UCLA (health law), and USC (geriatric law).[108] As new areas of the law, such as women's rights and the environment, came to the fore, law schools (drawing on government and foundation funding, as well as their increasingly flush budgets) developed new centers to provide public goods for the public interest law movement: training new generations of public interest lawyers, developing the intellectual foundations for future cases, and coordinating legal strategy through meetings and conferences.[109]

Law professors in this era contributed to the liberal legal network by helping to entrench the work of the Warren Court, culturally and intellectually. Law professors such as Alexander Bickel and Philip Kurland, who came of age between the mid-1930s and the mid-1950s, cut their teeth on legal realism and judicial restraint and consequently found the Warren Court's decisions starting with *Brown* and accelerating with *Baker v. Carr* difficult to square with these inherited commitments. The generation of liberal law professors who succeeded them, by contrast, rejected their predecessors' obsession with the "counter-majoritarian difficulty."[110] Whereas their forebears had rationalized *Brown* as a necessary but limited aberration, "Members of a new generation who went to law school during the Warren Court years and entered law teaching at Harvard and elsewhere during the 1960s—a group that included Jesse Choper, Bruce Ackerman, Ronald Dworkin, John Hart Ely, Owen Fiss, Frank Michelman, and Lawrence Tribe—were not haunted by memories of the old Court and viewed judicial activism even more tolerantly than did their teachers."[111] Legal liberals' realist predecessors were skeptical of lofty conceptions of rights, but this new generation sought to legitimate the expanded role of the judiciary ushered in by the Warren Court. While the faculty of Harvard Law were generally skeptical of the Court's activism, Fiss recalled that "even in those days it was understood that Harvard did not speak for the profession as a whole, and even less so for the young, who looked to the Court as an inspiration, the very reason to enter the profession."[112] This generation of law professors saw it as their duty to demonstrate the legal, and not simply political, character of the Warren Court's decisions.

> In the decades following the Second World War, particularly in the sixties, at the height of the Warren Court era, a new judicial doctrine arose to replace the doctrine that was associated with laissez faire capitalism and that was ultimately repudiated by the glorious revolution of 1937 and the constitutional victory of the New Deal. It embraced the role of the activist state and saw equality rather than liberty as the central constitutional value. Scholars turned to defending this new doctrine and in so doing sought to rehabilitate the idea of law in the face of the realist legacy. They sought to show that *Brown v. Board of Education* was law, not just politics. So were *Reynolds v. Sims*, *New York Times v. Sullivan*, and *Gideon v. Wainwright*.[113]

Armed with a revived understanding of law, this generation produced a series of major works that lacked the defensiveness of their elders, arguing that *Brown* demonstrated that a muscular role for the judiciary was indispensable to the cause of equality and justice, while also being above normal politics. Propelled by a progressive vision of history,[114] Dworkin, Tribe, Fiss, and others pointed forward to the completion of the Warren Court's vision as well as backward in legitimating its deeds.[115] The near-absence of conservative voices in law schools meant that this interpretation of constitutional law was nearly hegemonic. This was "a dominance so complete that every casebook, treatise, and handbook used to teach constitutional law in American law schools is the product of Democrats writing from Democratic perspectives."[116]

These legal scholars sought to ennoble the legal profession, making it a tool for the pursuit of justice rather than a mere lubricator of commerce. As Laura Kalman argues, this new conception of the law sunk deep roots in elite law schools.

> Law schools capitalized on the Warren Court. "Glossy admissions brochures entice some students into law school with promises that lawyers of the future, riding white chargers, will crusade against social problems," one student wrote. As a law student working with prisoners at Leavenworth, another future academic learned "that the federal courts are special. They are the most splendid institutions for the maintenance of governmental order and individual liberty that humankind has ever conceived." To the children of the Warren Court, "the law seemed like a romance." The editors of the *Yale Law Journal* said Earl Warren "made us all proud to be lawyers."[117]

A heroic conception of the law went hand in hand with a heroic role for the courts, and not incidentally an elevated status for law professors. This generation of liberal law professors, which Mark Tushnet caricatured as accepting the vision of the "lawyer as astrophysicist,"[118] meshed interdisciplinarity with the moral role of conserving and extending the Warren Court's accomplishments. An egalitarian understanding of the Constitution, with civil rights at its core, was for them part and parcel of a new legal professionalism. *Brown, Baker v. Carr,* and *Roe v. Wade* thus provided the text of a new civil religion, one in which elite law professors were the keepers of the true church. This role aimed left as well as right, against conservatives who attacked the Warren Court as lawless and the leftist legal skeptics in the critical legal studies movement, whom legal liberals attacked as preaching "nihilism" in their insistence that law was politics "all the way down."[119]

Sanctifying legal liberals' aspirations for the law was the powerful moral status of "rights" produced by the civil rights struggle and the image of a Warren Court that was simultaneously legally orthodox and substantively humane, whose actions rested on genuine authority as well as decent and civilized instincts. At the same time, the reputation of the institutions that they sought to reform, such as southern state governments, urban machines, and big business, was at a low ebb, and the ability of those institutions to compete in the cultural and ideological marketplace acutely limited. The place of legal liberals at the pinnacle of an increasingly well-resourced and influential legal academy gave their framing of legal politics real legitimating power, helping to preserve the role of legal liberalism in the legal profession even as its electoral grip was slipping away. The power of these ideas, which claimed to be above normal politics, would infuriate, frustrate, and ultimately mobilize conservatives in the years to come.

The Explosion of Liberal Public Interest Law

By the time that the Democrats' electoral dominance began to crumble in 1968, many of the pieces of the LLN were already well developed. This previous organizational development and network-building laid the groundwork for the final, and in policy terms most powerful, piece of the LLN: public interest law firms. Public interest law did not emerge spontaneously; the breadth, sophistication, and internal structure of these firms can be directly traced to the Ford Foundation's extraordinary strategic patronage. The LLN provided a supportive network and ideas, a more liberal judiciary swept away formal impediments to public interest law, and the Ford Foundation helped to tie these together by providing a major subsidy and strategic direction at the organizational generation stage.[120] The impact of public interest law was explosive, and it set the stage for the early countermobilization by conservatives.

The Ford Foundation's support for public interest law was anything but inevitable. The foundation was far from a monolith, divided between a staff closely tied to the liberal legal network and an establishment board intensely concerned with propriety and responsibility. The foundation's staff focused on persuading the board that public interest law was a sensible enterprise for the foundation. They argued that the foundation was already supporting the NAACP LDF and programming in indigent defense and legal education, and was generally pushing the bar to be more progressive and oriented to social reform. In addition, McGeorge Bundy had established civil rights and poverty as the foundation's overarching goals, and this provided an obvious justification for replicating the civil rights movement's legal approach with other groups (hence the foundation's support for the Mexican American Legal Defense and Educational Fund, the Puerto Rican Legal Defense Fund, and the

Native American Rights Fund). Finally, the foundation had active programming in areas such as communications and the environment, and this justified moving the focus of public interest law beyond ethnic and racial minorities to these new areas as well.

"Public interest" law, as distinct from civil rights or poverty law, presented some unique and very tricky issues for the foundation's leadership. The constituencies targeted by public interest law were not, on the whole, poor or disadvantaged, and thus not obvious targets of philanthropic support. It was here that increasingly popular critiques of interest group pluralism helped the foundation's leaders justify their support of what might otherwise look like direct political activity.[121] Bundy recalled that this new thinking first took hold in energy policy, but soon grew much broader.

> That grew out of a growing feeling [that] the public interest in analyzing it was not adequately represented . . . whereas the various or special interests were busy as can be, primarily but not exclusively, the commercial interests. . . . It's the old shoe-pinching argument of the democratic theorists that those whose interests are most closely affected are those who will pay the most attention . . . those . . . most attentive to their interests get there faster with more arguments than those who may in the end be just as much affected either as consumers or as workers or as students. . . . We encountered that problem when we moved into the policy aspects of public broadcasting; we encountered it again here in the energy case and its exists also in defense studies; in arms control studies; and I myself believe, it exists in the public interest law field. I think the Foundation is right to be ready to take a lively interest in those kinds of problems where there are plenty of people and forces and money to represent existing organized interests and not so much . . . that is unaffected by either personal or commercial or corporate or institutional interests. Broadly speaking, the Foundation doesn't have that kind of interest.[122]

This argument helped Bundy and the board reconcile the nonpartisan traditions of foundation philanthropy with the creation of a network of public interest law firms connected to liberal social movements. Instead of actively supporting one side in a political dispute, the Ford Foundation's role was simply a means of ensuring "balance" and an opportunity for arguments to be heard on both sides. It was well understood at the time, however, that public interest law would be in considerable tension with the Nixon administration. The program's original planning document noted that "whatever its other virtues may be, the prevailing attitude and view of the present Administration with respect to the meaning of the Constitution and the purpose of the nation has effectively shut off service in the Executive Branch of the national government as a viable outlet for large numbers of young people trained in the law who have public service motivations."[123] This illustrates one of the peculiar qualities of much of the LLN and the prevailing liberal consensus in elite circles and institutions. While in *substance* it often operated to support ideological and partisan causes, it was understood by many of its patrons and key participants in objective, neutral, nonpartisan, and nonideological terms. This framing of the legal liberal cause facilitated support from elite institutions and protected its tax status, and in later years it forced conservatives to devote resources to "exposing" the LLN's veiled ideological character.

The staff of the Ford Foundation had a second challenge in selling public interest law to their board: defusing potential concerns that the project was too politically hot for the foundation to handle. While the board was increasingly sympathetic to liberal causes, its members were by no means radical and in their professional life directed the most established institutions in American life. As a consequence, much of the structure of the public interest law firms supported by the Ford Foundation was put in place simply to neutralize possible opposition from its board. Sanford Jaffe, the Ford Foundation program officer in charge of the Government and Law Program from 1968 to 1983, recalls that the program's greatest challenge was the question of

> how do we [insulate] ourselves from . . . criticism both from some people on the Ford board and a lot of people from the outside? And that's really where we come across . . . an extraordinarily great idea. . . . I would go to a group called the Public Interest Law Advisory Committee and I would get their judgment as to whether or not this grant was a good grant . . . whether the people on the boards were really competent and they would be responsible people. So that way we would be able to tell the Ford board that, "Look, we have got these four very eminent people who have helped Sandy to make these grants." And then when we got attacked from the outside—which we did . . . I would be able to say, "Look, I got the advice of these four people." And who did we pick? We picked four ex-presidents of the American Bar Association. . . . [For example,] William Gossett . . . represented Henry Ford. . . . We had a sense that Henry Ford would be one of the difficult guys on the Ford board. The automobile industry might be a target of these law firms, who knew? . . . That became a key element to be able to say to Henry Ford if he had a problem, "Well, Bill Gossett—your lawyer—thinks that this is a worthwhile enterprise, he's joining us in looking at it." . . . I think without the structure I don't think we would have had a public interest law program. The Ford board, in my judgment, would have been very, very reluctant to approve the program.[124]

Jaffe also directly influenced the internal structure of the public interest law firms in order to assuage the foundation's board. The firms would have a litigation committee that would have to approve each case, and the committee would be made up of the same sorts of white-shoe lawyers as the Ford Foundation advisory committee.

And the theory behind that was, if somebody said, "Hey, these bunch of kids just out of Yale, or out of Harvard, or Columbia were suing, you know, the big auto companies or were suing the big chemical companies. Why'd these crazy Ford people give these kids a lot of money to do that? What do they know about this?" We'd say, "Now, wait a minute, they have a distinguished board and beside that they have a litigation committee and they cannot file a lawsuit unless the litigation committee's approved it." Now look who's on the litigation committee. Arthur Goldberg, you know was a former Supreme Court Justice, this person and that person and these are all senior partners at law firms.[125]

The foundation's program officers did all they could to give this potentially explosive program a smooth, establishment veneer. Beyond the elite lawyers on the boards of foundation and the public interest law firms, the program officers were able to point to previous victories against attacks on legal services (in the form of the "Murphy amendment," which would have given state governors a veto over legal services programs) as evidence that the establishment would, in fact, come to public interest law's aid when attacked:

A well organized lobbying effort to knock the Murphy amendment out of the OEO bill was mounted in the House. This unanticipated effort was powered by the fully mobilized, nationwide engines of the American Bar Association, supported by the staffs of the nation's law schools, and skillfully orchestrated by OEO Director Donald Rumsfeld and his deputies for Legal Services. . . . The ABA has been given total credit by the bill's managers for persuading a dozen or more congressmen of impeccable conservative hue and traditional antipathy to "poverty give-aways" to stand up for the Legal Services program before the outcome was clear.[126]

The transformation of the legal establishment gave public interest law a critical ally, assuring the Ford Foundation board that it would not be alone when the inevitable backlash came. Without this reassurance, the program would never have gotten past the foundation's board.

The second and closest-run episode in the development of public interest law concerned the firms' tax status. When the Ford Foundation was in the early planning process for its public interest law initiative, it was unclear whether these firms would be eligible under Section 501(c)(3) of the federal tax code, which grants tax deductibility to nonprofit, charitable organizations. Jaffe recalls that

Bundy said, "What if somebody hassles us about the charitable nature of this?" And you gotta remember, this was in a period of time in which . . . the only civil rights legal organization that existed, in my recollection, was the NAACP Legal Defense Fund. I mean, the Native American Rights Fund hadn't been created yet, the Puerto Rican Legal Defense Fund hadn't been created yet, wom-

en's rights law hadn't been accepted, there were no environmental public interest law firms at this point, so the notion of a group of lawyers having a pot of
money and then using that pot of money to litigate on behalf of the public
interest, some people thought might be a violation of the charitable tax code
that sets up charitable giving and all that business.[127]

The early foundation planning documents took this consideration very
seriously, and Jaffe reports that Bundy specifically directed him that "even
before we go to the Board . . we need an opinion from a very elegant,
first-class lawyer that says we can do this as a charitable thing."[128] Even
getting the opinion was difficult: the first lawyer the foundation approached declined, citing potential conflicts with the firm's clients.[129] The
early planning documents for public interest law make clear how uncertain the tax deductibility issue was. On the one hand, a report noted,
"At least at present, the term 'legislation' does not embrace the quasi-
legislative actions of regulatory and other administrative agencies,"[130] and
thus the actions of public interest law firms did not directly and explicitly
fall under the requirement that 501(c)(3) organizations not "attempt to
influence legislation." The tax code also permitted "public advocacy" by
tax exempt organizations, so long as it did not cross "partisan" or "legislative" lines. On the other hand, the same report noted that "Treasury
regulations do not explicitly authorize litigation in the courts by tax-exempt organizations, and thus contain no overt authorization for litigation
as the prime rationale for a tax-exempt organization."[131] The foundation
thought that the exemptions provided to the Center for Law and Social
Policy, the Center for the Study of Responsive Law, and the NAACP suggested that the IRS was on its side, concluding that "while clearly volatile
and unpredictable, the climate in Washington with respect to this particular activity appears, at present, to be improving."[132]

The climate was not, in fact, "improving." In March 1970, the IRS
gave the Natural Resources Defense Council tax deductible status, but
only on the condition that "the NRDC . . gain prior clearance on each
lawsuit it planned. The IRS would then be able to rule in each separate
case whether the NRDC was doing anything to jeopardize its tax deductibility."[133] Jaffe recalls that "it became a real hullabaloo and it would have
stopped our program right in the middle," as these restrictions would
have required that the firms surrender their 501(c)(3) status, damaging
their ability to raise funds from foundations and individuals.[134]

While the Nixon administration had a strong interest in preventing the
growth of tax-deductible public interest law firms, and communicated
this clearly to the IRS, this early effort at "defunding the Left" was no
match for the increasingly well-coordinated LLN. Two of the most important environmental officials in the Nixon administration, William

Ruckleshaus (then-nominee to head the EPA) and Russell Train, of the Council for Environmental Quality, came out against the IRS's ruling.[135] They were not alone in rising to public interest law's defense. Jaffe recalls,

> One of the things that was very helpful were our four advisors who, having been: a) ex-Presidents of the American Bar Association; b) all from extraordinarily well-positioned, prestigious law firms and all men of integrity and substance and so-forth began to make the calls that they felt it was necessary to make and to talk to people, point out the rightness of the law and the wrongness of their interpretation. . . I think it showed that there were forces aligned out there who felt that this was not something they wanted to see. I think it also showed that there was a lot of support from the bar.[136]

Such "men of integrity" did not exist just a few years earlier. Now, core members of the legal establishment had deep connections to the liberal legal network and were willing to put the force of the ABA and their own reputations behind public interest law. Just as was the case with defeating the Murphy amendment, this support made all the difference in swaying an elected Republican administration.

It is highly unlikely that public interest law would have gotten off the ground were it not for the support of the Ford Foundation. While some of these firms now have large budgets and thousands of members, in the late 1960s and early 1970s groups representing large, diffuse interests were still quite novel and the mechanisms of generating support unclear. Patron support allowed these groups to get past the difficult early stages of organizational formation, while allowing them to become active players in the policy process before building a mass membership base.[137] Would other patrons have emerged to support public interest law? It seems highly unlikely. Jaffe recalls that the large financial and reputational investment of the project led Bundy to seek partners in other large foundations, such as Rockefeller, Mellon, and Carnegie, but the controversial nature of the project led them to reject his entreaties.[138] This strongly suggests that, had the program officers not been able to effectively manage the difficult diplomatic work within the Ford Foundation, public interest law would have lacked a single major supporter. The foundation went beyond funding to provide coordination and advice. It sought to create a broad swathe of firms, distributed across the country and covering a range of policy areas, and identified organizational entrepreneurs willing to fill the holes in the public interest law network. It put budding public interest lawyers in touch with the legal establishment, recommended lawyers for their boards, and shaped their internal structure (going so far as to reject NRDC's original desire to have a communal leadership structure). The existence of a dense network of liberal public interest law firms was, in short, a highly contingent outcome. While changes in the opportunity

structure, as discussed in the next section, were necessary to the success of the enterprise, without the patronage of the Ford Foundation those opportunities would have lacked organizations capable of effectively exploiting them.

The Liberal Legal Network and the New Politics

Before the public interest law project got off the ground, the Ford Foundation staff could identify signs of support for public interest law in the courts, Congress, and administrative agencies, but for the project to have its full impact this support would have to increase substantially. Law "in the public interest" required changes in traditional legal concepts, such as standing, the definition of a class, and the allocation of legal fees, without which the firms would be stopped at the courthouse door. This was a matter of the greatest concern for the foundation's leadership because, as Jaffe recalls, if "the only guy who's got standing is the guy whose house is going to be impacted, then you can't do this kind of stuff . . . it would have been conceivable, had standing gone the other way, that it would have killed the movement then—or at least circumscribed it so much that it would have been very hard to bring a lot those kinds of class action cases."[139] Congress and the courts did, in fact, respond, making possible the impressive legal achievements of the era. The Center for Law in the Public Interest, Public Advocates, Natural Resources Defense Council, Environmental Defense Fund, Sierra Club Legal Defense Fund, Citizens Communications Center, Georgetown Institute for Public Interest Representation, League of Women Voters Education Fund, Education Law Center, International Project, Mexican American Legal Defense and Educational Fund, Native American Rights Fund, and the ACLU Women's Rights Project all started with Ford Foundation funding.

Shifts in the American political system in the late 1960s and into the 1970s made it much more accessible to the public interest law movement, helping solve problems of financing and providing protection when it was attacked. The public interest law movement was both beneficiary and contributor to what political scientists soon identified as "the New American political system" or the "new politics of public policy."[140] This new form of politics was tailor-made for the strengths of public interest advocates, while simultaneously disadvantaging those of their adversaries. What Daniel Patrick Moynihan had, in the early 1960s, called the "professionalization of reform" had become, by the end of that decade and in the decade following, the "legalization of reform."[141] The professionalization of reform that Moynihan noted in 1965 reflected a peculiar feature of the politics of politics in the 1960s and 1970s, which was the diminishing role of popular mobilization in setting the govern-

ment's agenda and the increasing role of ideas generated in the academy, professions, and government itself. Those who controlled the production of ideas and intellectuals, therefore, had a substantial competitive advantage.

Connected to this was the transformation of the American elite media. In the 1960s and 1970s a new generation of reporters appeared in America's newsrooms, and with them a changed conception of journalism. Journalists became eager to set their own agenda, and became open to those outside government who wished to use the news to introduce new issues into public debate or to challenge existing government policy. Stories of Americans demanding their rights, and challenging the discretion of government officials, fit nicely into this changed conception of the role of journalism, and actors within the LLN were well placed to take advantage of this openness. These new journalists shared the public interest lawyers' suspicions of corporations, regulatory agencies, and local government, making the media a substantial resource in using litigation to shape public perceptions and the government's agenda.

Congress, which was undergoing sweeping reform in this period, expanded public interest groups' access to government. A twenty-year movement to "open up" Congress came to fruition in the early 1970s, as the power of conservative committee barons was broken and a new Congress emerged in its stead, dominated by its subcommittees.[142] The subcommittees whose work was most important to the public interest law movement were typically led by those members with the most sympathy for the LLN, who used their position in Congress to protect and nurture it. These subcommittees were often staffed by young liberal lawyers with strong linkages (through the Nader and civil rights networks, for example) to allies across the government. Starting in the late 1960s, when liberals could no longer count on a sympathetic administration, Congress began to pass a number of low-profile legal provisions allowing for "citizen suits," loosening rules of standing, and facilitating public comment in regulatory proceedings, leading to more stringent agency regulation.[143] Few of these changes attracted much attention at the time, but the public interest law movement and its allies in Congress understood their importance, since they indirectly subsidized the practice of public interest law in regulatory and court settings and encouraged regulators to err toward stringency.[144] These shifts were possible because the decentralization of Congress had diminished the importance of "the floor" in Congress, transferring it to legislative "high demanders" in subcommittees. While regulated industries were high demanders on the specific implementation of regulations, they were unmotivated on broader issues since the impact of these procedural decisions on the corporate bottom line was distant and often difficult to trace.[145]

These changes in courts, bureaucracies, and Congress were all tied to the increasing centralization of policymaking in Washington.[146] Federal bureaucracies and courts came to supervise large swaths of policy, even in areas that remained under the nominal control of state or local governments. This centralization of policymaking diminished the value of broad-based, federated organizations and mass movements, but advantaged groups that were organized in Washington and networked into its web of agencies, courts, media, congressional subcommittees, and research organizations.[147] The centralization of government matched the centralization of the public interest law movement, whose lawyers "located themselves in Washington, D.C.—and, more specifically, in the once low-rent areas around Dupont Circle—[which] facilitated the opportunity for frequent interaction."[148] The Washington-based structure of the movement allowed for strategies and information to be quickly disseminated, networks to form, and ideas to be shared across the boundaries of Washington's formally separated powers. Information, networks, and proximity were central to this new centralized politics, and were, in the new politics of the 1970s, just as important as masses of active members or economic power.

The consequences of the emergence of the LLN for the outcomes of public policy were substantial and far-reaching. Lawyers associated with the welfare rights movement (most of whom worked for the LSP) convinced federal courts to oversee a revolution in welfare policy, which caused the percentage of eligible persons actually receiving welfare to more than double in a matter of a few years.[149] Lawyers for the NAACP LDF and the ACLU succeeded, for a time, in abolishing the death penalty.[150] Building on an initially judge-sponsored movement to reform prisons, the NAACP LDF, ACLU, and a growing network of law clinics and pro bono lawyers remade the American prison system.[151] Starting with *Griswold v. Connecticut* and concluding with *Roe v. Wade*, advocates were able to push abortion law from a trajectory of moderate, limited liberalization rapidly running out of steam to legalized abortion as the law of the land.[152] The ACLU Women's Rights Project achieved through the courts what it could not obtain through the constitutional amendment process: constitutional equality for women.[153] In a broad range of regulatory issues, from the environment to land use and the treatment of the disabled, public interest lawyers were able to maximize the impact of congressional enactments, despite the substantial costs these imposed on business and local governments.[154] Lawyers who spoke for a wide range of minority groups, especially Hispanics, were able to use a combination of regulation and litigation to incorporate themselves into the civil rights regime originally established for black Americans, despite an absence of mass mobilization.[155] American public schooling, especially in the areas

of discipline and student free speech, was transformed from a regime of almost total administrator discretion to one of pervasive legalization.[156] In perhaps the most emotional case of court-led policy change, judges mandated busing for racial balance in urban public schools, a policy that led to broad popular disapproval, and, in some cases, violence.[157] While a few of these policy changes were eaten away at the edges, what is remarkable is their original accomplishment and subsequent resilience.

Litigators were far from alone in these cases, drawing on a network of supporters in the legal academy, the bar, and the other professions. This network helped them fund, identify, and develop cases, establish their intellectual rationale, and provide the legitimacy that courts often assume from broad elite support. The power of this network came in large part because of the weakness of its opposition. In case after case identified before, defenders of the status quo were marked by their intellectual superficiality, their almost total lack of agenda control, an absence of information, and a vacuum in support from professional elites. Whereas liberals had specialized repeat-players defending their side in court, conservatives were often represented by relatively unsophisticated state government lawyers,[158] or representatives of business who were more interested in minimizing their costs than in long-term legal strategy.[159]

Finally, the combination of court action and the LLN served to insulate these reforms from reversal, even when they were unpopular or imposed large costs on concentrated, wealthy, organized groups. The LLN was well equipped for rapid mobilization when conservatives attempted to use their power in the elected branches of government to reverse liberal victories in the courts or the bureaucracy. The legal and intellectual resources available to conservatives at the time, by contrast, paled in comparison. The LLN's victories in court were also protected by the constitution's separation of powers. As Shep Melnick astutely explained, "By establishing a new policy status quo, the court shifted what might be called the political burden of proof within Congress. No longer was the burden on those favoring national uniformity and program expansion to build a coalition broad enough to pass new legislation. Now the burden was on their opponents to pass legislation to overturn the courts. Given the obstacles to constructing winning coalitions in Congress, this shift often proved decisive."[160] So long as liberals had disproportionate power over the agenda of courts and the institutions that supported them, conservative power elsewhere was a very limited countervailing force. As a result, liberals could achieve durable policy outcomes far from the center of public opinion (as in the case of busing and affirmative action) or that squeezed implementation of popular policies past where they would have gone otherwise (as was the case with disability and the environment).[161]

Conclusion

The development of the LLN into a formidable support structure for legal and policy change was not foreordained. Up through the 1950s liberals were largely outsiders in the professional bar. While the character of legal academia was changing in the 1950s, its liberalism was suspicious of courts, and few law schools had the resources to contribute to progressive social change. Legal aid was scarce, and public interest law did not reach beyond the ACLU and NAACP LDF. The Ford Foundation was becoming more interested in funding legal reform, but its interest was still in its nascent stages.

The development of the liberal legal network from these meager roots depended on a confluence of factors. First, the fear of state involvement in the legal profession, the incorporation of a new generation of more liberal lawyers, and the seismic impact of *Gideon v. Wainwright* caused the legal profession to alter its relationship to legal liberalism. Second, the social disruptions of the 1960s caused many American elites to see legal liberalism as the civilized response to challenges that would otherwise spill into the streets. Third, the courts and the federal government became substantially more sympathetic to legal liberalism, providing elite sanction for its goals (in the form of Supreme Court decisions) and subsidy for its organizational development. Fourth, in the wake of the civil rights movement, the idea of rights attained a powerful cultural status, making the political claims of legal liberals seem identical to morality, progress, and common decency, a part of elite common sense. Fifth, the rules of the game in American politics changed, in a way that durably advantaged the resources of legal liberalism. Sixth, elite foundations threw themselves behind the creation of the liberal legal support structure, providing critical funding and strategic coordination for its emerging infrastructure. By the early 1970s, these interacting factors produced an imposing structure for the production of liberal legal goals, one capable of sustaining legal liberalism's momentum even as the electoral status of its allies began to be challenged.

For much of its growth phase, legal liberalism was not a partisan project, drawing support as it did from elite actors in both parties. By the early 1970s, however, the party system was changing, as the issue context and coalitional dynamics of American politics started to change. Starting with Richard Nixon, Republicans began to recognize the value of assaulting legal liberalism as a strategy for realigning the party system. Small businessmen could be mobilized by resistance to the courts' aggressive decisions on environmental and health and safety regulation. Attacks on judges for their decisions on abortion, busing, and affirmative action decisions could be used to drive a wedge between urban ethnic Catholics and more affluent, socially liberal Democrats. Southern Democrats who just a few years earlier considered voting Republican a sin were attracted to the party's ranks by the Supreme Court's decisions on prayer in schools, desegregation, pornography, and abortion. At the same time, the Democratic Party began to change, as the liberal legal support structure became an ever-more important part of its elite stratum and its central commitments, such as women's, civil, consumer, and welfare rights and the environment, came to rival the party's older commitments to economic stabilization and unions. In the new party system that emerged in the 1970s, the liberal legal network became closely linked to the Democratic Party, while the Republicans attracted Democrats repelled by legal liberalism. In a telling example of this shift, Lewis Powell—who as president of the ABA had helped advance the cause of legal liberalism—became the author of a seminal report to the U.S. Chamber of Commerce calling for countermobilization against public interest lawyers, and eventually a Nixon appointee to the Supreme Court.[162]

While conservatives successfully used resistance to the courts to attract converts to their cause, they quickly discovered that disentrenching legal liberalism was an altogether more difficult matter. For example, in response to a lawsuit by the Center for Law in the Public Interest that stopped oil drilling by Armand Hammer's Occidental Petroleum, Hammer directly lobbied McGeorge Bundy to cut CLIPI's funding, had his lawyers contact CLIPI's trustees, and campaigned to cut its tax exemption. Despite being one of America's richest men, he was wholly unsuccessful.[163] The Nixon administration unsuccessfully sought to strip public interest law of its tax exemption, and both Nixon and Reagan made efforts to "defund the Left," but were able to do so only at the margins.[164] Conservatives slowly recognized that they needed to develop their own apparatus for legal change, one that could challenge legal liberalism in the courts, in classrooms, and in legal culture. How they did so, and the difficulties that legal liberalism placed in their way, is the story to which we now turn.

3

Conservative Public Interest Law I: Mistakes Made

OF ALL THE CASES of conservative legal mobilization examined in this book, none was more difficult or characterized by greater trial-and-error than public interest law.[1] While each step in the development of the Federalist Society and law and economics could build relatively smoothly on earlier ones, in public interest law conservatives had to overcome the legacy of their strategically inadequate initial response to legal liberalism. This chapter traces out the early—failed—conservative response to legal liberalism, the sources of its ineffectiveness, and the long process of strategic reevaluation its failings engendered.

Faced with a deluge of lawsuits from Naderite and Ford Foundation–supported public interest law firms it was far from obvious what response might be effective, and the founders of conservative PILFs lacked the experience and strategic sophistication to discover it. The conservative public interest law structure they did devise, with firms cartelized geographically, reactive to the agenda of legal liberalism, focused on amicus participation, and compromised by close ties to regionally powerful businessmen, produced meager results and was an obstacle to the emergence of more successful organizations. The first-generation firms' geographic focus and close ties to business limited their ability to specialize, develop a "public interest" reputation, and organize their litigation around a coherent set of ideological principles. Ultimately, as I will argue in chapter 7, power and decision-making in conservative public interest law passed from the businessmen who were dominant in the first-generation firms to a second generation of foundations, activist intellectuals, and conservative lawyers. This new alignment of patrons and organizational-intellectual entrepreneurs proved substantially more potent than their predecessors. This chapter examines the period of organizational trial-and-error that began in the early 1970s and continued well into the late 1980s. It sheds light on three elements of conservative elite organizational countermobilization: strategic errors driven by dominant movement interests and inappropriate models for action, lags in response to failure, and organizational learning through generational succession.

First, the conservative movement's responses in the law were poorly matched to available opportunities because of the interests, attitudes, and experiences of its core constituencies. The most mobilized interest of conservatives in the early 1970s was business, a problematic ally for the cause because of its unreliable opposition—and frequent support—for state activism.[2] While businessmen often sincerely believed in the ideology of anti-statism, they commonly detached this belief from their day-to-day behavior.[3] American businessmen also lacked the knowledge to effectively direct countermobilization in professionalized and intellectually dense fields. This close relationship with business put a taint on the movement, especially in a period dominated by the idea of the "public interest." Conservatives were further hampered by strategies that seemed natural or appropriate to its organizational entrepreneurs. Repertoires of action that the movement had used with success in other areas (such as electoral politics) were deployed in response to new problems, often without careful consideration of their effectiveness in new domains, while those with a higher probability of success were avoided because they violated strong collective normative commitments. Responses that drew on existing movement resources and organizational forms were preferred over those that required innovation and the empowerment of new kinds of leaders. These constraints help to explain why conservatives chose a geographically based, business-led strategy poorly suited to the task of legal change.

Second, the same forces that caused the conservative legal movement to devise a flawed organizational response to legal liberalism made rapid readjustment difficult, rendering flawed strategies durable despite their limited efficacy. While the market in interest group organization may "clear" over time, in the sense that ineffective approaches will lose support and more promising approaches will gain, the relationship between organizational entrepreneurs and their supporters means that initial responses may be very sticky. This relationship is likely to be characterized by asymmetric information, as supporters may have a difficult time monitoring organizational entrepreneurs and may not have a clear sense of what constitutes "success" or how to measure it.[4] As a result, inexpert patrons may be vulnerable to the existing organizations' self-interested assessment of their effectiveness. Conservatives overcame this problem over time, with the emergence of specialized patrons embedded in a network with multiple information streams, but it took more than a decade to do so.

Third, conservative movement leadership became more effective, adaptable, and legitimate when there was a shift in power from the movement's material base to those with primarily cultural and intellectual motivations. Organizational maintenance imperatives made it hard for incumbents to learn from failure, so learning happened through the creation of new organizations by "refugees" from the old. It is no accident that *all* of the senior leaders of the second generation of conservative public interest law worked at one time in first-generation firms.

The Origins of Conservative Public Interest Law

The rise of liberal public interest law in the late 1960s and early 1970s was seen by conservatives as deeply threatening. Liberal public interest lawyers established critical precedents in high-profile areas of constitutional law, threw obstacles in the way of conservatives' governing agenda, and used their superior organization, networks, and information to influence policy outcomes through litigation and intervention in the regulatory process (especially in the area of the environment). Conservatives' initial responses to the liberal legal network were direct reactions to all three of these dimensions of the rise of public interest law.

The first causes of conservative countermobilization were changes in constitutional law in civil rights, criminal procedure, and sexual and religious freedom. Liberal public interest law organizations pushed the Court to use constitutional provisions to liberalize policies and procedures, primarily at the state level.[5] These decisions threatened core conservative constituencies, such as religious conservatives or defenders of racial segregation. Even more ominously, they produced a shift in federalism, centralizing policymaking in a system where conservatives had seen their interests served by decentralization and separation of powers. Power was transferred from Congress, where conservatives could count on considerable support, to the Court, where they could not. Against these changes, conservatives initially mobilized almost exclusively in the electoral arena. Richard Nixon ran for president in 1968 promising to brake the Warren Court's activism by nominating "law and order" Supreme Court justices,[6] and by 1972, as the quote from Patrick Buchanan that graces this book's introduction makes abundantly clear, many conservatives believed he had succeeded.

Conservatives in government, especially Ronald Reagan during his stint as governor of California from 1967 to 1975, found their agenda obstructed by liberal PILFs, including those funded by the Legal Services Program. Reagan ran for office on a program of welfare reform, but soon found his changes challenged in the courts. Ronald Zumbrun, Reagan's deputy director for legal affairs in California's Department of Social Welfare, found that in defending Reagan's welfare reforms in court, "we were all by ourselves, with nobody to defend the program other than ourselves. We felt *we* were on the side of the public interest."[7] The wave of environmental public interest litigation provided an additional impetus to conservative legal mobilization. Unlike their predecessors in the NAACP Legal Defense Fund and the ACLU, these newer firms imposed large costs on businesses, ranchers, and other conservative interests, both directly (through regulation) and indirectly (by publicizing corporate wrongdoing, damaging corporations' reputations, and forcing defensive compliance).

Conservatives' inability to protect their victories in the polling booth or the profitability of corporate America without substantial representation in the courts led to the creation in 1973 of the first conservative public interest law firm, the Pacific Legal Foundation (PLF).

PLF drew support from the California Chamber of Commerce, whose members had become sensitized to the danger the public interest law movement could pose to business by the success of the Wilderness Society, Environmental Defense Fund, and Friends of the Earth in temporarily halting the development of the Trans-Alaska Pipeline in the early 1970s.[8] One of those businessmen, J. Simon Fluor, brought his complaint to Los Angeles lawyer (and future Reagan administration attorney general) William French Smith, who put Fluor in contact with Zumbrun.[9] The chamber of commerce recognized that corporations were at a substantial disadvantage in their battle with the liberal PILFs, as their in-house lawyers could never devote themselves full-time to business's collective interests. Legal liberals could also organize, at a time when tax rates were very high, through 501(c)(3) organizations funded by tax-exempt charitable donations, while individual corporate lawyers were paid by taxable funds. Drawing on his experience in government, Zumbrun hoped that PLF could obtain support from consulting contracts with state governments as well as financing from business.[10] Mimicking the rhetoric of its counterparts on the left, the Zumbrun-led PLF sought to represent the "other side" of the public interest. Unlike its liberal predecessors, PLF was created "not because they [conservatives] were disadvantaged in the legislative or executive arenas, but because they viewed conservatives as disadvantaged in the courts, where they believed that liberal firms had a 'moral monopoly' on the public interest."[11] PLF and its successors would be a shield, not a sword.

The most notorious indication of business's early strategic response to legal liberalism is a memorandum solicited by the U.S. Chamber of Commerce, written by soon-to-be Supreme Court justice and former ABA president Lewis Powell. Powell argued that business faced a challenge to its very survival, but that businessmen had "responded—if at all—by appeasement, ineptitude and ignoring the problem."[12] Powell recommended that the chamber of commerce hire a "highly competent staff of lawyers. In special situations it should be authorized to engage, to appear as counsel amicus in the Supreme Court, lawyers of national standing and reputation."[13] Powell assumed that business's problem was representative disequilibrium in the courts: when liberals were able to press their claims without effective probusiness rebuttal, courts inevitably sided with them. Powell did not propose that business use the law to create limits on government activism, but sought a return to the New Deal–era tradition of judicial restraint that business found it could work with. It would be over a decade before conservatives fully recognized that this tradition was beyond resuscitation and business would have to work within the new legal regime created by its adversaries.

The network of regional conservative PILFs that built off the experience of PLF shared Powell's strategic approach. PLF had expanded rapidly, taking on a number of high-profile cases and raising money quite successfully. PLF's staff wanted to take the organization national by creating branch offices across the country, a move that its board was afraid would stretch it too thin.[14] Leonard Theberge, a corporate lawyer who had been active in the ABA and conservative causes,[15] was asked by PLF's supporters to study the possibility of expanding the group's work nationally. This led to the founding, under Theberge's leadership, of the National Legal Center for the Public Interest, with the mandate of creating versions of PLF in the other regions of the country.[16] NLCPI originally operated out of PLF's offices in California, but soon moved to Washington, D.C.

NLCPI's most fateful strategic choice was to organize PLF's successors geographically rather than functionally, a decision that flowed from PLF's previous plan to open branch offices. NLCPI's founders also believed that regional firms could draw on local pride and business networks and establish their reputations through litigating issues of local importance. By granting a local monopoly in fund-raising, these firms would have a chance to grow without competing with their regional counterparts.[17] This cartel system would be maintained by a system of interlocking directorships, in which the president of NLCPI would serve on the firms' board and the presidents of the firms would serve on NLCPI's board. This structure was designed to prevent NLCPI from competing with its members (in particular by starting to litigate cases) and the regional firms from competing with each other (by allowing the president of NLCPI access to information about fund-raising and case strategy only available to board members). NLCPI would ensure that its members did not end up on opposite sides and adjudicate "border disputes" between the firms. In short, the network of first-generation public interest law was designed to stifle interorganizational competition.

NLCPI experienced organizational turmoil almost as soon as its member firms were created, with one faction of its board arguing it should go out of business and another interested in giving it an ongoing purpose. In 1979, former Ford administration assistant attorney general Michael Uhlmann was asked by Theberge to take over the presidency of NLCPI, a request that "had great appeal, especially in contrast to the commercial 'dry as dust' of private practice."[18] Uhlmann's vision for NLCPI put him into substantial conflict with the organization's members:

I had not thought through a programmatic agenda for NLCPI when I took over . . . it was enough for me then to be involved in trying to make a philosophical and rhetorical case for "conservative" public-interest law. . . . By the time I figured out what ought to be done, I could see that the NLCPI structure was not particularly well suited to its accomplishment. NLCPI had all the structural flaws of the Articles of Confederation—the regional entities wanted a weak central organization. . . . What they wanted from "central" was a national megaphone that would, from time to time, draw attention to their efforts, perhaps testifying before Congress occasionally, holding "national" conferences, etc. Above all, they wanted "central" to help them raise money, which would in be turn be redistributed to the regionals. The unworkability of this formula was compounded by the fact that most of the regionals were pretty thin entities to begin with. In fact, they were little more than tiny law offices whose principal function (as I later learned) consisted in filing amicus briefs within their bailiwicks. . . . The only one of the regionals that had a serious agenda, or that could make any serious claim to being a law firm, was Jim Watt's Mountain States operation, which tore a page from PLF and made itself into a force to be reckoned with. The others were feeble operations, big on rhetorical enthusiasm (which they would put forth before local business gatherings) but otherwise lacking anything resembling strategic vision or a way to achieve it.

Uhlmann and NLCPI parted ways when it became clear that he wanted it to abandon "coordinating" the behavior of regional firms and to go into business as a full-time, national public interest law firm. There was a powerful logic to Uhlmann's plan, but it was precisely what NLCPI's was designed—effectively—to prevent.

Uhlmann was replaced by in 1980 by Ernest Hueter, the former CEO of Kansas City's Interstate Brands. Hueter was actively involved in the Gulf and Great Plains Legal Foundation in Kansas City, later renamed the Landmark Legal Foundation. Hueter was approached by Joseph Coors, a fellow member of the National Association of Manufacturers' board, to replace Michael Uhlmann as NLCPI's leader. Coors made clear that he wanted NLCPI's president to be a respected businessman, who could reestablish businessmen's support of conservative public interest law.[19] The replacement of Uhlmann, an experienced and ideologically motivated conservative lawyer, with Hueter, a Midwestern businessman, was telling: the organization took a step in the direction of Washington-based, intellectual-driven leadership under Uhlmann and quickly jumped backwards. This leadership role for business, along with the movement's geographical structure, would set the template for the conservative public interest law movement's first two decades.

The Troubled First Generation

The experience for Chip Mellor and David Kennedy (who would go on to found the Institute for Justice) at the Mountain States Legal Foundation (MSLF) provides a useful case with which to examine the problems of the first-generation conservative firms because the organization had substantial advantages that its regional brethren lacked. MSLF was founded and financially supported by Joseph Coors, the conservative beer magnate who was also actively involved in building other parts of the movement's organizational apparatus in the 1970s. Unlike most of the other conservative firms, MSLF had a happy coincidence of geographical and functional differentiation: the states where it operated were those where public lands and related environmental issues were most hotly contested, and where the conservative legal movement's position on them had the strongest political support.[20] David Kennedy, the chairman of MSLF's Board of Litigation,[21] recalls that in the West there "was an enormous sense of political disenfranchisement. Therefore, with the lessons taught by the leftist activists of the sixties and early seventies in their use of the courts to obtain results which they were unable to obtain politically, there developed a movement to use the same tactics on behalf of more traditional, more conservative, more libertarian causes." Chip Mellor, a staff attorney for MSLF and for a brief period its acting president,[22] believes that this geographically focused grievance strongly differentiated MSLF: "One of the things that gave Mountain States an advantage that allowed it to be set apart from and more successful than its sister organizations was that it had a niche that it could successfully occupy and create an identity, a funding source, and some jurisprudence around. The other entities, to a greater or lesser extent, had a harder time developing a distinct identity. That led to problems in funding and focus of mission."

In its early years, MSLF had something else its sister organizations lacked: a powerful, dynamic leader, the soon-to-become-notorious James Watt. Watt drew attention to MSLF's cases, giving the organization a clear public presence, helping to attract talented lawyers to its staff, and building the trust and support of its board. After Watt left in 1981 to become Ronald Reagan's secretary of the interior, however, the flaws in the firm's organizational structure and legal strategy, which had been hidden under Watt's charisma, were exposed. David Kennedy comments, "When I compare . . . the quite carefully thought through and clearly articulate mission of IJ [Institute for Justice] with the more rudimentary thrust of MSLF, it's pretty clear that MSLF was starting from a basic complaint which was not carefully delineated or articulated." MSLF under Watt drew attention to its cause, but it was distinctly unsuccessful in directly using litigation to influence public policy.

The root of MSLF's difficulty in developing a coherent and effective legal strategy was in the tensions between individual business interests and conservative ideology—tensions that plagued all of the first-generation conservative PILFs. MSLF's board of directors was made up of three CEOs from each state, "either CEOs of their self-made companies, or mid- to upper-level executives with a larger corporation."[23] This leadership structure was largely driven by financial considerations, as all members of the board were expected to be either "financial contributors or at least to be active in fund-raising." Jefferson Decker has found that "in correspondence, foundation employees often thanked contributors for their 'investment,' not their 'donation' or 'contribution'; fundraisers targeted executives in specific industries and explained how Mountain States' legal work would 'directly affect' their cause."[24] In numerous cases MSLF took the logic of "investment" literally, preparing amicus briefs in support of its financial contributors.

The interests of local businessmen and the libertarian principles of MSLF's staff soon came into conflict with MSLF's challenge to Denver's grant of an exclusive cable television franchise to William Daniels.[25] Mellor recalls, "It was a great lawsuit. It was right at the time that cable television was in its infancy, and Denver was the cable capital of the world, and this was going to be the showcase system to demonstrate the potential of cable television to the world . . . [but] everybody was bought off on this thing. The business establishment, the political establishment, was very much behind it. But it was a violation of the First Amendment, so we filed suit." Mellor was answerable to a two-stage process within the organization: a Board of Litigation made up of practicing lawyers (who supported the suit) and the business-dominated board of directors.

> Some of them loved it, but there was a contingent from Colorado who said, "This is the wrong suit, you don't want to do this suit.". . . I was all for it, Clint [Bolick] was all for it, my wife—she wasn't my wife at the time—and our chairman [at the Institute for Justice], David Kennedy, was on the Board of Litigation, [future] Senator John Kyl, who was on the board. So we were all fired up about it. But it gored the wrong ox, it gored very powerful interests there, well connected to the Republican Party. The day we filed the lawsuit Joe Coors resigned from our board. Joe . . . thought this was not a good thing. It was not a cynical move on his part, and while he didn't like the idea that it was going to gore the people it was going to gore, he had much more of a feeling that "this is not what I founded MSLF to do. I founded it to take on the Sierra Club, not to do this sort of thing."

The Denver cable case exposed the division between the orientation of the businessmen on MSLF's board of directors and its staff and Board of Litigation. Reflecting the disconnect identified earlier between American businessmen's beliefs and behavior,[26] Daniels, a friend of Coors and the potential head of the Denver cable monopoly

> conceded that he understood and even sympathized with the principle which the staff was asserting, but argued that we had to "live in the real world" and, in the real world, municipal monopolies were the way it was going to be, so he was there to try to take advantage of the opportunity. . . . They failed to persuade this idealistic young organization that the real world had to be that way and . . . couldn't be changed. After all, we felt, that's what the entire purpose of this organization was, to change things from . . . the "unfair" status quo, to an order more consistent with . . . individual liberty and freedom from improper constraint, which we perceived as being all around us.[27]

Today, Mellor sees the Denver cable case as a "quintessential [Institute for Justice] case ten years before we formed IJ," but it didn't turn out to be an acceptable case for MSLF. "As the controversy and media coverage increased, contributions to the legal foundation dropped, especially from corporations. We persevered in court, but we were increasingly constrained by the Foundation from making our case aggressively in the media. Meanwhile, the screws continued to tighten on the funding front. In the face of this, the Foundation decided to abandon the fight."[28]

The MSLF experience taught Mellor lessons that he would spend the next decade trying to apply. The most important lesson was that, first,

> any organization worth its salt has to be dedicated to principle and not to expediency and political forces. Second, that the board of directors has to fundamentally understand the mission and be dedicated to that long-term mission, recognizing that there are going to be setbacks and difficult decisions along the way. Third, that fund-raising must never drive case selection, and you should never be beholden to anyone and that you have to be able to call your own shots. You have to gather around idealistic people who recognize the importance of the fight you are engaged in and who will pursue it with a passion that will allow you to have fun and overcome the obstacles.

The Denver cable case made it clear that free markets and business's interests were necessarily in tension. Conservative PILFs could not expect their business base to stand up for libertarian causes when they damaged the interests of specific firms. The key assumption of the first generation of firms, that the welfare-regulatory state could be turned back by mobilizing businessmen to defend their interests, failed under the stresses of real-life litigation. It would take Mellor a decade before he could create a new organization in which lawyers driven by ideology, rather than investors motivated by profits, would be in the driver's seat.

The Horowitz Report and the Problem of Business Influence

Mellor and Kennedy were not the only conservatives in the late 1970s who realized that something was seriously amiss in conservative public interest law. The most influential internal criticism came in a report to the Scaife Foundation by Michael Horowitz[29] that was subsequently distributed informally to conservative donors and activists.[30] The Horowitz Report had a powerful effect on conservative foundations and legal activists. Michael Greve, then a program officer at the Smith Richardson Foundation and later a founder of the second-generation Center for Individual Rights, recalls that

> there had for some time been a lot of dissatisfaction among conservative foundations about [conservative] nonprofit public interest law. . . . That didn't mean that all these places were losers. Some of them weren't, some of them were quite good. In general, there was a sense that the foundations had not gotten their money's worth. . . . There were reports that they had commissioned from outside people who had looked at this stuff, which had pretty much [agreed on the need for] specialization [and] more hardball litigation rather than amicus briefs. The [most important] document is the Horowitz Report.

The wide distribution of the Horowitz Report primed conservative foundations for new approaches and made them more skeptical of the projects they were already supporting. As a study of conservative organizational development in law prior to the 1980s and as an influence on it in later years, the Horowitz Report is worth examining in detail.

Horowitz's criticisms were direct and damning. "When visiting law schools" Horowitz found that "young men and women are tired, as is everybody, of the old answers. Yet, nobody has sufficiently offered young lawyers the sense that one can be caring, moral, intellectual, appropriately ideological, while at the same time being radically opposed to the stale views of the left."[31] While opposed to the liberal public interest law movement's goals, he was impressed by how it placed "its efforts on a higher moral plane than those of its adversaries and has thus engaged the loyalties of young attorneys and the national media."[32] This insight suggested the need to avoid a narrowly legalistic focus, instead attacking the "moral monopoly enjoyed by traditional public interest lawyers and their allies," thereby convincing young lawyers that conservatism and the public interest were not contradictions in terms. While the existing firms assumed that equalizing the contest over the public interest was simply a matter of who appeared in court, Horowitz recognized that the battle over the public interest was an intellectual contest over meaning and the moral reputations of ideological movements. Unable to compete at this higher plane,

"The conservative public interest law movement will at best achieve episodic tactical victories which will be dwarfed by social change in the infinite number of areas beyond the reach of its case agendas."[33] The conservative legal movement needed to stretch beyond the courts to the institutions that supported legal activism and generated movement reputations and intellectual distinction. Horowitz's report thus pointed beyond public interest law to the Federalist Society, of which he was an early supporter.

In the battle to transform legal culture, Horowitz discovered that conservatives were the victims of their greatest strengths, grassroots mobilization and the support of local businessmen, which encouraged the conservative public interest law movement's geographic division of labor. He observed, "The success of PLF led to the NLCPI model, which sought to replicate the least significant (and somewhat accidental) aspect of PLF—its regionally based character."[34] PLF's geographical orientation was not a secret to its success, but an obstacle, and certainly not a characteristic to be replicated.

> Washington is "where the action is" insofar as issues of public policy are concerned. A conservative public interest law movement should of course have, as one of its prime objectives, a radical alteration of that fact. Still, in maintaining its regional orientation, the conservative public interest law movement has essentially confused wish with reality, for it is in being more effective in Washington that the conservative public interest law movement can more effectively erode the power of its agencies . . . decision-making in Washington is, as is true with all human institutions, dramatically effected [sic] by personal relationships and ease of immediate access to decision makers.[35]

Conservatives had to adapt to the regime they sought to dismantle. That regime, centered in Washington, with policymaking conducted in the low-visibility, low-mobilization contexts of congressional committee hearings, agency regulatory operations, and informal relationships with interest groups and policy research organizations, foreclosed access to power by those based elsewhere. The national media, with its influence on the conventional wisdom of policymakers, was also based in Washington, and so firms interested in shaping the media's agenda and framing of the issues needed to have ongoing relationships with the Washington-based press. Situated far outside the Beltway, conservative PILFs lacked the ability to nimbly respond to opportunities, access information, and develop networks.

Even more important than this misdirected decentralization was the privileged role of business in the movement, which hampered its ability to seize the moral high ground and wage the battle of legal ideas. The firms' business-heavy caseload lent credence to their adversaries' argu-

ment that, far from being defenders of the public interest, they were nothing more than shills for conservative business interests. In fact, Horowitz agreed with the factual basis of this criticism, noting that "all too often, conservative public interest law firms serve as mere conduits by which monies contributed by businessmen and foundations are given to private law firms to assist it in the prosecution of 'its' cases. No practice presently engaged in by conservative public interest law firms is more inappropriate."[36] The source of this problem was the businessmen on the firms' boards, who saw their interests and that of conservatism as identical, and thus saw no conflict in having conservative public interest firms do their work for them.[37]

While this exposed the movement to claims of corruption and tax evasion, Horowitz was more concerned that it led conservatives to miss opportunities to influence the character of legal and policy debate. Those opportunities went well beyond those of interest to business, including social issues, poverty, and civil rights. Horowitz observed that there were "an increasing number of situations where businesses will seek federal support and subsidies to insure survival and to maximize their short-run interests. In such situations, 'conservative' positions will often be adverse to those of the businesses in question."[38] Businesses were highly risk-averse, hesitant to alienate their stakeholders by taking strong, ideologically charged stands, thereby producing "an adversarial confrontation between one party seeking principled, ideological gain, while the other, from the outset, seeks to limit losses, [a confrontation that] is inherently one-sided insofar as issues of precedent are concerned."[39] Conservative PILFs tended to reinforce this framing of the public debate, rather than challenging it. Business's leadership of the conservative legal movement, Horowitz concluded, harmed broader conservative interests in the law and was an obstacle even to its own long-term interests, and, as a result, business should limit itself to a purely financial role in the movement.

Freeing the movement from business would allow it to reach out to clients that fit the inherited framing of public interest law's mission. "It is clear," Horowitz wrote, "that only law-action centers which speak for such unrepresented parties as taxpayers, ultimate consumers and small businessmen, and which take positions (which may or may not be joined in by large corporations) against the growth of federal power and expenditures, can sufficiently articulate principled 'conservative' positions with a requisite measure of staying power and consistency."[40] To plausibly speak for these unrepresented interests, control of the movement needed to shift to lawyers with ideological and philosophical, rather than material, motivations. "The very decline in power of the American business community over the past decade, and the corresponding growth of a government-growth oriented, anti-business, traditional public interest movement is perhaps the best evidence that the skills in the business community are not well correlated with the skills involved in generating idealism and enlisting the intellectual loyalties of bright young men and women."[41]

Horowitz identified the university, rather than the corporation, as the key site of competition in the law. Universities, especially their law schools, Horowitz found, were the breeding ground of the liberal public interest law movement, where ideas were produced, strategies hatched, idealism shaped, and networks nurtured. Activists were motivated by their professors, the judges they clerked for, and the heads of public interest organizations, all of whom were motivated primarily by fundamental ideas of justice. If conservatives wished to compete in the public interest law arena, they needed to move their own intellectuals and entrepreneurs to the fore, since the primary battle was in the market for talented law school graduates. Links to law schools, rather than to business, were, as a consequence, vital in constructing the leadership of conservative PILFs.

Once they hired talented young lawyers, conservative PILFs needed to be able to stimulate them intellectually, which meant that "directors of conservative public interest law firms must only be those people capable of marshalling the enthusiasms of meaningful staffs."[42] These new leaders would be quite unlike practical businessmen, comfortable in organizations conducive to "an often impractical intelligence, a speculativeness of mind, often unfocused thinking, exceedingly unstructured organizations and the relative absence of hierarchy . . . the need for change in the above direction in the style and character of many conservative public interest law firms is not likely to be seen by many business leaders, but would be insisted upon by academics and others more regularly in contact with young men and women."[43] Even as conservatives were experiencing what Horowitz saw as an intellectual renaissance, the conservative academic community was nowhere to be seen in conservative public interest law. An inability to appeal to law students' idealism and organizational style led to the recruitment of lawyers who were "appallingly mediocre,"[44] graduates of lesser-known, regional law schools, with virtually no representation from the top-tier schools that fed liberal PILFs. To solve this problem, Horowitz wrote, "A dramatic change in the board and leadership profiles of conservative public interest law firms is a necessary first step, even at most successful conservative public interest law firms."[45] This was a repudiation of the dominant organizational model of the conservative movement in the 1970s and a shift in priorities that would accelerate in the 1980s as financial leadership of the movement shifted from businessmen to conservative foundations.

Conservative firms faced yet another set of structural obstacles to effective legal strategy, and these were the organizational maintenance impera-

tives that led to an unreasonable devotion of time and effort to activities, especially amicus curiae participation, that had little or no impact on legal or political outcomes. For Horowitz, business's emphasis on "measurable outputs" was a weakness where legal and intellectual combat was concerned, as it produced incentives for furious but strategically ineffective demonstrations of activity. Amicus briefs had the advantage of being cheap and quick to prepare, thereby allowing firms to show "participation" in a large number of cases, even when they were marginal to the outcome of the case. While admitting that there were instances where amicus participation made sense, Horowitz observed that "a high ratio of amicus participations on the part of a conservative public interest law firm raises a fair presumption that the firm is engaging in pufferies intended for naïve audiences of donors, and not truly doing meaningful work."[46] That "naïve audience" included businessmen and the diffuse audience targeted by direct mail, which has an even more limited ability to scrutinize the impact of groups they are asked to fund. Once firms got into this organizational maintenance cycle, little time or effort was left over for activities that might have had a significant impact on law and politics. Later critics of the first generation, like Chip Mellor, would trace even more serious consequences to the first generation's amicus addiction.[47]

Horowitz saw a target-rich environment for a conservative public interest law movement freed from structural impediments, especially in institutions controlled by liberals. Horowitz claimed that liberalism had become "a powerful establishment in American society which, in the name of speaking for the poor, has actually become the means of perpetuating the power and well-being of a middle-class group of well-paid and highly placed professionals, often through collusive and at times literally corrupt involvements with sympathetic government agencies."[48] This populist stance would allow conservatives to turn Naderite cultural resources—antiestablishmentarianism, suspicion of concentrations of power, claims of institutional self-interest, and temperamental populism—against liberal institutions.[49] This strategy would create opportunities for conservative firms to destabilize their opponents' material base and challenge their claim to monopolize the representation of the public interest.

In addition to attacking large, unaccountable institutions, conservatives could also draw on inherited understandings of public interest lawyering by defending large, diffuse, unrepresented interests. Among the issues Horowitz identified that would meet this criterion were the impact of regulation on small business and consumers, pornography, gerrymandering, deficit spending, and racial quotas. The specific issues were of considerably less interest to Horowitz than their long-term political po-

tential. Horowitz applied five basic tests of the attractiveness of an issue for the movement, which were whether it would

1. produce desirable political effects, in the sense of attracting potential constituencies for conservatism;
2. undermine the claim that liberals represented a trans-political public interest;
3. have plausibility as a matter of the public interest rather than wealthy private interests;[50]
4. exhibit idealism and provide an opportunity for conservatives to be seen on the side of the "good guys," which would also be useful for attracting idealistic young lawyers;
5. foster desirable policy outcomes, in the sense of limiting government power and empowering civil society.

While the business supporters of the first generation of public interest law thought in terms of discrete cases, Horowitz thought in terms of long-term political conflict, and judged cases by whether they weakened the institutional entrenchment of liberalism, and strengthened conservative organizations and causes.

Horowitz thought it especially vital for conservatives to represent clients who would associate conservatives with the underdog, individuals unjustly treated by large institutions, while simultaneously associating the Left with malevolent, unresponsive concentrations of power. In particular, conservatives needed to target "poor clients such as ghetto school children affirmatively interested in the maintenance of internal school discipline" and "ghetto public housing residents," who wished to "reestablish order in their neighborhoods." These cases "would sharply engage a traditional [liberal] movement which has essentially ignored the victims of ghetto disorder in its defense of the intended subjects of public sanction."[51] It would also help conservatives erase the stigma of racism and connect conservative legal activism to the increasingly sophisticated scholarship on race, poverty, and crime being produced by critics of the Great Society.[52] This scholarship, which would soon come under the heading of "empowerment,"[53] gave conservatives a plausible alternative on traditionally liberal issues, allowing them to claim that their legal activism genuinely represented the public interest better than did that of the Left.

The Horowitz Report's short-term effect on foundation support for conservative public interest law was primarily negative. In 1980, before the Horowitz Report was released, the staff of the Olin Foundation believed that the Southeastern Legal Foundation was "one of the better conservative public interest law groups, and one that the Steering Committee may want to support before the Scaife study [the Horowitz Report] is out."[54] By the beginning of 1982, the Olin staff was considerably

less impressed, observing, "As the Horowitz report indicates, this is not one of the more effective public interest law firms . . . staff recommends rejection of this general support proposal."[55] In 1982 the Olin Foundation responded to a grant request from the New England Legal Foundation by observing that "its staff is small and its director . . . is forced to spend most of his time fund-raising. Because of this, most of NELF's activity is limited to the filing of amicus briefs. A large number of amicus briefs are impressive to potential supporters, but these generally have little bearing on the outcome of litigation."[56] The Washington Legal Foundation (WLF) also felt the sting of the Horowitz Report. While not rejecting WLF's 1982 proposal completely, the Olin Foundation staff noted "WLF is more markedly a political organization than the other public interest law firms . . . and has not as yet had much influence on the legal profession itself. Horowitz also criticized WLF for using too many amicus briefs . . . and spending a sizeable proportion of its budget (about 15%) on direct mail."[57]

The Olin Foundation staff had clearly absorbed the core of Horowitz's critique, both its more obvious points (such as the use of amicus briefs) and its more subtle observations (such as the need for a more intellectual, idealistic approach to law). As a result, funding for other first-generation firms stagnated; it would be years before conservative foundations recovered their enthusiasm for the field. In fact, conservative patrons' skepticism of the field persisted as late as 1992:

> Staff is well aware of the Board's reluctance to make new grants for conservative public interest law organizations, and well aware of the good reasons for this reluctance. The bright hopes of ten years ago that conservatives could create effective counterparts to the liberal groups that have taken their policy agendas to the courtroom, such as the American Civil Liberties Union and the Sierra Club, have produced more disappointments than successes. The loose network of law firms has not been conspicuously effective, well-organized or stable.[58]

This experience was not wholly negative, since it primed the movement's patrons for new approaches to legal change. When a new generation of organizational entrepreneurs, such as the Federalist Society and second-generation PILFs, showed that they had learned Horowitz's lessons, foundations were ready and willing to fund them.

The Capital Legal Paradox

While Horowitz was unsparing in his attack on the conservative public interest law movement, he made an exception for one firm: the Capital Legal Foundation (CLF). CLF anticipated almost all the strategic and

organizational innovations that were put into practice at the Center for Individual Rights and the Institute for Justice a decade later, but collapsed in on itself, despite its strategic foresight, just a few years after Horowitz's praise. This makes CLF a very valuable case, for two reasons. First, it demonstrates that the failure of first-generation firms was due less to the absence of an effective strategic template for conservative public interest law and more to the unwillingness or inability of CLF's counterparts to recognize the superiority of its model and adapt their organizations accordingly. Second, CLF's eventual collapse demonstrates the substantial constraints that the immature conservative infrastructure imposed on even a firm with a strong and innovative strategy.

CLF was established at the same time as the other regional firms, and was undistinguished until Dan Burt, a successful Massachusetts lawyer, took the helm in 1979. As Jim Moody, his colleague at CLF, puts it, "It was Dan with the vision, now best embodied at IJ, that government and especially unwise regulation was there to basically help the established and entrenched aristocracy with collateral damage to the 'little' people, or the economically or politically unpowerful." Burt brought a coherent strategic vision to CLF, combined with a critique of the administrative state that echoed the liberal public interest law movement that he had once been a part of. CLF under Burt was more libertarian than its traditionally conservative counterparts, giving it a framework that detached it from business—a framework that, in fact, led it to take cases in which business was being protected or subsidized at the cost of consumers.

CLF anticipated (and may have influenced) many of the critiques made in the Horowitz Report. First, CLF was based in Washington, locating it close to the national bureaucracy, media, opinion leaders, and lawmakers. Second, CLF shared Horowitz's conviction that conservative PILFs needed to establish a principled image as the populist enemies of large concentrations of power. This required a very different relationship between case selection and fund-raising than that of other first-generation firms. "Dan ran interference," Moody said, "and made it *very clear* that our positions and actions were to be guided by the merits and not by *any* money-related concerns; he'd gladly sacrifice money for taking the right position."[59] Third, through litigation, Burt's book on the Nader network,[60] and attacks on the nomination of Nader ally Reuben Anderson to head the Administrative Conference of the United States, CLF argued that liberal firms were compromised by their cozy and dependent relationships with government, just as liberals had claimed that conservative firms were illegitimate because of their ties to business. Fourth, CLF focused on direct litigation as the route to long-term legal and policy change since, as Moody recalls, "Dan's vision [was] to directly represent clients as this . . . leads to better control of issues, record, etc. [although it] is *much*

harder and more expensive."[61] For example, CLF defended a group of homeworkers (the "Vermont Knitters") against Department of Labor regulations that threatened to put them out of business, attacked federal agricultural marketing orders, and effectively challenged FCC content and balancing rules in broadcast license renewal decisions.

This approach made CLF extremely popular with foundations and protected it from the reconsideration of investment in first-generation firms that occurred in the aftermath of the Horowitz Report. From the beginning, the Olin Foundation was impressed with Burt, whom it saw in 1980 as a "very bright, aggressive, former Naderite who understands how the Nader organizations work and uses the same tactics for conservative causes,"[62] and in 1982 as the head of "probably the most effective of the conservative firms operating at the national level," noting Horowitz's praise of the organization.[63] CLF was regularly given the Olin Foundation's highest rating—a record no other public interest law firm could match—and its budget increased steadily in the early 1980s even as other conservative firms faced financial instability.

In 1982, CLF was presented with what seemed like a golden opportunity to establish conservative public interest law as a force to be reckoned with. General William Westmoreland was the subject of a 1981 CBS *60 Minutes* segment that claimed he knowingly falsified reports of enemy troop strength. Westmoreland believed the claim was libelous and shopped his case to several high-profile lawyers, all in vain.[64] At the same time, Leslie Lenkowsky of the Smith Richardson Foundation (SRF) was contacted by a friend at CBS News, who was "appalled" by what he read in an article in *TV Guide*[65] attacking the *60 Minutes* report. According to Lenkowsky, SRF "had been working with Burt, had paid for his Nader book. And I passed the tip to him. He in turn spoke to Dick Larry at Scaife, who contacted a D.C. PR man . . . who knew Westmoreland." The case was attractive because it promised to humble the "liberal media" and present an opportunity for the Supreme Court to revisit its decision in *New York Times v. Sullivan*, which set a very high bar for libel claims.[66] In addition, there was a genuine moral offense at CBS's reporting, shared widely on the right at the time. Jim Moody "recall[s] vividly the sense of outrage we all felt at the depth of the CBS lies, a truly calculated and deliberate effort to rewrite history to a different agenda. Sure we knew it would be [very difficult] but we just couldn't in all conscience *not* take the case," even though they were aware that the case was a stretch for an organization like CLF.

Before the case was tried Burt's gamble looked like it would pay off. Because of the damage inflicted by the *TV Guide* article, CBS was in the uncomfortable position of needing to prove, in the words of its general counsel, "that in fact your broadcast was well founded. And therefore

you had to defend the journalism as well as the law. We were in a public battle as well as a legal battle."[67] Although even CBS realized the case was dangerous, *Westmoreland* did not play to CLF's organizational strengths. CLF had to raise money for *Westmoreland* as it tried the case, a distraction even for an experienced libel lawyer, which Burt was not.[68] Exacerbating CLF's competitive disadvantage was CBS's extremely talented and well-funded legal team headed by David Boies of Cravath, Swaine. Despite these disadvantages Burt embarrassed CBS in the court of public opinion prior to the trial, using the discovery process to pry embarrassing documents out of CBS, including an internal investigation (the "Benjamin Report") critical of the program.[69] Burt's aggressive handling of pretrial publicity and his promise that "we are about to see the dismantling of a major news network"[70] made him a cause célèbre in the conservative movement.[71]

Partially due to Burt's less-than-stellar performance in court, the case concluded with a disappointing settlement in which CBS granted Westmoreland neither money nor a retraction or admission of guilt. Despite this, Moody believes the case was a success, as "the discovery and scholarship associated with the case proved CBS lied and did so deliberately in a very agenda-driven and deceptive way, violated many of its own internal news guidelines. Westy's reputation was vindicated, even without the payment of damages." On the other hand, after investing the largest sum of money ever put into a conservative public interest law case, CLF obtained a meaningless settlement that made it difficult for the firm to argue that the case had been a success.

CLF's failure at the trial stage points beyond the firm to problems with the entire conservative legal movement at the time. First, CBS was a prestigious institution with extremely deep pockets and the finest legal defense money could buy. CLF, on the other hand, had to raise enormous sums of money for the case, since it lacked the pro bono assistance of a large private law firm, while also conducting the litigation and directing the public relations that went along with it. A more experienced and better-funded firm would have used the Westmoreland case to embarrass CBS through the discovery process and then moved it into the less resource-heavy appeals process, where it could focus narrowly on enticing the Supreme Court to revisit *New York Times v. Sullivan*. CLF, despite very heavy fund-raising, could not even fully cover the cost of the trial itself. While many observers at the time accused Burt of being outlawyered by Boies into accepting a vacuous statement by CBS, by the time the trial concluded it was clear that Westmoreland was going to lose. Therefore, going to the jury and getting an unfavorable verdict only made sense if CLF was prepared to invest the next few years in the appeals process. It would have been nearly impossible for CLF to survive long enough to do

so. By the time the case concluded, without even going to appeal, CLF was $400,000 in debt and had suffered reputational damage from the popular (if not wholly accurate) sense that Burt had mishandled the case. Michael Greve concludes that "Dan Burt bet a terrific outfit on Westmoreland—and lost." The fact that CLF's very existence was at stake in a single case underlines the difficulty PILFs faced in litigating highly fact-intensive cases against large, well-defended institutions without the ability to draw on the free resources from lawyers in private practice.

The failure of CLF in the Westmoreland case also points to two strategic problems that conservatives would confront over the next few years. First, the case was based on the theory that the dominant media could be shamed or litigated into what conservatives thought was more dispassionate, less ideological reporting. The Westmoreland case showed that CBS would stand up against attempts to alter its reporting through libel actions, and the public relations from the case did not seem to put a dent in the popularity of *60 Minutes*. As a consequence of the seeming futility of this strategy, conservatives began to focus on developing their own alternative media, supporting campus newspapers, the *Washington Times*, and, a decade later, the *Weekly Standard* and *Fox News*. This strategy would pay substantial dividends by the 1990s, in a way that the strategy of critique never did. Second, the Westmoreland case points to the lack of depth within the conservative movement at the time and the difficulty in maintaining a legal movement without the support of an effective professional insurgency. While Dan Burt may have been one of the best conservative legal minds at the time, he was wholly inexperienced in libel law. Today, as a result of the networks created by the Federalist Society, a high-profile personality such as Westmoreland with an exciting case could attract at least a handful of talented lawyers with experience in libel law, ready and willing to provide their skills and the resources of their firm.[72] In the early 1980s, when the Federalist Society was in its infancy, no such network existed, which explains why CLF got the case in the first place.

While the fallout from the Westmoreland case and Burt's desire to return to private practice killed CLF, it would be too easy to write it off with the rest of the first-generation firms. In fact, as argued earlier, CLF had a strategic design and litigation strategy that resembles the best of the second-generation conservative firms. Beyond its own achievements, CLF also recognized many of the legal opportunities that the Institute for Justice and the Center for Individual Rights took advantage of half a decade later. Still reeling from the failure of *Westmoreland*, Burt in 1985 presented an ambitious plan for the future of CLF to the Olin Foundation that proposed a new initiative to attack "self-help barriers" created by government, drawing on the then au courant idea of "empowerment."

While CLF could not get this initiative off the ground, the general approach and justification for the project were identical to those proposed by CIR and IJ years later. CLF argued that the issue of poverty could provide conservatives with legal traction, positive public relations, and the potential to embarrass liberals. "In short," wrote Burt, "many of the regulations aimed at 'helping' or 'protecting' the poor in fact perpetuate a culture of dependency that deprives them of the skills they need to enter the mainstream of our society."[73] CLF would use the law to win tangible victories for the poor and demonstrate the idea that government action itself was responsible for persistent poverty. Reflecting Horowitz's insights, CLF claimed that legal activism could influence popular ideas and reshape the conventional wisdom. In its last years, CLF also proposed other initiatives that would be fully developed by later law firms. It proposed to defend "the right to practice your profession," which, along with the Vermont Knitters case described earlier, has remarkable similarities to the "Ego Brown" case (defending a black Washingtonian's right to shine shoes) that made Clint Bolick's name at the Landmark Legal Foundation and the Institute for Justice.[74] This suggests that conservative public interest law in the early and middle 1980s did not lack strategically sound legal opportunities, but *was* faced with insurmountable organizational problems in establishing the resources, networks, and tactics to match its ideas.

Not long before CLF closed its doors, Burt, at the prompting of Richard Larry of the Scaife Foundation, addressed the question, "Is There a Future For Conservative Public Policy Litigation?" Not surprisingly, Burt's answer was a qualified yes. He admitted that even the best of the first generation of conservative litigation was not designed primarily to change the law. "Although we won most of our court and administrative litigation . . . many of these cases were brought to change attitudes, and raise money. Indeed almost all conservative public policy litigation to date has been brought to change public and judicial attitudes, since this is a prerequisite to changing the law, and with an eye to their fund raising appeal. . . . What we need to do now is convert these changes in attitude into changes in law."[75] Burt observed that five years of Reagan appointments to the bench meant that the opportunity to change the law existed in a way that it did not a few years earlier. Anticipating Charles Epp's arguments, Burt argued that changes in the composition of the courts would lead to only limited legal consequences without corresponding shifts among conservative litigators.

> Judges don't legislate, they must have specific cases before them to rule on. The new attitudes toward welfare, entry barriers and so on cannot become part of our law, cannot be institutionalized, if the disputes that arise when these attitudes clash with the laws of the last 50 years are not brought before the new judiciary. The policy litigators must turn from the high visibility, big press cases

of the last eight years and bring repeated cases in their area of special concentration, which they are prepared to litigate and relitigate until they change the law. . . . CLF has done this in a number of areas—most notably in the field of agricultural marketing orders. But as you know from that fight, it is long, arduous, and often undramatic labor. . . . In the process we have also raised marketing orders as an issue in the press and with the public. At the same time we hurt our fund raising in two ways. First Sunkist, our chief opponent in the marketing order fight, urged our corporate contributors to stop supporting us. I reckon they cost us $75,000 or so a year. Secondly, the issue wasn't "sexy," and did not attract individual or "gut" conservative money.[76]

Finally, Burt concluded that business could not be mobilized to defend free markets. In fact, as seen by CLF's efforts to eliminate agricultural marketing orders (a New Deal–era policy establishing production quotas) business could be the conservative movement's most determined foe.

Corporate America never had a long term view of public policy litigation. It sought relief from an immediate problem, and that happened. The Reagan years have taken the immediate public pressure off the business world, and hence eliminated the pressure to support policy litigation. Thus the policy litigators have seen a substantial part of their funding disappear. This has been especially serious to CLF, since its program never included litigation aimed at pleasing business, as opposed to supporting free markets. For example, a long-time CLF corporate contributor cut its contribution from $20,000 to $5,000 in the last two years. Its public policy executive told one of our directors before the last cut: "You'll have to take more cases that appeal directly to the business community if you want our support." . . . The general public [through direct mail] will fund highly visible attacks on liberal "sacred cows," but it will not sustain a large, careful slog through the courts that results in fundamental, long range legal change. It will not do so because this sort of fight is undramatic, subtle, and not easily understood.[77]

CLF clearly understood the organizational bind that faced conservative public interest law, but had no answer to it beyond a request that conservative foundations substantially increase their support. CLF recognized the solution to the problems of conservative public interest law, but it would take a new generation of firms, and the deepening of the conservative support structure, to take advantage of this strategic breakthrough.

Charting a New Course

Chip Mellor moved on from the Mountain States Legal Foundation to the Department of Energy, a thankless task for a libertarian, while his colleague Clint Bolick went to work in the Reagan administration in

Clarence Thomas's Equal Employment Opportunity Commission. Government service was a part of neither's long-range plans, but developing an invigorated form of conservative public interest law was. Starting in the mid-1980s, and drawing on Horowitz's critique and their own experience, Bolick and Mellor began to devise a strategy and an organizational design to guide a new generation of conservative PILFs. This process would produce many of the insights that Bolick and Mellor drew on in founding IJ, influence the future leadership of CIR, and convince conservative patrons that public interest law was not an intrinsically futile project.

Before they left the Reagan administration, Mellor and Bolick began planning a law firm, the "Center for Constitutional Litigation." Their original planning documents are striking in their scant emphasis on "judicial restraint," which was still dominant in conservative jurisprudence, and their insistence that courts should energetically protect a libertarian understanding of constitutional liberties.

> In the American system of government, the courts are designed to safeguard basic liberties against the passions of the other branches of government. Unfortunately, the judiciary has abandoned this vital responsibility while assuming the role of a super-legislature, imperiling those very individual rights with whose protection it was entrusted. Leading this effort is a highly sophisticated advocacy movement with a well-defined legal and social agenda. The philosophy of this movement now permeates legal academia and much of the judiciary, and no effective, principled alternative has yet been developed to challenge its agenda. Thus, any comprehensive movement to advance liberty must include as a vital component an organization designed to restore and expand judicial protection of these principles.[78]

Bolick and Mellor recognized that their opposition was a well-organized liberal legal network rather than a disconnected set of cases. Countering that network required a serious intellectual critique, principled constitutional philosophy, and organizations capable of acting across the entire range of venues that feed into legal change. With the MSLF experience clearly on their minds, Mellor and Bolick declared that "the Center's efficacy in achieving this goal is directly dependent upon its steadfast commitment to principle and rejection of simple expediency. This requires methodical effort with a long-range strategy to be implemented through carefully developed litigation. The Center and its supporters must be prepared to make a long-term commitment."[79] Making that long-range strategy a reality required that the proposed firm's patrons eschew using public interest law to achieve their short-term economic or political interests in order to facilitate their long-term interests in a constitutional order of limited government. The keys to stretching out the firm's time horizon were severing fund-raising from case selection and identifying patrons who would accept outcomes from litigation campaigns years or even decades out.

Bolick and Mellor identified a range of areas ripe for litigation, such as civil rights, free enterprise, property rights, contracts, torts, education, and telecommunications. They had no doubt that the opportunity structure for conservative litigation was permissive, but it could not be exploited without significant strategic and organizational innovation. Their first innovation was to be strategic rather than reactive, selecting issues "in concert with movement think-tanks, academicians, and legal experts," focusing on concerns that had the greatest potential for creating useful precedent, rather than those of interest to their donors. This strategy would bring conservative intellectuals closer to the center of legal activism than they had been in the past, and require that the firm's lawyers be informed by and contribute to scholarship. A close relationship between intellectuals and lawyers was essential since "in some mission areas, it will be necessary to lay extensive scholarly groundwork before litigation is commenced. . . . One of the Center's most important functions will be to produce law review articles, to sponsor and provide speakers for law-related seminars, to work in concert with other legal scholars, and to coordinate with think tanks within the movement. Such an approach will ensure the intellectual integrity of the Center's program and of the precedents it successfully establishes."[80] This intellectual orientation reflected the lessons of the Horowitz Report (which they knew potential grant-makers would have read) and the insight that a clearly defined, intellectually informed strategy was an organizational maintenance device: the clearer the principle upon which litigation was based, the less risk of being pushed and pulled by short-term considerations or pressured by patrons.

Bolick and Mellor's second innovation was to organize the proposed firm *functionally* by issue instead of *geographically* by region. This change reflected a crucial lesson they had learned from the Left, which was the need for careful, strategic client selection. Despite the fact that conservatives had previously criticized the Left's "venue shopping," Bolick and Mellor recognized that this was essential in using law strategically to produce large-scale change. "After a strategy is devised, the Center will typically initiate litigation in multiple jurisdictions. This approach will increase the likelihood that favorable fact-situations and forums can be found, and that a conflict may emerge among the circuit courts leading to possible resolution by the Supreme Court."[81] The more functionally specialized the organization, the more regionally opportunistic it could be. The first generation of firms made the opposite calculation, being functionally promiscuous but regionally focused.

The 1985 proposal never made its way to any potential funder, but it was a critical step in the development of the second generation of conservative public interest law. Mellor presented the proposal to David Kennedy, who, "in his gentle but firm way . . . convinced us that we weren't there yet in having really thought it through enough or in having the management and fund-raising experience to pull it off."[82] At the same time, Mellor was recruited from the Reagan administration by Anthony Fisher, the patron of a far-flung network of think tanks in the United States and abroad, to head the Pacific Research Institute (PRI). Mellor's move to PRI, soon after the 1985 proposal was written, gave him an opportunity to "try to develop and focus the concept further while learning how to manage and fund a nonprofit," and a home for a new project, the Center for Applied Jurisprudence (CAJ), that became the principal planning tool for the Institute for Justice.

The original grant proposal for CAJ, sent to all of the major foundations on the right, began with a forceful call for change in the conservative legal community. The proposal made clear that "the courtroom is and will continue to be a policy arena, regardless of President Reagan's success in transforming the judiciary."[83] Success in elections and the consequent appointment of judges would not transform the courts, because the legal liberal movement, "unlike the conservative movement[,] has developed a cohesive and pragmatic ideological program with support from legal academia, supplemented through a sophisticated public interest law network." Liberals compensated for their declining electoral power through a powerful network of legal organizations, while the absence of a similar network on the right meant conservatives failed to capitalize on their increasing power over judicial appointments. As Horowitz had also observed, the conservative firms that did exist were notably ineffective.

> Conservative public interest law organizations were, and in some important cases continue to be, a significant first step in advocating concepts of free enterprise, private property rights, and individual freedom in the courtroom. But the effectiveness of conservative public interest law has been impaired by at least three factors: 1) the need to learn on the job since it was a new approach to advocacy; 2) an ad hoc, uncoordinated approach to case and tactics selection, guided generally by conservative principles, but rarely as part of a comprehensive, philosophically consistent long range strategy; and 3) a "discomfort factor" toward such litigation in the general legal community and among judges.[84]

Mellor told conservative patrons that the firms they supported were insufficiently intellectual and principled and that their meager long-term impact was a function of their reactive posture, defined as they were by their opposition to the Left rather than their own vision of social justice. A clearer set of principles would allow conservatives to set the legal and political agenda and define the terms of public debate. In what amounted to movement heresy at the time, the proposal embraced a proactive stance for conservative litigators and an assertive role for federal courts. This was bitter medicine for a movement raised on "judicial restraint" and "strict construction," but it was necessary if conservatives were to cease the futile exercise of playing defense in the federal courts. Consequently, the CAJ proposal recognized the necessity of convincing conservative judges and executive branch officials, who had grown up under these older ideas, to accept the unfamiliar and seemingly exotic sources of doctrine that this new generation of litigators would present in court. Without establishing the intellectual weight and coherence of these ideas outside of court, in the institutions where legal norms are legitimated, they would produce limited results on the inside, even from judges with a conservative temperament.

The CAJ proposal emphasized the project's intellectual dimensions, in particular the prominent legal scholars who would participate.[85] This was a sign of the conservative legal movement's maturation. Assembling a group of prominent conservative legal theorists and lawyers with government experience would have been almost impossible a decade earlier, but by the mid-1980s the conservative movement had developed a cadre of activists and thinkers whose primary commitment was to a set of ideas rather than the defense of particular interests or constituencies. Their common belief was that advancing the conservative legal movement required the elaboration of conservative ideas rather than the further mobilization of conservative interests. Idealism *was* strategy.

The CAJ proposal assembled three task forces of intellectuals and lawyers: on the First Amendment, on economic liberty and civil rights, and on property rights. Papers written by the chair of the task force laid out the issues at stake in the area, which were then critiqued by the task force and its collective judgment assimilated into a book. While the books would be the responsibility of the authors alone, the process was designed to build consensus within the movement. As Mellor recalls, the purpose of organizing the task forces was

> to create a buzz, to get people excited about what we were up to, then to enlist the involvement of these scholars and recognized authorities in their respective areas. I wanted to grow our own talent; I didn't want to bring in someone who was already recognized as having this scholarship or this point of view, so all we were doing is giving an old dog a new platform. I wanted to get something new and dynamic going that would shake up the tradition a little bit and draw upon the good ideas from a variety of different people. So bringing those authorities in got us their expertise, but it also got them invested in our success. They . . . became . . . very excited about this. Many of them . . . have continued to play important roles in the Institute for Justice.

These books would combine substantive legal and policy arguments with strategic judgments about how to organize a legal campaign. In particular, the books would emphasize:

1. Model case development including possible timing, forum, ideal parties, and appellate considerations
2. Timing and placement of significant law review articles and related publications
3. Exposure and debate in the legal community, academia, and the general public
4. Cooperation with other groups or endeavors, e.g. law and economics, the Federalist Society, Institute for Humane Studies, and conservative litigation groups[86]

CAJ's proposed legal strategy integrated the transformation of legal culture and ideas with strategic public relations and coalition building. Cases and legal strategy would be chosen for maximum public impact in areas that held the potential to attract new groups to the conservative fold.

Michael Greve, at the time the program officer at the Smith Richardson Foundation in charge of the CAJ grant, recalls that "the SRF grant unquestionably demonstrated that Chip is a very good fundraiser. What's more, he made good on the grant. . . . That undoubtedly helped him to establish IJ." CAJ not only helped Mellor think through the organizational and strategic questions in public interest law, it also demonstrated to the foundation community that he was capable of organizing and delivering on a major project—thereby helping to alleviate suspicions inherited from the Horowitz Report among conservative patrons of public interest law entrepreneurs. The CAJ had a broader impact than laying the foundation for IJ, as it influenced the thinking of the larger conservative network. Greve recalls, "The sessions I attended were on First Amendment and Equal Protection. Former mostly on commercial speech; dominated, intellectually, by Mike McConnell and Lillian BeVier. Latter dominated by Clint Bolick, then still on a racial neutrality riff. [There was] lots of advice (from Jeremy Rabkin, Nathan Glazer, yours truly) to get off it and to push 'black entrepreneurship' instead." While Bolick would continue to push race neutrality in his publications, IJ followed the advice of the CAJ task force in its actual litigation. The CAJ networking was important for Greve as well. The early CIR grant proposals stressed his participation in the CAJ's task forces, and noted that "CIR's Directors have spoken with William ('Chip') Mellor, PRI's President, and he has agreed to make the PRI's Task Force strategies available to the CIR."[87] This sent a signal to conservative patrons that money invested in CIR would not lead to a reprise of the errors made by earlier firms.

Just as important were CAJ's more diffuse impacts. "What I really got out of it was a confidence builder," says Mellor. "It's not that I knew all the legal issues, I didn't by a long shot, but I expected to learn those. What I was really in need of at that time was the reassurance that there was fertile ground there. . . . I needed confirmation, but they told me it was even more fertile than I realized." Speaking of CAJ, Greve argues that

> the original project [didn't] dictate any particular result, position, or even emphasis. For example, Clint [Bolick] later wrote a screed against local "Grassroots Tyranny," which is light years from my own and CIR's perspective on federalism and local government. More significantly, perhaps, IJ would never represent the people CIR represents, but behind that product differentiation lays the judgment that you've got to get back to the constitutional norms. So in that sense, the project really was a marker.

The search for a new strategy of conservative public interest law that began with the Horowitz Report culminated with the CAJ project, giving the movement's organizational entrepreneurs the confidence to set up new firms, and its patrons the confidence to fund them.

Idealism as Strategy: The Strategic Vision behind the Institute for Justice

The most important book to emerge from this project was Clint Bolick's *Unfinished Business: A Civil Rights Strategy for America's Third Century*.[88] At Clarence Thomas's EEOC, Bolick had been deeply involved with the development of conservative thinking on civil rights. After leaving government he moved to the Landmark Legal Foundation, where he put the CCL and CAJ framework into action, pursuing libertarian goals with clients, including African-Americans, who were not typically associated with conservatives. Drawing on this experience, Bolick developed an argument that prefigured the strategy behind all of IJ's most prominent cases.

Unfinished Business was relentlessly optimistic in tone, highly sanguine about the role of the judiciary, and characterized by a total lack of defensiveness that was both temperamental and strategic. Bolick argued that "a strategy that consists mainly of resisting the civil rights establishment's agenda is by nature a losing strategy . . . a reactive posture allows the other side to define civil rights in terms of its own agenda and to claim the moral high ground."[89] Bolick embraced the empowerment fad popular among a handful of younger Beltway conservatives while also distancing himself from the mainstream of the conservative movement, evidence for which was Bolick's quoting of Stuart Butler that "confidence is not engendered [among black Americans] by conservative attorneys chasing firetrucks to see if any members of the Teamsters Union are upset about affirmative action."[90] Bolick understood that in civil rights, perhaps more than in any other area, an image of goodwill was a precondition for having conservatives' intellectual argument taken seriously.

> Those who have resisted the civil rights policies of the past quarter-century have been accused, often justly, of offering no alternative. The lack of a coherent, credible, and comprehensive alternative leaves us in the untenable position of arguing either that all of our nation's civil rights problems have been solved or that the major civil rights issue of our time is the plight of white firefighters victimized by reverse discrimination. If that is our response, our detractors may be excused for calling into question our commitment to civil rights.[91]

The repetition of the "white firefighter" trope is illuminating. Bolick took as axiomatic the modern activist state's assumption that policies need to be justified in terms of their impact on less privileged groups. Sixty years of government activism had shifted the ground of politics, and so, for conservatives' argument for limited government to be heard, they would have to justify their policies against the standards of their liberal opponents.

While Bolick did not argue against opposing affirmative action (he would later become famous for calling Lani Guinier the "quota queen"),[92] he claimed that the conservative cause on civil rights was better served by identifying blacks, not whites, as its beneficiaries. Even if this strategy did not advance Republican electoral fortunes, it would produce clients with "stories" more compelling to the courts and the media. While a client's racial identity should be irrelevant from a conservative point of view, Bolick argued that "given limited resources, public interest litigators should represent the most disadvantaged individuals and should try whenever possible to find a plaintiff whose plight outrages people."[93] He claimed the authority of the civil rights movement as justification for his emphasis on an affirmative role for federal courts. Against the conservative consensus in favor of judicial restraint, Bolick asserted that

> as our nation's founders recognized, the legislative and executive branches are especially susceptible to majoritarian and special interest influences. Since civil rights are by definition individual rights . . . the ultimate guardian of those rights, when the other branches of government have failed adequately to protect them, is the judiciary. I recognize how imperfectly the judiciary has provided that protection to date . . . but those considerations, it seems to me, speak in favor of increasing our activities in the courts rather than diminishing them.[94]

Bolick called, without apology, for judicial activism, on the grounds that liberals could not be defeated by putting the activist court genie back in the bottle. In sharp contrast to the visionaries who inspired the first-generation conservative PILFs such as the Pacific Legal Foundation, Bolick claimed that success would come only through judicially enforced constitutional rights, which could act as a counterweight against the "majoritarian and special interest influences" that preserved liberal policy preferences.

Bolick extended the CAJ proposal's argument that public interest lawyers needed to establish clear long-range goals, and to judge "every individual case . . . against those principles and goals to keep the program on course. Otherwise, the public interest law firm becomes just another law firm."[95] Bolick had learned from the Left that victories in court that established no clear precedent for future cases could set the movement back, while "defeats can advance the strategy by creating splits among jurisdictions (thus increasing the odds of Supreme Court review), by providing guidance in fine-tuning strategy, and by creating public support that may translate into future triumphs."[96] For conservatives to counter the Left in court, they needed to establish "counterrights" of their own, with precedential value that could push back the scope of governmental intervention.[97] An amicus strategy, even if successful, could only stop assertions of liberal rights in particular cases. A more powerful strategy was to use the law as a sword rather than a shield, expanding the judicially recognized meaning of the First Amendment and the takings clause, for example, to put liberals on the defensive. Conservatives of the second generation had a few examples of this approach, none more powerful than the Pacific Legal Foundation's successful litigation in *Nollan v. California Coastal Commission*, which applied the takings clause of the Constitution to government conditions on the use of property.[98] *Nollan* signaled that conservatives could do more than play defense, that the newly reshaped federal courts would allow them to create counterrights of their own.

The final, and, for organizational purposes, most important insight that Bolick (drawing heavily on Mellor's experience and judgment) presented in *Unfinished Business* was the centrality of organizational design. Opportunities were not enough if they were squandered by short-term organizational maintenance imperatives.

> It is absolutely essential that groups dedicated to such goals understand the respective roles of fundraising and case selection. Funds are raised to support the cases—not vice versa. This rule is critical not only for the organization's integrity, but also for the mission's success. While no public interest group can afford to overlook funding realities, allowing such concerns to dictate or heavily influence case selection confused ends with means. . . . Too often, public interest law firms have lost sight of their original goals, ultimately viewing the perpetuation of their particular programs as ends in themselves and engaging in mercenary tactics to advance their programs even at the costs of the very principles

that are their reason for existence. Such organizations are not only worthless, they detract from those who are sincerely committed to principles by diverting scarce resources and by fostering cynicism about the entire movement.[99]

By learning from the Left and from their own experience of the dynamics of legal strategy, and combining these lessons with an organizational form capable of supporting those lessons, conservatives could make the courts into a powerful instrument for political change.

Conclusion

The sources of the first generation's ineffective reaction to the rise of legal liberalism can be found in the character of the conservative movement in the 1970s. Conservatism's strengths were its activists at the state level, especially its network of small to medium-sized businessmen. These assets were electorally potent, since the federal character of Congress and the Electoral College mirrored the movement's resources. The changes in American politics described in chapters 1 and 2, however, devalued those resources when it came to legal and policy change. In this new regime, conservatives had few resources appropriate to the system they sought to influence, which privileged ideas, legal tactics, access to Washington networks, and the ability to influence the mass media. In this regard, conservatives compared poorly to the Left, whose assets were precisely those rewarded by this new political system. The new American political system was well adapted to influence by the "new class" of intellectuals and professionals, a class in which conservatives were all but entirely unrepresented.

Conservatives were also hampered by their alliance with the business community. Conservatives had counted on business, whose bottom lines were being attacked by liberal public interest law, to be the natural constituency for countermobilization. What they had not anticipated was the way that American business had adapted to the structure of the activist state. America's business leadership had learned to make the expansion of government activity work for them, or at least to minimize its impact on their bottom line. Both Mellor and Kennedy at MSLF and Burt at CLF recognized that business's interest in keeping its access to anticompetitive arrangements could make it the enemy of free markets. Those businessmen sufficiently motivated to support the movement were insufficiently sophisticated in the new mode of legal politics to effectively guide it, and they lacked interest in the broader range of conservative legal opportunities. Reorienting the relationship between conservative public interest law and business would, therefore, be a necessary precondition for organizational success.

The problems with first-generation public interest law went beyond the predominant role of business. The larger challenge was that change in professionally dense areas like the law requires context-appropriate networks to provide personnel that can develop legal ideas and strategy, identify and bring cases, take maximal advantage of legal precedents in bureaucratic rule-making, and raise money from foundation and governmental sources. It was here that conservatives were weakest. Even if the businessmen who supported the first-generation firms had been more sophisticated than they were, they would have lacked the foot soldiers to devise an alternative as effective as their liberal opponents. It would take the development of a conservative legal network, of the sort that the Federalist Society would create in the early 1980s, for conservatives to have the public goods to support an effective legal movement.

Finally, the experience of the first generation of public interest law suggests the importance of agenda control in the new American political system. Liberal public interest law organizations were designed to control the legal agenda and to use even marginal precedents to keep their adversaries on the defensive. Conservatives fell into a trap by presenting the "other side" in an institutional context—the courts—where power comes from defining the terms of debate and choosing the terrain on which the battles will be fought. By organizing reactively, conservatives guaranteed that they could only slow down the advance of legal liberalism, but not stop or reverse it. Only when they reoriented their activity to support "counterrights" of their own could conservatives take advantage of the opportunities of the new American political system.

Seizing those opportunities required new ideas and new organizations. To gain control of the legal agenda, conservatives needed to escape the bounds of judicial restraint, which stated what courts should not do rather guiding where they could legitimately act. Judicial restraint was the natural ideological match to the strategy of providing the "other side," since both aimed to resuscitate the legal status quo ante. Legitimating an active role for the courts in defending individual rights would require a much greater role for intellectuals in the conservative legal movement, since transforming what judges considered reasonable and appropriate was as important as the design of specific cases. Conservatives would have to change the ideas of legal elites before they could effectively change the behavior of courts.[100] As subsequent chapters will show, this is why conservatives of the second generation sought to rebuild their legal movement around intellectuals and academics, and significantly diminish the role played by businessmen and Republican politicians.

4

Law and Economics I: Out of the Wilderness

DOES THE FIELD OF LAW AND ECONOMICS even belong in a book on the conservative legal movement? Many of the field's most prestigious practitioners are quite liberal and motivated primarily by a desire to make law an empirical discipline, rather than an instrument of conservative or libertarian ideology. That said, there can be no doubt that many conservatives, especially foundation patrons, saw in law and economics a powerful critique of state intervention in the economy, and a device for gaining a foothold in the world of elite law schools.

To understand the place of law and economics in the larger conservative legal movement, it is necessary to begin at the University of Chicago Law School, the home of scholars such as Richard Posner and Richard Epstein and the training ground of many of the movement's most important early practitioners and entrepreneurs. From there, our story moves on to the myriad projects of Henry Manne, who scored the first real entrepreneurial success for the movement through his economics programs for judges and law professors, and his Liberty Fund conferences on law and economics. Manne's programs at Rochester, Miami, and Emory emerged at roughly the same time as conservative public interest law, but were rooted in a very different model of legal change. Businessmen dominated conservative public interest law, but in law and economics they provided money without taking a significant leadership role, a role that was tightly guarded by the movement's intellectuals. Whereas conservative public interest law assumed that the way to counter legal liberals was by providing the "other side" in court, the law and economics movement sought to undermine the intellectual foundations on which its arguments, and its claim to represent the public interest, were based.

Throughout this chapter, there are false starts and failed efforts at institution building, to go along with some impressive organizational successes. Even more interesting, this period shows that the conservative movement was far from internally homogenous—internal conflict and suspicion between movement patrons and entrepreneurs helped to sink one of the movement's most ambitious efforts at institution building, Manne's project of building "Hoover East" in the suburbs of Atlanta. A close study of the early organizational history of law and economics shows that conservative countermobilization was not governed by a "grand plan" hatched all at once. Instead, movement patrons opportunistically supported organizational entrepreneurs who seemed to have found a crack in the edifice of legal liberalism. Only later did these opportunistic decisions gel into a coherent strategy that could then be applied in other cases.

Building the Mother Ship: The Creation of Law and Economics at Chicago

The organizational history of law and economics, like so much of the modern conservative movement, begins with the University of Chicago. While it has since found other homes, Chicago has always been the spiritual center of the movement, especially for those who see it as a critique of government activism as well as a method for studying law. Chicago provided a home for law and economics to develop even when its ideas were regarded with intense skepticism and hostility in the larger academic and legal world.[1] As a result, the field was ready when the law schools and policymakers became more open in the 1970s.

Law and economics began at Chicago by accident, rather than as part of a larger ideological plan. The first economist in the University of Chicago Law School was Henry Simons, who "published little and was not a popular teacher"[2] but "had a few good friends in the law school like Wilber [Katz] and [Malcolm] Sharp" who managed to move Simons from the economics department to the Law School in 1933.[3] The irony of Simons's appointment was that what passed for law and economics in most law schools at the time was part of the progressive project to question the theoretical foundations of classical economics and the legal doctrines informed by it.[4] It would have been hard to find a character less sympathetic to this approach than Simons, who was a representative of the "Old Chicago" economics of Frank Knight and Jacob Viner. By the late 1930s Simons had become, like many others of libertarian instincts, genuinely spooked at what he saw as threats not just to the free market, but the free society. Simons, who helped arrange for the publication in the United States of *The Road to Serfdom*, agreed with Hayek that economic planning posed a danger to personal and political liberty; in the words of Aaron Director, he "thought that doomsday was upon us."[5] Simon's "doomsday" was set in motion by a growing state that pulled academics into its maw, a trend that threatened both the quality of public policy and the freedom of universities.

> The prevailing drift toward increasing participation of professors as bureaucrats, as governmental or business consultants, and as Round-Table exhibitionists is, I think, tragically mistaken and wholly ominous for democracy. . . . It means not only bad government—democracy of cheap debate and mere

technical maneuver, instead of government by intelligent, truth-seeking discussion—but bad Universities as well. The alternation of professors between action and inquiry, as occasional, temporary bureaucrats or part-time consultants, involves accretions of power and prestige and often large additions to full-time academic remuneration. . . . The consequent perversion and distortion of academic standards and University functions thus becomes pervasive.[6]

The increasing reach of the state meant that universities no longer set their own priorities, but became corrupted, albeit softly and subtly, by a state that had outstripped its proper bounds.

While Simons was not appointed to the Law School because of his ideology, he was a Chicago economist through and through, committed to helping to save capitalism—if it could be saved. While his book on taxation was considered a serious contribution at the time, he devoted a substantial percentage of his time to less academic pursuits aimed at preserving free enterprise.[7] On the one hand, Simons published *A Positive Plan for Laissez-Faire*, which by the standards of the time was highly market-oriented but which is markedly lacking in orthodoxy by contemporary standards.[8] George Stigler quipped in this regard, "It's true that he was the man that said the Federal Trade Commission should be the most important agency in government, a phrase that surely should be on no one's tombstone. . . . Yet, relative to the hectic, excited days of the thirties he was leaning the other way."[9] Simons represented what is best understood as the evangelical element of Chicago economics, embodying the same spirit that inspired Milton Friedman in his public intellectual work and the Chicago economics department's famous (and in some quarters notorious) collaboration with the Catholic University of Chile.[10] By 1945, Simons's concern for the future of free societies had become acute, as had his anxiety about the fortunes of classical liberal thought.

> With the scattering of the "Austrians" and the vastly changed complexion of economics at Cambridge and Harvard, this intellectual tradition . . . is now almost unrepresented among the great universities, save for Chicago; and it may not long be well represented at Chicago. It still has its firm adherents, to be sure; but its competent representatives are widely dispersed and isolated from one another, in academic departments or governmental bureaus where they are largely denied opportunity for cooperation with like-minded scholars, or for recruiting and training their successors.[11]

Acutely aware of their isolation, classical liberal thinkers initiated projects aimed at identifying allies and networking domestically and internationally, the most important of which was the Hayek-founded Mont Pelerin Society. The overriding object of the Society was to cement a network of classically liberal thinkers of all countries; "the contacts which the meetings provide and the exchange of opinions between members which the mere existence of a list provides should remain the main function of the group."[12] Hayek's proposal assumed that the "scattering" was a more or less permanent state of affairs, and proposed to correct for it by networking those advocates for classical liberalism that still remained.[13]

Simons's plans at the University of Chicago were driven by a vision different from Hayek's libertarian *internationale*, looking instead to what we might call "remnantism," the idea that in a fallen world a "saving remnant" of those still committed to right thinking should be preserved until the folly of corrupt ideas was definitively revealed.[14] Driven by this more pessimistic sense of the prospects for classical liberalism, Simons proposed, in a document sent to Hayek and intended for eventual consideration by the Volker Fund,[15] "There should, I submit, be at least one university in the United States where this political-intellectual tradition is substantially and competently represented—and represented not merely by individual professors but also by a small group really functioning as a social-intellectual group."[16] An institute, staffed by libertarian professors and with funding for research support, visiting lecturers, seminars, and visiting fellows, would bring together "the best economists and political philosophers of its 'school' from all over the world."[17] With the concern about capture by central administration that would later characterize the administrative entrepreneurship of Henry Manne, Simons insisted that his institute "should be set up, not as part of the University of Chicago but independently, with its own governing body and its own funds. It should be located at Chicago, however, only after reasonable assurances of close and friendly relations with the University; and it should be free to move elsewhere if effective or fruitful cooperation later proves unattainable."[18]

For the future of law and economics at Chicago—and beyond—the most important part of Simons's proposal was its proposed leader: "Aaron Director is not only the ideal person to head the Institute; he is available and would be willing to undertake the task even at financial sacrifice."[19] In a letter to Hayek, Simons confided that the project was "contrived . . . largely for what one might call ulterior purposes . . . to get Aaron Director back here and into a kind of work for which he has, as you know, real enthusiasm and superlative talents."[20] While Simons's institute never materialized, the discussions surrounding it did succeed in bringing Director to Chicago, through the beneficence of the Volker Fund. Director recalls that

> Hayek . . . met a person called Luhnow, who was then responsible for a lot of money in the Volker Fund. He persuaded Luhnow to give a certain sum of money to establish a center that would promote private enterprise. It was earlier decided that Chicago was the only place that was likely to accept such a project,

and it was also decided that the law school was the only part of the University of Chicago that would accept such a project. Henry Simons was the one that suggested to Hayek that I should be the person in charge of the project. Apparently the dean of the law school, Wilber Katz, then wrote in one condition. It was that I should be permitted to teach one course in the law school. The course, of course, was economic analysis. Henry Simons had tired of teaching it by then and had been trying to get the law school to get me to teach it. There I was with this project, which never amounted to much, teaching this course on Economic Analysis and Public Policy.[21]

Despite the failure of his institute, by obtaining a position for Director in the Law School, Simons planted the seed for a quite unintended growth, Chicago-style law and economics.

When Aaron Director came to the Chicago law school, the newly invigorated field of antitrust was being taught by Edward Levi, an alumnus of Thurman Arnold's "brain trust" at the Justice Department. One of Director's duties at the Law School was coteaching the then-mandatory antitrust course with Levi. In a story that became a Chicago legend, while Levi taught the cases four days a week, Director would spend the fifth day telling "us that everything that Levi had told us the preceding four days was nonsense. He used economic analysis to show us that the legal analysis would not stand up."[22] Robert Bork recalls that this course had the effect of recruiting a significant number of students to discipleship in the nascent movement: "A lot of us who took the antitrust course or the economics course underwent what can only be called a religious conversion. It changed our view of the entire world. . . . We became Janissaries as a result of this experience."[23] Bork's comment, while somewhat obscure, is telling: the Janissaries were Christian prisoners of war who converted to Islam and formed the elite corps of the Ottoman Empire. While only a handful of Director's students were as motivated as Bork, there was something in the power of these ideas that impelled those who had learned them to a life of evangelism—both intellectual and organizational—on their behalf.[24] A set of ideas that lacked the intrinsic potency and breadth of Chicago-style price theory would have been unlikely to produce such voluntary efforts on behalf of the cause.

Director's influence reached beyond his own classroom, and in those early days began to wind its way, through his impact on students and the faculty, into the rest of the Law School as well. Henry Manne recalls that

at this very moment, a strange thing happened. . . . In classes we began talking more about economics. Aaron Director began having a clear, direct influence on certain members of the faculty. Every afternoon there was a tea well attended by students and faculty. . . . Most of us stood around talking to Aaron Director. A lot of the discussion of how you might talk about law and economics started at those teas. . . . It began showing up in classes. In my last semester, I thought I was very lucky to have a seminar with the most famous law professor in the country at that time, Karl Llewelyn, who gave a seminar in jurisprudence. He thought he knew everything about everything. He thought the TVA was one of the greatest things that ever happened. Well, those of us who knew something about economics started raising some questions about it, and he became apoplectic. He turned beet red, he slammed his book shut, stormed out the door, and turned around and said, "Just wait until my first-year elements class gets here, then we'll have a real jurisprudence seminar!" That was a revealing moment.[25]

Director's influence was such that he continued to recruit converts for law and economics, even after he retired from teaching. Posner, who met Director at Stanford in 1968, recalls that "he was . . . a Socrates-like figure in the sense that he wrote very little . . . [but had] a very penetrating style of discussion. He wouldn't let you get away with anything. Most of what people say in conversation [is] casual nonsense, and he didn't tolerate any of that. He was polite but he was very firm and a real teacher."

Director's influence deepened with the creation of the *Journal of Law and Economics*, and the establishment of a research program in antitrust. The Anti-Trust Project was the first great entrepreneurial success for the movement, allowing Director's ideas, which would have been locked up in his writer's-blocked brain, to be disseminated to the larger world through the project's fellows.[26] In addition to laying the intellectual foundations for law and economics, it is also gave the field a solid organizational base. "The economic analysis of law was no longer an idea but a fact. The *Journal of Law and Economics* existed. There were law and economics fellowships with the whole program financed by the Volker Fund. Furthermore, and this was extremely important, there were now law professors who took an active part in the program, at first Ken Dam and Edmund Kitch, later to be joined by Richard Posner."[27] Law and economics' origins in antitrust are also an important explanation for the movement's success. Law and economics "was viewed as a very narrow hole in the dam geared mainly to antitrust where it was perfectly appropriate. At that time there was probably less resistance than might have emerged later when the whole operation burst forth in ways that weren't forecast by the people involved."[28] Law and economics was able to find a place in legal education because "this was an activity involving the appointment of maybe one economist. It might be interesting. It did not have clear implications for someone who was, say, teaching property."[29] The combination of an academic entrepreneur (Director), a group of disciples (the Anti-Trust Project fellows), a willing patron (the Volker Fund), and a "hole" in the edifice of legal education (antitrust) prevented law and economics from dying in the crib.

Ronald Coase would build an even more impressive base for law and economics on Director's foundation. It was the combination of the chance to extend Director's ideas and the opportunities available in Chicago that led Coase to the Law School.

> When I came to the University of Chicago, I regarded my role as that of Saint Paul to Aaron Director's Christ. He got the doctrine going, and what I had to do was bring it to the gentiles. And I don't think I would have ever come to the University of Chicago had it not been for the existence of the *Journal of Law and Economics*. That's what I wanted to do. I wanted to get what Aaron started going so that the whole profession [would be influenced by these ideas]—and when I say profession, I mean the economics profession; I have no interest in lawyers or legal education.[30]

Coase's ideas showed how economic reasoning could apply to the entire legal system, and his editorship of the *JLE* demonstrated these broad applications. At the time, it was extremely difficult to place economically informed articles in major law reviews,[31] but Coase could run the *JLE* proactively, soliciting articles that extended economic analysis of law to social regulation, intellectual property, education, minimum wage policy, unionization, property rights, broadcasting, and industry structure. In the 1960s, the *JLE* provided coordination and coherence to the movement that would have been absent if its adherents had to publish in pure economics or law journals. Coase's work with the *JLE* also meant that, when an intellectual entrepreneur par excellence arrived in Chicago, he could draw on a deep foundation of preexisting scholarship.

The Externalities of Richard Posner and the Takeoff of Law and Economics

While the work of Director and Coase helped to establish law and economics as a respectable field, it was the emergence of Richard Posner that made it an academic phenomenon of the first rank.[32] First and foremost, the breadth of the ambition of Posner's major work, *Economic Analysis of Law*, signaled to the legal academy that law and economics could identify major defects in traditional approaches across the entirety of legal scholarship, thereby inducing others, especially prospective law professors, to follow his lead. Second, Posner legitimated law and economics as a mainstream field by setting off so many arguments with legal academia's incumbent scholars. Third, because he was publishing in so many different fields, Posner created a strong incentive for even the unsympathetic to become competent in law and economics, if only to argue with or understand what he was saying. Fourth, Posner helped to create a small industry by cofounding the economic consulting firm Lexecon, thereby creating a demand for persons trained in law and economics, as well as educating lawyers in the usefulness of the field. Posner's work, in short, produced a positive externality for the movement, by increasing the demand for its scholarship and removing blockages to its supply.

After graduating from Harvard Law and clerking for Supreme Court Justice William Brennan, Posner went on to a series of important posts in the federal government, concluding at the Solicitor General's office, where he handled antitrust matters. Up to that point, Posner's career trajectory pointed to a bright, if conventional, future in the liberal academic establishment. At the Solicitor General's office, Posner began to be exposed to the possibilities of law and economics, when as the head of a Telecommunications Task Force he worked with the economists Leland Johnson and William Baumol, and the law and economics pioneer William Baxter. As a consequence, he says, "By the time I went on the teaching market and I was hired by Stanford I knew I wanted to do economic analysis of law." What was not clear to Posner was what a career in economic analysis of law looked like. Reflecting on his arrival at Stanford in 1986, Posner recalls,

> I noticed the name Aaron Director on the door of an office, and I knew the name because I read a little book that . . . mentioned [him] . . . disapprovingly, but indicating that he had an interesting point of view. I thought that since I was going to do antitrust I would meet this fellow so I went and introduced myself, and soon realized that this is a very smart person. I mean, Lee Johnson was a good economist, but Aaron was a really exceptional person.

In addition to influencing him intellectually, Director also brought Posner into contact with his Chicago network. After Nixon was elected president in the fall of 1968, George Stigler was asked to set up a task force on antitrust, to which he appointed Coase and Dam of Chicago, and, on Director's recommendation, Posner. Posner's connection to the network deepened even further when Stigler taught at Stanford that same fall. Bill Baxter was also teaching law at Stanford, and introduced him to the work of Guido Calabresi, which "was a real eye-opener, this idea that you could use economics to talk about tort law."[33] This was also the year that Gary Becker published his famous article on the economics of crime.[34] Taken together, these simultaneous influences suggested to Posner that if economics could be applied beyond antitrust, to torts and criminal law, then there was no area of law immune from its scrutiny. While his year at Stanford opened his eyes to the potential of law and economics, its equally durable impact was to pull him into the network that would land him an appointment at Chicago in the fall of 1969.

Becoming the Richard Posner who would go on to apply economic calculation to all areas of social life involved more than a new methodology. Given his background as a Brennan clerk and Johnson administration lawyer, he embraced a new ideology as well.

> I would say I was looking for an academic niche, but it is of course the case that people like George and Aaron and Milton, Gary Becker, Harold Demsetz, they're extremely conservative. . . . I'd been very liberal up until then, but I didn't like the student unrest of the late sixties and the general leftism. . . . I didn't have any particular belief in the Vietnamese, all this left-wing stuff and riots and all that, so I was unsympathetic, but as late as '68 I did vote for Humphrey. I didn't vote for Nixon, but gradually I swung around [so that] in the seventies I was very conservative, and so certainly part of my interest in economics analysis of law . . . by the seventies was an effort to reform the law and make antitrust more economic and less political, which would narrow it necessarily. . . . So I think the conservative and the normative side of it was a factor, but I think the most important was just that these people seemed very smart, analytically. This is different from . . . their political views . . . this reflex hostility [to government]. It was a reaction of course to overregulation. . . . They seemed smarter than lawyers . . . and in particular they were smarter in the sense they had much better sharper analytical tools for dealing with law rather then the standard legal vocabulary, so that was really the decisive thing, and that was more important than the normative [side].

Looking back at Posner's epochal *Economic Analysis of Law*, it is hard to miss this weaving together of the ideological and methodological sides of law and economics. Posner's tone was brutal, implying that traditional approaches to law were based on little more than muddle-headed liberal benevolence. Economic liberalism had become a sedative to serious discussion of first principles, and the legal profession and the law itself needed to be administered a dose of shock therapy to awaken itself.[35] The conservatives that Posner began to associate himself with seemed willing to confront reality directly, and they had a methodology that allowed them to do so.

Economic Analysis of Law helped to move law and economics from its relatively low profile in the 1960s to its ubiquity in the 1970s and 1980s. While leading liberal legal scholars largely ignored the previous generation of law and economics scholarship, they felt compelled to respond to Posner. George Priest observes that, despite its weaknesses,

> Posner's efficiency-of-the-law project . . . had great intellectual influence—defined even in market terms—because it electrified the academy by compelling

them to learn something about law and economics. Here, Calabresi had an important role as well. Calabresi and Posner both had substantial influence over the market for law and economics through their decade-long debate over the importance of efficiency as a value. Note, however, that this influence derives not so much from the originality of any idea or from its attempted refutation, but from the debate itself. It was the debate between the Chicagoan and the Yalie, the conservative and the ultraliberal, which had the influence. . . . Both parties embraced the core of economic analysis as a mechanism for thinking about legal problems; they simply differed in that embrace in many respects. At heart, what was important in the Posner-Calabresi debate was the economic analysis that they agreed upon. Observers could side with one or the other combatant regarding their differences. To do so convincingly, however, each observer had to learn the common areas of agreement.[36]

The Posner-Calabresi debate convinced legal scholars that, if they did not update their analytical toolkit, they might be left behind. Michael Graetz of Yale Law School recalls that Posner played a critical role in the diffusion of law and economics "because he was saying, 'You may think you can ignore it in procedure, but you can't ignore it in procedure. You may think that family law doesn't apply here, but you can't ignore it there. In criminal law you can't ignore it.' By the mid-1970s young scholars at least thought it was something that you had to read and understand." Finally, the fact that one of the participants in the debate was at Yale Law School helped to strip law and economics of the perception that it was an entirely conservative, University of Chicago project. "In the academic world generally, certainly in the law school part of it, anything out of Chicago economics at that time was ideological. It wasn't really scholarship. But here was someone who never set foot in Chicago at that time writing the same kind of thing. . . . Well that gave a kind of respectability [to the field]."[37]

Economic Analysis of Law signaled that traditional legal approaches were vulnerable and that substantial reputations could be made in challenging them. As Roberta Romano has convincingly argued, the legal academy's approach to corporate law, for example, was intellectually vulnerable in the late 1960s, but the efforts of Henry Manne and Ralph Winter to apply economic concepts to the field were ignored at best and ridiculed at worst.[38] Because of his sheer visibility, Posner could not be ignored. Douglas Baird, a student at Stanford Law in the mid-1970s and later dean of the University of Chicago Law School, recalls that Posner reshaped the structure of legal scholarship.

In the early seventies, people like Posner would come in and spend six weeks studying family law, and they'd write a couple of articles explaining why everything everyone was saying in family law was 100 percent wrong. And then the replies would be, "No, we were only 80 percent wrong." And Posner never got things exactly right, but he always turned everything upside down, and people talked about law differently. . . . By the time I came along, and I wasn't trained as economist, it was clear that . . . doing great work was easy. . . . I used to say that this was just like knocking over Coke bottles with a baseball bat. You had the article *du jour* club. You could just go in and write something revolutionary and go in tomorrow and write another article. I remember writing articles where the time between getting the idea and getting it accepted from a major law review was four days. I'm not Richard Posner, and few of us are. I got out of law school, and I was interested in bankruptcy law, which was inhabited by intellectual midgets. . . . It was a complete intellectual wasteland. I got tenure by saying, "Jeez, a dollar today is worth more than a dollar tomorrow." You got tenure for that! The reality is that there was just an open field begging for people to do great work.

Economic Analysis of Law suggested to young scholars that the future belonged to law and economics, and that traditional doctrinal scholarship was no longer the unquestioned route to success in the legal academy.

On top of this, expectations for scholarly production among law professors began to increase considerably in the 1970s, and Posner's remarkable productivity showed that law and economics was an approach that fit these increasingly strict tenure standards. No group was more effected by this than the editors of elite law reviews. "If you were a student who was interested in going into law teaching, in the mid- to late 1970s your education would include editing law review articles of Posner and Easterbrook. . . . If you look at the articles that were published in the field in this period, people like Posner were just crushing people and leading the pack. That's the cutting edge that people like me were exposed to."[39] Finally, Posner influenced the legal academic pipeline because, in comparison to the first generation of law and economics scholars, he had sterling establishment credentials, and his success destabilized the model of what constituted the career of an elite legal scholar. Posner recalls, "I was someone who had very conventional legal credentials. . . . I was a great student, I clerked for the Supreme Court, I worked for the Solicitor General, so I was a sort of model law professor type, but instead of writing conventional law professor stuff I was writing economics, so if I was doing that . . . then people began to wonder what exactly is the standard law professor's career?" Posner's example suggested that there was no risk, and potentially great reward, in a career in law and economics.

Posner was also instrumental in exploiting the business potential of law and economics, by cofounding (with Richard Landes and their student Andrew Rosenfield) the economic consulting firm Lexecon in 1977.[40] The firm, which now has a staff of over one hundred, offices in five cities, and clients that include many of the nation's major corporations and top law firms, provides expert witnesses and economic analysis on litigation and regulatory matters. The increasing comfort of judges with economic analysis, in large part a function of the surging legitimacy of law and economics scholarship, has made economic consultants almost mandatory for large companies involved in complex litigation. Michael Mandel has identified three forces leading to increasing demand for economic consulting: the boom in litigation, economic deregulation, and mergers and acquisitions. Romano adds to Mandel's list the increase in complex financial deals beginning in the 1980s, which stimulated market demand for law and economics practitioners and provided natural experiments with which to test its claims.[41] Writing as the economic stakes involved with the law were increasing, Mandel argues that "lawyers and judges have become much more comfortable with economic reasoning," a phenomenon he attributes to the spread of law and economics in law schools, and the Law and Economics Center's seminars for federal judges (for the LEC see below).[42] Given the stakes involved, firms have been willing to spend enormous amounts for economic expert witnesses: Mandel provided a low estimate of the market in 1997 (just at the largest firms) of $300 million, "almost certainly larger than the payroll for the full-time faculty at the top 25 economics departments."[43] In 1994, consulting fees for top economists at Lexecon were $300 an hour, and some estimates suggest they have doubled in the years since then.[44] The lucrative nature of the field created a substantial demand for both lawyers and economists trained in the area, putting pressure on law schools to produce students familiar with the subject.

Posner influenced the legal scholarship market on the supply (of scholarship) and demand (by law schools and firms) sides, and in the process helped lead law and economics from the margins to the academic mainstream. It would take skillful organizational entrepreneurship, however, to make the most of the opening that Posner and others had created.

The Birth of an Intellectual Entrepreneur: Manne at Rochester

While Coase claims the mantle of the St. Paul of law and economics, Henry Manne, along with Posner, has an equally strong claim to having evangelized the gentiles.[45] As the movement's first organizational entrepreneur, Manne increased the audience for law and economics scholarship in the academy and on the bench. While there were larger forces encouraging law and economics, Manne's activities are essential in explaining the rapidity and depth of its diffusion in the 1970s and 1980s.

Manne made his reputation as a legal scholar at George Washington University, producing work on corporate law that was (and continues to be) controversial. In the mid-1960s, Manne argued that hostile takeovers are the most effective device for the control of management[46] and that insider trading is an efficient mechanism for extracting information from inside the firm.[47] On the basis of these publications, Manne was offered an endowed chair in the University of Rochester's political science department, then under the leadership of the legendary William Riker, who had made it the "mother ship" of rational choice theory, the application of microeconomic theory to political institutions and processes.[48] In addition to being a member of the political science department, Manne was asked by then-president W. Allen Wallis to take over the planning of a new, fully interdisciplinary law school with a strong emphasis on law and economics. The planning documents Manne generated show the two sides of law and economics, its nonideological critique of legal education and legal scholarship and an ideologically charged attack on government interference in the economy. While the law school was never built, its failure led Manne to direct his entrepreneurial energies into wholesale reform of the legal academy, and his plans for Rochester provided the template for his deanship of the George Mason University Law School fifteen years later.

Manne's formal proposal for the law school emphasized the nonideological component of law and economics. He noted that criticism of the standard law school curriculum was not of recent vintage, but could be traced back to the rise of legal realism, which led naturally to interdisciplinarity; as there was no uniquely "legal" discipline, the law was best approached through the methods of the social sciences. This intellectual critique, Manne argued, had now become a professional necessity. The specialization of law and the complexity, differentiation, and regulation of the economy made law schools' focus on appellate advocacy skills unsuited to the world of working lawyers.[49] While this was a compelling critique, it had not yet influenced the core of legal education.

> In spite of the consistent responsible criticism of both the form and the substance of modern American legal education, the traditional mode continues to prevail. . . . This process produces a graduate with a somewhat mechanical approach to legal problems and little comprehension of the social, political and economic realities of his subject matter. The modern American political system has placed responsibilities on lawyers for which this traditional program has not adequately equipped them.[50]

No one would create new law schools that resembled the current model, but it was impossible to unwind existing institutions and substitute something new in their place. "Introducing a program of this sort with a completely new law school is quite different from attempting to introduce such a program into an existing law school . . . it is almost impossible to change the institutionalized patterns of a traditionally-oriented law school. . . . This would not be the case with a program adopted from the beginning with a faculty who were sympathetic to it."[51] While newness in a highly reputation-sensitive field like education could be a liability, Manne proposed to make it his chief asset. "There is no vested bureaucracy, no tradition-bound alumni, and no contented administrators without strong motivation for change. It is, happily, relatively simple to institute vastly improved educational programs in a new law school, whereas it might be impossible to get leadership on such matters from existing schools."[52]

The core of Manne's alternative was law and economics. In Manne's view, while other disciplines had become attractive to law professors,

> no other social science discipline can begin to match the relevance and importance of economics for the training of modern lawyers. . . . The idea should be to infuse the entire curriculum with economic sophistication. Law graduates who plan on careers in government, in business or with business law firms should be equipped to analyze the problems they confront with rigorous analytic techniques of both law and economics. If this training can be successfully accomplished, it would be safe to predict a heavy demand for these graduates.[53]

The attractiveness of the law school to future graduates was only a part of the story, however. Equally important was the potential that the approach had for attracting the support of American business.

> On very few occasions have law schools sought direct support from industry. The law school at the University of Chicago has done successful fund raising from corporations, as has Yale. . . . But these two, and undoubtedly other cases not know to the writer, are the exceptions rather than the rule. Almost every corporation today has considerable in-house legal work; the general counsel has become an increasingly important figure; and the promotion of general counsels into higher executive offices is quite common in American industry. Thus a law school especially designed to serve the needs with which these men are familiar could strike a responsive chord that many other law schools do not.[54]

By taking advantage of this untapped resource and leveraging the resources of Rochester's well-developed business school and economics department, Manne proposed to create a new law school that could compete with the elites of legal education. "If the University of Rochester established a law school along the lines proposed here, it should be possible in a few years to achieve an academic status which would otherwise take many years and considerably more money."[55]

Building such a school would require a great deal of money, and not just clever ideas. Manne's plan assumed the attractiveness of the school's law and economics focus to American business. It was here that the other side of Manne's project, and law and economics itself, revealed itself most clearly. Especially instructive in this regard was Manne's correspondence with Pierre Goodrich, the wealthy Indianapolis founder of the Liberty Fund. The two men's shared assessment of the state of American education, and legal education in particular, is vividly expressed by Manne's observation that

> the Augean stables were cleansed by diverting a stream of water through them. . . . The educational world is such a mess today from the libertarian point of view that a cleansing is certainly long overdue, but one strong stream of attractive conservative philosophy might just be able to sweep things clean. One law school dedicated to propositions like those you propound . . . would do more to discipline all the other law schools (and conceivably other segments of the university) than anything I can think of.[56]

Manne clearly saw himself, as Simons did, as part of a true-believing remnant, comparing the potential for his law school to that of the Chicago economics department.

> I frequently recall my own experience at the University of Chicago from 1949 to 1952. I received my first serious introduction to libertarian views there. The man most responsible for my education in libertarian values was Aaron Director, the economist in the Law School. But consider the state of economics education in the United States at that time. With the exception of perhaps six to eight people at the University of Chicago and four or five more scattered around the country, there was literally no remnant of libertarian philosophy in academic economics in America. Had that Chicago group not existed, I think that today's growing popularity and respect for so-called "Chicago economics" would not exist. That is not to say that libertarian values would have disappeared from the face of the earth, or that Chicago economics perfectly embodies those values. But it is to suggest that from a small tough nut, like that group at Chicago, vastly larger and more important things can grow. Actually I believe that the law school world is even more ripe for this than economics was twenty years ago. A single generation of lawyers from one school dedicated to true liberal values could turn the American legal system back into a productive and desirable channel. At least it would be a start, and that is more than is happening elsewhere at present.[57]

This letter makes clear what Manne's proposal did not, that the Rochester Law School would provide a home for those who believed in "true liberal values," and, like Chicago, would send out missionaries to the unchurched. It would do what Yale Law School had done for modern liberalism: provide an intense environment for the development of ideas, and a training ground for the lawyers who would disseminate them. "Hopefully all our students will become educated in the true implications of law for free men in a free society. If we do succeed in that goal, we shall certainly be the only major law school in the United States even addressing itself to the problems of law in the free society."[58] Manne was clear that if this project was not undertaken at Rochester, it was exceptionally unlikely that it could be put into place anywhere else, as Rochester was "one of the few major universities in the United States that has a significant number of professors who are strongly oriented toward the free market philosophy and the free society."[59]

A sympathetic faculty only dealt with the internal problem. More daunting was attracting external support for a law school with a distinctly libertarian edge.

> We have a tremendous fund raising problem ahead of us, since so many founda-
> tions and individuals will not support what they consider a "conservative" law
> school, and I will not dishonestly propose something to them while I plan to
> establish something else. I have no interest in founding "just another law
> school," and certainly no interest in furthering the statist characteristics of our
> leading schools. . . . Nothing would make me more proud than to be able to
> name our law school the Pierre F. Goodrich School of Freedom Under Law.[60]

The traditional reliance on alumni makes raising money for a new law school a risky proposition, but Manne believed that law and economics would allow Rochester to raise money from conservative donors, like Goodrich and the (then still conservative) Pew Foundation. Raising that kind of money was a full-time, presidential-level job, but despite Allen Wallis's strong commitment to the project—he donated half a million dollars to the project—his time was increasingly absorbed in conflict with the university's faculty.[61] While fund-raising problems and the opposition of the local bar[62] killed Manne's plans at Rochester, his failure redirected his entrepreneurial activities to the larger world of legal academia. Henceforth, he would operate within existing law schools while mounting an ideological and pedagogical critique of them.

Manne's greatest entrepreneurial success at Rochester were his Economics Institutes for Law Professors. The seminars brought law professors together for three and one-half weeks (later reduced to two) of intensive training in microeconomics: "No effort was made in the early versions of this course to relate economics directly to the law: that was to be left entirely to the law professors, each armed with a copy of Posner's *Economic Analysis of Law*."[63] Manne's motivations for starting the program were complex. On the one hand, the ideas themselves were so powerful that they produced a powerful motivation for spreading them to others: "I was all excited by the power of the economics that I had learned. It was totally new. It wasn't the economics I learned in college, it wasn't even the economics I had learned from Aaron Director. This was

. . . the economics of property rights. . . . I thought that if law professors learned this, it would really change things." Manne's alienation in the legal academy meant that he also had more self-interested motivations for spreading these ideas to law professors. Having failed to receive an offer from an elite law school and unable to start his own, Manne focused on making himself part of the mainstream by exercising influence from the outside: "Over time I educated over 650 law professors, and I dare say I became friendly with a great number of them. So slowly, this idea that Henry Manne was some kind of a kook—and it was strong—[declined]. . . . This was wholesaling it. I thought that then, and I used it to sell it [that way] too." Unable to supply legal education himself (retailing), he could supply the suppliers, law professors themselves (wholesaling). In the process, Manne gradually evolved into a network entrepreneur, focusing on the dissemination of ideas and the creation of a coherent community of law and economics scholars.

The seminars worked on both the supply and demand sides of law and economics. On the supply side, the seminars provided law professors with the skills to introduce economic concepts into their scholarship. As a later section will make clear (see "Early Adopters: UVA and USC"), the Manne programs substantially helped certain law schools, such as the University of Virginia, develop a core of law and economics scholars. The scholarship of Ralph Winter, then a professor of law at Yale and later a judge on the Second Circuit, and Douglas Ginsburg, then a professor of law at Harvard and now chief judge of the D.C. Circuit, took on a strong law and economics coloration soon after they attended Manne's seminars.[64] Warren Schwartz of UVA Law attended the first Manne seminar and recalls, "As an intellectual matter, I had a very serious itch that I did not have the theoretical foundation for. . . . In particular, I was teaching regulated industries from the typical casebook which simply disclosed what the regulatory law was. It simply didn't make any sense to me. I was very much in the market if you will for some theoretical coherence. I went to the [first seminar] at Rochester, and it was for me a just a very exciting awakening." Perhaps the most direct impact was at the University of Toronto. Manne recalls, "I got a call from . . . Michael Trebilcock. He was from New Zealand, and had been teaching at University of Toronto Law School, and the province of Ontario just put up a quarter of a million dollars for a program in law and economics, and he'd been selected to head it. He said, 'But I've never studied economics. Could I come to your program?' He did, and went on to head what was one of the strongest law and economics programs in the world."

Just as important were the effects on the demand side. At the simplest level, the seminars helped law professors understand economics and integrate it into their teaching, even if they did not produce it themselves. In addition, the tenured professors who made the law school hiring decisions were wholly untutored in economics, and because of ideology or incomprehension were resistant to hiring law and economics scholars. Eroding this blockage in the academic hiring market was a key objective of the seminars for law professors. In order to have maximum impact, Manne "would not take a single professor from any law school. They had to come in a minimum of pairs, and the more the merrier, because I knew exactly what would happen, they would go back and get laughed at, as I had been at GW. . . . If there were two or more, they could support each other. In the first program there were six from UVA, four from Yale, two from Harvard, Indiana had three or four." Steve Eagle, who was one of Manne's earliest hires at the George Mason Law School, also believes that the seminars had this effect, saying, "Even those who went to the program and went back to their home schools, and did pretty much what they had done before, had an exposure to law and economics, and it made it easier for them to accept hiring people in the law and economics field, made them more comfortable and conversant in law and economics scholarship. . . . It spread the idea that law and economics was an important part of the law professors' world, even if the individual didn't participate." Michael Graetz, then at UVA Law and one of the program's earliest graduates, recalls,

> I remember even now a handful of people from around the country who you met who became important people in their fields. I think they created lots of networks, lots of people stayed in touch. . . . It created a group of true believers. . . . If you look at key first-generation people of a certain age cohort of that time, you'd find that they had been through the Manne school at some point, because he did it for a long time. . . . It made them more sophisticated consumers. . . . It created lots of networks. . . . Henry certainly reduced the transaction costs to people becoming competent at least as readers if not as producers. And he got enough people interested to be producers. So he played a catalyst role.

The Economics Institute for Law Professors spurred the creation of more scholarship, increased the audience that was receptive to it, and reduced the hostility to its practitioners. By demonstrating organizational success, Manne's first program also made it much easier for Manne to raise money for later, even more ambitious programs.

What gave the program for law professors even greater momentum was the ease with which Manne was able to raise funds, a pleasant surprise after his experience at Rochester. Manne had tried and failed to launch a similar program at GWU, but between 1968 (when Manne left GWU) and the early 1970s business had become much more open to supporting law and economics.

This time when I went for fund-raising, I wanted $100,000, and I thought I could handle a fund-raising job of raising $10,000 from ten of them [major corporations]. I wrote to eleven, and I related it heavily to antitrust. At this point, the world knew that Chicago economics was the only thing that could possibly save them from an antitrust debacle, and I related it strongly to that. I said it was a way to get these ideas across to a large number of law professors who create the lawyers and government officials. Well, of the eleven I wrote to, within a few weeks I had $10,000 from ten of them, and the last $10,000 came in a few weeks later. It was the U.S. Steel company. I called the guy and said, "I can't use your money," and he said, "No, don't do that." I gave the extra to the university.

Manne was riding the same wave as conservative public interest law's early entrepreneurs, but, in sharp contrast, Manne was raising money from corporations for long-range, free-market-oriented activity. This fund-raising success would be even more important in subsequent years, as Manne's programmatic ambitions increased.

Spreading the Gospel: The Creation of the Law and Economics Center

By 1973, Manne had definitively concluded that he could be "far more effective in some activity other than waiting around here indefinitely to open and administer a law school."[65] Manne's opportunity for greater effectiveness arose at the relatively undistinguished law school of the University of Miami, under the deanship of former University of Chicago law professor Soia Mentschikoff. The new dean was eager to put the school on the map, and despite her ideological reservations about Manne's intellectual approach, she agreed to give him "the necessary autonomy to run a free-market oriented research, teaching and conference center," which would "do scholarly research in free market alternatives to the regulatory approach so pervasive in our legal system today."[66] Manne's experience at Miami shows the opportunities and constraints that existed for conservatives in the legal academy of the 1970s and early 1980s.

While Manne had been considered a marginal, even eccentric, character in the legal academy of the 1960s, by the mid-1970s his star was rising. Manne credits the shift to the increasing credibility of free-market economics: "I had become respectable at this point. . . . You know who I credited for that? Milton Friedman. At an AALS meeting in about 1969 or 70, two young professors that I didn't even know were walking ahead of me, and they were talking about me. And I heard one of them say, he's not a conservative kook, he's like Milton Friedman! Milton made the world safe for people to talk about free market [ideas]. . . . Now I was respectable—she [Soia Mentschikoff] wouldn't have touched me two years before—and it wasn't accidental that she called me the same year that Yale did." The rising tide of Chicago was raising all boats, Manne's included, by removing the stigma associated with libertarian ideas. In his last year at Rochester, the offer from Yale Law School that Manne had waited so long for finally came through.

> At that point, I finally had an offer from Yale. I got a call from Ralph Winter. He said . . . we want you to come visit as a prelude to a faculty appointment. . . . I said Ralph, you're two weeks and five years too late. . . . Two weeks ago I agreed with Soia Mentschikoff that I was going to start this new center at Miami . . . [and] you're five years too late for me to give a damn. That was one of the truest things I've ever said. Because for the first fifteen years I was dying to get to Columbia or Yale Law School.

Why did Manne turn down a visiting appointment at Yale, then as now the pinnacle of legal education? Resentment at the elite legal institutions that had refused to make room for him played an important part, but Miami's relative backwardness offered opportunities that even a law school as strong as Yale could not match.

> The relative weakness of the University academically is paradoxically an advantage in that same regard. At a stronger University or law school, where I would not be the most prominent professor, it is very unlikely that I could promote a program of this sort without considerable resistance and interference from other members of the law faculty, the economics department, and from the University administration. It is unlikely that an opportunity like this one would ever be presented at any other major university in the United States.[67]

Miami, unlike Yale, was not in a position in the legal academic market to allow its ideological scruples to interfere with an opportunity for national attention.

The Law and Economics Center (LEC) that Manne created at Miami was remarkably ambitious. In addition to the economics program for law professors, the LEC hosted an economics program for federal judges, a fellowship program for students with economics training to obtain a law degree, and topical conferences supported by the Liberty Fund. These programs transformed law and economics from an idea to a movement with real organizational breadth.

The Olin Fellows program brought recent PhD's in economics to Miami to receive a fully funded law degree, supplemented with a specialized curriculum in law and economics. The objective was to produce economists that law schools could hire, at a time when JD/PhD's were very rare in legal academia. The alumni of the Olin program remember the Law and Economics Center as a heady intellectual environment. Fred McChesney, professor of law at Northwestern University and certainly the most distinguished alumnus of the Olin Fellows, recalls, "It was fabulous. People coming in, going out, giving short courses, giving long courses, giving papers, conferences, it was electric, just electric. . . . Buchanan came in, Coase came in. . . . Guido [Calabresi] came in. . . . You'd be walking down the hall, and there'd be Gary Becker, there'd be Armen Alchian, there'd be Harold Demsetz. . . . You want to talk to them? Go in and talk to them. Anybody who was somebody was down there at some point." None of the other LEC Olin Fellows ascended as far as McChesney, but the program had other successes, the most important of which was producing the core of the faculty that Manne recruited in his first few years as dean of GMU Law School. In Manne's view, the success of the program has to be judged relative to its location at Miami and later at Emory.

> I always thought that the Olin Fellowship program was central to the whole idea of the Law and Economics Center. . . . Indeed, I think I might go so far as to say that I do not think the Center could ever have had the success it did without the galvanizing and energizing influence of the Fellows. . . . I was confident that the uniqueness of the program and the growing reputation of the Center, as well as a lot of money in a fairly bad market, would get us decent students. It worked; the Olin Fellows were regularly in the top 10 percent of their law school classes. . . . After all the dust settled, sixteen of the thirty-three Fellows at Miami and Emory ended up in academia, some in business schools but mostly in law. One [Fred McChesney] is today a very distinguished chair professor at Northwestern; one is a mainstay of law and economics at George Mason. . . . One had a chair at Kansas Law School before he took (and then dropped) the deanship at Chapman's business school (he now runs a very successful program in economics for state judges for the Brookings-AEI Joint Center); one was a very prolific and successful economist at Clemson until he died a few years ago; one was my associate dean and a very successful professor at GMUSL. . . . One (who finished his law degree at Chicago) is a professor at U Penn Law School; and one became the academic VP at the University of Texas—Arlington after a successful teaching career. . . . Consider, if you will, the rather amazing list that I just presented. These were law graduates of Miami and Emory law schools (though to be sure some had very prestigious PhD degrees), and I suspect that this is more academics than those two schools have produced in total during their entire existence.

Stated in these terms, there is no question that the Olin Fellows program was a success. Soon enough, however, conservative movement patrons, the Olin Foundation especially, asked themselves whether success relative to weak institutions was enough.

More unambiguously successful were the Liberty Fund conferences and the economics programs for federal judges. The Liberty Fund conferences, which ran from 1975 to 1985, brought law and economics practitioners and others together for intense conferences on a single subject. As a letter from Manne to the Earhart Foundation explained, part of the motivation for the conferences was LEC public relations: "The great advantage to us of these programs is that they rapidly acquaint both the economics and law school worlds with our existence, and they generate an excellent book of papers and proceedings with the Center's imprimatur."[68] More important were the networks the conferences created between scholars in economics and law who rarely ran in the same professional circles. The Liberty Fund conferences were of critical importance to younger scholars, integrating them into the budding law and economics network. George Priest, now at Yale but then at the University of Puget Sound Law School, recalls that the conferences

> gave younger people an opportunity to interact with senior people, and it created a cadre of law and economics types that proved to be very helpful. I met Bob Bork at the "Fire of Truth" Conference,[69] and spent a lot of time with him there; Ed Kitch took me to a conference once when I was a research fellow [at Chicago] and I met people from UCLA, USC, and other schools. And after I did very well in some of these conferences, Henry Manne started soliciting articles from me for the conferences. That gives you even more prominence, and encourages you to work harder. Getting a thousand-dollar honorarium to write a paper then was a lot. I drooled over it. It was very helpful.

Attendance at the Liberty Fund conferences also increased the perceived market value of law and economics practitioners, increasing their status in their own institutions and the likelihood that they would be recruited by other, more prestigious institutions.

> These conferences both enhanced existing markets and created markets of their own. Within a law school, again because of the rarity of academic conferences, it was a distinction to be invited to an academic conference of this nature; to be asked to deliver a paper was a special distinction. Thus, attendance at one or more of Henry Manne's conferences greatly enhanced the positions of law and economics scholars within existing schools and with other schools to which they might be recruited. . . . They created markets that vastly enhanced the position of many of us in the field (including myself).[70]

Charles Goetz, who became a major figure in law and economics at Virginia, is especially impressed with the networking functions of the Liberty Fund conferences.

They were very important to me, because I very quickly got to know the other people who were interested in this stuff spread out across the United States of America. I met the people who were players at that time, and who you might want to have exchanged a paper [with] and so forth. I met people whose stuff I then knew enough to read. One example that strikes close to home is that I met George Priest at those conferences. He was a young guy out in Siberia, at the University of Puget Sound. I remember being very excited by George, and recommending him to the appointments committee at the University of Virginia.[71]

The Liberty Fund programs were also important for purely intellectual reasons. They provided detailed feedback to scholars working in law and economics, identified areas for new research in a field still in its infancy, and provided opportunities for ideas to germinate. In the absence of a geographic center other than Chicago, the Liberty Fund programs provided otherwise isolated scholars with the intense, face-to-face interactions necessary for intellectual ferment and creativity.[72]

Manne's most famous programmatic achievement was, without a doubt, his Economics Institute for Federal Judges. Started in 1976, soon after Manne arrived in Miami, these were a direct spin-off of the institutes for law professors, which Manne concluded were successful and worthy of extension to other audiences (before the first seminar for law professors, in fact, he conducted programs for congressional staff and was considering programs for law review editors, journalists, and even clergy).[73] The draw of the program, especially before it developed a reputation among federal judges, were its price (free), luxury accommodations (the first was held at the Ocean Reef Club in Key Largo, and later seminars were held at equally attractive locations), and high-quality instructors, including Milton Friedman, Paul Samuelson, Armen Alchian, Harold Demsetz, Paul McAvoy, and Martin Feldstein.[74] The inclusion of Samuelson was especially important, since it gave the seminars cover from charges of ideological imbalance.[75] Manne was careful to limit the course to microeconomics, and to avoid any direct applications to legal issues. Charles Goetz, a professor in later programs, recalls that this limitation was not designed to avoid accusations of influencing judges' decision-making, but for pedagogical reasons.

> The economics program for judges was pretty much straight economics. The competitive model, capital values, discounting to present value, that sort of thing. Henry Manne was concerned that judges were uncabinable if you tried to bring any kind of express legal applications into the picture. Classes would wind up being discussion of law rather than economics. Putting it bluntly . . . judges are pretty hard to control. They're petty monarchs in their own courtroom. They're not like ordinary students.

For two and a half weeks (reduced to two weeks a few years later), federal judges would be marched through a tightly compressed course in micro-economics. In addition to the formal teaching sessions, Manne encour-aged his faculty to mix informally with the judges in order to encourage intellectual interchange and engagement with the material.[76] At its height, in 1990, the Economics Institute for Federal Judges had hosted 40 percent of the federal judiciary, including Ruth Bader Ginsburg and Clarence Thomas, and sixty-seven members of the federal courts of appeals.[77]

The LEC's seminars for federal judges have not been without contro-versy. First, the seminars for judges, like those for law professors, were held in first-class locations with opportunities for recreation in the afternoon. This led to accusations that the seminars were junkets intended to influence the decision-making of judges. Second, critics argued that the seminars violated codes of judicial ethics, because they were funded by corporations that judges could face as litigants. This was the charge of a challenge to the programs brought to the Advisory Committee on Codes of Judicial Conduct in 1980 by Charles Halpern, the cofounder of the Center for Law and Social Policy at the Georgetown University Institute for Public Interest Representation. Henry Butler, a close associate of Manne's over the years, recalls that this challenge did lead to a change in the financing of the program. "In the process of discussing the LEC's finances, Manne commit-ted to the Judicial Conference that the LEC would not use corporate contri-butions to pay the direct expenses of the judicial education programs spon-sored by the LEC. All direct expenses for the judges programs would be paid for with contributions from private foundations not affiliated with corporations. Corporate contributions would be used to cover LEC over-head and other activities, such as the Economics Institute for Law Profes-sors and Law for Economics Professors."[78] Ending direct corporate contri-butions to the seminars has not satisfied the LEC's critics, especially those in the liberal legal network, who have continued to publish widely publi-cized reports purporting to expose them as a form of judicial corruption.[79] In recent years, this controversy has heated up, although it has focused primarily on the seminars run by the Foundation for Research on Eco-nomics and the Environment, which has successfully rebuffed accusations that participation in its programs is ethically improper for federal judges.[80] In fact, Manne made a point of avoiding telling his supporters that there were any direct impacts on judges' decision-making from the programs. He recalls "a family foundation out in San Francisco that gave us a lot of money, and finally withdrew it. They said that 'you've taught us that foundations oughtn't give money if you can't show results. Well, we want you to show that you're getting some impact from your judges' program,' and I said, 'You're going to take that one on faith, because one thing I can't do is claim to be having any impact on how judges decide cases.' "

Manne always recognized that the effects of the judges programs were diffuse—rather than trying to change judges' decision-making on particular cases, he was hoping to make them, at the margin, more open to economic reasoning across the board.

Despite all the controversy that has swirled around them, Manne is convinced that his program for judges has had less impact in spreading law and economics than the Liberty Fund conferences or seminars for law professors, noting that "the ultimate intellectual payoff [of teaching judges], while perhaps more immediate, could never be as great as would teaching the teachers."[81] That said, Manne is convinced that the judges program was important, but as much for the attention it brought to the LEC and the legitimacy it gave to the larger enterprise of law and economics as for the actual impact on judges' decision-making: "Law professors and lawyers have almost a mystical regard for judges, so if they were taking economics, it had to be okay."

Manne's programs required enormous funding, well beyond what a university like Miami could raise on its own, and he was concerned that the LEC might raise money that would be diverted to purposes other than those of free market programming. In response, Manne chose the risky strategy of relying on annual funding, rather than building up an endowment.[82] In a letter to his supporters, Manne explained that

> there should be no permanent endowment funding for the Center. Grants can be conditioned on my continuing as the Director of the Center, and funds for individual professorships can be conditioned on the chair's being occupied by a specific individual. This approach, however, leaves the Center somewhat vulnerable, since its long term future is always in doubt, and this can be debilitating. . . . In effect, what is required is good faith on the part of supporting foundations and agencies that they will not unexpectedly withdraw financial support from ongoing Center programs.[83]

Manne's success at Miami, and to a degree at Emory as well, was in part due to his impressive ability to extract resources from foundations and, to a degree that has not been replicated in other cases examined in this book, from corporations, without compromising his vision of the LEC's programming. The LEC's fund-raising success was partially owed to being founded before the explosion of conservative groups in the late 1970s and early 1980s.

> There wasn't much competition for that money—the competition came with these think tanks that were beginning to start up. . . . [At Scaife] Dick Larry always understood in some way what we were about, [but] what he really did was he liked Dick Ware, the program officer from Earhart, who pioneered a way of philanthropic giving that made more sense than anything. Find people

they trusted and give them money when they could use it. . . . Dick Larry often used to say that I was always welcome to come in and make applications, because I had always done well with them in the past. He never was able to articulate why he liked what I had done, but it had always worked.[84]

At least in this early period, and to some degree even today, conservative and libertarian foundations operated on the basis of "feel" and trust. They identified people they agreed with and in whose competence they had reasonable confidence, and did not ask a lot of questions or require extraordinary documentation. These patrons recognized that in the law, outcomes were long-term and difficult to reliably trace, and thus relied on informal evaluations and reputations developed within the small network of conservative founders and organizational entrepreneurs, rather than more formal, bureaucratic methods.

Equally important as foundation support was Manne's success in corporate fund-raising. In the early years of the LEC approximately three-quarters of its support came from foundations and one-quarter from corporations, but Manne was so successful in raising corporate money that by the end of the decade the balance of support had been reversed (despite level funding from foundations). As chapter 3 showed, business in the early 1970s had become frightened by widespread challenges to corporate capitalism, a fear that Manne successfully exploited. Manne's initial insight into corporate fund-raising was that the modern firm's intellectual capital was concentrated in its general counsels, who had advanced degrees and were required to think about the corporation's social, political, and legal context. While these general counsels could not give very large gifts, they "had their power of donation. . . . It was usually a small pot; they had twenty-five, fifty thousand. A lot of our gifts were five to ten thousand dollars. If you got one hundred donations, that's pretty good."[85] Working with corporate counsels allowed Manne to sidestep corporate philanthropy offices that tended to be more sensitive to the firm's public relations. Establishing this broad donor base also meant that Manne did not have to worry about offending any particular firm. Diversity thus provided an effective defense against capture by its corporate donors.

Manne's fund-raising needs at Miami were considerably larger than they were at Rochester, and his strategy had to adapt accordingly. Fortuitously, soon after arriving in Miami, Manne met Bill Weston, who had worked for J. Howard Pew (the benefactor of the Pew Family Foundation) at the Sun Oil Company. Manne recalls that

I met him once at a conference some years earlier. . . . I'd say a month or so after we got to Miami, he walked in the front door, said he wasn't doing anything, but he knew what I was doing and he'd like to help. . . . We were going lickety-split trying to raise money, and at that point the mechanics of getting money out of corporations wasn't clear. Fund-raising isn't a one-person job; you needed someone to do all the advance work, and that's what he was willing to do. Plus, he knew government affairs people—that's another office that often had money to give. Bill Weston was so good, the line I gave to general counsels he gave to government affairs people, and he would get them to take a longer-range view than they had. He really beefed up our fund-raising.

Manne's connection to Weston gave him a staff member with networks that allowed him to see possibilities for raising corporate money that were invisible to most academics. Manne and Weston's networks allowed them to set up a fund-raising apparatus separate from, and thus not easily cannibalized by, the University.

Manne made a direct appeal to corporation's long-term self-interest, but—in sharp contrast with the first generation of public interest law—in the service of programming that he had designed for his own purposes. Law and economics was attractive to corporations who recognized that the growth of federal regulation was not a fad. Whether the appeal was to antitrust, which hit at the core interests of large corporations, or the new "social regulation" of the early 1970s, regulation was inescapable, growing, and connected to a powerful support structure in universities. Manne remembers that both he and Weston agreed that

> we were not asking for charity. We didn't even believe in corporations making charitable contributions. Corporations had a long-range interest in what went on in universities, and if they didn't begin tending to it, it was going to jump up and bite them. This was an easy line for the lawyers, because I could talk about antitrust, the work that was done in product liability. . . . There were other areas that the solid academic work academic guys were doing would be useful to these guys, but they didn't know anything about it. . . . To learn that this could go on, and that this thing could be introduced in court was very impressive to them. They had seen it already at this time in antitrust, you could always use the antitrust example. . . . Weston did very much the same thing. He'd talk to the government affairs people about getting materials they could use in their work that they weren't getting out of the university world at the time. Law and economics . . . would be on their side, to put it very simply. Not that we were tailoring things for their needs, but we were doing something that they ought to buy.

Manne recognized that corporations could also be motivated to contribute, despite the incentives to free ride, by leveraging their desire to "keep up with the Joneses."

> Believe me, we always made them feel guilty about being free riders. We'd tell them that others were supporting this, it was going to benefit them whether or not they contributed, but others would look down on them. They were very

sensitive about that. There was a community among those people. They all wanted to know, "What did so and so give you?" It would sometimes be a company in their industry, but more likely it would be a company whose size and importance they thought was like theirs. Like Sears might want to know what did Exxon give. . . . If we could get an existing contributor to write letters to people he knew at other companies, that was like social charity. . . . You give to my pet charity, and I'll give to yours.

Law and economics gave Manne and Weston a language through which they could communicate with businessmen in terms they understood and that made the long-term, relatively untraceable outputs of the LEC seem like a good investment. "We were in business. Here we were producing this stuff, trying to market it to you. Often we talked about it in those terms, and this was something they understood. A few of them articulated it as if they were entering into an informal contract to buy something. It was an inchoate product, it wouldn't be measured very easily, but the thing came to be understood."[86] This common language was the cement that got corporate donors into the door, and kept them there in the LEC's early years. Finally, Manne had a taste for fund-raising, an exceedingly rare trait among academics of any ideological stripe. "What you were doing was really like sales work, calling on people face to face, offering your product and seeing if you could interest them. I grew up in sales, so I did like it."

Manne's successful fund-raising allowed the LEC to expand rapidly. By early 1975 he reported to Richard Ware of the Earhart Foundation, "I can only preface the details by stating that we have been successful in this organizational year beyond even my usually optimistic expectations. I believe that we are already at the point I initially anticipated for our third year. We have enough money pledged, assured, or on hand to begin every specific program and project mentioned in the Prospectus sent to you last fall."[87] Unfortunately, the LEC could not completely insulate itself from the Law School, or the University as a whole. As Manne recalls, "In more general terms, we weren't a good fit. We were too good an operation, too intellectually high-powered to be at the University of Miami." The dean of the Law School, Soia Mentschikoff, appeared to have been threatened by the growth of the LEC, and attempted to limit its operations in a number of ways. Manne wrote to the president of the University in early 1980 that his relationship with the dean had totally broken down. "Singlehandedly—unless you want to take part of the credit through inaction—Soia has destroyed my ability to manage personnel by raising tensions and lowering morale to the breaking point. Every important member of the LEC faculty and staff has actively sought other employment in the last six months because of their fear of Soia and their realization that the university administration is either unwilling or unable to provide security for them. . . . I give up."[88] Manne maintained much of the LEC's momentum by going over the dean's head to the university president, but by 1980 his relationship with Miami was damaged beyond the possibility of repair. Manne was looking for a way out, and was receiving offers to move the LEC to other schools.[89]

In early 1980, Manne began negotiations with Emory University, and by August of that year they were complete. The LEC's exit was far from amicable: a timeline in Manne's files of the LEC's transition to Emory reports that, on November 12, the president of the University fired Manne as head of the LEC, and that, on the following day, "Tensions became very high at the Center as armed guards were posted, locks were changed on various doors. Dr. Manne's Secretaries were told to leave the building, file cabinets were taped up, and Drs. Moore and Aranson were ordered by Dean Walton to vacate their offices."[90] Conflict was especially severe over fund-raising. Manne began to raise funds for the LEC at Emory while still at Miami, while the University of Miami used the LEC's mailing list to solicit contributions from its donors. This suggests the importance of Manne's decision to avoid raising an endowment. Had he done so, he would have been faced with years of conflict with Miami over its status, rather than less than a year of severe but limited acrimony.

Despite the controversy that swirled around the LEC and Manne's battles with administrators at Miami, a very powerful organizational foundation was laid for the law and economics movement in these years. When the Manne programs were combined with the intellectual breakthroughs being made by Richard Posner and Ronald Coase, among others, law and economics had both a set of ideas whose power was increasingly recognized and an elaborate network of programming to diffuse those ideas throughout legal academia and the judiciary. It would turn out to be a potent combination.

Early Adopters: UVA and USC

While law and economics made only small strides at elite schools beyond Chicago in the 1970s, it became a major force in the law schools at the University of Virginia and the University of Southern California. This breakthrough was due to four factors: the move toward interdisciplinarity in legal scholarship; the presence of creative, entrepreneurial deans looking to increase their law schools' status; at USC, and to a lesser degree UVA, an institutional connection with nonlawyers working in the public choice tradition; and the impact of the Manne programs in equipping law professors with the basic skills to conduct law and economics scholarship.

The combination of these factors allowed UVA and USC to attract unusually strong faculties at a rapid rate.[91] Of particular importance for moving the field into the mainstream, only a few of the scholars who were influenced by law and economics at UVA and USC shared the strongly libertarian instincts of its Chicago progenitors.

By the early 1970s, criticism of law schools as intellectually vacuous and unsuited to the research expectations of the modern university began to reach a critical mass. This same period was the high point of faith in the social sciences, and these disciplines were obvious candidates for filling the hole in legal scholarship that critics had identified. Combined with these factors, the transformation of gender equality expectations put pressure on the informal approaches to hiring in elite institutions. Richard Posner recalls, "Certainly the way I was hired, it was a network . . . people knew each other and so the people hired were all white males. When that was challenged, the question was, 'Well, if you're not going to hire the white males that you know, what are you going to use as your criteria?' So they moved to criteria which seem more objective, having to do with productivity and so on—using that for hiring or for promotion gives the law school some insulation from complaints about discrimination." The rise of interdisciplinary scholarship and an emphasis on scholarly production created an opportunity for lower-ranked institutions to dramatically improve their national reputation. Robert Scott recalls that "this is a time when there was a big transformation in American legal academics . . . the integration of the law school with the rest of the university. With that integration of interdisciplinary work came the integration of university standards for productivity. All of a sudden writing original scholarship became the sine qua non of a successful academic. I'm not sure it was happening everywhere. I visited at Columbia in 1987, and it was just beginning to happen [there]." Law schools more focused on their institutional aspirations than their existing constituents could dramatically improve their reputation by responding to this shift, because many top schools continued to believe that the preeminent responsibility of the law school was to the profession, not to the academy.

Taking advantage of this opportunity required leaders with the instincts and authority to put interdisciplinary law scholarship at the center of their school's mission. At UVA, that leader was Monrad Paulsen, the author of the best-selling casebook in America.[92] Paulsen believed "it was supremely important that the law school be engaged not merely in vocational training, but in serving as an integral part of the university."[93] Michael Graetz recalls that "Monrad was really transformative in pushing people on scholarship. Monrad would go around asking, 'What are you working on?' What he was doing was trying to hire younger faculty, a faculty much more engaged in scholarship." But while "Monrad was really supportive of the law and economics group . . . he was not a law and economics person. Monrad was a real intellectual, he was interested in ideas." Paulsen's strategy for transforming the law school at UVA was to "create an appointments structure that gave a lot of power to the appointments committee, and then stacked it with the younger people who he thought were the more ambitious people in the law school. . . . He was willing to take risks that many deans might not, in those days, have been willing to take."[94] By the standards of legal academia, Paulsen was a genuine entrepreneur, willing to disrupt existing organizational forms and practices in order to take advantage of opportunities that other market actors, especially schools above him in the law school status hierarchy, could not.

At roughly the same time, USC hired Dorothy Nelson as dean. Like Paulsen, Nelson was not a law and economics scholar, but she was committed to building the law school, and willing to take risks to do so. "By 1967, attrition had reduced the number of tradition-minded senior faculty [at USC], and the appointments process had come under the control of a diverse group of younger and more senior faculty united in the view that law was about ordering social processes. . . . The understanding could be theoretical or practical, philosophical or economic, but it should not be merely doctrinal."[95] Michael Graetz recalls that Dorothy Nelson "basically turned the appointments process over to the faculty. This was a point where you had a group of faculty who were basically into the 'Let's build USC' mode. So they were looking for interesting scholars. They were also looking for something that looked cutting edge, and law and economics at the time was pretty cutting edge." USC could compete by playing what George Mason University Law School later called "moneyball," hiring scholars who were undervalued by the market and ignoring the credentials by which faculty at the time were typically judged.[96]

> They weren't as interested in the superficial credentials that would mark a good appointment in the old system. They probably couldn't have competed for Supreme Court clerks or guys who finished first in their class at the Harvard Law School. So they were looking for people who were really smart and intellectually interested, but for whatever reason whose academic career was a little more academically checkered, who chose not to clerk or who went to a lesser law school. They were willing to make their decisions based on the quality of the mind and the ambition of the individual, and were willing to trust that instinct, rather than what was at one time the sine qua non, which was being a very good law student.[97]

A willingness to seek out the unorthodox made USC a magnet for those committed to the intellectual transformation of legal scholarship. Graetz recalls that "when I went back to USC in 1979, I had an offer from Chicago, and I decided that USC was every bit as interesting a faculty as

Chicago." Douglas Baird similarly recalls that when he graduated from Stanford in the mid-1970s, "I desperately wanted a job at USC because I didn't think I could get a job at Chicago. I wanted to be where the action was, and if it wasn't Chicago, a close second was USC." USC took an approach that some law schools were willing to accept at the margins, and by making it the dominant theme of the school USC created a huge competitive advantage. While the story was not simply one of law and economics—the school was open to other disciplines as well—no field was as mobilized to take advantage of the opportunity.

USC, and to a lesser degree UVA, became early adopters of law and economics in part due to their connection to the rising centers of public choice scholarship. Public choice in economics and rational choice in political science apply rational, hedonistic, behavioral assumptions to the decision-making of government. While law and economics scholars devoted much of their attention to demonstrating the inadequacy of existing legal frameworks, public choice purported to explain that inadequacy by focusing on the motivations of political actors.[98] The public choice connection at USC came through its close relationship with Caltech, where a number of law faculty (including Graetz, Schwartz, and Levine) had joint appointments.[99] Levine recalls that "the Caltech group profoundly influenced and greatly broadened my notion of what interdisciplinary work entailed. They gave me a perspective and analytical tools with which to address the obstacles that prevented adoption of regulatory policies that would produce efficiency gains. . . . It helped explain the seeming paradox that a careful economic analysis of law and policy, however eloquently and persistently put forth, did not seem to carry the day politically and influence real-world outcomes."[100]

UVA Law was in the same university that gave birth to the "Virginia School" of public choice, including economists James Buchanan, Gordon Tullock, and Ronald Coase. Former UVA faculty members Michael Graetz, Jerry Mashaw, and Warren Schwartz recall that there was a significant influence of the Virginia School on the economically minded professors in the UVA law school, through the meetings of a reading group called Pegasus that connected them with the public choice scholars at Virginia Tech and UVA.[101] Charles Goetz, however, recalls that, by the time he arrived in 1975, the connection with the economics department was much less substantial than it would have been just a few years before, given the exodus of the Virginia School that began with Ronald Coase in the early 1960s and was largely complete by the early 1970s.

At that point Tullock was at Rice, Coase was at the University of Chicago, Buchanan went off to UCLA. . . . The reason why there wasn't much interaction with the Department of Economics was, there were still some people like Bill

Bright and Leland Yeager, but there was a big falling out in the Department of Economics itself, so by the time I arrived in 1975, if you spoke to the people who were on one side of the wall, the other people became your enemies. It was that bad. I basically was unable to have any interaction with the economics department at all, in those years, nor do I recall anyone who did.

Therefore, while there was some cross-fertilization with the Virginia School, it does not appear to have been the main conduit for economic thinking in the UVA Law School.

The most important connection between the Virginia School and UVA Law was Goetz himself, who had been a professor of economics at Virginia Tech, the home of Buchanan and Tullock's Center for the Study of Public Choice. Goetz got on Virginia's radar screen when he met Warren Schwartz at a talk in Blacksburg, where Schwartz recalls that "he just knocked my socks off, and I thought, 'This guy would just be perfect for a law school,' which I got right. I don't remember exactly how, but Virginia decided they would like to hire an economist, and I was assigned the task of finding one. . . . The first person who visited was Isaac Ehrlich.[102] . . . We offered him a job, which he declined. Then I thought of Goetz." Goetz was a student of Coase, Buchanan, and Tullock at Virginia in the early 1960s, but when he moved to the Law School, he quickly committed to being more than the economist on the law faculty.

> The one difference between me and the other early people in law and economics is that I . . . decided that I would give myself at most four or five years to learn enough law that the people on the faculty, my colleagues, would regard me as a legal scholar, as opposed to just an economics guy grafted in there. I made a very concerted effort to learn the closest equivalent of microeconomic theory in the substratum of law school discussion, the fields like contracts, tort law, civil procedure. . . . That meant that I could then talk to people in different areas who often came to me for some kind of advice or insight. . . . Just to give you one example: This seems incredible now, but back in 1975, the whole notion of the applicability of the prisoners' dilemma and game theory . . . to legal problems was new. . . . Even people who had been to Henry Manne camp had no knowledge of elementary game theory, and that turns out, as the years go by, to be an important tool in legal analysis.[103]

In addition to spreading economic concepts in the law school, Goetz became part of one of law and economics' most fertile collaborations, with Robert Scott. Goetz recalls,

> I had an office on the third floor . . . and I could hear an argument between Bob Scott and Warren Schwartz over liquidated damages. . . . Economists had been hostile to liquidated damages, thinking, wrongly in my view, that liquidated damages would impede efficient breaches. Scott and Schwartz were arguing

over this, Scott arguing in favor of liquidated damages, at least under certain circumstances. I remember once jumping up and walking down the hall and saying to Warren, "Bob is right, and I can prove it." By the next day I had an economic model; several of them became incorporated into the article. . . . That argument in the hallway wouldn't have taken place in a lot of places.

While the Manne seminars created a common language for the UVA faculty, the presence of a skilled economist on the faculty meant that economic theory could constantly feed into the intellectual life. Schwartz recalls that "Charlie [Goetz] was very much the tutor for all the rest of us." Robert Scott believes that these "arguments in the hallways" were very important in his own development as a law and economics scholar.

Warren Schwartz had an important role because he . . . spent most of the day chatting with colleagues. I remember several lunches with Warren and [others] . . . in which my first memory was someone talking about Coase, and I had no idea who Coase was, so if I was going to be with these guys I'd better know a little bit about what they were talking about. So I did take that occasion to get . . . the first edition of *Economic Analysis of Law*. I read Ronald Coase's "Problem of Social Cost." . . . So I was knowledgeable about the nascent law and economics movement, but I hadn't integrated it significantly into my own scholarship. . . . I started writing an article on the constitutional regulation of procedural due process that was subsequently published in the *Virginia Law Review*. In the course of conversations with a number of colleagues, Mashaw certainly was an important one. . . . I read more and that article was my first law and economics article. . . . That article was written in the academic year 1974–75, and that spring Graetz and Jeffries and I signed up to go to Florida for Henry's program.

Proximity breeds creativity by facilitating unplanned interactions and arguments and increasing the emotional intensity of scholarly interaction. At UVA, adding additional people with common interests (especially those who combined complementary intellectuals skills with broad interests) produced increasing intellectual returns.[104]

The other explanation for the rapid spread of law and economics in Virginia's faculty was the disproportionate impact of Manne's Economics Institute for Law Professors. According to Manne, "In the first three years the program, we had half of the UVA faculty, and that's because Monrad pushed it. I would take anyone Monrad nominated." Dean Paulsen was a close friend of Henry Manne's, a drinking buddy at AALS meetings and a former summer roommate at UCLA in the late 1950s, so it was natural that he would turn to Paulsen to help drum up interest in the economics institutes. Goetz recalls that the impact on the Virginia Law School "was enormous, because Manne managed to attract to these

summer programs some of the really big names in the law, not just big
names of those who were already established, but those who were up
and coming, like Jerry Mashaw and Graetz, and they became quite excited about economics. The Manne summer camps were important in
the sense that they gave some of these people who were early attendees
a common language, and they were able to find linkages that cut across
the substantive fields." It was that common language that structured the
intense intellectual environment that produced some of the most important figures in law and economics over the next few decades: Graetz,
Scott, Mashaw, and Warren Schwartz were among the UVA attendees in
the early years of the program.[105]

Of the two programs, UVA seems to have been able to hold onto its
position as a leader in law and economics, while USC has declined somewhat. Both schools developed Olin Law and Economics Programs, but
UVA retained many of its core faculty for decades, while USC lost most
of its faculty and was not able to match UVA in recruiting new law and
economics scholars. In 2001, as the Olin Foundation began to wind down
operations, it reported that, at UVA, "the Law School's dean, John Jeffries, is an enthusiastic supporter of the Program and has made the financial commitment necessary to sustain the Program at a level of funding at
least half of the current budget."[106] UVA Law built its impressive reputation with the assistance of law and economics, and it appears that it has
become an institutionalized commitment of the school.

A Beautiful Dream: Trying (and Failing) to Create Hoover East at Emory

His relationship with the University of Miami having become acutely
unpleasant, Manne began looking for a new location for his Law and
Economics Center. The opportunity to move the Center to Emory University came with the appointment of Tom Morgan (an alumnus of the
professors' institute) to the deanship of the law school. Morgan knew
that Manne was eager to move and, upon becoming dean, "the first thing
he did was approach me about coming to Emory." When Manne made
his move to Emory, the University had just begun its rapid move up the
ranks of American higher education, driven by the Woodruff family's
(the owners of the Coca-Cola Company) extraordinary donation of
$100 million in 1979. Manne arrived a year later and, in 1981, President
Jimmy Carter took a position at the University, dramatically increasing
its visibility.

Emory seemed in 1980 to be the ideal location for the Law and Economics Center: a university rapidly growing in prestige and wealth in the

most important city in the Southeast. Manne's programming increased substantially in his first few years at Emory, and he had a strong ally in Morgan, who put the LEC at the core of the Law School's research agenda. Morgan's 1981 Status Report on Emory Law argued that

> with the coming of the Law and Economics Center to Emory, the Law School has an unparalleled opportunity to become what few law schools even aspire to and fewer even come close to being: a school with sufficient breadth of view to be called a school of jurisprudence. Emory will have a natural advantage in bringing together a group of first rate scholars interested in applying the rigorous logic of economics to the study of law, and should exploit that advantage to the extent possible.[107]

The Olin Foundation, Manne's most important patron, was also encouraged by Manne's move to Emory, noting that "the Center at Emory will enjoy a much better faculty, the stature of a much finer University, and the close cooperation of the Emory administration."[108] Manne had at Emory what he lacked at Miami—a sympathetic dean and a university rapidly increasing in prestige—to accompany his patron support. What he lacked was the most basic, but essential resource in academia—space. As banal as this may seem, it was a fight over space that eventually led Manne to fall out with Emory's administration, and more critically, with the Olin Foundation.

At the start, Manne's relations with the Emory administration were very warm. "[President James T. Laney] welcomed the center, agreed to put up a million dollars. . . . My error [was that] I didn't really know before I got there how inadequate the facilities were. We had eight or ten people, and there were some in the law school, in that little tiny house. It was inadequate." Just as it became clear that the LEC needed more space, Manne learned that an architecturally remarkable facility, the Simmons Building (also known as the Gulf&Western or Jones Bridge building), twenty miles away from the Emory campus, had come onto the market.[109] Along with housing all of Manne's staff, the building had space for the LEC's seminars and room for other activities.

> At that time, the Simmons company, an Atlanta bedding company, sold out to ITT, a very generous supporter of the Law and Economics Center—they were very interested in antitrust. . . . Simmons had built the most glamorous building I had ever seen. . . . It was all redwood, copper, and glass, sitting on 125 acres of virgin forest, on the Chatahoochie River, which was a trout stream at that point, twenty miles out from Emory, in Gwinnett County, which was just starting not to be an outlier. You could tell the real estate was going to go up there. ITT acquired this building, and decided it was too glamorous for any of their subsidiary companies. . . . One of the guys told me about it, maybe we could

make a deal. There was something in the tax laws called a bargain sale, in which by manipulating numbers, a piece of property is sold at a discount price, and the difference is allowed as a charitable contribution for the corporation. The arithmetic worked out. . . . It was almost ready-made for my more ambitious plans for it.[110]

Manne quickly approached John M. Olin about supporting the purchase of the building, a request that he received sympathetically, based on his previous support with Manne and his friendship with Robert Woodruff. He directed Manne to submit a formal request to the Olin Foundation.[111] Manne approached President Laney with the idea, and "Jim approved it. He said, 'If you raise the $3 million, I'll get you the $1 million and we'll buy it.' "[112] Laney wrote in May 1982, "I can't tell you how pleased I am with the work you have done to date to develop Emory's Law and Economics Center and particularly to find a more adequate physical facility . . . We all join with you in your enthusiasm for the Simmons Building on Jones Bridge Road in Gwinnett County and believe this would make an excellent addition to both the Center and the University."[113] With both the Olin Foundation and Emory's leadership on board, Manne believed the way was clear to buy the building.

Manne believed that the purchase of the Simmons Building would turn the LEC into a major component of the free market organizational infrastructure. In May 1982, Manne made clear to John M. Olin that the building represented a rare opportunity for the conservative movement.

What I have reference to is the whole cause of free market and conservative ideology in American universities. There is literally only one academic building in the country housing a number of respected and influential conservative scholars. That is the Hoover Institution at Stanford University. And successful as the Hoover Institution has been, it has always lacked a certain influence because of its location on the West Coast and because, as a one-of-a-kind institution, many intellectuals do not take it seriously. The building we want for the John M. Olin Law and Economics Center would be an East Coast anchor of conservative intellectual thought comparable to the Hoover Institution on the West Coast. Indeed two such activities, geographically separated, would lend more credibility to the work of each. Because of our special emphasis on economics for lawyers, law professors and judges a properly housed John M. Olin Center would likely become one of the most influential academic operations of its kind in the world, one to which the most distinguished thinkers would repair on visits or research leaves. Further, the Center would become a world focal point for conferences and other programs concerned with the free enterprise system. I believe that this kind of presence would be a more significant association for your name than merely a building or the Center as it presently operates.[114]

Manne believed that the ideological instincts of American university administrators made this opportunity very unusual, one that if squandered could not be easily replicated.

> I am not sure that many people understand how completely left-leaning American universities are today. Emory in that regard is no better nor worse that the rest of them. It is simply understood and accepted by most administrators, professors and trustees that American universities will be dominated by people with extremely liberal views. . . . Our president, Jim Laney, is thoroughly confused by the appearance of a successful and intellectually respected conservative activity like the Law and Economics Center. Nonetheless, the people running our universities are trapped to some extent by their finer, older traditions; they must tolerate dissent, even when it is most distasteful to them, as with anyone proclaiming the virtues of individualism and free enterprise. But toleration is not support, and it is rare for a university to make things easy for a group with our point of view. The Hoover Institution has been a festering sore for a number of left-wing academics at Stanford for years, as in a smaller way has the Law and Economics Center, both at Miami and at Emory. But if we can fund our own way and maintain high standards of work, there is literally nothing they can do except brood about our expansion and our influence. But a lot of people here are unhappy with the prospect of the Law and Economics Center having such a handsome facility; they understand very well that we will be a much more potent intellectual force if we make that move. Unfortunately, without the move, we may disappear altogether. In other words, we hang precariously between an enormous increase in our importance and a possible slide into obscurity.[115]

Some discount probably should be applied both to Manne's hopes for the Simmons Building and his fears if its purchase fell through: he was, after all, trying to convince John M. Olin to increase his financial contribution to its purchase. That said, Manne seemed to sincerely believe that conservatives were strangers in American higher education. What opportunities they had came from institutional norms of "fair play" that provided small openings for conservative mobilization, but only if those cracks were skillfully and expediently taken advantage of.

It is difficult to say whether this perception of Emory's administrators (and to some degree those of other institutions as well) was accurate. Laney had every reason to be unsympathetic to a major conservative project at Emory, especially one connected to law and economics. Laney was a political liberal and close to President Jimmy Carter—the Carter Center was located next to Emory and was envisioned to come under its management after Carter's retirement.[116] Laney was also a believing Christian of the liberal, social-justice-oriented variety, having studied under Niebuhr at the Yale Divinity School in the 1950s. One indication of Laney's beliefs can be seen in a speech he gave to the United Methodists (the denomination that sponsored Emory) in 1992: "Our dominant philosophy also has a down side—a kind of unrestrained individualism that ignores the social fabric. It tends to spawn an ethos of disregard. Individuals pursue their own interests, but those interests are sometimes terribly self-centered. The last few years have revealed what the excesses of laissez-faire individualism lead to when there is not a concomitant concern for larger responsibility."[117] Laney imagined the university as a corrective to individualism, a community dedicated to moral improvement and growth.

The program of the LEC, by contrast, was devoted to the "laissez-faire individualism" that Laney found so distasteful. Worse, with private funding and a building off campus, it would have been difficult for Laney to exercise meaningful control over Manne's empire-building. Manne concedes, "I'm sure he saw that this would be Henry Manne's empire, trading on Emory's name, and he wouldn't be able to control it. And he was a control guy. If I'd been president, I'd have been a control guy. . . . Given my proclivities, if, say, Ralph Nader had wanted to do the same thing, I think I would have put stumbling blocks in the way." Manne and his staff, in fact, believed that the Simmons Building *would* insulate them from the University's control. Lewis Rockwell, an LEC staff member at the time, wrote to Manne in March 1982,

> I vote for Jones Bridge. . . . It would be far easier to raise money, because of Jones Bridge, than because of an ordinary building here. At Jones Bridge, we would have the premier meeting facility in the conservative world. No one—not Hoover, not AEI, not Heritage—could compete with us. The building itself would raise money for us. . . . We would not be putting our trust in modern universities and the kind of people who administer them. We would have all the advantages of the university connection, and very little of the disadvantages. Here on campus, we would be having continuous troubles with the administration, just because of the nature of the people in it.[118]

Roger Miller, who had been with Manne since the founding of the LEC, concurred in this latter judgment, stating that "the reliance on the good will of a few individuals is a weak basis for locating on campus."[119] Manne told Michael Joyce early on in the negotiations that

> an activity like the L&EC requires very careful and delicate tending in any respectable American university. The instincts and the politics of most people who manage universities run contrary to everything we stand for. We have certainly not escaped their attention at Emory, nor do I think we would at any university of this quality. To some extent we are and will always be strangers on a campus: actually we are "free riders" on an edifice that is run by our ideological enemies. All of this is by way of saying that my decision to go for the Simmons Building was designed to give us a degree of security here that we certainly do not have

at present, could not likely secure elsewhere, and could not have with President Laney's alternative proposal for a small office building on campus.[120]

Manne's deep suspicion of his own university and his conception of academic politics as a battle with his "ideological enemies" explains his high-wire efforts to salvage the Jones Bridge location and the conflicts they engendered.

With the purchase of the building reasonably far advanced, Emory's administration withdrew its support for LEC's off-campus location. The Olin Foundation's account of these events claims that, in July 1982, "the Board of Trustees of the University rejected the Simmons Building as a location for the Law and Economics Program. They apparently thought the building was too far from the campus. . . . Laney, we gather, concurred in this judgment."[121] Following on this rejection by the board, Laney proposed that the foundation put up $1.5 million to match the university's $1 million, which would be used to build an on-campus facility for the LEC, a building that would also house the economics department. This new offer may have been driven by predictable administration desires to use outside money to cover ordinary university functions. The Olin Foundation was unsympathetic to paying to house the economics department, and the university revised its proposal, with the foundation paying $1.5 million to build the facility and the university donating $1 million to endow the LEC. While this was going on, the purchase price for the Simmons Building dropped to $2.5 million—the exact amount that Olin and Emory had on the table—and Manne tried to convince Laney of the merits of shifting back to the Simmons Building option.[122]

Confused by the "mixed signals" coming from Emory, the staff of the Olin Foundation invited President Laney in October 1982 to speak with the foundation's steering committee. "Laney was advised by the Steering Committee that it was up to the University to decide once and for all which of the alternatives it preferred. . . . At the meeting, Laney made a strong pitch for the Simmons Building."[123] However, in this meeting, Laney was informed by Olin Foundation president William Simon that the foundation would support the university's preferred location,[124] thus contradicting his understanding that the foundation's support was contingent on the off-campus location, and in the process undercutting Manne's position and credibility. Laney reversed course and, in November, the University officially requested support for the on-campus location. "Manne objected immediately to this decision, stating his strong preference for the Simmons Building. He told Laney that he would not cooperate with the proposal, and would inform the Foundation of his objections."[125] In fact, Manne proposed to the foundation that he be allowed to purchase the building independent of the university, a proposal the foundation rejected.[126] Laney took Manne's actions as a personal affront. "By your action in recent days, you have failed to acknowledge and abide by my decision and have subverted Emory's efforts to raise money for an on campus location. It is a matter of record that you informed the John M. Olin Foundation that you opposed the proposal which you originally drafted on the University's behalf for the on campus solution. Your conduct in this instance is unacceptable and clearly would not be tolerated from any other member of the University community."[127] Convinced that the University and Manne were not on the same page, the Olin Foundation Steering Committee withdrew its support from the project. It was at this meeting that the foundation also decided to pull its funding from the LEC's Olin Fellows program and to pursue the possibility of creating law and economics programs at elite law schools, which will be discussed in detail in chapter 6.[128]

His relations with Emory's administration in tatters, Manne made a last, desperate gambit to establish the Center as an independent operation. Separation from Emory only increased the scope of Manne's ambitions, and he entered into a partnership with his old friend from the University of Rochester, Richard Rosett, dean of the University of Chicago business school from 1974 to 1983, to form the "Chattahoochee Institute." Rosett's stature in the academic community (he was later appointed dean of arts and sciences at Washington University), combined with his friendship with Manne, made him a natural choice for helping to resuscitate the project.

Relieved of the connection to a university, Manne proposed to move the LEC's programming beyond training judges and professors, to include virtually all senior-level decision-makers in America. Manne observed that, traditionally, knowledge diffused to decision-makers in one of two ways: publication in scholarly journals or through traditional classroom teaching. To these Manne proposed to add a third:

> Courses tailored for senior level executives, attorneys, and government officials, taught by scholars selected for the importance and influence of their scholarship and for their skill in teaching. Examples are courses in economics for corporate counsel, finance theory for executives with an engineering background, regulatory law and theory for chief executive officers who must take positions on pending government proposals, or accounting and marketing for trustees of not-for-profit organizations. The Institute will provide a communications shortcut, enabling business and government leaders to become sophisticated consumers of new ideas that ordinarily reach them along conventional routes.[129]

The objective of these programs was to counteract what Manne saw as the liberal bias in the information that executives received, in the process reshaping the perspectives of American decision-makers.

Expanding the LEC's training programs was only the beginning of Manne's plan for "Hoover East." The institute would play host to other sympathetic organizations (such as the Mont Pelerin and Philadelphia Societies, the Atlanta Lexecon office, and smaller conservative foundations) as well as providing a home for new organizations, such as an international law and economics association and an association for economic expert witnesses. The new institute would also use its expertise in economic consulting, providing assistance in the selection of expert witnesses, and helping "translate" between economists and lawyers. On top of these initiatives would be an aggressive research program with visiting scholars, sabbatical programs, postdoctoral fellowships, and an expanded research staff.[130] Manne proposed to push the combination of entrepreneurship and free market research much further than he had before.

By May 1983, Manne and Rosett believed that their Hoover East plan would reach fruition. Rosett wrote Manne at the time that "the excitement still is not fading. I have examined the idea from every angle I can think of and its appeal grows steadily. I have tried to work out a plan that will allow us to move ahead with some confidence that the Chattahoochee Institute will come into existence and that it will have the importance it deserves." The risk of the institute's plan, given its detachment from an academic institution, clearly weighed on Rosett. "You will see that I am giving myself more than one option and as much safety as I can manage. I expect that you will want to do the same."[131]

What finally killed the efforts of Rosett and Manne to bring the Hoover East project back to life was the implacable opposition of William Simon. Manne asked Rosett to go to New York to make a final pitch for the newly redesigned project, but Simon turned him down flat. Rosett recalls, "I went to the Olin Foundation and talked to Mike Joyce and told him what I wanted, and he said, 'You ought to talk to Bill Simon.' He ushered me into a room where I met Bill Simon for the first time. . . . He told me there were no circumstances where he would support any activity of Henry's." Despite John M. Olin's personal support for the project, Simon had lost trust in Manne due to the crossed signals coming from Emory, and, given Simon's dominant position in the foundation, that meant the Simmons Building project was finished. As many involved with the foundation agree, Simon was a man of strong opinions, who relied on his gut instincts, and he had decided (perhaps on the basis of imperfect information) that the foundation should burn its bridges with Manne.[132] It was only due to the support of other members of the board (including George Gillespie, Olin's private lawyer) and some of the staff, that the foundation continued to support the seminars for federal judges despite Simon's hostility.

Manne aimed high and he fell hard. He lost any chance of acquiring the Simmons Building, the funding for his Olin Fellows program was eliminated, and the finances of the LEC were withering. The distraction of the Simmons Building negotiations had taken an especially heavy toll on the LEC's previously careful nurturing of its financial supporters. The LEC depended on Manne's personal connections, reputation, and attention, and once these became frayed, the momentum of the LEC began to stall. By 1984, Manne was forced to plead with foundations to maintain his core programs, the economics seminars for law professors and judges. The Olin Foundation grudgingly agreed that

> Manne is not without his weaknesses as an administrator, and has probably brought the bulk of his economic woes upon himself. Still, staff is sympathetic to this particular request [for the judges institutes]. . . . While the precise impact this economic training has had on legal decision-making is difficult to gauge, many recent decisions reflect a sound understanding of economic principles, and indicate how important it is that judges have a background in economics. One such case in point is the recent decision by the Ninth Circuit Court of Appeals to reverse the District Judge in the State of Washington on a comparable worth ruling. The decision explicitly reinforced the supremacy of market forces in determining wage and price values. . . . Staff thinks the cancellation of the Economics Institute would represent a significant loss to the legal community.[133]

While the "sexiest" programs from the point of view of the foundation were maintained, much of the rest of the LEC, especially its training of students, had unraveled.

> The main thing we lost was the fellowships, and the fellowships just gave a spark to the whole thing. . . . We lost a lot, and [had we stayed at Emory] I'm not sure it [the LEC] would have survived. I sure didn't like the idea of staying on as a full-time law professor at Emory. Tom Morgan by that time had left; in my last year there was another dean there. He had moved on to be the dean at George Washington. The new dean didn't have a clue what it was all about.[134]

By 1983, Manne had lost his opportunity to create Hoover East, and the Law and Economics Center, which just a few years earlier was one of the conservative movement's most impressive assets, seemed to be coming unraveled.

Conclusion

By the early 1980s, law and economics was becoming part of the mainstream of academic law. The meteoric rise of Richard Posner gave the movement a bona fide intellectual superstar, whose notoriety forced the rest of legal academia to take law and economics seriously and sent powerful signals to young scholars that prestigious careers could be forged in this once-exotic field. Posner's work built on the foundation laid by Director and Coase, which points to the importance of the Chicago Law School's role in nurturing law and economics in its early years, despite the fact that it was still out of fashion in the larger world of legal academia. Had Chicago not performed this function, it is unlikely that law and economics would have experienced the explosive entry into the legal mainstream made possible by Posner's emergence. At the same time that the Posner phenomenon burst on the legal academic scene, the movement developed important outposts at Virginia and USC, where budding law and economics practitioners could learn from, compete, and collaborate with each other. Just as important, the law and economics professors at UVA and USC were not Chicago-style libertarians, and as they moved on to more prestigious law schools, they helped eat away at the perception that the approach was simply thinly veiled ideology. This legitimated law and economics in the legal academic mainstream, and opened the way to its institutional advances in the 1980s and 1990s.

Of equal importance was the entrepreneurial work of Henry Manne, who successfully operated on both the demand and supply sides of the movement. Manne's institutes for law professors equipped a remarkable number of legal academics with the techniques necessary to apply law and economics to new fields, and increased the receptivity of the profession to those scholars' insights. At the same time, Manne's programs for federal judges ensured that many members of the federal bar could understand the concepts that these professors were developing, which meant that the courts would not have to wait on a wholly new generation of judges to absorb these new theories. Of even greater long-term significance, Manne's programs helped to build networks of law and economics scholars across the country in a period when most of the movement's personnel were widely scattered across the country and isolated in their home institutions. When this intellectual and network entrepreneurship was combined with the increasing scope of law and economics' ambitions, the stage was set for entry into the legal mainstream in earnest in the 1980s and 1990s.

The 1970s and early 1980s were a period of remarkable organizational success and significant setbacks for law and economics. Given how scarce entrepreneurial skills are in the academy, had Manne invested his talents in pure scholarship (as he might have, if he had been appointed to an elite law school in the late 1960s), it is far from certain that anyone else would have built the movement's organizational infrastructure. It was only because of the still-powerful barriers to entry to the legal academy that

Manne's efforts were deflected in this direction. In his organizational entrepreneurship, much of Manne's success came from trial and error, and
not from a grand plan. In the area of fund-raising, Manne only slowly
discovered how to draw large sums of money from corporations without
compromising the intellectual focus of his programming, something that
the leaders of the conservative public interest law movement were not
able to do. Despite his success in raising money and building enthusiasm
for the movement, Manne's path was not without obstacles. At both
Miami and Emory he operated under administrators who were not enthu-
siasts for the project of law and economics, and his conflicts with them
limited his entrepreneurial reach. In a series of events that show that the
movement was far from a well-oiled "giant right-wing conspiracy,"
Manne had an almost complete falling out with the Olin Foundation by
the early 1980s. In short, the organizational successes of law and economics in this period were far from inevitable, might not have occurred without Manne's specific skills and commitment, and were limited by internal
conflict within the conservative movement itself.

   Ironically enough, however, it was this very conflict that set the stage for
the next steps in the movement's organizational evolution: the creation of
the Olin programs in America's elite institutions and the resurrection of
Manne's plan to build a law and economics law school. We will return
to these programs in chapter 6.

5

The Federalist Society: Counter-Networking

THE FEDERALIST SOCIETY IS ACKNOWLEDGED, by friend and foe, to be an organization of extraordinary consequence. Liberals, fearing a "giant right-wing conspiracy" in the law with the Federalist Society at its head, have been alarmed by its role in judicial selection and have devoted significant time and resources to producing detailed studies of the organization.[1] On the right, conservatives have lavished praise on the Society for helping to "turn the tide" against liberal control of the legal profession, the law schools, and the courts.[2] Others are impressed simply by the federal judges and Supreme Court justices, top conservative legal professors, and prestigious private lawyers who attend its annual meeting. All of this focus on the Society's members—the articles they have written, decisions they have handed down, presidents they have hunted—leaves the Society as an actual, working organization somewhat in the shadows.

This chapter, by contrast, focuses primarily on the Federalist Society itself, asking three fundamental questions about its development and place in the larger conservative legal movement. First, what explains the rapid growth of the Society, given the dismal fortunes of the conservative public interest law organizations described in chapter 3? How did it avoid falling into their "organizational maintenance" trap? Second, why did the Society's leaders choose to act as intellectual and network entrepreneurs rather than orient the organization more directly at legal change? Third, what explains the growth over time in the Society's functions and ambition?

The key to answering these questions and correcting misconceptions about the Society is the concept of "boundary maintenance." There is a strong tendency in most of the popular writing on the Society to conflate the activities of the organization itself with those of its members. For example, during the Clinton impeachment saga it was common to read that the president was being hunted by "Federalist Society lawyers." This was true in the sense that many of the president's pursuers were Federalist Society members, but false in the specific sense that the Society as an organization was not involved.[3] Nevertheless, it is probably the case that the networks produced by the Society made such activities easier than they would otherwise have been. I suggest as much below, describing these as the "indirect outputs" of formal Society activities. The Society has been faced with opportunities to expand into the activities its detractors claims it engages in, and has refrained from doing so because of concerns over organizational maintenance. An organization that did what many people think the Federalist Society does would not, and could not, look like the Society that exists today.

What is it, then, that the Society does? It is best understood as a provider of public goods (in the welfare economic sense) to the conservative legal movement. First, it engages in *recruitment* of law students and practicing attorneys who can identify with and participate in the movement. Second, it invests in the *human capital* of members through frequent debates, which acquaint them with conservative legal ideas and heighten their intellectual self-confidence, and through their participation in its student, lawyer, and practice groups, which provide leadership experience. Third, the Society produces *cultural capital*, in that its activities facilitate the orderly development of conservative legal ideas and their injection into the legal mainstream, reducing the stigma associated with those ideas in institutions that produce and transmit professional distinction. Fourth, and perhaps most importantly, the Society is a producer of *social capital* in the form of networks that develop as by-products of Society activities. In the absence of an organization like the Federalist Society, these movement public goods would be produced in a haphazard, uncoordinated, and redundant fashion, if produced at all. Organizational entrepreneurs would have seen their transaction costs escalate significantly, to the point where some activities would not have been worth pursuing.

Why did the Society's activities cohere around these functions and not others? To explain this, I pay particular attention to the choices its leaders made in shaping the Society's organizational structure. While it is probably true that, given the context of the early 1980s, some organization of conservative lawyers would inevitably have formed, it was not predetermined that it would look like the Federalist Society or that it would effectively manage the organizational maintenance problems that face all such projects in contemporary American politics. It matters a great deal that the opportunity to build a network of conservative lawyers was seized by the particular individuals who formed the Federalist Society. Had others been the first movers, it is highly unlikely that the organization would perform the functions it does. The importance of leadership in the conservative legal movement is even clearer when the Federalist Society is compared to the first generation of conservative public interest law firms (as discussed in chapter 3), which had a very different sort of leadership, and very different outcomes.

The key decision this entrepreneurial cadre made was to narrow its mission to facilitating the activism of its members and influencing the character of intellectual debate rather than directly influencing the actions of government itself. The Society has aimed to deepen the character of legal thought in conservative circles, rather than proposing doctrines of its own. It has tried, through its activities, to make conservative lawyers aware of each other, thereby activating latent resources for the conservative legal movement, rather than plan overall movement strategy and organizational development. It has sought to make conservative lawyers aware of opportunities for political and legal participation but has not itself engaged in litigation or lobbying. The Federalist Society, in sum, has pursued an indirect approach to legal change, one that operates as a focal point for discussion and as a safe harbor for individuals who feel isolated from the mainstream of American legal culture. This strategy of indirection was dictated by its initial organizational commitments to intellectual debate and a desire to serve as a hospitable environment for the entirety of the conservative legal movement. Indirection has served the organization well. The leadership of the Society has been happy to see the fruits of its labors harvested by other organizations, which have been able to take advantage of the networks and resources the Society has produced. The key to understanding the Society's ability to attract resources despite their diffuse outputs has been their close relationship to patrons willing to invest for the long term.

To understand the role of the Federalist Society in the conservative legal movement, it is necessary to focus on how it solved some basic problems of organizational design, in particular the establishment and maintenance of organizational boundaries. As I argued in chapter 1, the modern activist state created a change in the character of modern parties. With more of the governing apparatus outside of direct electoral control, partisan mobilization has shifted to new sites of contestation, such as the professions and the universities, where many of the key resources for elite political change are rooted. Understanding the Federalist Society requires that we situate its rise and development as part of a larger effort to mobilize against the entrenchment of the liberal legal network. The critical factor in explaining why opportunities are seized or lost in this sphere of political competition is the decision-making of organizational entrepreneurs, and here the movement was lucky in the character and continuity of the individuals who founded the Federalist Society. Had people with other interests and abilities filled the organizational space taken by the Society, the history of conservatives in American legal institutions could have been very different.

Founding the Federalist Society

The Federalist Society was founded by a small minority of law students embedded in what they saw as a hostile institution, America's law schools. For both strategic and personal reasons, the Society's founders

responded to this hostility by creating an organization with a central commitment to intellectual debate. This founding organizational mission has
been sustained by a leadership cadre that has, with only small adjust-
ments, controlled the Society for its first quarter-century and will, in all
likelihood, do so for another two decades.

The first Federalist Society activity was a symposium on federalism at
Yale Law School held in April 1982. At the time, active conservative law
student organizations existed at Yale, Chicago, Harvard, and Stanford,
although not all of the chapters were formally known as the Federalist
Society. The inspiration for the symposium was the organizers' belief
that "law schools and the legal profession are currently strongly dominated by a form of orthodox liberal ideology which advocates a centralized and uniform society. While some members of the legal community
have dissented from these views, no comprehensive conservative critique
or agenda has been formulated in this field. This Conference will furnish
an occasion for such a response to begin to be articulated."[4] The conference was intellectually ambitious but organizationally modest: none of
the organizers anticipated that the symposium would lead to anything
like the modern nationally organized and funded Federalist Society. As
Lee Liberman Otis recalls, "We did not know [we were] starting a national organization when we started this. Basically what . . . we at Yale
and we at Chicago thought about this [was that] we were starting organizations at our schools." The original proposal showed the modest expectations that accompanied the first conference: "If it is successful, we
would hope to make such a conference annual or periodic occasions for
reflection on the ways in which the law and the development of legal
principles affect society."[5] While the earliest ambitions of the Society's
founders were intellectual rather than organizational, hints of its eventual function as a network of conservative lawyers were in evidence even
at this time. The organization provided financial support for students to
come to the symposium from law schools across the country, and its
organizers announced their hope that they would "participate in the discussion following each address, and would also have the opportunity to
exchange ideas with the speakers between meetings, during the informal
reception and over meals."[6] Networking was built into the organization
from the beginning.

The founding symposium of the Federalist Society attracted enormous
attention in the national press, in the conservative movement, and among
conservative law students. Gary Lawson, at the time a law student at Yale,
recalls that

> once the stuff all dropped in our laps, of course we're going to do some-
> thing. . . . We had student groups in 1981 writing to us and saying, "How do

we start an organization?" What are we going to do, say, "We're going to have this conference at Yale and then disappear"? It all really started with conferences. The major event was the conference in 1982, but we started that with the idea of having one panel. We had Bork and Winter at Yale, Scalia and [Professor Edmund] Kitch at Chicago and we thought, "Wouldn't that make a fun panel on federalism?" That just steamrolled into a whole conference. We had people from other schools calling us up, wanting to be part of the conference. We had people who wanted to come in from a thousand miles away and start their own chapters. That was the first sign that there was something there. There's a void in that market waiting to be filled.

Steven Calabresi also uses a market metaphor to explain the emergence of the Federalist Society, to some degree underplaying his role as an entrepreneur and emphasizing instead the existence of an enormous untapped demand for an organization.

My original objective—I started the Yale Chapter when I was a second-year student at Yale Law School—was to have some good debates, to bring some conservative speakers to Yale, where I don't think any conservative voices were being heard, force faculty members there to confront the ideas by debating who we were bringing in. . . . We held a conference in 1982; it was held by the folks at Chicago and by the folks at Yale. The folks at Chicago were friends of mine from my undergraduate days at Yale—Lee Liberman Otis and David McIntosh. Our conference was covered by *National Review* and suddenly conservatives at fifteen other law schools began calling us and telling us they wanted to attend the conference and they wanted to form chapters too. That was a process of almost spontaneous generation. It turned out there was an enormous demand at other law schools for the kind of thing we felt a demand for at Yale.

Conservative law students alienated in their home institutions, desperate for a collective identity, and eager for collective activity provided a ripe opportunity for organizational entrepreneurship. What was undetermined at the time, however, was how this opportunity would be directed, and by whom.

By the end of the summer of 1982 the Society's founders were well on the way to tapping into this unmet demand by attracting funding from conservative foundations. In a letter to Richard Larry of the Scaife Foundation in August 1982, Lee Liberman Otis noted, "While there now exist a number of organizations which are beginning to provide a counterweight to the liberal public interest law groups, no comparable effort has been made at the law school level."[7] Echoing Michael Horowitz's broadside from two years earlier, the Society's founders pointed to the intellectual vacuum at the core of the conservative legal counterestablishment, and argued that changing legal culture through the education, recruitment, and development of young conservative lawyers was an essential counterpart to investments in litigation. Changing legal culture required shaking the self-confidence of liberal lawyers by challenging their perception that they had a monopoly on serious legal thought. An October 1982 proposal observes that by "encouraging conservatives to present their ideas more articulately and more vocally, it [an organization of conservative law students] could cause others to listen to these views more attentively, and, perhaps ultimately, to question some of the liberal positions which are being presented as the law."[8] Conservatives were insufficiently "articulate" and their ideas poorly developed, and the budding Society claimed that they could build an organization that could help make conservative ideas both convincing and respectable.

Early on in its development, the Society looked to create a membership larger than law students. In its original 1982 proposal, the Society proposed a tripartite organizational structure, composed of student, law faculty, and lawyer divisions. While speakers, symposia, and publications were at the core of the Society's mission, these purely intellectual activities did not exhaust its ambitions. Number 5 in the proposal's list of activities was placement, which it claimed was dominated by the liberal legal network: "Conservatives have long bemoaned the fact that clerkships to prominent conservative jurists have often gone to people with liberal views. Similarly, it has been contended that far too many legal posts in governmental offices (even those not controlled by civil service regulations) have been held by liberals under Republican administrations. Finally, it is generally acknowledged that there is an insufficient number of conservative law school faculty."[9] A placement service run by Professor James McClellan of the University of Virginia was proposed, along with a "job exchange section" in the Society's newsletter. The proposal was prescient in its prediction that "simply through its existence, the Society can be expected to create an informal network of people with shared views who are interested in helping each other out in the placement sphere. It will in fact be one of the national organization's goals to develop key relationships with judges, legislators, governmental counsels and practitioners. To some extent, through the Yale symposium, this has already begun to take place."[10] From its founding, the Society's leaders hoped that "simply through its existence" conservatives might gain sway over jobs in conservative administrations and in the courts. Early in the Society's development it crowed to patrons about members' success in obtaining prestigious clerkships and other positions,[11] but it looked for its greatest impact in placement to come as a by-product of the Society's other activities, rather than as an explicit, formalized function of the organization.

While they did not direct the Society's development, the support of senior members of the conservative legal movement was essential in this period. By the fall of 1983, the Society had a permanent office and a full-time director, Eugene Meyer.[12] Perhaps the most important elite sponsor of the Society in its early years was then-professor Antonin Scalia, who first helped connect the Yale and Chicago contingents with the conservative law group at Stanford,[13] helped them with fund-raising, spoke at their first conference,[14] hosted visiting Harvard Law Federalist Society members at his home when the Society had its conference at the University of Chicago Law School, and facilitated the Society's early move into an office at the American Enterprise Institute. Michael Horowitz also played a critical role in getting the Society off the ground, no doubt recognizing that it was doing what he had called for in his report to the Scaife Foundation.[15] As Lee Liberman Otis recalls, Horowitz

> found us after we started. . . . He was really excited to find out that this thing existed. And he was full of ideas, people he knew. . . . He did help us a little with foundations, but also I think he helped us with just meeting other conservative lawyer types in Washington. For example, I clerked with a fellow named John Schmidt who became deputy counsel to Vice President Bush. Mike Horowitz came up with the idea that John should meet Boyden Gray who was then counsel to Vice President Bush. He just knew everybody, basically, and so if we were looking for speakers or things like that he would be able to help us with stuff like that.

Finally, Kenneth Cribb, first as an advisor to the attorney general and then as assistant to the president for domestic policy, was an early an important ally in the Reagan administration. Cribb recalls,

> I was always looking for people who would come and work on the president's agenda without self-calculation, and that describes these Federalists. They're loyal to a philosophical principle that Reagan was trying to accomplish, and they weren't trying to [ideologically] position themselves for personal gain, so they were very valuable. . . . In any event, after Meese had been appointed attorney general . . . Judge Bork said there's one person you must hire when you're setting up the Justice Department, and that's Steve Calabresi. . . .So he was the first one brought in, and he became a special assistant to the attorney general, then David McIntosh, who was practicing law in Los Angeles. . . . So I hired David second; he was also a special assistant to the attorney general.[16] Lee [Liberman Otis] had been hired independently by William French Smith at Justice, so she was there when we came over in 1985. . . . In terms of the signal it sent, [hiring the Federalist Society founders showed that] the Reagan administration thinks what they've accomplished in terms of founding the Federalist Society is important, and worthy, and we're going to give them good jobs. I think a third

sense is that young, idealist-oriented students saw that you could win that way, you could succeed if you acted honestly on the basis of your ideals, as opposed to maneuvering and telling people what they want to hear and playing both sides of the street. It was a signal that if you do the right thing you'll go further than if you manipulate. It's a good moral example.[17]

Society membership was a valuable signal for an administration eager to hire true-believers for bureaucratic hand-to-hand combat.[18] In addition, by hiring the Society's entire founding cadre the Reagan administration and its judicial appointees sent a very powerful message that the terms of advancement associated with political ambition were being set on their head: clear ideological positioning, not cautiousness, was now an affirmative qualification for appointed office. In its early years Federalist Society membership carried a stigma within legal academia, but it was precisely the willingness to bear this stigma that made Society membership a valuable signal of true-believership for conservatives in government.[19]

The nascent Federalist Society was beginning to connect conservative law students from across the country, and the involvement of Scalia, Horowitz, Cribb, and Gray connected the Society to the conservative legal establishment. In recognition of how far the organization had come, just four years after its modest founding journalists were already describing the Society as part of the "Conservative Elite."[20]

Building Chapters

The Federalist Society moved rapidly to open chapters in as many significant law schools as possible. This could be done spontaneously, up to a point, by building on the outpouring of interest produced by the Yale symposium. The Society's founders sought to guide this budding movement even before they developed a national office, by distributing "How To Form a Conservative Law Student Group," a document that provides a window on the Society's early goals and methods.

David McIntosh recalls writing the document with Otis "literally a few weeks before the first conference, because people were asking and we realized, 'This is an opportunity, we're bringing fifty people together, let's have at least something they can take home with them to think about how to do it.' " The document emphasized the Society's intellectual mission to "stimulate thought and discussion about the applications of conservative principles to the law."[21] Cognizant of the wide range of conservative thought, the proposal noted that the Yale Federalist Society "provides a sense of community for its members who span a broad ideological spectrum which includes traditionalists, fusionist conservatives, libertarians, objectivists, classical liberals and Straussians." Aware that these ideological divisions posed significant dangers to the movement, the proposal recommended that student chapters

> should not use the adjective "conservative." This is for several reasons. There is no need to become involved in disputes among conservatives, libertarians and other factions about what they call themselves. A number of people may be hesitant about identifying themselves as conservatives, although they may share most of your views. Additionally, although it is important to have some ideological identification among members of the groups, a number of non-conservatives may want to come to your events and participate in the group, and there is no need to make them feel uncomfortable. . . . Finally, if the group wishes to issue statements on national or law school policies, or even if it does not, it will have greater credibility if the name does not make the group appear too unobjective.[22]

This passage points to two fundamental dynamics in the Society's early development. First, the founders had a strong desire to avoid factionalism. Previous conservative student groups, like Young Americans for Freedom, were rife with such conflict, to the point that their energies were squandered in internecine conflict. "One of the easiest ways for groups of students interested in politics to fail to accomplish as much as they would like," the paper observed, "is for them to become bogged down in internal politics."[23] The Society was obviously aware of such a danger, and from the beginning consciously tried to avoid it.[24] As McIntosh recalls, "I noticed that there was often a tendency for conservatives to be critical of each other, and . . . some of that was product differentiation, but some of it was [that] culturally it is a lot easier to get into a fight with a fellow conservative because you're both outliers to the mainstream of American culture. It's a lot harder to get into a debate or a fight with the law school or legal establishment." Second, the Society sought to make its ideas attractive to those not previously affiliated with conservatism. Factional infighting ran the risk of turning off outsiders, a serious danger since the personal experiences of Society leaders convinced them that "conversion" was possible. Steve Calabresi recalls that

> there was definitely a feeling of conversion, that . . . there were people who could be turned around. Most law students had grown up in liberal families, had gone to good schools where the viewpoints being heard were mainly liberal and . . . they were essentially liberal out of lack of awareness of conservative ideas. Some of that was fueled by our lack of personal pasts in conservatism. . . . I was originally a moderate Democrat, and I was persuaded by Reagan that conservative ideas were right, but I was definitively a liberal who became a

conservative. Lee Liberman was definitively in the same position, David McIntosh was in the same position. We tended to assume that if we could make the transition, other people could also, so long as we made a good persuasive argument for the things we believed in.

The Society's leaders thought there was a constituency for their ideas beyond the hard core of self-identified conservatives. Convincing them, not simply providing succor for the hard core, was the principal objective of the Society.

The Society's emphasis on debate, rather than just sponsoring conservative speakers, was evident from the beginning. The original "how to" document makes the motivation clear: "You are more likely to convince people of your viewpoint if they feel the other side has been given a fair hearing."[25] As Calabresi recalls, "If you just bring a famous conservative and the audience hears that but thinks, 'Well, sounds good to me, but I think one of my professors probably could have critiqued it and then I would have understood where they were wrong.' By having the professor there on stage with them they get to see it and evaluate the ideas."[26] Otis, Calabresi, Lawson, and McIntosh had all been active members of an undergraduate debating society, the Yale Political Union, an experience that each of them identified as important in shaping their ideas for how to organize the Society. McIntosh remembers that "Lee, Steve, and I as undergraduates and Gary when he was at Yale [were] very involved in a debating society [which] meant that we embraced the classical liberal notion that a debate about ideas is a healthy thing because the truth will emerge from that. And that strong belief . . . led us to instill it as an organizing principle for the organization. We're all very politically oriented people, so [without that experience] you could have seen a different ethic. There was also a genuine intellectual commitment to debate." Gary Lawson notes that "you don't have an interesting discussion if you don't have people disagreeing, [if you have] pep rallies." Eugene Meyer argues that the debate orientation came about because "we think in a fair debate these ideas are really strong and we'll win. Two, if it's a really fair debate and you keep losing, you sure better figure out why if you're intellectually honest. [One example is] original intent and original meaning. To some degree some of these discussions and debates led not all but most conservatives to abandon original intent and adopt original meaning."[27] An orientation to debate also had the consequence of moderating factional conflict. Despite their differences, in debates conservatives and libertarians would find themselves agreeing with one another more than with the liberals on the other side. The original, foundational commitment to debate made the organization open and attractive to outsiders, moderated factional conflict and insularity, and had a tendency to prevent the members' ideas from becoming stale from a lack of challenge.

After having established a strong foundation of student chapters, the Society moved on to develop its lawyers division, beginning with its first and most important chapter, in Washington, D.C. The D.C. chapter was founded by Stephen Markman, a young conservative lawyer serving as a staff member of the Senate Judiciary Committee. Markman was approached by active members of the Society in early 1985, Michael Horowitz in particular, because his position on the Judiciary Committee gave him strong connections to legal conservatives in the administration and on the Hill. As Markman recalls,

> I thought it would be a way in which we could provide a greater focus for those individuals who shared . . . conservative judicial and constitutional values, and of course I knew there were a great many people in Washington who did in fact share those values, but it was all far more amorphous back in those days—there was no regular meeting group. There'd been a couple of aborted efforts by the Heritage Foundation and some other groups to have that kind of meeting, [and while] they did serve their own purpose, there really was no principal focus for people who shared those views.

In its early years, the D.C. chapter helped conservatives across government shape the movement's still fairly underdeveloped legal ideas by facilitating freer debate than is typically possible within the day-to-day routines of the executive branch and Congress. Markman believes that the intense interactions facilitated by the D.C. chapter played a key role in the evolution of "originalist" jurisprudence.

> Ed Meese at this time had originated not the idea, but the nomenclature of original intent jurisprudence. This was later refined, refined I believe in a very useful way to original meaning jurisprudence, but remember at this time the stuff of debate was still kind of the old Nixonian terminology of strict contructionism and law and order jurisprudence, and this was a very clumsy way of referring to the ideas I think united people who congregated around the Federalist Society. I think that one of the interests in getting together was trying to try to refine our debate, to try to render more sophisticated what it is we were talking about, and many of our speakers contributed to that. I think the language of interpretivism or textualism or original meaning jurisprudence—these things were all aired and the subject of a great deal of discussion at Federalist Society meetings.

Steven Calabresi believes that the Society has had a continuing impact in shaping the evolution of conservative thought, and speeding the transition from the older tradition of judicial restraint.

Before we existed there were a handful of conservative scholars, but they weren't in contact with each other. By bringing them together, putting them on debates and things, I think we've to some extent helped to bring together a homogenous, mature set of conclusions on things that people on the right agree on, about how particular legal problems should be addressed. One example might be the takings clause of the Fifth Amendment. I think at the time that we started there were some members of the Federalist Society, some of our leading scholars, who were very skeptical of expanding the takings clause. They thought it violated judicial restraint, they thought it might hark back to a return to *Lochner v. New York*. I'd say in particular Robert Bork and Antonin Scalia, who were very involved in this from the beginning, were very hesitant about expanding the takings clause. Then there were people like Richard Epstein who thought everything was a taking. . . . Both of those positions have gradually been rejected by most members of the Federalist Society, so today most members of the Federalist Society believe there are some things that are regulatory takings, and in that sense the takings clause has been expanded beyond where it was in 1981. Even Scalia now on the Supreme Court goes along with that view and has written cases like *Nollan*.[28] That reflects to some degree the interest in the takings clause among Federalist Society members. . . . That may be a case where having conservatives and libertarians . . . debating this issue and fleshing it out, and having members listen to it, has led to the emergence of a position that was not the original position of either of the advocates of that matter.

By encouraging intense and sustained interactions among its members, the Society—in particular, its D.C. chapter—has created the deliberative conditions necessary for convergence in the ideas of the conservative legal movement's various factions.

While it is easy to emphasize the networking function of the Society, the most significant fact about the Society is what its networks center around. The sense that something is at stake in the speakers and debate that the Society sponsors gives the Society an emotional and intellectual edge. Especially for those members of the Society who had participated in it during their law school years, the D.C. chapter provided sustenance in what could easily be an intellectually stultifying environment. McIntosh recalls, "I was a young lawyer in government and [the D.C. chapter meeting] was a great opportunity to see friends who were spread around the Reagan administration and hear a debate similar to what we had done at the Society meetings or the national conferences, when your daily activities didn't let you do that as much. So I think there was a sense of people missing that academic debate, and this was an opportunity to keep being involved in that."

The most important by-products of the D.C. chapter's intellectual debates were the networks it created across the federal government. The

D.C. chapter helped overcome the atomization and lack of coordination that is an unavoidable danger in our "government of strangers."[29] Markman recalls that networking "was obviously one of [our] interests—it was also . . . to try to identify more individuals who shared those values with whom one could seek assistance . . . knowing somebody in the Commerce Department who shared your perspectives [was very valuable]." Based on his experience as head of President George H. W. Bush's Council on Competitiveness, David McIntosh found the D.C. chapter's networks especially valuable in overcoming the intrinsic informational challenges of coordinating action across the executive branch.

> Our formal role [was] to ensure that the president's policy preferences were taken into account in the agency rule-making, and yet we had no staff, half a dozen people by the end and some staff support from technical people at OMB who monitor these regulations. Being able to attend the Federalist Society lunch and hear from people who were either at an agency or at a law firm working on some of this issues meant that I had a much better sense of what was happening on issues that were taking place. . . . One of the folks at OMB told me, . . . "David, you've been getting the mushroom treatment." And I said, "What do you mean?" and he said, "You're kept in the dark and fed shit." And by that he meant the information flow was being controlled by the agency and we were expected to at the last minute ride herd on this for policy reasons. So having a group of people who were friends and talked freely with each other opened up an alternative information source.

The D.C. chapter reduced the transaction costs of governing as a conservative. It allowed Society members to identify allies in other agencies, thereby facilitating the flow of information, helping ideas to germinate and spread, and allowing members to escape from the "agency view." As we will see later in this chapter, this network function of reducing transaction costs (especially those connected to the search for information) has also been vital where judicial appointments are concerned.

The Growth and Funding of the Federalist Society

Whether one focuses on its budget, members, or programs, the Federalist Society has grown dramatically over its first two decades. How did the Society manage to finance this growth given its diffuse and hard-to-measure goals? The secret to the Society's success is the diversity in its sources of support, in particular the (financial and in-kind) contributions of its members and the long-term support of conservative foundations.

The Federalist Society budget has gone through four basic phases, which can be identified (as in figure 5.1) by funding plateaus. The first,

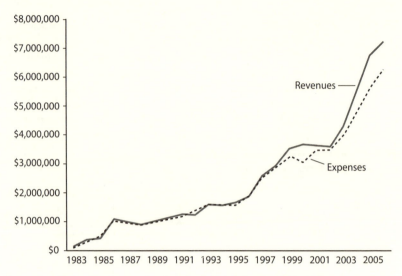

Figure 5.1. Federalist Society Budget (in 2006 dollars), 1983–2006

from 1982 to 1986, saw the organization's budget go from around $120,000 (measured by revenues in 2006 dollars) to a little over $1 million by 1986, where it stayed for the next few years.[30] The next big jump was between 1989 and 1993, when the budget rose to $1.6 million. Fund-raising steadily increased from 1993 to 1997, as the budget exceeded $2.5 million, and the growth since then was gradual before sharply accelerating in 2001. The Federalist Society's activities, with the exception of its two national meetings, are conducted primarily through its student chapters (in law schools), lawyer chapters (by city), and practice groups (organized by functional interest). The growth in the student and lawyer chapters can be seen in figure 5.2.[31] In a shift from the evolutionary pattern of the lawyers and student chapters, the Society's fifteen practice groups were created at the same time, in late 1995, funded by a $100,000 grant from the Wiegand Foundation.[32] Since then, the practice groups have created subcommittees, but the basic structure has remained the same.

The Society's membership tracks the expansion of its budget and chapters (see figure 5.3).[33] It evened off somewhat in the mid-1980s, increased dramatically in the wake of the Bork nomination, and went up enormously during the Clinton administration.[34] The latter finding may be somewhat surprising. The Society's skeptics typically argue that it is a "job network" for conservatives, but some of its strongest growth occurred during a period when the Democrats controlled executive branch appointments and the power to nominate federal judges. Thus, it is rea-

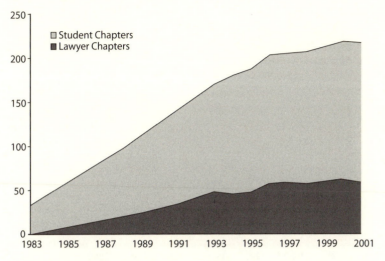

Figure 5.2. Federalist Society Chapters, 1983–2001

sonable to hypothesize that the Society is most effective when Republicans are *out* of office. Conservatives may be drawn to the organization more when it is least powerful, as a forum in which challenges to existing government policy can be developed, relationships formerly established in government can be maintained, and networks can be preserved when governmental office is no longer there to provide ongoing contact and esprit de corps.

Discovering a way to fund the growth the Society has experienced over the last two decades, without distorting the goals of the organization, has been one of its most fundamental challenges. The Federalist Society has flourished in part because of its increasingly wide base of support. The Society is less dependent on third-party support than almost any similar organization, because of its members' substantial in-kind contributions and membership dues. The leaders of the student, lawyer, and practice groups are, for the most part, not compensated,[35] even though they put in tens of thousands of hours a year performing Society-related tasks.[36] Lee Liberman Otis notes that "if you try to cost out the in-kind contributions of members, it is enormous, because they are all lawyers, so their time is very valuable." The Society recognized early on that building its membership base was essential to its success. In a letter to Michael Joyce in 1984, Eugene Meyer observed that "in the long term, we intend to obtain a significant percentage of our funding from members of the legal community. This is why we feel developing some activities involving lawyers is essential."[37] While the Society created its Lawyers Division for

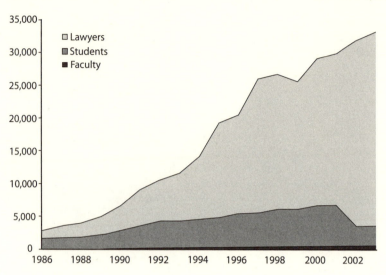

Figure 5.3. Federalist Society Membership, 1986–2003

other purposes, the desire to identify a pool of donors who had a personal connection to the Society played a significant role. Today, over two-thirds of the Society's high-dollar ($1,000 or more) individual contributors are Society members.[38]

Despite the substantial resources represented by Society volunteers, the organization has always needed to raise money. Like most of the institutions of the conservative legal movement, this funding came from a handful of relatively small conservative foundations, while support from business or law firms only came much later, after the Society's basic organizational norms and structure had congealed. Through October 1983, the Society spent a grand total of $103,000, 95 percent of which came from six conservative organizations, and 5 percent from dues and fees.[39] Meyer believes that the key to the Society's fund-raising success has been the distinctiveness of conservative foundations.

> [Foundations usually ask] What have you done? Well, we've helped change some of the debate on the Constitution. But what have you *done*? I can't answer that in the type of compelling way . . . [such as] Senator So-and-So wouldn't be a senator but for this, or even such and such a bill wouldn't have passed. . . . That's true of policy organizations generally unless they are lobbying organizations. . . . There's definitely in the philanthropic community a big emphasis on measurable results. I understand that. The only problem I have is that you have to have the judgment to know what sort of measurement you can reasonably expect for certain kinds of goals. The leading conservative foundations have

had more of a long-term outlook. . . . That is what foundations should be for. . . . You can understand that if you're doing a new group, a certain percentage of your grants will fail, the group won't work, and you have the same costs that any other entrepreneur in the business world has—that's the way business works. If you can choose intelligently you'll start some really good businesses or really good organizations.

Conservative foundations were especially vital in the Society's early years, when funds from corporations were scarce, and they have stayed with the Society ever since. Foundation leaders had been exposed to the Horowitz Report's message that conservatives needed to focus on legal ideas and the recruitment of law students, priming them for the pitch that the Society's leaders brought to them. James Piereson at the Olin Foundation, Michael Joyce at Olin and then later at the Bradley Foundation, and Richard Larry at the Scaife Foundation established personal relationships with the Society's leaders, creating bonds of trust that permitted a more aggressive and long-term style of grant-making than would have been possible without them.[40] With less need to focus on fund-raising in its early years, the Society was able to eschew direct mail and corporate support and focus its energies on its members and the programming and services of interest to them.

As soon as it established itself as a permanent organization, the Society sough to increase its organizational reach by using elite supporters such as Bork and Senator Orrin Hatch to expand its donor base beyond foundations. A 1985 letter from Otis to Abraham suggests that Hatch supported aggressively expanding Society fund-raising from an early point.

Brent Hatch (son of the Senator) says his father was very impressed . . . [with] the caliber of the people in the Society, and wanted to know what he could do to help. In particular, he thought we could do a lot with "real money." Brent unfortunately told him that he thought we had already raised $300,000, and didn't think we needed help; but I'm sure that misimpression can be corrected. David [McIntosh] thinks we should make a blueprint for a $1 million organization and present it to Hatch. . . . In any case, I think we should meet with Hatch sometime next week, while he still remembers his enthusiasm.[41]

A 1988 memo shows that the follow-up with Hatch must have been successful; he was one of the first two successful prospects for a Federalist Society Development Board.[42] A central goal of this project was to create a board of trustees that could contribute or commit to raising $50,000, as well as a National Legal Advisory Council, whose members would commit to $10,000.[43] Both of these new committees were intended to broaden the reach and networking of the Society, as well as provide intelligence on "the organization's perceived reputation within various sectors of the legal community."[44]

Boundary Maintenance

All organizations have to determine the boundaries of their membership and mission. While some scholars have argued that political organizations have a natural tendency toward growth, rooted in the self-interest of organizational leaders, the development of the Federalist Society suggests that this is far from an iron law.[45] The key to the Society's boundaries has been its self-imposed prohibition on "position taking," a constraint that distinguishes the Society from ordinary interest groups and explains why it has repeatedly turned down opportunities to grow. This section will identify two of these foregone opportunities—a proposed litigation center and rating of nominees for the federal bench—and show how the Society has regulated its members' behavior and limited the use of the Society for the personal interests of its leaders.

At the beginning of the George W. Bush administration, a number of Federalist Society members who were nominated for positions in the Justice Department were quizzed about the organization. For example, Viet Dinh, who was being considered for the position of assistant attorney general, was asked by Senator Richard Durbin (D-Ill.), "So is your belief that the Federalist Society does not have a philosophy, a stated philosophy, when it comes to, for example, the future course of the Supreme Court?" Dinh responded, "No, I do not think it does have a stated philosophy, to my knowledge. It may very well have. I just simply do not know. I know that the Society has a very diverse membership of people who think very critically about these issues, and I know that I've gotten into many, many disagreements with members of the Federalist Society on these kinds of issues. So I do not think that an official policy would be possible, even if desirable."[46] In a similar exchange, Edith Brown Clement was asked, "Do you share a judicial philosophy with the Federalist Society?" to which she replied, "I am unaware of any judicial philosophy articulated by the Federalist Society."[47]

Any number of reporters and columnists found these denials to be unconvincing, and depending upon what one means by a "judicial philosophy," they were. There is no question that the Federalist Society is held together by some very broad, overarching principles, the generality of which is suggested by Sen. Orrin Hatch's (R-Utah) description of the Society's philosophy: "The Federalist Society espouses no official dogma. Its members share acceptance of three universal ideas: One, that government's essential purpose is the preservation of freedom; Two, that our Constitution embraces and requires separation of governmental powers; and, three that judges should interpret the law, not write it."[48] Meyer notes that the distinction between these "principles" and "policy positions" is far from obvious.

The statement, "We don't take positions" is more accurately, "We don't take policy positions." In other words, when we say in our statement of purpose that we are interested in the current state of the legal order and separation of powers, the rule of law, individual freedom, and [that] certainly the role of the judge is to say what the law is, not what it ought to be—obviously those are positions. Those are the positions we take. Beyond that, the fact that something promotes individual freedom doesn't mean we're going to support it. . . . Does that broad set of principles affect what our programming is? Of course it does. It's designed to bring those things to the fore. We make sure in our program . . . that those general principles are strongly advocated in addition to other principles. That's where we stop. But once again, where we stop and someone else picks up can make the line seem fuzzy.

This denial of position-taking could easily be seen as a ruse, but this would be a critical mistake, since stopping short of drawing out the policy or legal consequences of its principles serves vital organizational maintenance, enhancing the Society's role in the larger conservative movement.

Michael Oakeshott's distinction between enterprise and civil association is useful for clarifying this point. Enterprise associations are defined by their goal: members join because they agree with its goals. Civil associations, on the other hand, provide a common venue, resolve disputes, and establish rules for interaction. Oakeshott observed that the mode of civil association is very difficult to maintain in a pure state, since at some point people need some general notion of why the forum that the procedures make possible is desirable, some assurance that it is oriented toward a morally defensible end. On the other hand, a pure enterprise association has a tendency toward collapsing in on itself, becoming insulated and antiparticipatory. All organizations that seek some form of membership, therefore, usually end up between these poles.[49]

The Federalist Society has positioned itself primarily as a civil association, focusing almost exclusively on fostering debate and providing services to its members. While its critics have often interpreted its role through the frame of other Washington-based organizations, the Federalist Society is *not* an interest group, and it does not engage in many of the activities its opponents attribute to it. This is not because the organization finds anything intrinsically wrong with such activities—it works closely with organizations that involve themselves in litigation and judicial confirmation battles, and these activities are made easier because of the networks the Society has fostered. The Society could not involve itself directly in these activities, however, and preserve its organizational structure and distinct mission. The vital distinction here is activities the Society actually engages and those that we might call "externalities" of its core function.

A useful example of how the Federalist Society has consciously limited its mission is its consideration in the mid-1980s of a litigation center. This would seem to be a natural extension of the organization's mission, given that Michael Horowitz's criticism of conservative law firms was still fresh in the movement's mind and that the Center for Individual Rights and the Institute for Justice would not be founded for years. In addition, as Meyer notes, "If you get a group of lawyers with a broad set of principles, what do lawyers do? They sue someone. We had litigators involved with us; they wanted to use their talent. A lot of our lawyers were involved in pro bono work." However, the litigation center never got off the ground, and other organizations stepped in to fill the void. Why didn't the organization take advantage of this opportunity to expand its reach?

The litigation center was seriously considered, and hints of interest in the idea even appeared in the Society's original proposal. That proposal, written when the Society's organizational form was still inchoate, stated, "As its statement of purpose indicates, the Federalist Society is being founded in no small measure to advance such concepts as judicial restraint and the rule of law. In order to effectively achieve that goal it may be helpful for the Federalist Society to submit amicus curiae briefs in appropriate cases."[50] Interest in the idea increased in 1985, an indication of which is a letter from Irving Kristol to Eugene Meyer observing, "I am not a lawyer and really have no opinion about a pro bono litigation center or lawyers groups—but, in the abstract, the prospect pleases."[51] This letter appears to have been in response to a memo written that year suggesting projects for the litigation center, including "locating appropriate cases," "conducting litigation projects," and "participating in think-tank seminars." It notes that "we expect to be able to raise initial grants from foundations who have given money to the Federalist Society. Senator Hatch has indicated enthusiasm for the project and will assist in fundraising for the Center." It proposed that the center incorporate in November 1986, hire a staffer by April 1986, and begin selecting cases soon thereafter.[52] Finally, there is a 1986 "Status Report"[53] that notes, "The Federalist Society has available today a $75,000 grant from the Scaife Foundation, the terms of which would permit expenditures toward initial funding of the Litigation Center." In addition, the Society's files include plans for a conference designed to produce a "compendium of ideas for use by Federalist Society Litigation Center."[54] Pointing to the findings of the Horowitz Report—another sign of the report's importance to the conservative movement—the memo noted the disappointing results of existing conservative firms. "Although the movement's success has received mixed reviews, it has clearly not achieved the widespread conservative shift in legal policy that was originally intended." Society members have somewhat different recollections of how seriously the litigation center was considered. Gary Lawson, a longtime member of the Federalist Society's board of directors, recalls, "We pretty quickly put the kibosh on it on the theory that it would compromise the mission too much. . . . My recollection is that . . . there was some foundation that expressed interest in six-figure funding of a litigation group. So we had to consider it." On the other hand, both Otis and McIntosh believe that the proposal was considered quite seriously. Otis states,

> I think we did think about it reasonably seriously, and I remember what happened in my mind was at a certain point I realized [that] if we do this we are going to be filing briefs, and there [will] have to be the Federalist Society's name on it, and people are going to want us to take a position. . . . You have different schools of thought. [We have members who] would really like the takings clause to reach certain kinds of government regulation . . . and then we have other people in the organization who feel strongly that it's not the case. And so officially the brief is going to have to say one thing or the other, and [as a result] there were going to [be] people who are going to be really mad, and then what? I remember fairly clearly going through that thought process and thinking . . . we're going to have to kill this thing.

David McIntosh adds that the opportunity costs of starting a litigation center were a significant factor, given that the Society was just getting off the ground.

> The energy to make something like that work was a lot more than we had anticipated and therefore we'd have to make some explicit choices. Do we want to now spend a lot of our time and effort and resources in developing a litigation project at a point when there existed other conservative litigation entities? And it would take away and diminish our abilities in the programming we were doing on campuses, starting the lawyers chapters. . . . It forced a choice of where you put your resources in an organization, and we went to the core strengths.

A litigation center could have also jeopardized the participation of many of the Society's members, especially those in government. Suggestive in this regard is a 1985 letter from a senior Reagan administration official noting that he would have to resign from the organization if it pursued such an initiative.[55]

As a partial substitute for a litigation center, the Society created, in the mid-1990s, a pro bono law clearinghouse to connect conservative and libertarian lawyers with ideologically sympathetic pro bono opportunities. The initiative was initially modest and poorly funded, but the Society has recently increased its ambitions in the area considerably through the creation of the Federalist Society Pro Bono Populi Center, funded largely by a grant from the Brady Foundation. The Society's increased focus on pro bono law was driven by interest from its members, who "complained a lot about the kind of pro bono activities that are available. If you're going to do pro bono work you want to do something you feel strongly about, and they didn't feel they were getting as much of that as they'd like."[56] The question was whether it was possible to reconcile the Society's desire to be responsive to its members with its mission to facilitate debate. The creation of the passive matching system has allowed them to do so. Using a computer matching system, the Society connects members with organizations who have submitted cases without taking any role in case selection, a point strongly emphasized in the project's grant proposal. "Because the Society will not screen participants, it makes no representations regarding the qualifications or legal experience of particular lawyers involved. All we do is encourage the initial contact." Furthermore, the proposal noted that "furnishing information to public interest groups should not be construed as the Society's endorsement of either the group or the specific project involved."[57] While this project is somewhat at odds with the Society's primary mission of fostering debate, it fits well with its increasing role of countering what it sees as the influence of the liberal legal network on the organized bar (discussed in greater detail below in the section "A Counter-ABA?").

The Society saw the project as an opportunity to correct a significant imbalance between liberal and conservative public interest law. Just as the Federalist Society has accused the ABA of being ideologically biased, it has recently claimed that pro bono law in major firms is systematically diverting valuable resources to legal liberals, while providing almost nothing to lawyers on the right.[58] Chapter 2 provides some support for this argument, since it shows that the liberal legal network has thousands of lawyers willing and able to handle public interest law cases, fed through the pro bono system and trained in law school clinics. Despite all their other strengths, conservatives continue to have little of this sort of infrastructure, and as a result conservative law firms only have the manpower to take cases likely to set a significant precedent. The need to correct this "disparity between these two philosophical sides in the number of lawyers who follow up on victories made by the public interest groups with whom they agree"[59] was the most important motivation for the Society's expansion of its involvement in pro bono law. By matching lawyers in its network with interesting but non-precedent-setting cases, the Society told its patrons that "lawyers will work thousands of extra pro bono hours in these cases, thereby dramatically expanding the ability of our public interest groups to defend the Constitution and promote free enterprise by connecting them with a new generation of volunteers."[60] This project is probably the farthest the Society has strayed from its mission of fostering debate to actively organizing conservatives for political and legal activism. The Society has gambled that it has created a means by which it can support conservative pro bono law while respecting its carefully policed organizational boundaries.

No conviction about the Federalist Society is as tenacious as the belief that it plays a key role in Republican administrations' selection of federal judges, especially since the Bush administration limited the role of the ABA. This is another area where the distinction between the Society as an organization and as a network is essential. The Society *has* considered issuing its own ratings of judges, in response to pressure from members. An early memo[61] describes a proposal for "Recommendation and Evaluation of Judges," in which the Society would "develop recommendations for appointment to the U.S. Court of Appeals for all circuits. . . . Each recommendation will be accompanied with a short statement about the candidate, his record, and his strengths and weaknesses."[62] The memo also suggested that the Society "make every effort to contribute to the examination of potential judicial appointments whom we hear about before their actual appointments." The memo makes it very clear why the Society considered such a project:

> Judicial candidates are perhaps less thoroughly examined than most candidates for public office. This is true both with regard to their judicial philosophy and the intellectual caliber of their thought and writing. Their integrity usually receives exemplary review; but integrity alone is not enough. The Reagan administration provides an example of the importance of such review. While most of its judicial appointments have been excellent, a few have shared the philosophy and judicially activist orientation of many of the Carter appointees. There are many reasons for these appointments, but we hope that our evaluation of judges will contribute usefully to the store of knowledge from which judicial appointments are made.

In the absence of a mechanism to systematically determine the judicial philosophy of nominees to the bench, the memo assumes that Republican administrations would fail to nominate reliably conservative judges. Outside government, but with a formidable network of "its own advisory board, its recent graduates, and law professors, lawyers and law students with whom the society has had contact and who share the society's basic purposes," the Society would have access to information on the judicial philosophy of potential nominees inaccessible to government officials.

Meyer recalls that Society volunteers "keep saying, 'We think the ABA is biased in the way it does judges; we need something to counter, to show that there is an alternative.' And they say that the Federalist Society is the natural thing to do that." The proposal was never acted upon, because of doubts about the effectiveness of such ratings: "How seriously would such ratings be taken? What's our qualification for doing it? It's a large

logistical [project]. The fact of the matter is how it would be perceived."
Despite the ambition of some members that the Society act as counter
to the ABA, it lacks the dispassionate, neutral professional reputation
necessary for effectively rating federal judges. The Society has the power
to vigorously challenge the reputation of the ABA—which it has done
successfully enough that the Bush administration ceased cooperating with
ABA review of judicial nominees—but it has not been able to reform the
ABA or provide a viable alternative to it.

While the proposal to rate federal judges was rejected, formal involvement in judicial selection may have been rendered unnecessary by the
growth of the Society's network. First, Society members have assumed
important positions in the judicial nomination process. Steven Markman, who as assistant attorney general in Reagan's second term was
responsible for judicial nominations, suggests that the Society network
helped to identify and expand the pool of potential conservative nominees for the bench.

> When you look early in the Reagan administration in the first term, sure, every-
> body knows that Professor Scalia at the University of Chicago or Professor Bork
> at Yale shared this approach to the judicial role, but it was not a deep team at
> that point, and . . . the Federalist Society really did help to not only identify
> additional [candidates], but . . . it also helped to create more individuals who
> found these views attractive. Once you get past people like Professor Easter-
> brook, and Professor Bork, and Professor Scalia, there was a lot of confusion
> as to the other appellate court nominees, and District Court nominees as well,
> and I think the Federalist Society helped to identify, to track, people who proved
> to be . . . capable of filling those positions.

Lee Liberman Otis, who in the first Bush administration directed the
White House Counsel's work on judicial nominations, argues that the
Society dramatically improved the quantity and reliability of information
in the hands of conservatives involved in judicial nominations. The Society had "[a] lot of people who were sympathetic to what we were trying
to do on the courts whom one could call and ask for thoughts about
various candidates, or for thoughts on candidates that would make good
judges. . . . It was a source of information in both directions, both positive
and negative."

Republicans also have used Society membership as a criterion in making executive branch appointments. A former official in the George W.
Bush administration recalls that

> Precisely because the law schools and legal establishment are so liberal, mem-
> bership and especially leadership in the Federalist Society is a costly signal of
> commitment to legal conservatism, and so as a result it is also a valuable signal.

So, if someone is willing to stick their neck out to be a member of the Federalist Society, then they can be counted on to have some commitment to conservative legal ideas and the conservative movement that someone else does not, say a local Republican Party hack. When I was hiring at [an executive agency], we would not only look for whether someone was in the Federalist Society but whether he or she actually attended monthly Federalist Society lunches or were at Ted Olson's annual barbecue, signs that they were willing to bear a cost for the signal.[63]

Like the D.C. chapter's role in the diffusion of information within the federal government, the Federalist Society's network reduces the transaction costs of acquiring information about the quality and ideological preferences of potential nominees to the federal bench and executive branch. This networking effect, combined with the presence of active Society members in senior positions in Republican administrations, is much more important in the selection of personnel than any active role the organization plays as an organization. Meyer concludes, "If we have succeeded in the ideas part . . . and people have come to share ideas, and . . . get to know each other, we're not irrelevant to what they end up doing. I wouldn't go farther than that, but I would go that far."

While the informal role of Society members and networks is surely its most important role in judicial selection, the Society has increased its formal role over the last few years, and this has required careful attention to boundary maintenance. Starting with the Roberts nomination, the Society did become more involved in the debate over judicial confirmations, but in a way that maintained its short-term institutional neutrality. Meyer describes the new role for the Society as primarily about enabling public education:

[In the Society] there a bunch of people who are . . . experts in [the role of the courts] and clerked on the Court and have constitutional law expertise, [and] they really would be people who should be out there talking to the media. [So], one, we were making them available, and number two, we've gotten some PR help to make them available. Our feeling is that the role of the Court is one of the central things that we talk about, and it will facilitate the public discussion a lot to get some of these people out there. So we are doing [this] as an organization not in the sense that these people are representative of our organization, but in the sense that we're very much trying to get these people out into the media so [the most eloquent views on the subject] get heard. But beyond that, we as an organization don't do anything.

This strategy is reminiscent of how the Society has managed its role in pro bono law. In pro bono law, it wanted to increase the contribution of Society members to conservative public interest law firms, while in judicial selection it sought to shape the debate over Republican nominees to the bench by increasing the availability and quality of conservative commentators available to the news media. In neither case was the Society "neutral": it wanted to increase the effectiveness of conservative public interest law and the success rate of conservative nominees to the federal bench. In both cases, however, the Society sought to avoid involving itself in a way that would lead to conflict with its members, who might disagree with any particular case brought by a public interest law firm, or with specific judicial nominees. As a result, the Society has fallen back on its role as a network entrepreneur, facilitating the participation of its members and in the process increasing the impact of the rest of the conservative legal movement.

While the Society has limited its formal role in judicial confirmations, its task of projecting its organizational neutrality has been complicated by the increasing involvement of Leonard Leo, the Society's executive vice president and director of its Lawyers Division. Along with Ed Meese and Jay Sekulow,[64] Leo closely advised the White House in the choice of John Roberts, Samuel Alito, and, more controversially, Harriet Miers.[65] Leo had previously been involved in partisan politics as the head of Catholic Outreach for the Republican National Committee, but his deepening involvement in judicial confirmations in Bush's second term led him to take a leave of absence from the Society, since that deeper role has made it "hard[er] to separate him from the organization."[66] While the Society was eager to distinguish its formal involvement in the Roberts nomination from that of Leo's more direct role, the nearly unanimous support Roberts received from Society members meant that tension or confusion was unlikely. The Miers nomination was entirely different, as her strongest opponents were Society members such as Robert Bork, Randy Barnett, and John Yoo. The tension between Leo's role in the Society and his support for the Miers nomination came to a boil with the publication of a long *Wall Street Journal* article. The article reported that "Roger Pilon, vice president for legal affairs at the Cato Institute, a libertarian think tank, was fuming in his Washington office when the Miers nomination was announced. When he saw Mr. Leo on television, defending the nominee and identified as a Federalist Society officer, Mr. Pilon picked up the telephone and complained to the society's president, Eugene Meyer. Mr. Meyer had already called the television network to complain, both men recall."[67] Meyer is quick to point out that all of his members understood, when it was explained to them, that Leo's role was in his own personal capacity and that he took a leave of absence precisely to avoid making it seem as if the Society was actively supporting the administration's judicial choices.

The very complications that Leo's role in judicial confirmations has created for the Society is a sign of the importance of its boundaries and the consequences of an apparent breach. As McIntosh observes, "My view—and I am the most politically oriented in the board—is [that] once you cross that Rubicon [of active involvement in judicial confirmation], the nature of the organization changes, and so we have to remain disciplined and say, 'No, we're going to participate, but we have a larger function of making sure these ideas are debated in the legal culture.' " David McIntosh recalls that deciding precisely where the activities of the Society in judicial nominations should end and where that of its members should begin was a major subject of debate within the Society's leadership.

> Now a step over the line which we . . . consciously have decided not to do in the organization would be having a group . . . geared to support a particular nomination, a particular process for that nomination. And again it came down to wanting to be faithful to not taking positions. It requires discipline—let's put it that way—because you've got members who are interested in engaging more fully in the political process of a confirmation. You've got political entities that look to the Federalist Society favorably who say, "Can you guys participate?" And we say, "No, our mission is limited to this."

The Society clearly is "political" and partisan in one sense, in that it seeks to advance legal goals with strong support in the Republican Party and little support among Democrats and to increase the effectiveness of conservative organizational entrepreneurs whose activities are largely consistent with those of the Republican Party. As the Miers nomination shows, however, the Society's network is also capable of disciplining party leaders when they are seen as going soft on conservative legal principles for short-term or personal political reasons. This disciplining function does not mean that the Society is set apart from the party system; in a system in which parties have become defined by ideology, this is a critical mechanism through which elected officials are held responsible to the party's elite strata.

How did the Society maintain such a clear, consistent, and limited mission over time? Much of the explanation has to do with its remarkably stable leadership cadre. Of the six members of the Society's board of directors, Steven Calabresi, David McIntosh, Gary Lawson, and Eugene Meyer have led the Society from its inception, while Brent Hatch and Kenneth Cribb became active in the leadership of the Society soon thereafter. The Society has had only one full-time president, Eugene Meyer, and the co-chairmen of the Society's Board of Visitors, Robert Bork and Orrin Hatch, have had some relationship with the Society from its inception. This consistency of leadership is no accident, as vacancies on the board of directors are filled by the board itself, a decision that emerged early in the Society's development. The July 31, 1982, organizational meeting minutes indicate a decision that "the Board of Directors will be self-perpetuating and will be comprised of students and lawyers. . . ." Interestingly, that sentence originally was concluded with "each serving a one or two year term."[68] Had this become official Society policy, it would have eliminated the continuity of leadership that has allowed the Society to manage its organizational boundaries and protected the Society against short-term pressures for expansion. As Gary Lawson explains,

> The reason we've succeeded . . . is that the same people who ran it twenty years ago, and the same people who will run it twenty years from now . . . all have a very clear vision of what this organization should do, which is promote ideas. Bring debates into the law schools, bring debates into the legal community, and everything else that happens, we'll take it. . . . If you ever view this as a device for organizing and galvanizing or anything else, it will blow up, and we all know that, and we're not going to let that happen. . . . If anybody wants to try to move the focus of this organization . . . they're going to run into a brick wall immediately.

This stability of mission and personnel would not be surprising for most contemporary political organizations, but the Federalist Society is *not* a nonparticipatory "association without members."[69] Quite to the contrary, the Society's strength comes from the direct participation of its members. In this sort of participatory organization, leadership elections might be thought essential, as they encourage member mobilization and ensure leadership legitimacy.[70] In the case of the Society, however, ideological competition with legal liberalism substitutes for internal competition among conservatives and weakens the virulence of intragroup ideological conflict. In addition, the norm against "position taking" and the focus on intellectual debate reduces the need for ideological factions to mobilize to protect their position. That said, it might have been expected that as the Society grew from a small group of friends to a large, less intensely connected group, the legitimacy of its tight leadership cadre would come under suspicion, as was the pattern for many participatory groups of the Left.[71] Conservatives, however, may be more willing to judge the legitimacy of leadership by the fruits of their labor; so long as the Society seems to be working, they see no reason to challenge its authority structure. Finally, while the Society's national office prepares lists of funded speakers, the chapters themselves choose whom to invite, who their leaders will be, and what activities they will engage in. These factors, taken together, explain how the Society has been able to maintain the high level of participation that is necessary to its core networking mission, while simultaneously preserving a stable leadership cadre that can maintain the organization's boundaries.

Organizational Outputs: Direct and Indirect

As was hinted at before, to understand the Federalist Society requires close attention to the distinction between its direct and indirect outputs. The most significant direct output is debate: over half of the organization's funding goes to sponsoring speakers and its national meetings.[72] The indirect outputs of the Society network are best understood as the conservative movement's return on the social capital produced by the Society's debating activities.[73] None of the Society's effects on the politics of judicial nominations, networking, placement of members, or facilitating connections across government is denied or foresworn by its leaders. That said, the Society could never have produced these effects had it pursued them directly. By limiting its programming, and thereby nurturing a reputation for intellectual seriousness and distance from short-term partisan politics, the Society has, perhaps paradoxically, been more effective in serving the political goals of its allies than a more directly partisan organization ever could have been.

The orientation to debate discussed above (see "Building Chapters") was not the only model available to the founders of the Society. When it was created, the other model, especially for campus organizing, was represented by the *Dartmouth Review*. Calabresi argues that

> we've tried to remain in dialogue with the organizations we're trying to compete with on the left. One thing we very much did not want to do when we started going was turn into another *Dartmouth Review*. We thought that the *Dartmouth Review* was a forum where conservatives got together and had fun by acting like caricatures of themselves and taking all sorts of extreme positions and making themselves the objects of hatred and alienated everybody. We wanted to be engaged in constructive dialogue with liberal institutions. The underlying premise of the Federalist Society was that if we could just get liberals to think about and talk about our ideas enough, we might persuade them that we're right. So we want to be a reasonable organization like AEI, an organization of thoughtful and intelligent people, an organization that's engaged in dialogue with people on the left, not an organization that's a caricature of what conservatives could be. That's colored us with the ABA; it's been the case with law schools, with law firms. We've always attempted to be in dialogue with the organizations that we're competing with, in part because we hope to influence them to some extent.

The rejected *Dartmouth Review* style of conservative organization was outrageous, attention-grabbing, and ideologically extreme. Former *Review* editor Dinesh D'Souza claims that the *Review*'s strategic insight was that "by staking out a kind of far-right position, the *Review* has legiti-

mated a wide range of positions in the middle."[74] Reminiscent of the strategies of the far Left in the 1960s, by baiting liberal institutions to censor
it, the *Review* sought to uncover their concealed ideological bias and inherent repressiveness. This repression would repel students from the Left,
and the *Review*, by stretching the ideological range far to the right, would
tend to pull the center along with it. Despite the *Review*'s visibility in
the early 1980s, the Society's founders rejected this approach. Federalist
Society members are regularly reminded by their leaders to be cordial and
well mannered with their ideological opponents. While this is driven in
part by what the Society's leaders consider appropriate, it is also informed
by the assumption that ideology has a personal component, that people
are initially attracted to or repelled by the character of an ideological
movement's representatives rather than their ideas. The Society's strategy
was, therefore, to generate for legal conservatism a reputation as more
rational, open-minded, intellectual, and idealistic than its opposition, and
as a result to attract individuals who share these temperamental characteristics, even if they were, like much of the Society's leadership in an earlier
ideological phase, vaguely liberal.

This emphasis on intellectual debate is, again perhaps paradoxically,
the key to the Society's ability to fulfill its more directly political goals.
Calabresi argues that the Society was designed to be a "conservative university without walls," recognizing the critical political functions produced by modern higher education.

> We've tried to replicate the function that major universities serve on the left of
> creating a community of people with similar views on similar issues. We've
> tried to do that by holding debates and meetings, particularly panel discussions.
> We've definitively tried to keep the organization more of an intellectual organi-
> zation, as an organization that debates ideas, puts people in touch with each
> other, and forms friendships, networks of friends, rather than crossing over the
> line of actually lobbying for a bill in Congress, or taking a position in an amicus
> brief before the Supreme Court.

Gary Lawson argues something similar, noting that "the mere fact of having a gathering place, a place where people can, twice a year on the national level and however many times on the local level, gather, of course
has that consequence. That's not something we ever tried to stop or stifle.
It's always a by-product, an incidental consequence of 'at last there is a
conservative legal organization out there.' " Calabresi takes a somewhat
less passive approach than Lawson to the indirect effects of the organization, emphasizing the network-building functions of the Society's formal
activities, and also suggesting that these were intended, and not just desirable unintended consequences. One important goal of the Society was

letting conservatives know who's out there in the conservative movement, so you build up networks of friends and associates who are all on the conservative side of things. The hope is that people will collaborate on projects on conservatism and law in the future, but that collaboration will only get started if the friendships are there and if people know who's out there in the conservative community. Basically the situation we face is that at any given law school there may be ten or fifteen conservatives, and they may know each other but they wouldn't know other conservatives at other schools but for the existence of something like the Federalist Society. Similarly conservative lawyers are scattered all across the country, but there may be only one or two or three in any given firm. By having an organization like the Federalist Society you bring all those people together, they form friendships, they start working together, they start collaborating on things, and before you know it you have a powerful network of people who are working on programs of social change. Basically one thing we concluded was that the Left had very powerful networks of Harvard and Yale Law School, or past Supreme Court clerks who tended to be liberal, and those networks on the left tended to be very effective . . . at influencing legal developments in a liberal direction. . . . So hopefully what we've done is create a major network on the right of people who like to talk about law, talk about legal issues, who will get together and act on legal issues. And it's all very decentralized—they're not acting according to a program. . . . They [Society members] tend to be libertarians or social conservatives and they will naturally tend to collaborate with each other on conservative legal developments.

Networking versus intellectual engagement may be a false dichotomy, since the Society is, first and foremost, a network cemented by intellectual and philosophical commitment. The Society's assumption has been that serious intellectual stimulation and opportunities to meet other legal conservatives will generate strong bonds of friendship. Once these activities are in place, the Society networks do not need any direction from the center.[75] By increasing the probability that conservative lawyers will interact with others of similar views and interests, the Society helps members share ideas, provide tips on opportunities for activism, and share leads on employment.[76] Through repeated contact with other conservatives, the Society's networks reinforce ideological commitment, transform general attitudes into well-formed philosophical commitments, and as a consequence make members more willing to defend their views publicly.[77]

The Society's networks also increase the willingness of members to be open about their identity as conservatives.[78] Many of the Federalist Society members I have spoken to refer to conservative lawyers as being "in the closet," and the comparison to homosexuals is quite instructive.[79] The Federalist Society tie, with its picture of James Madison, serves a similar function to a pink triangle bumper sticker or lapel pin, signaling to those "in the closet" that their identity is not shameful and that there are others out there like them. In the process, it helps transform what would otherwise be a stigmatized identity into a badge of pride and in the process creates a deep emotional attachment to the organization. This function was, of course, more important in the Society's early years. Gary Lawson recalls,

> People don't understand what the law schools were like twenty years ago. It was much more important to bring people out of the closet. We started with six people at Yale. We were the six who would self-identify as anything other than far left. Four traditional conservatives, one libertarian—me—and one classical conservative, Hayekian. In terms of speaking up in class, that was basically me, and the reason for that was that anyone who said anything out of the orthodoxy would get hissed. Not only did the professors not do anything about it, but some of them we strongly suspected were complicitous in that. Someone like me, I reveled in it because I liked being the bad guy. It would be uncomfortable for someone [else].

This account of the situation at Yale seems hyperbolic not because Lawson is engaged in victim-mongering, or because Yale was a strange outlier—no less a figure of the Left than Duncan Kennedy confirms that a similar situation existed at Harvard Law School[80]—but because the Society (in conjunction with changes in the larger culture) has been so effective in shifting the tone in America's elite law schools. As an early grant proposal describes it, the purpose of the organization was to "reduce the necessity of conforming. To be outside the liberal network will no longer mean having to sacrifice all of the benefits. In days of conservative administrations, our network will even be able to offer advantages that the other cannot."[81] Solidarity and collective action would, the Society's founders hoped, encourage conservatives to show their ideological stripes.[82]

One important consequence of declining preference falsification among conservatives has been an increasing willingness to pursue ideologically driven pro bono work. Calabresi observes, "I've just kind of casually noticed that significant numbers of Federalists who are out practicing . . . in firms try to find conservative pro bono work, and I don't remember that going on to that degree twenty years ago." Being embedded in a network of fellow believers provides social support for taking on controversial cases, helps lawyers identify sympathetic allies in their firm, and gets members' names into circulation among those with relevant cases. By reducing the stigma of legal conservatism and creating durable networks between its members, the Federalist Society also reduces search costs for conservative litigation organizations. As Chip Mellor, the president of the Institute for Justice argues, the Federalist Society "attracts a wonderful array of talent, bright and committed conservative and libertarian lawyers who are looking to apply their philosophy through their legal training in some fashion. All of them have a certain awareness of the kinds of issues that we deal with. They're a tremendous talent pool that's out there ready to be mobilized in some fashion." One clear example of the importance of the Society's role in reducing the transaction costs of identifying conservatives is the Institute for Justice's recent move to create state-level chapters. Mellor observes that, in deciding where IJ should set up state chapters,[83] the critical factors are "a viable conservative and libertarian state think tank, constitutional provisions that are not gutted in terms of their potential for advancing liberty, a strong Federalist Society presence, a medium-sized state with both a nonpoliticized and a noncorrupt judiciary." The Federalist Society provides public goods for organizational entrepreneurs like IJ, goods that are vital given that identifying conservative lawyers is an expensive and time-consuming task that serves the interests of all conservative organizations but would not be cost effective for any of them to produce on their own.[84]

A Counter-ABA?

From early in its history, the Federalist Society has had to decide how it should relate to the grandfather of all legal organizations, the American Bar Association. While the Society made some efforts to influence the ABA directly, this approach was almost wholly ineffective. The Society has chosen instead to harshly and repeatedly criticize the ABA, damaging its legitimacy as the representative of the legal profession, and added activities that replicate some of the professional bar's functions, such as networking and professional development. Driven by the Society leadership's personal anger at the defeat of the Bork nomination, this "counter-ABA" strategy has become an increasingly central part of the organization's mission.

It has always been an article of faith within the Federalist Society that, as its 1983 proposal put it, "Under the guise of nonpartisan and even non-controversial law reform proposals, both the state bar associations and the ABA have played crucial roles in developing a legal agenda which sometimes strangles dissent."[85] In its early "Three Year Plan," the Society set out as a key goal of its newly created Lawyers Division to

bring together and coordinate conservative activity within the ABA. This will involve using the ABA national, state and city conventions as both a recruiting ground and a platform. . . . [We should] determine which sections of the ABA our members are involved in. We will concentrate our activities in one or two of these sections. In the long term, making conservatives from around the country aware of each other's existence and encouraging them to become active in a section of the ABA where they can help tip the balance of power will be a means through which we will improve the ideological balance in the ABA.[86]

As early as 1984, the Society's leaders recognized that this strategy of infiltration for ideological balancing was insufficient.

In addition to activities within the ABA, we will pull together conservative lawyers outside the ABA and use the Federalist Society as a national conservative legal organization which would do on a smaller scale many of the things the ABA does, such as pronouncements or ratings concerning appointments to legal positions or comments on developments affecting the law. At present most Americans and even many knowledgeable observers think the ABA is conservative itself. This way at least some other legal organizations could be quoted to show that the ABA's view that "we have to take the Meese nomination head-on" is not the only legal viewpoint.[87]

The "many knowledgeable observers" that the Society referred to in this document even included the conservative foundations that were funding the organization. In a 1984 letter (which may have sparked the comment above), Thomas Main, a program officer at the Smith Richardson Foundation, remarked, "In your last letter, you claim the ABA has a liberal bias, which I found rather surprising. I had been under the impression that the ABA is a relatively conservative organization. I would like evidence of this bias."[88] Before the Society could make the case for becoming a "counter-ABA," it had to convince the conservative movement that a need existed in the first place.

The Society's relationship to the ABA combined revealing the ABA's ideological character with using that revelation to inject competition into the market for representing the profession. The latter objective is evidenced in a grant proposal from 1985, which predicted that "the very existence of an organization with some reputation for scholarliness which expressed alternative views would help undermine the influence exercised by the organized bar on the legal and political communities. It would undercut the bar associations' monopoly on respectability and provide a vehicle for publicizing the partisan nature of much of their work."[89] The Society thought that this approach would be especially influential on those outside of the conservative movement. Consider this passage from the first issue of the Society's *ABA Watch*:

One of the most disturbing social trends of the last two decades has the growing politicization of institutions that were once praised for being impartial and "above politics." One by one, leading American institutions, from our courts, to the academy, to the media, have become vehicles for achieving political objectives. This trend is no doubt alarming to many members of the legal community. . . . For decades, public officials have generally believed that the organization is objective and apolitical. To this day, on matters involving legal policy and appointments to the bench, the ABA receives the utmost deference from most legislators.[90]

Many issues of *ABA Watch* have bemoaned the "liberal bias" in ABA activities, from its amicus briefs in such cases as *Grutter v. Bollinger* to its ratings of federal judicial nominees. The Society's core argument, however, is that having any principled position is inappropriate for a professional organization intended to represent a wide range of members. The Federalist Society has staked out a rhetorical position in favor of "neutrality," no doubt knowing that any kind of rigorously applied neutrality would require a dramatic restriction of the ABA's mission. The Society has taken advantage of a bind that the ABA, and to a degree all professional organizations, face. While the idea of professional neutrality has entered into terminal decline, the ABA's justification for its existence presumes that such a neutral role *can* exist. This bind has provided a very effective opening for the Society's attacks on the organization.

The drive to turn the Federalist Society into a counter-ABA picked up momentum after the defeat of the Bork nomination in 1987. Calabresi believes the nomination injected a powerful emotional charge into the organization, rooted in the close personal connection that Bork had forged with the group.[91]

> It was tremendously energizing for conservatives, having a martyr, basically. That's the only way of describing it. . . . Bork was a person who forged extremely deep friendships with a large number of people. He had been an active spokesman for thirty years before his nomination, he'd been around for a long time, he knew all the leading conservatives in the conservative legal movement. We [had] been his students or his law clerks, or worked with him in the SGs office, been colleagues of his when he was a judge. . . . People felt a tremendous loyalty to him; he was one of these unusual people who inspires a real loyalty, one that I feel today. In fact I named my oldest son Robert, I'm sure because of my admiration for him. . . . People didn't set about to make Bork a martyr because it would be politically useful to the conservative cause to have a martyr. People genuinely felt outraged. They felt the way if their father or mother had not been confirmed to the Supreme Court, or some close personal friend. There were a lot of people who felt this way and nursed their sense of grievance, and it became a martyrdom situation.

That sense of martyrdom translated into a powerful motivation to use the Society to get revenge on the liberal legal elites who were seen as responsible for Bork's defeat. While the organization has continued to conduct its intellectual activities, Calabresi believes it has given an impetus to the counter-ABA functions of the Society:

I think one question that we struggled with in the mid- to late eighties was what direction our lawyer's division should go in, whether we should try to be a conservative alternative to the ABA. I think the Bork nomination failure pushed us [in that direction], forming practice groups in various areas where practitioners in communications law or administrative law could get together and talk about their fields, basically trying to increase our membership so that it was closer to the size of the ABA. I think we became much more interested in being a conservative alternative to the ABA after the Bork fight in part because one of the key things in the Bork fight was that the ABA committee split on giving Bork a well-qualified rating for the Supreme Court. Four or five members of the ABA review committee said he was not qualified or that he was only qualified, not well qualified, so the ABA was seen as playing a role in Bork's defeat. That made us want to be more of a conservative alternative to the ABA. In that sense we became more political than we had been before the Bork confirmation fight, because before that we did not have so concretely the goal of being a conservative alternative to the ABA. After the Bork fight we did to a greater extent.

Most social movements have a seminal moment of injustice that motivates their members to greater exertions: homosexuals remember Stonewall, blacks images of John Lewis being beaten in Rock Hill, feminists the Clarence Thomas hearings. These moments of injustice serve essential organizational functions. They are often ritualized and remembered, nursed as grievances and used as motivation for extracting extra effort from group members. They can also, as in the case of the Bork nomination, serve as catalysts for organizational change and the intensification of effort. Before the nomination, the organization's budget had leveled off. In the four years after it, the Society's budget doubled, in large part due to the "Bork effect." A Development Planning Meeting memo from October 1990 notes, "A special appeal to the Federalist Society mailing list signed by Judge Bork has been the most successful ever. Receipts total $17,250 and are matchable. Another grant of $10,000 from the Foundation for American Studies came in after receiving this letter."[92] Other fundraising memos mention the importance of Bork's support to the Society's fund-raising efforts.[93]

In addition to the growth of the Society's Lawyers Division, the most important institutional shift in the organization since the Bork nomination has been the addition of the Society's practice groups. The Society currently operates fifteen practice groups, examining subjects from administrative law to telecommunications,[94] roughly the same set of topics that the Society began with in 1995. In contrast to the lawyer and student chapters, the practice groups were the result of planning rather than gradual evolution, driven by the Society's reaction to, and attempt to partially substitute for, the ABA's "Sections." The original proposal to the E. L. Wiegand Foundation, which funded the practice groups' start-up costs, makes the motivations for the practice groups clear, and shows that the Society's criticism of the ABA is not simply a rhetorical ploy, but is sincerely believed by its leaders. The objectives of the practice groups were the following:

1. To develop a mechanism by which like-minded lawyers with practices in particular areas can meet to exchange ideas. Existing groups that try to bring lawyers together on the basis of their work in specific areas of law— i.e., the organized bar—almost never focus on topics that are of importance to lawyers interested in traditional legal values. . . . It is no surprise, therefore, that a significant number of talented attorneys will not (and perhaps cannot) use meetings of the ABA and other existing bar groups to seek out lawyers who share their principles.

2. To facilitate a more in-depth analysis of how traditional legal principles should inform judgments in particularized or specialized areas of legal practice. . . . The organized bar has no apparent interest in such ideas— even at the simple level of raising them through debate—and it is therefore very difficult to use existing institutions as a springboard for serious discussion.

3. To create and bring together networks of lawyers in major areas of legal practice who, through projects of mutual interest, can counterbalance negative trends that are developing due to government action, judicial overreaching, or leftward pressures by the organized bar. The leadership of the organized bar is, by and large, captured by the Left. Consequently, there are limits to how much leadership those interested in traditional legal principles are able to assert through the organized bar.[95]

The practice groups reflected the frustration of the Society's members with the ABA's perceived blending of professional status with an ideologically motivated agenda, and the hope that by reflecting the ABA's structure on the right the Society could perform for conservatives the same functions that were performed for those on the left by the ABA. In replicating the structure of the ABA's organized sections, the Society has also duplicated many of its functions. The practice groups organize panels at the Society's annual meetings, operate subcommittees for the discussion of more specific areas of law, maintain websites that keep members up-to-date on new cases in their area of interest, publish newsletters that provide a forum for the groups' most active members to disseminate their ideas, direct members to new articles and books within the ideological umbrella of the organization, and publish transcripts of practice group panels. The Society also believed that by providing continuing legal education opportunities for practice group members, the new division would "attract attorneys who might not otherwise be exposed to our activities,"[96] since they could justify to their firms devoting their time to Federalist Society projects in their specific areas of interest that they could not with its more purely intellectual debates.

These conferences, which are held across the country, also help to create a stronger national network of conservative attorneys interested in specific areas of law, by giving them the opportunity to create personal connections along functional lines. In the Society's view, the practice groups are designed to link

> leading practitioners to one another, as well as to public policy leaders. Practice Groups . . . facilitate networks that enable lawyer members to become active in the issues that matter most to them—issues where they can have an impact. . . . A number of Practice Groups are establishing pro-bono networks that connect lawyers with opportunities for pro-bono service in their practice areas. The Criminal Law group, Environmental Law and Property Rights group, and the Free Speech group have all initiated these valuable referral networks.[97]

The practice groups represent the Society's effort to organize functionally as well as geographically, in order to facilitate more active, policy-relevant interactions between members, and to allow for a more intensive form of involvement with the Society than is available in the Lawyers Division. An example of the sort of interaction that the Society was looking for is indicated by an instance where "on their own initiative and behalf, several members of the Administrative Law group responded to a request by the Senate Governmental Affairs Committee to review draft legislation, culminating in the completion of a memorandum to Committee staff."[98] In addition, the practice groups' newsletters and white papers fill the middle-range void between the work of legal scholars and the typically nonstrategic activities of lawyers in private practice.

The work of the Society's practice groups is the closest it has gotten to active involvement in public policy. Even here the group maintenance imperative still exists, in the insistence that members are involved "on their own initiative and behalf," without the imprimatur of the Society itself. When the practice groups were created, there was substantial concern that they would cross the line into position-taking, and thus break the organization's boundaries. Lee Liberman Otis recalls, "I was nervous that practice groups would really have trouble not taking positions. . . . I think what they end up doing is exchanging ideas of their areas of practice, and serving as organizational mechanism for people to get to know each other, who then if they want to go out and take positions together and [pursue] cases, they know each other and they can do that." Even with the more ambitious set of activities associated with being a "counter-ABA," the Federalist Society is still a professional organization designed to serve the interests of its members, albeit with an open appeal to one part of the ideological spectrum. This concern for avoiding conflict explains why, even though it has added counter-ABA functions to its original mission of encouraging intellectual debate, the Society has focused on facilitating rather than directing political, legislative, or litigation work.

Whatever reservations the officials of the Society may have about its role as a counter-ABA after the Bork nomination, other members of the conservative movement came to see it that way. Michael Greve, a founder of the Center for Individual Rights, argues, "It's actually a sort of serious counterinstitution to the American Bar Institution. . . . It's nothing official. It's just people know each other. . . . None of it is conspiratorial, that's just how the world works. Just as liberals have their own institutions—they're called universities, or the ABA—so conservatives have theirs."

The Federalist Society is still far from a true alternative to the ABA. It has a small percentage of the ABA's budget, a fraction of its membership, and lacks the ABA's structural role in the legal profession. That said, the Society is clearly doing more for its members than operating as a debating society. Its practice groups help conservatives develop alternative approaches to law and public policy, and its Lawyers Division fosters social networks that make conservative lawyers less dependent upon the mainstream bar. It is increasing its role in helping conservative lawyers fulfill their obligation to do pro bono work for conservative and libertarian causes. It is not yet a complete alternative to the ABA, but it is closer to fulfilling this function that it was fifteen years ago.

Back to the Law Schools

The Federalist Society began in the nation's law schools, and while its programming has expanded dramatically, it has never lost its focus on legal education. At the top of the Society's list of complaints with the legal establishment has been the perceived exclusion of conservative faculty in American law schools. For most of its quarter-century history, its response remained at the level of critique, but over the last few years the Society has sought to directly address the representation of conservatives in legal education. The fortunes of this project are a useful prism through which to evaluate the future of the Society and its effort to undermine the liberal legal network.

In 1996, James Piereson of the Olin Foundation asked Eugene Meyer whether there was anything that the Society could do to alter the ideological balance of America's law schools. Meyer spoke with Gary Lawson of Boston University, who told Meyer that his one-year fellowship at Yale Law School was vital to his success in obtaining a teaching job. The Olin Foundation had been operating its own fellowship program, which provided funding for a year of leave for professors in a wide range of disciplines (including law) prior to submitting their tenure file. Meyer and Lawson's idea was even more ambitious than this, since it proposed using foundation support to improve the success of conservatives at the front end of the hiring process, and not just at the back end of the tenure process.

The market for potential law professors is quite different from that in the arts and sciences. Whereas applicants for jobs in political science or English can demonstrate their scholarly potential through their dissertations, this is only possible for the minority of law teaching applications with JD's or PhD's. A large number of applicants to the legal academy take jobs in government or law firms before applying for teaching positions, rather than going directly into teaching. As proof of scholarly impact has become more important in law school hiring, the ability to get time off to write before entering the legal academic market has become increasingly important. A 1999 proposal for the Olin Fellows program argued that the process by which time to write is allocated is biased toward those on the left.[99] "Fellowships do exist, but they are difficult to obtain and usually are closely controlled by fairly senior professors who share, even more than the average law school academic, the prevailing left-wing orthodoxy that dominates the academy. Therefore, if these opportunities are going to exist for students dedicated to principles of the rule of law and limited government, a new fellowship program is necessary."[100] The proposal noted that the conservative movement had already been successful in placing students in law and economics, but that in other areas of law the conservative infrastructure was much more limited.

> The few fellowships generally available to conservative students are in law and economics. As a result, this has been the one area of law where conservative scholars have had good opportunities—largely because of the excellent John M. Olin Law and Economics programs that exist in many leading law schools. Unfortunately, generally conservative perspectives in teaching are just as desperately needed in most other legal subjects. In addition, there is some tendency for any conservative teaching law to be pushed into law and economics. Therefore, while there should be great pride in the build-up in that area, it is crucial to reach into other parts of the legal academy as well.[101]

The Olin Fellows program represented a new stage in conservative movement philanthropy in legal education, and to some degree in higher education more broadly. Conservative organizations, like the Intercollegiate Studies Institute and the Institute for Humane Studies, have long provided grants for like-minded students in PhD programs, to encourage them to complete their studies in a timely manner. The Olin Fellows program is a step beyond these programs or the Olin pre—tenure review fellowships, in that they are designed to attract the brightest young conservatives into academic work and equip them with the qualifications to compete for the top jobs in legal academia. Where most previous conservative initiatives with university faculty, therefore, involved strongly supporting the few conservatives who managed to work their way into academic positions, the Olin Fellows program seeks to actively place them in those positions in the first place. The Society's strategy with the Olin Fellows program builds on the assumption that has governed most of the Olin-funded efforts to influence higher education, which is that change filters down from the top.[102] Meyer observes that the Society's standards for the fellowships are very high. In response to applicants from lower-status institutions, he says, "I am going to be fairly blunt. I know the situation if someone says, 'I was first in my class at Dayton Law School . . . and I have written some op-eds on legal issues. . . . I clerked for a district court. . . . That's great, but honestly almost everybody who has gotten this has clerked for the Court of Appeals. A number have clerked for the Supreme Court. If their resume doesn't look like they'd be competitive for the Supreme Court, chances aren't good." Because of the importance of marks of distinction in legal academic hiring, the Society almost always limits its Olin Fellows program to candidates from top law schools with impressive clerkship and restricts the schools at which fellowships can be used to those at the top of the law school pecking order.

It is still too early to tell whether the Olin Fellows program has been effective, and in any case it is very difficult to disentangle the impact of the program from the influence of a changed legal culture or greater willingness of law schools to consider hiring conservatives. Table 5.1 shows the fellows from 1997 to 2006, along with the schools that they graduated from, where they took their fellowship, who they clerked for, and their current teaching position, if any. Of the thirty-one Olin fellows, all but ten now have academic teaching jobs. Did the Olin fellowship program play a role in placing these conservatives in the legal academy? It is difficult to know. On the one hand, the best placements among the Olin Fellows have been those with a Supreme Court clerkship (and a law degree from Notre Dame, Harvard, Yale and Chicago) or a PhD in economics (Michigan). It would be surprising if candidates like this did not get an academic teaching position of some sort. Their success could simply be a sign of the impact of conservative Supreme Court appointments on the legal academy, and thus a strong argument for a direct connection between electoral and academic change. In addition, at least some law schools, especially Harvard, have made a clear push to hire more conservatives: at almost the same time that Harvard Law hired

TABLE 5.4
Olin Fellows, 1997–2006

Name	Fellowship and Year	JD from	Other Degree?[a]	Appellate Clerkship	Academic Job[b]	Primary Focus L&E?
Allen Ferrell	Harvard 1997	Harvard 1995		"Kennedy SC/Silberman, DC Circuit"	Harvard	Yes
Adrian Vermeule	Georgetown 1997	Harvard 1993		Scalia SC/Sentelle, DC Circuit	Harvard	No
Erica Worth Harris	Virginia 1997	Texas 1996		None	None	Yes
Geoff Manne	Chicago 1998	Chicago 1997		Arnold, 8th Circuit	Lewis&Clark	Yes
Matt Stowe	Texas/Cornell 1998	Harvard 1996		O'Connor SC/Lutting, 4th Circuit	None	No
Keith Sharfman	Cornell 1999	Chicago 1997		Easterbrook, 7th Circuit	Rutgers	Yes
Scott Angstreich	Georgetown/Harvard 1999	Harvard 1998	M.Phil.	Ginsburg, DC Circuit	None	No
Julian Ku	Virginia 1999	Yale 1998		Smith, 5th Circuit	Hofstra	No
Thomas Lambert	Northwestern 1999	Chicago 1998		Smith, 5th Circuit	Missouri	Yes
Rachel Barkow	Georgetown 2001	Harvard 1996		Scalia SC/Silberman, DC Circuit	NYU	No
Nicholas Rosenkranz	NYU 2001	Yale 1999		Kennedy SC/Easterbrook, 7th Circuit	Georgetown	No
Laurence Claus	Northwestern 2001	Queensland 1991	D.Phil.	Easterbrook, 7th Circuit	San Diego	No
Amy Barrett	GWU 2001	Notre Dame 1997		Scalia SC/Silberman, DC Circuit	NotreDame	No
Adam Mossoff	Northwestern 2001	Chicago 2001	MA	Wiener, 5th Circuit	Michigan State	Yes

Name						
David Moore	Chicago 2001	BYU 1996		Alito SC/Alito 3rd Circuit	Kentucky	No
Jennifer Braceras	Harvard 2001	Harvard 1994		Winter, 2nd Circuit	None	No
Ilya Somin	Northwestern 2002	Yale 2001	PhD	Smith, 5th Circuit	GMU	No
James Prescott	Harvard 2003	Harvard 2002	PhD	Garland, DC Circuit	Michigan	Yes
Charles Keckler	Northwestern 2003	Michigan 1999	PhD	Boggs, 6th Circuit	None	No
Donald Kochan	Virginia 2003	Cornell 1998		Suhrheinrich, 6th Circuit	Chapman	Yes
Robert Miller	Yale 2003	Yale 1997	PhD	None	Villanova	No
Jeffrey Manns	Harvard 2004	Yale 2003	D.Phil.	Wilkinson, 4th Circuit	None	Yes
Chaim Saiman	Harvard 2004	Columbia 2001		McConnell, 10th Circuit	Villanova	No
John Pfaff	Northwestern 2004	Chicago, 2003	PhD	Stephen Williams, DC Circuit	Fordham	Yes
Brian Fitzpatrick	NYU 2005	Harvard 2000		Scalia SC/O'Scannlain, 9th Circuit	Vanderbilt	No
Nathan Sales	Georgetown 2005	Duke 2000		Sentelle, DC Circuit	George Mason	No
Elizabeth Harmer-Dionne	Harvard 2006	Stanford 1998	M.Phil.	None	None	No
Charles Fischette	Penn 2006	Virginia 2005	MA	Walker, 2nd Circuit	None	No
Christopher Newman	UCLA 2006	Michigan 1999		Kozinski, 9th Circuit	None	No
Michael Risch	Stanford 2006	Chicago 1998		None	West Virginia	Yes
K.A.D. Kamara	Northwestern, 2006	Harvard 2004	PhD	Hartz, 10th Circuit	None	Yes

[a] Completed or Near-Completed
[b] Tenure or Tenure-Track

former Olin Fellow Adrian Vermeule away from Chicago, they also hired John Manning and Jack Goldsmith. While all three had sterling qualifications, there are also indications that conservatives' rhetoric of intellectual diversity also helped create a climate in which their hiring seemed institutionally prudent.[103]

While the opportunity structure for conservatives in the legal academy may have become more permissive over the last few years, in interviews with a number of the Olin Fellows I was told that the fellowship had a substantial impact on their career trajectory. A couple of the fellows mentioned that they used the fellowship to support work on a second degree, while a large number of them thought the networks they developed while a fellow, the experience of faculty seminars, and the prestige of the fellowship made a difference in obtaining an academic job. One fellow's assessment of the impact of his fellowship was "that it had a substantial impact. I became better acclimated to legal academia (as opposed to my prior graduate work). . . . I made contacts and developed friendships with academics that have proven invaluable in both professional and personal terms, and I made great strides in becoming a legal scholar. More important, I acquired the knowledge and skills that made it possible for me to succeed in obtaining a full-time academic position the year after my fellowship (and I received multiple job offers)."[104] One very highly placed fellow observed that he thought it was unlikely that he would have gotten an academic job without the fellowship, because "there would be no time to write."[105] This fellow had not published any articles before his fellowship year, but he was able to finish two articles that year and start a third. Laurence Claus, with degrees from Australia and Britain, observed that the fellowship "gave me an opportunity to write a substantial piece of U.S. constitutional law scholarship and to explore the US entry-level teaching market. Without it I probably would have taken an academic position in Europe and would have entered the U.S. academy, if at all, only much later as a lateral appointment with an already-established reputation." Finally, a fellow from a less highly ranked law school observed that the fellowship "taught me how to approach scholarly topics, it provided an opportunity to learn about game theory, it gave me the chance to make contacts with top-notch scholars at least one of whom has continued to serve as a mentor, it added a top-notch school to my resume, and it allowed me to write and place well two pieces."[106] It is still early in the history of the Federalist Society's Olin Fellows program, but there are some signs that it has helped, at the margins, to alter the ideological composition of the legal academy that caused the Society to come into existence in the first place.

Conclusion

The Federalist Society was founded to dislodge what it saw as the "hegemony" of liberalism in the key institutions of the legal profession, and as such has been a critical component in the larger conservative mission of scaling back liberal successes in the courts. The aspiration of some in the Society's leadership, and perhaps more outside it, that the organization should become a "counter-ABA" is part of the larger conservative movement's objective to break what it sees as the liberal control of many of the institutions of modern America.[107] The Federalist Society represents, without a doubt, the most vigorous, durable, and well-ordered organization to emerge from this rethinking of modern conservatism's political strategy. In fact, it would be difficult to name a case of conservative mobilization outside of economic and foreign policy, with the exception of welfare reform, that has been as successful as the Federalist Society.[108] If anything, the success of the Society has been more impressive than the project of welfare reform. Conservatives had a powerful political resource in public opposition to liberalized welfare policy, but have not been able to draw upon a similar popular engagement with matters of judicial philosophy, apart from occasional distaste for specific liberal initiatives in the courts. Transforming the courts, therefore, required a strategy of elite rather than popular mobilization. Conservatives had to create a web of intellectual, political, and network entrepreneurs who could generate new legal ideas, dedicated activists, litigation centers, and connections between individuals across the country that could certify individuals as ideologically suitable for positions as clerks and judges.

The Federalist Society has played a critical part in building the support structure of the conservative legal network. The success of the Society was not predetermined, but has been the product of the careful strategic leadership of a tight network of individuals who have been with the organization since its founding, in tandem with the foundation executives and the well-placed senior members of the conservative legal community who assisted the Society at critical junctures. The success of the Society is in large part a product of its self-limitation, driven by its leaders' strong commitment to intellectual debate and determination to avoid expanding into areas that would introduce divisive controversy between its philosophical wings. This success can also be traced to the effectiveness of the Society's peculiar organizational structure in reconciling the goals of a large participatory membership and an insulated leadership cadre. This leadership cadre has been able to effectively impress norms of "rational debate" on the Society that set it apart from other conservative membership organizations. These norms have enhanced the Society's effectiveness in persuading outsiders, maintaining dialogue with liberals, and, as a consequence, reducing the stigma attached to its ideas.

Perhaps the greatest success of the Society is one that must be seen as double-edged. It has vigorously attempted to expose the "hidden" ideological bias behind the ABA and America's law schools. These were once essential parts of the "American Establishment," a set of interlocking institutions that exercised substantial influence over American society, generally but not always in a liberal direction.[109] While the Society, along with other parts of the conservative movement, has helped weaken the power of this establishment, it has, counter to its typical members' philosophy, further weakened the idea that there are any "neutral" standards, and in particular any institutions that can be counted upon to defend them. This is an outcome that should not, in the main, be laid at the feet of the Society's leaders. The strategy adopted by the Society was, in large part, dictated by the difficulty its leaders faced in infiltrating the primary institutions of the law. As a result, they had little choice but to directly attack those institutions, expose their underlying ideological orientation, and present themselves as an alternative to them. The consequence, however, is that neither the Federalist Society nor its enemies on the left can count on the authority or legitimacy that the institutions of the law once held in American life. Partially as a result of the Society's challenge to the liberal legal network, the law has become wracked by seemingly unending ideological conflict, making it even harder to move toward the Society's understanding of the rule of law as something that transcends the ideological conflicts of the day. The Society's activities have injected competition into the legal profession, but not, at least for now, a new establishment.

6

Law and Economics II: Institutionalization

> I have the strong feeling that the economic analysis
> of law has "peaked out" as the latest fad in legal
> scholarship and that it will soon be treated by the
> historians of legal thought like the writings of
> Laswell and McDougal. Future legal historians
> will need to exercise their imaginations to figure
> out why so many people could have taken most of
> this stuff so seriously.[1]
> —Morton Horwitz, Professor of Law, Harvard
> University, 1980

FOR A GOOD DEAL of the period covered in chapter 4, the question that
loomed over law and economics was not whether it was right or wrong,
but whether it was worthy of being considered seriously at all. Among a
large part of the legal academic community, law and economics was
thought to be the province of libertarian eccentrics, a nihilistic project to
undermine the normative foundations of American law, or simply unfamiliar and vaguely threatening. This atmosphere of stigma meant that
elite law schools did not feel the need to make room for the field or its
adherents, and its ideas could be legitimately ignored. The strategic challenge of law and economics, therefore, was to remove the field's stigma
and force a debate on the merits. The engagement of a huge swathe of
legal academia with Richard Posner and the increasing prestige of market
solutions to policy problems (even among liberals) played a large part in
erasing this stigma. Henry Manne's seminars for judges and law professors built on these changes in the environment by reducing the mystery
and threat associated with law and economics, associating the idea with
the prestige of federal judges and equipping law professors to intelligently
engage with and contribute to the field.

By the time this chapter opens, in the early 1980s, law and economics
had become a legitimate if still controversial part of the legal academic
community. Law and economics was no longer "off the wall," but it was
still a distinctly minority approach even in its core areas of private law.[2]
Today, law and economics is dominant in private law and plays an im-

portant role in much of the rest of legal education. The law schools of
Harvard, Yale, Chicago, and Stanford boast over a dozen law and economics practitioners each, organized into well-funded research centers.
In just twenty years, an economics-focused law school with a libertarian
spirit at George Mason University went from nothing to the *U.S. News*
top 40. While critical legal studies, its great combatant for the mind of
the legal academy, has been all but vanquished, law and economics continues to increase in its influence.

Some have argued that the explanatory power of the economic approach, the changing nature of legal problems, and the spread of scholarly
standards to professional schools made this success inevitable. But it is
difficult to account for the speed and thoroughness with which law and
economics ripped through legal academia without accounting for the role
of organizational entrepreneurship and creative patronage.

Especially important in moving law and economics from a barely tolerated minority to a dominant presence in legal academia was the Olin
Foundation's two-decade-long investment in law and economics programs at the top-ranked law schools in the country. Olin believed that
law and economics represented a rare crack in the liberal legal network,
a beachhead for conservatives otherwise locked out of the elite legal academy. Beginning in a period when most of those schools had only a handful
of law and economics scholars, Olin's strategic patronage increased the
visibility and prestige of law and economics, intensified the networking
and productivity of its practitioners, and drew ambitious future law professors into its sphere. In a profession intensely sensitive to prestige and
distinction, the presence of the Olin programs in elite law schools sent a
powerful signal to institutions further down the academic pecking order
that to "keep up with the Joneses" they needed to hire students trained
in law and economics. Due in substantial part to Olin's patronage, law
and economics moved rapidly from an insurgency to a part of the legal
academic establishment.

Ironically enough, Olin's remarkable support of law and economics
came at a time when the ideological character of the field was moving
well beyond its libertarian roots. Law and economics at the elite level
came to resemble disciplinary economics in its overall ideological coloration.[3] This represented a substantial shift from the prevailing opinion in
law schools but a far cry from law and economics' former free-market
enthusiasm. This shift raises the question of how much Olin's support
transformed law schools, and how much elite law schools transformed
law and economics.

Quite a distance from the Olin Programs' ivy-covered confines, a very
different model for reshaping the law was developing at an obscure com-
muter school in the suburbs of Northern Virginia. While the Olin Founda-

tion judged that supporting law and economics at the nation's elite law schools was the key to transforming legal culture, Henry Manne's effort to build an economics-driven law school at George Mason University was informed by a very different strategy. Unlike the Olin programs, which were characterized by a focus on methodological sophistication and disciplinary legitimacy, GMU Law carried forward the more libertarian variant of law and economics that Manne first encountered at the University of Chicago. Manne's law school at GMU would test whether conservatives could influence the legal mainstream by building a place of refuge for law and economics' original libertarian spirit rather than by burrowing from within at existing law schools. On the one hand, GMU is an unquestionable organizational success—it is difficult to identify any law school in the last forty years that has moved so far, so fast. Where its broader ambitions to influence the character of legal education are concerned, however, the jury is still out.

A Foothold among the Elite: The Olin Law and Economics Programs

John M. Olin was as establishment a figure as one's imagination could fabricate. Olin vacationed and socialized with America's corporate elite and through the 1960s his philanthropic activities were not markedly different than those of other wealthy Americans. Olin was especially generous to his alma mater, Cornell, and was a member of its board of trustees from 1954 to 1966.[4] It thus came as a shock to Olin when, in 1969, Cornell's buildings were seized by armed black students, who squeezed curricular and other changes from frightened university administrators.[5] The events at Cornell led Olin to suspect that the administrators of traditional charitable institutions no longer shared his conservative values. George Gillespie, Olin's private lawyer, recalls that his client "stopped giving to Cornell at about that time . . . [and] his philanthropy turned to what he called the preservation of liberty and the free market system." The resignation of Henry Ford II from the Ford Foundation board in 1976 reinforced Olin's skepticism of traditional philanthropy, and convinced him that the typical, family-run, perpetual foundation model was a poor fit for this new kind of strategic conservative philanthropy. It was at this point that Olin contacted William Simon, who had been the secretary of the treasury in the Nixon and Ford administrations. Gillespie recalls that Olin "admired Simon's way of addressing problems, which was very directly and almost strident." Olin trusted that Simon shared his own conservative vision, and he appointed him to direct a new foundation designed to ensure fidelity to his intentions. James Pierson, the executive director of the Olin Foundation from 1985 to 2005, recalls that

John Olin did not set the foundation up as a family foundation; these tend to be outlets for family charities, do not have a strong point of view, and are usually ineffective in accomplishing anything important. . . . John Olin created a foundation with a purpose. He appointed various business associates to the board who shared his philosophy, hired Simon as president, and told them to spend the money in a generation. These early decisions allowed the foundation to stay on track until it closed a generation after his death.

Rather than trusting the goodwill and judgment of traditional institutions, Olin sought to direct his money to individuals that shared his ideological convictions and appeared to be doing important work, primarily in the world of ideas.

By the 1970s, John M. Olin feared for the future of the capitalist system that had made him so wealthy. This fear led to his aggressive grant-making, and to Henry Manne. Olin was so impressed by the Manne programs in law and economics that he sought to use them as a model for additional foundation programming. The July 5, 1979, minutes of the Olin board of trustees report that "Mr. Olin introduced a discussion of whether law-economics programs similar that of Henry Manne at the University of Miami can be established elsewhere. During the course of discussion, it appeared to be the view of a number of trustees that it is difficult to emulate or even transplant successful programs. What is needed, rather, is to identify institutions and individuals with leadership qualities who are willing to establish centers for the study of free market economics, including centers promoting interdisciplinary approaches."[6] Soon thereafter, Olin encouraged Cornell's law school to lure Manne and the LEC to Ithaca. While there was not an explicit promise that Manne's appointment would lead Olin to reopen his wallet to Cornell, the possibility that it would made this a matter of intense interest on the part of the law school dean and the president.[7] Ultimately, the proposal was thwarted by a coalition of liberal and conservative faculty who opposed law and economics.

The failure of the Cornell gambit deeply frustrated Olin and the foundation's trustees. The minutes of the March 27, 1980, board of trustees meeting report that "after considerable discussion, in which displeasure in Cornell's actions was voiced by a number of the Trustees, the Trustees authorized Mr. Joyce to communicate with Cornell the sense of disappointment the Trustees felt in Cornell's unwillingness to appoint Dr. Manne." The aborted project of bringing Manne to Cornell confirmed Olin's earlier disappointment with the university's leadership, and, when combined with his reading of trends in American politics, led him to believe that the hour for American capitalism was very late. A letter written by Olin in 1980 to the president of Cornell University indicates his state of mind at the time.

I enclose with this letter a copy of an article which appeared in *Business Week*, April 23, 1980, entitled "Marxists on the campus—in the faculty." . . . I cannot help but feel a situation has developed at Cornell which needs very very serious study and correction. The article . . . points out in rather sharp detail the infusion into the higher educational structure of our country of scholars stemming back to the 50s and 60s with definite left-wing attitudes and convictions. It matters little to me whether the economic development is classified as Marxism, Keynesianism or whatnot—the fundamental involved is the increased development since F. D. Roosevelt's 1932 presidency and following World War II of socialism in our country. There is ample evidence of the growth of liberalism/socialism, which words I regard in our country as synonymous, and unless this trend is halted, I very much fear the 1980 decade will bring about very very serious problems in our own country. . . . I now have the privilege of reflecting rather in great depth upon the problems which are facing all of us and it is for this reason I felt I wished to write this letter to you rather emphasizing my concern about the situation which I feel exists at Cornell, triggered by the recent law college faculty left-wing rejection of Doctor Manne and his Law and Economics Center . . . which brings into sharp focus the divided responsibility and authority existing now between the Board of Trustees, your administration, and the faculty, which is a cause of deep study upon my part and great concern to me. I am definitely of the opinion the situation now existing can only worsen and may result in the intrusion of organized labor into our faculty with its concomitant problems of contract negotiation to closed shop eventually resulting in socialism taking over. I feel very strongly the time has come for a thorough analysis of the existing situation and the development of an alternative and remedy for correction be instituted as promptly as possible.[8]

For Olin, the problems of America's economy and universities were increasingly of a piece, and law and economics seemed to offer an opportunity to remedy both. Bolstering this support was Frank O'Connell, Olin's former labor lawyer and the first executive director of the Olin Foundation, who was intimately aware of the interface between law and economics and as hostile as his boss to government regulation and labor unions.

Law and economics was the Olin Foundation's first effort at strategic philanthropy, and its ambitions in the area increased with the foundation's ballooning assets. As enthusiasm for the Manne programs waned (as described in chapter 4) the board's interest in gaining a foothold in the top law schools grew. In an early sign of the foundation's acute concern for academic distinction, "In 1981, Olin Board member George Gillespie expressed his concern that many of Manne's Olin Fellows were entering private law practice rather than the academy, and those who chose to become professors were not able to secure appointments at the nation's best law schools."[9] By 1983, when the board definitively pulled support from the

Simmons Building project, the foundation had decided to seek out other outlets for its beneficence. This shift from lower-status institutions to the American elite was reflected in all of the foundation's programming. As early as the late 1970s, the board had concluded that funding smaller conservative schools had little impact on the national debate. "The work of these schools, however laudable in its intentions, makes little or no difference in the hearts and minds of Americans as regards attitudes toward free enterprise, nor do their faculties, alumni, and students tend to influence the climate of opinion . . . our hull has acquired a few barnacles and it may now be time to scrape down the hull."[10]

Pulling support from Manne's programs was consistent with this process of "scraping down the hull," but personal factors also played a role. The members of the foundation board were, like John M. Olin, men of America's elite. Piereson recalls that

> our trustees were focused on elite institutions because by and large this is where they went to school. [Richard] Furlaud and [Peter] Flanigan went to Princeton; Gene Williams went to Yale; Gillespie to Harvard Law School; Chuck Knight to Cornell. . . . These trustees wanted us to work with elite institutions, not so much because they were influential but because this is the world they lived in. From my own point of view, I felt that we could have greater influence if we could penetrate these institutions, because they are emulated by other colleges and universities of lesser stature. Thus, the trustees and staff came to the same conclusion via different routes.

This elite-focused strategy was also influenced by a desire to honor John M. Olin, with whom much of the board was personally close. The minutes of a 1981 Olin Foundation Steering Committee meeting report that in a discussion of the Olin Fellows at Emory, Gillespie suggested that Henry Manne "be contacted to encourage stricter criteria be used in selection of future participants in this program, especially if John M. Olin's name is to be associated with the Center."[11] The meeting prior to the foundation's decision to eliminate the Olin Fellows program at Emory observed that the "SC [Steering Committee] thought that a fellowship program bearing Mr. Olin's name might be better pursued at an institution of greater influence and reputation."[12] While the Olin Foundation was certainly in the business of strategic philanthropy, therefore, it was not wholly lacking in the traditional philanthropic motivations of burnishing the benefactor's memory.

The effort to bring law and economics programs to elite institutions was, at least at the start, an initiative of the foundation's board. As James Piereson recalls, "Mike Joyce [the Olin Foundation's executive director from 1979 to 1985] was not all that sympathetic about law and economics. I've talked to Mike about this. He thought it was too abstract or theoretical. He was more interested in the intellectual combat you find in the magazines. However, our board members were very interested in working with these law schools." George Gillespie recalls supporting law and economics "was really not a staff initiative. . . . The board took a greater interest, and understood more fully what we were doing than in some of the other programs." At the same meeting where the board agreed to withdraw its support from the Olin Fellows at the LEC, they decided that

> efforts should be made to identify one of the top dozen or so law schools in the United States at a university with an outstanding economics department whose law and economics faculties would support institution of a law and economics program similar in scope to that which had been offered at the University of Miami Law School and Emory University Law School for law students who might be known as John M. Olin Fellows. The trustees emphasized in the course of their discussion the desirability of emphasizing both the quality of the institution—law school and economics department—and the quality of the students and faculty who might be invited to participate in a John M. Olin Law and Economics Program.[13]

With that decision, the Olin Foundation's project to inject law and economics into the nation's elite law schools was launched.

The foundation's aggressive expansion of its programming in law and economics reflected its newly increasing ambitions. At the January 22, 1981, board meeting, William Simon "stressed the importance of staff using its imagination in evaluating and planning the Foundation's programs,"[14] leading to a major effort at long-term planning. A November 1982 report to the trustees, which Piereson recalls was "heavily influential in shaping the subsequent direction of the foundation," laid out this new approach. The report noted that grant-making had declined over the previous few years because of the dearth of attractive applications. As a consequence, the staff noted that "in the future, the Foundation may have to increase its efforts to seek out high quality projects."[15] In contrast to its previously passive approach, the report recommended that the foundation should operate more like a "venture capitalist, who seeks new and more productive investments for his funds. He initiates opportunities. Following this model, the Foundation's staff could begin to search out new projects, discuss them with the Steering Committee and Board of Trustees, suggest them to qualified individuals or organizations, and use Foundation grants to make them realities. . . . Where the Foundation has attempted this, as in the creation of the Law and Economics movement, its efforts have been successful."[16] This entrepreneurial turn was facilitated by the foundation's steadily increasing assets. As Piereson recalls, "After John Olin died in 1982, almost $60 million came into the Foundation from his estate. He died at precisely the point when the long bull market of the 1980s took off. When I came in as executive director at the end of 1985, those assets had increased to $100 million at a time when we were spending less than $5 million per year. I had the latitude of spending a lot of money very quickly without everyone in the world knowing we had it. Otherwise we would be inundated with proposals, but instead we were able to pick our spots, and allocate this money before the wide world knew we had it."[17] Law and economics would be the most important target of the foundation's entrepreneurial ambitions and loosened purse-strings.

The first of the new Olin programs began with a meeting between the foundation staff and Professor Gerhard Casper of the University of Chicago Law School. Piereson recalls that "Gillespie and Simon at a Steering Committee meeting told Mike [Joyce], go out to Chicago and get a law and economics program at Chicago. It was not something Mike would have done on [his] own; they told him to do it." After meeting with Casper, he says, "We did make a grant to Chicago, and that became the prototype for others. There was faculty research, visiting lecturers, student fellowships, some other things which would provide a basis for the group to grow in the law school. . . . Eventually we did develop the idea that we could influence legal education more broadly this way, by funding these programs at several important places."

The decision to start law and economics centers at elite law schools represented a turn to a more directive, strategic form of patronage. With a professional staff and a broad portfolio of supported projects, the foundation could serve as a focal point for learning and feedback in the development of the conservative movement's intellectual infrastructure. The foundation was especially alert for opportunities to influence legal education: just as it was supporting conservative students in elite law schools through the Federalist Society, law and economics offered entrée into the faculty. Piereson recalls,

I also had the view that it was important to get into the law schools. I felt they were very important institutions, and it was important to have some sort of presence there. Remember, by now the Federalist Society had started, so you had student groups forming. Because of that, you had a way to bring various speakers in and activities. The law and economics thing now seemed like a way to work on the faculty side and the curriculum. As time passed, the Federalist Society chapters did work very closely with the law and economics people on the faculty. They became their advisors and so on. A lot of them became speakers in Federalist Society activities, like Richard Epstein. So they worked on parallel tracks. . . . I would have preferred to do something in constitutional law, but you couldn't really do that; you didn't have enough people inside the universities, inside the law schools, to do that. If you said to a dean that you wanted to fund conservative constitutional law, he would reject the idea out of hand. But if you said that you wanted to support law and economics, he would see that as a program with academic content and he would be much more open to the idea. Law and economics is neutral, but it has a philosophical thrust in the direction of free markets and limited government. That is, like many disciplines, it seems neutral but isn't in fact.

The foundation's leaders did not have a strong sense of the subtleties of the field, especially the differences between libertarians trained in law like Epstein and the rising generation of law and economics professors—many of whom had PhD's in economics—more interested in doing work that was respectable among professional economists. In their defense, the foundation's leaders were also realistic about how much they could direct the evolution of the field or pick and choose whom to support. Law and economics seemed like the opening in the world of elite legal education that they were looking for, and they quickly committed serious resources to the project.

After Chicago, the foundation went to Yale, where it was able to take advantage of the presence of George Priest, a prolific Chicago-trained scholar who had recently arrived at the law school. Before Olin began supporting law and economics at Yale, there was a small law and economics presence on the faculty and only the nub of an institutional structure. Priest recalls that while there were people at the law school with an interest in law and economics (Guido Calabresi, Robert Bork, Ralph Winter, Bruce Ackerman, and starting in 1983, Jerry Mashaw),

> there was no institutional feature at all. [Dean] Harry Wellington, largely as a fund-raising effort, created something called the Program on Civil Liability, of which Guido [Calabresi] was supposed to be the director, and they were going to raise corporate money. Well, anyone who knows Guido's views knows he is pretty liberal if not radical. So they raised a little money, but not a lot. When I came here, the year after I came here, I headed that program. Guido had never written on business; he wrote on accidents, and the only connection to business came through insurance. Harry Wellington had some ties from the insurance industry, and he raised some money from there for civil liability reform. But Guido wasn't business oriented, and I was, it wasn't so much conservative as it was a more business practical orientation. So I raised some money, and we had some conferences.

Thus, while law and economics was certainly not absent from Yale, "It still wasn't much of an institutional presence." The Olin Foundation moved law and economics at Yale from a primarily research-based project of a few professors to a much more wide-ranging program capable of

making a substantial imprint on the culture of the school. Priest concludes, "What the Olin Foundation did was [provide] an infusion of new
money, which we used for a workshop, a journal, student scholarships;
we brought fellows in. It was not controversial in the slightest, because it
brought in a lot of money, and schools can always use money."

The foundation hoped to make law and economics an institutionalized
part of Yale Law School, and by 2000 the staff thought they had succeeded. An Olin grant proposal record concludes that

> staff considers the law and economics program at Yale to have been an excellent
> investment. George Priest is a preeminent scholar in the law and economics
> movement, and his students have achieved remarkable success. Sixty-one for-
> mer JMO Fellows hold professorial positions at American law schools; 11 for-
> mer JMO Fellows have clerked for the U.S. Supreme Court, one for the Supreme
> Court of Australia and two for the Supreme Court of Israel; 105 JMO Fellows
> have clerked for Judges on the U.S. Circuit Courts of Appeal; 66 JMO Fellows
> have clerked for Judges on U.S. District Courts; and seven JMO Fellows have
> clerked on state supreme courts. This is one of our most influential Law and
> Economics grants (along with Harvard and Chicago) and staff believes the Yale
> program is well worth sustaining after we close our doors. Moreover, Dean
> Anthony Kronman has written a very strong letter. . . . in which he commits to
> raising an endowment for a chair in Law and Economics as well as for other
> programs at the Center. Clearly, he is doing all he can to assure the permanency
> of the program.[18]

The foundation believed that its support for law and economics at Yale
had delivered what the Manne programs had not—a substantial impact
on America's legal elite (especially students, who were always a greater
concern for the foundation than was faculty research) and an entrenched
position for the field at the nation's top law schools. On the other hand,
some of this perceived success with students was simply a function of
attaching the Olin brand to future lawyers who would have ended up
succeeding regardless. In fact, at least some of the Yale John M. Olin
Fellows, such as current Yale Law professor Reva Siegel, were anything
but sympathetic to the foundation's goals. Where Henry Manne's prominent position at less prestigious institutions gave him almost complete
control over the direction of his programming, the Olin programs in
elite law schools like Yale were under much greater pressures to adapt
to their surroundings.

The success of the Olin programs in the 1980s was, in large part, a
consequence of investments made in the previous decade. As Piereson
recalls, "There was not much else going on in law and economics [in the
1970s] other than Manne's programs. At that time, we could not have
spent much more in law and economics. In . . . the eighties [law and eco-

nomics scholars] began getting jobs at very good places, and they could mount these programs. Priest was at Yale, Shavell went to Harvard. All you needed was one or two people in a law school, and they could begin to build." Some of the seeds of the growth of law and economics in the 1980s had been planted at Chicago, and others by the Manne programs. Both Priest and Cornell's Jonathan Macey had been active participants in Manne's Liberty Fund conferences, and a number of the alumni of Manne's economics seminars for professors had moved into top teaching positions. The rise of "fundable faculty" in law and economics was, therefore, not exogenous to conservative patronage, but to a significant degree a consequence of its earlier work.

Equally important in explaining the foundation's decision to set up law and economics programs at the top law schools were the advantages of law and economics' ideological ambiguity. Imagining the difficulties in starting similar centers at the nation's top law schools in "originalist jurisprudence" is sufficient to make this point clear. Pierson observes that "you couldn't get into the law schools with programs targeted at constitutional law. . . . When you went in with law and economics, you didn't need to specify anything about the content; the content took care of itself, because economics is what it is. If you went in with constitutional law, you wouldn't want Larry Tribe constitutional law, you'd want Bob Bork constitutional law. But you couldn't go in and say that." Also helping law and economics programming avoid direct opposition was its concentration in the early 1980s in areas that were not on the cutting edge of the nation's cultural wars—such as antitrust, torts, and economic regulation—and that were widely acknowledged to be intellectually weak and thus a relatively soft target.

Law and economics was also interesting to the foundation's board in a way that constitutional and other hot-button areas of the law were not. Gillespie recalls that "law and economics, even though I'm not an economist, I can understand the analysis that goes into it, and it seems right to me. . . . I don't read Supreme Court decisions on the progeny of *Roe v. Wade*. It doesn't interest me. . . . It had to do with the kind of board we had. . . . John Olin was first and foremost a businessman, and this is a business approach to the law." While the staff were, if anything, more motivated by constitutional questions, the board made the final decisions, and their heart was clearly in law and economics. The board's interest, combined with the presence of law and economics professors at the top law schools, made it an attractive candidate for the foundation's growing funds. This set the stage for the foundation's ambitious effort to change what was then the nation's most influential law school—Harvard.

Law and Economics and the Battle for Harvard Law School

Where the Olin Foundation's main goal at Chicago and Yale was to accelerate trends that were already in motion, its ambition at Harvard Law School was much more audacious. At Harvard, the Olin Foundation sought nothing less than the ideological redirection of the law school, and the defeat of its most dynamic faction, critical legal studies (CLS). The foundation's leaders believed that Harvard played a pivotal role in the nation's legal profession, and that its control by CLS would give the Left a powerful platform for shaping the development of the law. In these conservatives' minds, law and economics was the only movement capable of providing an intellectually respectable alternative, and the foundation committed millions of dollars to its support. While other factors played an important part in the defeat of CLS over the next two decades, the Olin Foundation's patronage of law and economics at Harvard certainly played a critical part.

Because of its size and prestige, Harvard Law School has an outsized impact on American legal culture and the character of the legal professoriate.[19] The foundation also became interested in developments at Harvard for reasons that had little to do with the intrinsic merits of law and economics, but a great deal to do with concerns that board members (especially Gillespie) had with trends among the school's faculty—especially the growth of CLS. While CLS was a sweeping movement, a few of the beliefs of its adherents deserve our attention. First and perhaps most crudely, CLS was an effort to create a community of left-leaning law professors seeking intellectual sustenance, community, and power in numbers.[20] Second, CLS supporters saw themselves as the true inheritors of legal realism, arguing that law was essentially indeterminate and consequently its interpretation was "politics all the way down."[21] Third, the belief that law was reducible to politics drove CLS scholars like Morton Horwitz to demonstrate the ways that the law, far from being neutral, had supported the interests of the powerful, especially business.[22] Fourth, CLS supporters believed that the ideology of legalism and rights had de-radicalized social movements of the left, directing their protest into safe, "liberal" channels incapable of achieving their transformative goals. Finally, CLS trumpeted the belief that not only was the "personal" political, but so was the "professional." Genuine radicalism required that the law schools' role in perpetuating "hierarchy" be exposed and that they be transformed into sites for political resistance.[23] The challenge these tenets represented for both legal liberalism and modern conservatism proved, for a time, powerfully stimulating to scholarship as well as activism.

The growth of CLS was an unintended effect of the effort in the 1970s to inject greater intellectual energy into Harvard by attracting young, intellectually exciting professors. Derek Bok, the president of Harvard when CLS faculty were hired, recalls,

> I think we did recognize that they had different views, which was regarded as a strength, because the law school, like many other law schools throughout the fifties and sixties had been, while full of very bright people, was characterized by a uniformity of approach that a number of people thought was intellectually unfortunate. One of them was Erwin Griswold, so this wasn't any effort to get more liberal voices per se. Erwin of course was a very staunch Republican conservative of the old school, liberal on civil liberties, conservative on economic matters, but he felt there ought to be more diversity in the faculty, and that was a common view. People saw the appointment of people like [Roberto] Unger and Morty Horwitz, who had historical training and Duncan Kennedy as a step in that direction.[24] They tended to have different intellectual approaches. . . . It wasn't thought of in left-right terms at all.

By the late 1970s, however, Bok and others sensed that while hiring Unger, Horwitz, Kennedy, and others had increased the intellectual dynamism of Harvard, it also created a deep conflict over the direction and control of the school. By the time that CLS became a topic for discussion within the Olin Foundation in 1984, many observers wondered if the movement was on its way toward control of Harvard. Particularly alarming to graduates of the old Harvard Law was Duncan Kennedy, who proposed using first-year classes, such as his class on torts, to "teach our students that bourgeois or liberal legal thought is a form of mystification."[25] Even more disturbing, he encouraged young lawyers (in the *Harvard Law School Bulletin*, a publication read by alumni), to "reconceive the internal issues of firm hierarchy as an important part of one's political life, fighting the oligarchy of senior partners, opposing the oppression of secretaries by arrogant-young men who turn around and grovel before their mentors."[26] Such statements were to be expected from the students, perhaps, but from professors at a school that was famous for the rigor—some would say the sadism—of the faculty? Lawyers like Gillespie were not especially concerned that Kennedy would succeed in injecting his acolytes into firms like Cravath, Swaine & Moore. Gillespie recalls, "I didn't care about that—it wasn't going to happen, or at least I didn't regard it as a risk." Kennedy's real threat was to what men like Gillespie saw as the traditional, civilized place of Harvard within the legal profession. To them, Kennedy represented a kind of professional barbarism.

The publication of an article in the *New Yorker* by Calvin Trillin, claiming that supporters of CLS had enough support to block appointments, convinced the Olin Foundation board that the situation at Harvard had become critical.[27] The May 22, 1984, minutes of the foundation report that George Gillespie "asked that staff consider what could be done in the area of critical legal issue studies at Harvard University and suggested that they confer with the most reputable scholars known to them in this field to prepare a presentation to the Trustees for discussion at May 31 meeting."[28] At that meeting, the board of trustees agreed that it should seek "to support scholars at leading universities who are able to advance the intellectual case against the CLS movement through public lectures and debates, publication and research" as well as "emphasize support of assistant law professors in the John M. Olin program of support for the untenured faculty."[29] Harvard Law professor Philip Areeda was invited to the next board meeting to help the foundation develop its strategy.[30] Areeda was not a law and economics scholar, in the contemporary meaning of the term, but a "traditionalist" deeply committed to Harvard's inherited understanding of the purposes and means of legal education.[31] Areeda's close friend Derek Bok confirms that he was deeply shaken by the conflict at Harvard Law.

> There were even times when he was thinking of leaving the law school because he found it personally unpleasant. It focused particularly on the appointments process, where critical legal studies were always pushing their people, and of course that created great resistance on the other side, and by the end a lot of people lost their objectivity because they were consumed in this kind of battle between those people who thought . . . they could take over the law school. Probably not the most realistic view, but some of them entertained it, and were pushing for more and more faculty members who were part of their group, and this infuriated people on the other side. There was never a complete breakdown, but there was a lot of bitterness and unpleasant debates, unsatisfactory outcomes, in the sense that it became hard to get anyone through, which caused Phil a lot of anxiety and upset.

Areeda had the good fortune to have Bok and Gillespie, his old law school friends, as allies in the project of countering CLS. Gillespie recalls,

> I was a friend of Phillip Areeda. . . . We were together on the *Harvard Law Review*. He was a year ahead of me; he was a classmate of Sam Butler's [Gillespie's partner at Cravath, Swaine]. Sam was very active in Harvard affairs over time. Derek Bok, the president of Harvard, was also on the *Harvard Law Review* with me, also a class ahead of me, a classmate of Butler. . . . Sam talked quite a bit with Derek . . . and I invited Phil Areeda to sit and talk with us at the foundation about the critical legal studies problem, and how that could be turned around.

While Areeda was increasingly losing control of the situation within Harvard's walls, his alliance with the Olin Foundation allowed him to, in effect, expand the zone of conflict. Without this alliance, he might have simply given up the fight.

The Olin Foundation board's meeting with Areeda cemented its determination to use law and economics as a counter to CLS. In December 1984, members of the board met with the dean of the Law School, James Vorenberg, and Professor Steven Shavell "to discuss the possible establishment of a law and economics program at Harvard Law School . . . those present at the meeting (Samuel C. Butler and Messrs Gillespie and Joyce) had focused on the possible law and economics program as a counter to the Critical Legal Studies Group within the Harvard Law School faculty. Mr. Gillespie also reported that he and Mr. Joyce had strongly suggested that any such program at Harvard Law School should include a significant emphasis on student programs."[32] Gillespie was especially interested in the example of the newly created Olin program at Yale, asking in January 1985 "if this program could be suggested as a model to Harvard in planning a like program."[33] By March 1985 the foundation approved a grant of $917,000 over three years to support law and economics at Harvard Law, the money to be spent on student fellowships, visiting speakers, workshops, research funds, and conferences. The law and economics program went from original expressions of concern (May 1984) to funding (March 1985) to implementation (fall 1985) remarkably rapidly, which was a necessity in a context as volatile as Harvard Law School in the mid-1980s.

When the foundation first became engaged with the situation at Harvard, the group of law and economics scholars at the school was limited to Steven Shavell and Louis Kaplow. Shavell recalls that the foundation board members "did not tie their support to particular pet projects. They really gave us freedom to develop our programs as we saw fit, the only real constraint being that, usually, they wanted a certain [percentage of their funds] to be spent on students as opposed to faculty research." From the start, the Olin Foundation was not particularly engaged with the particular ideological or methodological coloration of law and economics at Harvard, assuming that it was generally sympathetic to markets and that it was futile to seek control over its substance in any case. As Shavell notes, the foundation's more pressing concern was that its programming reach students, which is a sign that its focus was on the character of the law school, not the substance of scholarship. On this dimension, the Olin funding was a success, giving a small group of lawyer-economists a much larger footprint on the culture of Harvard than they would have had without it. As Duncan Kennedy recalls, the Olin program provided

something to affiliate with. If they're going to create a law and economics counterinsurgency, it means that they're going to have unbelievable resources available to do it. And they had a genuine organizational talent. . . . They created, using the Olin money, a genuine community. The money wouldn't have done them any good if they didn't have the capacity to organize through the law and economics workshops. . . . Everybody who did law and economics in the country came to the workshop. Students could come to the workshops. . . . They [produced] . . . the impression that there's a national thing even though there's only two people there.

The Olin funding came at a time when CLS—despite its extreme claims—seemed to be the only source of genuine intellectual ferment in Harvard Law School. The "traditionalists" were in no position to provide an alternative to CLS, wedded as they were to older, less intellectual traditions in legal scholarship. Law and economics scholars like Shavell and Kaplow, on the other hand, could compete with CLS on its own intellectual terms, and with funding from the Olin Foundation they could provide an alternative community for students who recognized the exhaustion of the traditionalists.

At the same time that Olin initiated its support of law and economics at Harvard, the Federalist Society launched a very public effort to convince the legal profession that Harvard Law was out of control.[34] Much of the Society's 1984 conference at Harvard was devoted to attacks on CLS, and this came hot on the heels of the publication of Trillin's article and the exit of traditionalist Paul Bator for Chicago, who pointed to battles with CLS as the reason for his move. This effort to heighten the perception of crisis reached a crescendo in May 1985, in a debate at the New York City Harvard Club sponsored by the Federalist Society that pitted Kennedy and Abram Chayes on the left against Paul Bator and Robert Clark on the right. The Society's advertising for the event was, itself, an important part of its strategy to publicize the "crisis" at Harvard. It trumpeted CLS's supposedly outrageous views and told Harvard alumni that the Society believed that it was "important to bring to the attention of alumni the pervasive effects this movement is having at Harvard Law School."[35] At the panel, both Bator and Clark pressed the point that, in addition to its rejection of "science, business and the legal profession," CLS had a damaging effect on Harvard, making it difficult for the faculty to make offers and encouraging candidates to reject them.[36] Extending the offensive after the symposium, the Society had transcripts of the event sent to all New York—area Harvard alumni. George Hicks concludes that the Federalist Society event "initiated a strong wave of alumni support for getting things back under control, and it identified Clark as someone who would fight back."[37]

The perception of crisis helped CLS's foes to further expand the zone of conflict, linking the beleaguered anti-CLS faculty members with allies outside the University. CLS's opponents combined this outside support with a well-positioned internal ally, Harvard president Derek Bok. Bok denies that his concern with CLS was due to alumni pressure, arguing that his involvement with the Law School was due to

> the situation itself. What I really feared was not alumni reaction, what I feared was that people like Phil would just get upset and leave, which I am sure would have upset the Law School, but what I really feared was that the Law School would be greatly diminished. . . . I got more involved in the appointments process because I had lost a certain degree of confidence in the objectivity of the process because people on both sides were so engaged in the battle with the other side that . . . people's judgment[s] were being influenced by political and tactical considerations rather than a dispassionate view of the quality of the candidate. So I did something that hadn't been done before, which was on a few occasions insisted on having an ad hoc proceeding where we brought in people from outside the Law School faculty, which is a common procedure but not used in the memory of man in the Law School. But we imposed it anyways, in the case of a few appointments that . . . circumstances suggested needed a dispassionate review.[38]

While alumni played a role in Bok's decision, insofar as they were part of an unwelcome public relations problem for the university, it seems more likely that Bok became involved for a simpler reason: no Harvard president would wish to preside over the implosion of one of the university's most important assets. This public relations problem reinforced Bok's instinct toward institutional conservation. Bok was a Cold War, "vital center" liberal, and as such was closely attuned to the threat to liberal institutions that could come from the left.[39] Kennedy believes that the memory of the conflict-ridden 1960s played a role as well. "In this period, there's still the smell of gunpowder, there's still a dim haze in the skies over Cambridge." It is not difficult to imagine that someone like Bok would be alarmed that a faction with as little interest in institutional preservation as CLS could attain veto power at Harvard Law School.

With the resignation of Dean Vorenberg in 1989, Bok had an opportunity to appoint someone who would do what the previous dean had not done—get the situation at Harvard under control. Clark's scholarly work had drawn on law and economics (even though he lacked the technical skills of Shavell and Kaplow), and the Olin program represented a major institutional commitment opposed to CLS's vision of law. It thus made sense for Clark to build up law and economics, both because of its inherent merit and because it could act as a counterweight to CLS. Before Clark became dean in 1989, there were five law and economics faculty at the law school (three of which were appointed after the creation of the Olin program): Steve Shavell, Lewis Kaplow, Lucian Bebchuk, Reinier Kraakman, and Howell Jackson. During Clark's term of office, hiring in the area accelerated, as Kaplow was placed on the appointments committee and law and economics hires were made in 1992 (Bruce Hay), 1994 (Christine Jolls, Einer Elhauge), 1995 (W. Kip Viscusi), 1997 (John Coates), 1998 (J. Mark Ramseyer), 1999 (Mark Roe and Allen Ferrell) and 2002 (Guhan Subramanian). Law and economics became a major faction in the law school, and the alliance of many of its members with the traditionalists made it difficult for CLS to get appointments of its own. Dean Clark and his allies in law and economics succeeded in reducing CLS to a small minority, no longer a significant power in the school's decision-making. Just a few years after its initial investment, the foundation's staff concluded that their investment had been a success, both in fostering a movement sympathetic to free markets and in shifting the balance of power in the nation's most visible law school. The staff wrote to the foundation's board in 1993 that

> when we began supporting Law and Economics some years ago, our goal was to create programs in the leading universities in the hope that this investment would establish the field as a legitimate area of study in schools all over the country. Our initial hopes have been fulfilled: Law and Economics has become a major field of specialty in the law schools, and has had a pervasive effect on legal thinking not only in the law schools but also in the courts, in business and in government generally. In addition, Law and Economics gives us an important foothold in law schools that we would not have otherwise. Conservative students tend to gravitate to professors in law and economics, and the discipline provides an intellectual framework within which to criticize the doctrines that are taught by liberal and left-wing faculty (by far the majority in most law schools). Our program at Harvard has been very successful in the years since it began in 1985. Initially, there were only two or three faculty with any interest in the field and the Dean at the time was unsympathetic. Since then, however, the number of students in the field has increased dramatically and the presence of Law and Economics in the curriculum has expanded as well. The number of faculty with expertise in Law and Economics has also grown; currently the school has eight faculty members whose main specialty is Law and Economics, and another five who have substantial involvement with the field. This makes Law and Economics one of the largest specialty areas within the School. . . . Thus, there is good reason to believe our investment has paid off well at Harvard.[40]

Dean Clark, who shared an interest in thwarting CLS, agreed with the staff's assessment, telling William Simon in 1994 that "the Foundation's support has played a crucial role in *restoring* the academic soundness of Harvard Law School, an institution whose influence on law and legal education is indisputably enormous."[41]

The Olin Foundation's money was certainly not the only cause of law and economics' success at Harvard. Once the field came to be seen as a major movement in legal education, having established a significant position at Yale and Chicago, Harvard's traditional desire for preeminence put pressure on the school to make additional hires in law and economics. This pressure would have been present whether the Olin program had been established or not. One suggestive indication that the Olin program was far from irrelevant, however, is the number of Harvard law and economics faculty who were trained at Harvard, and thus were able to take advantage of the resources of the Olin program. For example, Elhauge received his JD from Harvard in 1986, Ferrell in 1995, Hay in 1988, Jolls in 1993, and Subramanian in 1998. The Olin program played an important role in attracting Harvard students into law and economics and training them sufficiently that they could be hired as professors at Harvard (and elsewhere). Interestingly, none of the law and economics faculty hired in this period came from Chicago. This may have been due to the ideological stigma that attached to Chicago-style law and economics, but a more likely hypothesis is that Harvard simply has a very high propensity to hire its own graduates. By building up law and economics at Harvard, the Olin Foundation deepened the pool of law and economics practitioners from which Harvard law professors are traditionally drawn. Had the law and economics faculty members at Harvard depended on recruiting faculty from other institutions, it is unlikely that they could have built up the field at Harvard so rapidly. The consequence of that would have been a smaller law and economics bloc, and with it a smaller anti-CLS contingent.

The internecine conflict between CLS and law and economics at Harvard was an important part of the larger battle over the last twenty-five years for control over American legal culture. The Olin Foundation entered this battle less because of its commitment to—or even understanding of—law and economics, and more because it saw the fortunes of law and economics as tied up with the direction that the legal profession would take over the next few decades. As I argued in chapter 1, elite law schools help to generate the legal ideas that shape the long-term development of doctrine, provide students with the intellectual capital, professional distinction, and networks that they draw on in their subsequent careers, and produce the next generation of law professors. A movement without a significant presence at Harvard and Yale law schools will, therefore, be hampered in building a support structure for legal change. The Olin Foundation's support of law and economics at Harvard was driven by its fear that the Left might use the Law School to produce these critical resources for itself and deny them to conservatives. The foundation's staff would have preferred to throw their support behind other forms of legal scholarship that were closer to their conservative principles, but in the battle to repel the CLS offensive, law and economics was the only weapon available.

The Olin Programs and the Diffusion of Law and Economics

From Harvard, Yale, and Chicago, the foundation quickly moved to spread Olin programs in law and economics to other elite law schools. The fact that these leading schools had developed strong, well-funded programs in law and economics sent a signal to the rest of elite legal education that this was now a respectable, mainstream field of legal scholarship, since no field that had a presence at these schools could be considered "off the wall." In fact, the presence of law and economics at Harvard and Yale suggested that the field was now a part of any respectable law school's portfolio. The foundation was now pushing against an open door. Nevertheless, openness to law and economics did not necessarily translate into the kind of major investment in an area that can transform the character of an institution. For that to happen in elite institutions, substantial outside subsidy was required, which was precisely what the Olin Foundation provided.

In the wake of the foundation's support of Harvard, Yale, and Chicago, the Olin programs in law and economics spread very rapidly: Penn in 1986, Stanford, Berkeley, and Virginia in 1987, Columbia, Duke, Georgetown, and Toronto in 1989, Cornell in 1992, and Michigan in 2000.[42] Despite the increasing popularity of the field, these programs would not have developed as quickly, or had as much impact in elite law schools, were it not for the support of the Olin Foundation. From January 1985 to January 1989, approximately $4.45 million was donated by the major conservative foundations to law and economics (including the Manne programs), of which only $736,000 came from sources other than Olin. While support for law and economics would broaden somewhat in subsequent years (see figure 6.1), Olin was the dominant decision-maker in the area, with other foundations piggybacking on its leadership.[43] It is highly unlikely that any of the other conservative patrons had the will or means to get these programs off the ground, and no major law school showed much interest in funding such programs themselves.

After Harvard, Yale, and Chicago, Stanford was the law and economics program that had the strongest internal support and that received the most generous funding from the Olin Foundation. By 1987, when Stanford Law submitted its first proposal for a law and economics center, the faculty already included eleven professors of law and economics, a number of whom also held appointments at the Hoover Institution.[44] A letter from the Law School's dean, Paul Brest, accompanied Stanford's initial application and frankly stated, "One of my priorities as Dean is, to put it immodestly, to develop the preeminent integrated curriculum in law, economics and business."[45] Stanford received an initial grant of $870,733

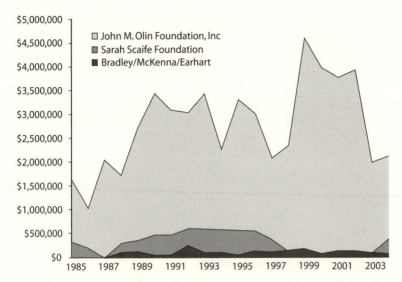

Figure 6.1. Foundation Funding for Law and Economics (in 2004 dollars), 1995–2004

for its first three years, and continued to be among the most richly funded of the Olin programs in law and economics. As was the case at Harvard and Yale, the place of law and economics in the context of the larger ideological environment at the University was never far from the Olin Foundation's mind, as a grant proposal record from 1996 shows. "Stanford is, overall, a less conservative institution than the University of Chicago. But first-rate people who understand and respect markets are a significant presence—at the law school, the economics department, the business school and the Hoover institution. The law school, for example, has thirty-eight faculty members, twelve of whom make the insights of the law and economics movement an important part of their teaching and scholarship."[46] The foundation saw supporting law and economics at Stanford as a way of putting its support behind the relatively conservative portion of the university's faculty.

The other reason for the foundation's strong support of law and economics at Stanford was its perceived impact on other institutions, through the production of teaching faculty. The foundation's staff reported in 1986 that "one mark of his [Mitch Polinsky's] success is that the number of students choosing to pursue both a JD and a PhD in economics has doubled since the early years of the program. Moreover, many of the students concentrating in law and economics are the most intellectually able and conscientious in their class, according to Prof. Polinsky. Graduates of the Olin program have gone on to teaching positions at Berkeley, Harvard, Yale and Michigan."[47] The foundation shifted its law and economics programming in the direction of elite institutions precisely because it thought that these institutions dictated the agendas and produced the faculty for all the other schools lower on the academic food chain. The foundation's 2002 retrospective analysis of its grant-making in law and economics recalled that "trustees saw support for Law and Economics as an opportunity both to advance cutting edge scholarly research as well as to gain a foothold for market economics and limited government in the law schools, whose faculties tended to be very much on the left. . . . The Foundation made these grants on the 'trickle down' theory, expecting that if all the best schools mounted programs in the field, others would feel the need to follow."[48] The foundation clearly believed that its Stanford grants, along with those at Chicago, Yale, and Harvard, had succeeded in influencing the rest of legal academia, and also in further entrenching law and economics in the law schools' curricula. In one of its last grant reports, the foundation staff reported that

> Stanford Law School is a place that takes law and economics very seriously, and our program has had the full support of the Dean, Kathleen Sullivan. Although she will be stepping aside shortly as Dean, she assures us in the attached letter (as well as in two visits to our offices) that Law and Economics is such a critical part of the Law School that any new dean is bound to be equally supportive. . . . [Polinsky and] Sullivan are determined to raise the funds required to continue the program indefinitely. They have pledged to match any grant we might now make, and to do so on a 2:1 basis for a gift in excess of $2.5 million. Assuming a new dean is appointed who is sympathetic to Law and Economics (and Stanford's president assures us this will be the case), staff would enthusiastically recommend continued support for this program.[49]

Law and economics, which had never been particularly controversial at Stanford, was now effectively institutionalized.

At Stanford, the Olin Foundation saw supporting law and economics as a way of enhancing the resources of an already distinguished group of law professors sympathetic to market economics. Berkeley, as a 1987 staff report noted, was another story.

> The law and economics program is not at this point very well developed. It consists primarily in the activities of two professors, [Robert] Cooter and [Daniel] Rubinfeld. Staff met with Rubinfeld, and was not overly impressed, but thought that he might be able to give some impetus to the law and economics movement at Berkeley. . . . From our contacts in the field, staff has discerned that Rubinfeld and Cooter are well regarded, but not considered among the top scholars. . . . Given these considerations, staff thinks a small grant would be warranted if strategically placed to encourage the growth of law and economics.[50]

Given that the foundation was not overly impressed with the personnel at Berkeley (a judgment that, in retrospect, was obviously unwarranted and, as with some of the foundation's other judgments in law and economics, not particularly well-informed), why did they choose to put one of their few Olin centers at Boalt Hall? The staff's evaluation of Berkeley's 1994 application makes its motivation clear.

Boalt Hall is one of the two best law schools on the West Coast (Stanford is the other), and is also one of the very few academic schools/departments at Berkeley with a conservative presence. Staff believes it is important to maintain an intellectual beachhead at Berkeley in the form of our Law and Economics Program. At Berkeley, as at other eminent law schools, most of the faculty lean to the left; our Law and Economics program is a strong counterweight, providing intellectual support for rational inquiry, free markets, and skepticism about what government can achieve. [Name redacted] notes that Berkeley faces a great deal of funding pressure because of the shortfall in local funds, so that the infusion of Olin money could make a big difference in keeping Law and Economics alive here.[51]

The foundation's motivation for supporting law and economics at Berkeley was not idiosyncratic, as staff evaluations of law and economics programs at Georgetown and Columbia at roughly the same time demonstrate.

Our grant to Georgetown represented an opportunity to strengthen and expand a small but sound program in Law and Economics at a law school which is in a unique position (on Capitol Hill) to draw upon the law and policy resources of Washington. . . . The last time this proposal came up for funding two years ago, staff had mixed feelings about it because the quality of one conference was questionable and the law school had recently disciplined a student for revealing that admissions office data showed minorities were admitted based on less stringent criteria than white students.[52] Since then, however, staff has gained confidence in the program, in part because of the praise with which [name redacted] speak of it. . . . Moreover, Georgetown is an important school, and it undoubtedly behooves us to "keep a candle lit in the darkness," by continuing to fund law and economics inside the school.[53]

Prof. [name redacted] . . . agrees that Columbia is very strong on corporate law, and has a great deal of respect for some of the Law and Economics professors like John Coffee and Mark Roe. But his impression was that the program may be suffering some directional drift and he advised keeping a close watch on it. He thought it was worth continued support, however, because it is important to have a foothold for free-market thinking at Columbia Law School.[54]

The foundation supported law and economics at Berkeley, Georgetown, and Columbia for the same reason that it plowed money into Harvard:

because it saw the program as an opportunity to shift the ideological balance in the university at large, as well as in the law school. At Berkeley, for example, the foundation judged that Cooter and Rubinfeld were well positioned to influence the future of the law school, noting that they had both served on major appointments committees, while Oliver Williamson was head of the Faculty Senate.[55] Four years later, the foundation was impressed with the inroads that law and economics had made at Berkeley, noting that the program "has assumed an increasingly prominent position at Boalt Hall, and there are currently ten economists on the law school faculty."[56] An outside evaluation of the program from one of the leaders of law and economics concluded that "the program there is quite strong and has in many ways . . . a Chicago flavor. . . . There is not a huge amount of top flight brilliance, but there is a lot of very solid competence with real intellectual energy. . . . The faculty has really turned itself around for the better in the last couple of years. Overall I think the program is behind the industry leaders, but certainly within the top ten."[57]

Did the increasing presence of law and economics at Berkeley, to take one example, have the influence on the ideological character of the law school that the Olin Foundation hoped it would? While Cooter was clearly on the libertarian-conservative side of the ideological fence, Rubinfeld was a Democrat and served as assistant attorney general for antitrust in the Clinton administration. Cooter believes that, despite the fact that many law and economics professors like Rubinfeld considered themselves Democrats or liberals in national politics, what really matters is their placement within the distribution of law school and university opinion.

> The faculty perceives Dan [Rubinfeld] as being conservative while knowing that he's a liberal Democrat, and it's because he's an economist. In the debates among the faculty, you may be in favor of affirmative action, you may be as in favor of affirmative action as the law allows, like Ian Ayres, but you're still an economist. You just can't accept the bull about regulation and control, the nirvana theory that social programs are going to work because they're well-intended. This stuff just doesn't fly. . . . If you have any judgment about how you evaluate data, whatever your prior beliefs, you're going to come out pro-market in a way that a lot of people in a society are not. I think law and economics is inherently pro-market, and less inherently conservative. Certainly the distribution of sentiment in the ALEA [American Law and Economics Association] is shifted to the right, relative to American law schools, probably relative to the American public.

Law professors with economics training also differ from other law professors where decision-making on internal university matters is concerned.

On our faculty, and on many faculties, the strongest leftists are also the strongest proponents of what I call "other values." By other values I mean not the traditional values by which the quantity and quality of scholarship is to be evaluated. . . . For example, if you apply those standards, it's going to be hard to achieve your affirmative action goals. So as a consequence, the economists are all committed to those traditional research values. . . . We have a common framework, and that framework is antagonistic to the other values approach to choosing faculty members. That's one of the reasons that a person who is a liberal Democrat but an economist will be perceived as a conservative by the rest of the faculty.[58]

While relatively few of the hires that Berkeley has made in law and economics would be considered conservatives, what really matters in a university are faculty preferences on issues internal to the university.[59] So while law and economics *has* lost the ideological fervor that it once had, at places like Berkeley the law and economics liberals are to the right of the rest of the faculty. While that may not be exactly what the Olin Foundation thought it was getting, their support for law and economics probably has had the effect of shifting the ideological dynamics in elite law schools.

The kind of law and economics that was dominant at Harvard, and that increasingly characterized the Olin programs at other universities, differed significantly from what was being taught at Chicago and George Mason. While it is perhaps too simple a formulation, Chicago-style law and economics was not just more libertarian than what evolved at Harvard, it was more of a "lawyer's" version of the field, as opposed to the more economist-dominated Harvard variant.[60] A 1990 report to the Olin Foundation from a major figure in the field made it clear that law and economics had changed dramatically since the foundation first committed to it.

When the field started getting underway in the late 1960s and early 1970s, its leading practitioners painted with broad and bold strokes. . . . The more recent developments in the area have been somewhat different. There are fewer manifestos in support of the discipline, and fewer wholesale attacks on its soundness and operation. It is no longer fighting for a place within the curriculum, but has secured powerful beachheads in multiple areas: all the common law subjects (property, contracts and torts), procedure litigation and settlement, corporate law, bankruptcy and secured transactions, criminal law. Similarly, the techniques of analysis have changed. . . . While the overall level of economic sophistication on faculties has grown, there is probably a greater gap between the cutting edge of research on the one hand and the knowledge of the ordinary law professor on the other. The faculty then [*sic*] tends to go into the area is often armed with both a law degree and a PhD in economics. In consequence of the level of formality and abstraction, there are conspicuous barriers between what is done and understood by law and economics types of the one hand, and the rest of the legal academic world on the other hand.[61]

Fifteen years later, these trends have only increased, to the point where most newly minted law and economics practitioners now have dual degrees. While the field is still certainly to the right of the rest of legal academia on economic matters, this is because its ideological distribution increasingly resembles that of the discipline of economics, where even liberal Democrats are substantially more sympathetic to market arrangements than most of their academic colleagues. In short, the number of true believers has declined as the field has become more professionalized. Given that law and economics' impact has occurred as the field has become more ideologically mainstream, did patrons like the Olin Foundation really get what they were looking for?

To answer this question, we need a relatively compact understanding of what the patrons of law and economics programs wanted, as compared to the preferences of the academics who were actually running them. At least in the case of the Olin Foundation, the motivations were fairly clear. First and foremost, the foundation believed that the state of legal education was in grave danger, which was far from a trivial concern for an organization whose board included partners in the whitest of white-shoe law firms. By supporting law and economics, the foundation hoped to establish a "foothold" in the law schools for conservatives, and to provide a "counterbalance" against liberals. Second, law and economics was just one part of conservative foundation efforts on university campuses. Law and economics was a way to get conservative-leaning faculty inside the university, where they could affect campus debate and governance, at a time when the barriers to other forms of legal conservatism were much more considerable. Third, the foundation hoped that, through its grants to students and its programming in the law schools, the Olin programs would alter the socialization of the next generation of lawyers, making them less sympathetic to government management of the economy and more able to press the case for the free market. Fourth, the foundation believed that law and economics could have a salutary influence on law itself, raising doubts about the efficacy of regulation and providing intellectual support for a legal system more supportive of free markets.

The interests of law and economics professors, by contrast, have only a partial overlap with those of their patrons. While a number of the law and economics professors hired in the 1980s and 1990s were avid supporters of free markets, many were not, and this trend only accelerated as the field became more mainstream. For the professors who staffed them—even those who were more conservative—the most prominent motivation for building the Olin Centers was purely academic. Professors doing work in law and economics found the subject stimulating and important for future lawyers to understand, wanted to build a research infrastructure for themselves, and hoped to produce high-quality research. Only a few university administrators, such as Harvard's Dean Clark, seem to have shared the Olin Foundation's ambition to use law and economics to reshape the politics of their institutions, but by the 1990s most recognized that supporting law and economics was necessary in order to keep up with the market leaders. In short, the Olin Foundation was more concerned with the indirect effects of law and economics—on the law school, the university, and society and government—while the professors were interested in their direct outputs, such as facilitating scholarly production and debate, and increasing the prestige of their field. The relationship between the Olin Foundation and its law and economics programs was, in short, a marriage of convenience, albeit one that brought substantial benefits to both sides.

A Home at Last: The George Mason University School of Law

Over the last thirty years, conservative patrons interested in reshaping higher education have focused on gaining a presence in elite institutions by supporting student organizations, such as the Federalist Society and undergraduate conservative newspapers, and by building research programs around conservative professors. This focus on elite schools was driven by the belief—especially strong at the Olin Foundation—that intellectual credibility and distinction are produced by only a handful of institutions. This explains the foundation's repeated concern that it create a "foothold" or "beachhead" and "keep a candle lit in the darkness" at top-ranked schools. Henry Manne's project of building George Mason University School of Law (GMUSL) represented a very different approach to influencing the legal academy—building an alternative institution from the bottom up rather than influencing the legal academy from the top down. While the Olin programs represented a "Fabian" strategy of slowly burrowing into mainstream institutions, GMUSL followed a "Gramscian" approach of creating a parallel institution where more libertarian professors could hone their ideas without the compromises associated with elite institutions. The consequence of the Fabian strategy of the Olin Foundation was that, as the previous two sections showed, law and economics came to adapt to the norms of elite institutions, becoming more technically sophisticated, closer to mainstream economics, less accessible to lawyers, and more ideologically heterogeneous. Starting from scratch at GMUSL, Manne was able to build an institution infused with a "Chicago" flavor—less methodologically formal, more oriented to shaping doctrine and public policy, and more openly libertarian. A close examination of Manne's experiment in Northern Virginia, therefore, provides a useful study of the challenges and opportunities associated with one important approach to legal and educational change.

By the mid-1980s, Manne's opportunity for institution-building at Emory was finished. As Manne puts it, "I was sort of coasting." It was then that Manne received a phone call from the economist Gordon Tullock, who had, along with James Buchanan, built a public-choice-oriented economics department at George Mason University, the new state university in Northern Virginia. The University, led by its president, George Johnson, had acquired a low-status law school based in Washington, D.C., and was considering what to do with it. Steve Eagle, an associate dean under Manne, recalls that "the University president at the time was interested in putting the University on the map. I'm not sure he was interested in putting it on any particular continent. He wanted the law school to make a splash. If he could have gotten someone in a totally different field than law and economics, he would have done that. As it was, George Johnson spoke with Jim Buchanan and Gordon Tullock, and both of them told [him] that Henry was a hot property." The perception that Manne was a successful organizational entrepreneur and had an ambitious plan already developed for legal education made him immensely attractive to Johnson. Initially, Manne was uninterested.

> I said, "Gordon, . . . one thing I would never do was go into an existing law school, because I couldn't stand it. They'd run me out on a rail in a year anyways." Gordon said, "Well, come up to talk to George and tell him about your ideas on legal education anyways." This was 1985. As a favor to Buchanan and Tullock I agreed to go up and talk to Johnson. They were already there and they were trying to help Johnson. They had a hidden agenda; they were going to find conservatives for him. He didn't mind it, because he had heavy financial support from Republican interests in Northern Virginia. At any rate, he was very persuasive, and, given my condition, I was susceptible too. I gave him the program that I would do. It was basically the Rochester program limited to Law and Economics, which at this point really looks good. It's the big hot field in law, but no one had ever thought about building a law school around it. That's what I told him I wanted to do, but that I couldn't do it with the faculty he had there.

Manne quickly recognized that the weakness of the existing law school, and Johnson's desire for an immediate jolt to the University's reputation gave him an opportunity that most academic entrepreneurs can only dream of: liquidating the law school's existing commitments and starting anew. The previous dean of the school told the faculty, "I want you to get out and practice law. You get no extra money from me for writing law review articles." Just the opposite of what any school would be doing. That played beautifully into my hands, because what George was telling me, that he'd make some money available to me to buy out faculty, really was beginning to make sense. . . . I didn't tell anyone, but I planned to get rid of every nontenured professor. . . . George convinced me that I could create a new kind of law school there, even though there was an existing faculty. . . . I started thinking about it. . . . It became attractive as soon as I saw that there was a chance of doing what I wanted to do at Rochester.

In building a new law school, Manne had some important advantages. First and foremost was the LEC. "No one had ever heard of George Mason Law School, but lots of people had heard of Henry Manne's Law and Economics Center."[62] The LEC ensured that the re-formed school would begin with a widely recognized research program, along with the still vibrant program for federal judges. Second, the weakness of the inherited law school allowed Manne to act quickly, before opposition to his plans could organize. Eschewing the usual advice given new deans to slowly build the faculty's trust, Manne decided to conduct a bloodbath. He immediately fired every nontenured faculty member, offered buyouts to others, and gave a few of the survivors the opportunity to receive advanced degrees in economics. Manne recalls that George Johnson instructed him to " 'act fast, do anything you want to do now, because by next April they'll be organized.' I took his advice . . . and within two weeks I had announced these departures, and, exactly as he said, by April the cabal had started, but it was too late, because there weren't enough of them left." Acting quickly also had the advantage of freeing up resources to aggressively add new professors, many of whom he knew through the Economics Institute for Law Professors.

> Because of my familiarity with law professors who had been through the law institute, I knew a bunch of guys who stayed in touch with me, because they had really glommed on to the field. And they were at places where they weren't happy. . . . So I got Larry Ribstein, who was at Mercer, doing great corporate work which they didn't appreciate. [Michael] Krauss was at McGill doing tort law and economics, and being very underappreciated. I got Frank Buckley, who was out in western Canada, who had already spent some time at Chicago, and an economist who had been through our program, Bill Bishop. . . . Then I hired our former Olin Fellows: Henry Butler, Steve Crafton, and later Lloyd Cohen and . . . Bruce Johnsen. Then I hired a couple of economists, got a name from Harold Demsetz, Bruce Kobyashi. He came that year. At that point we had more PhD's in economics on the George Mason law school than any other law school in the country.

On top of selecting faculty who accepted his vision, Manne also made clear that GMUSL would not be a democracy. "I had an important and identical discussion with all of them. . . . We're going to be a law and economics law school. We're going to have specialized tracks. . . . I'm going to run it. We're going to have faculty meetings when and if necessary, but this is not going to be a faculty-run operation. In blood every one of them signed on. It's what they wanted, what any good academic wants, for an administrator to run the thing and let them do what they're interested in." The availability of underplaced law and economics faculty, Manne's networks, and the reputation of the LEC allowed him to rapidly build a sympathetic faculty and avoid effective internal challenges to his plans.

Manne's plan for the law school closely followed his earlier design at Rochester: specialization, a pervasive role for law and economics, and the introduction of required classes in quantitative methods.[63] The law school at GMU, in short, would not look like any other law school in America. These innovations, however, led to problems with the school's application for admission to the Association of American Law Schools.[64]

The visiting committee of the AALS that began to scrutinize the school in 1989 was impressed with the school's rapid progress in its first two years, but had two concerns: whether the school had the resources to support its track system and the racial and gender balance of the faculty. The committee was especially concerned that "the dearth of minority and women candidates interested in pursuing law and economics might preclude an effective hiring process geared towards diversifying the faculty at George Mason."[65] When interviewed by the committee, Manne argued that he had aggressively sought out women and racial minorities, but that his insistence on a law and economics faculty limited the pool he could draw from. At this point a member of the AALS committee asked whether, if that was the case, there was something flawed about the overall conception of the school. "Is having a racially and gender diverse faculty as great a priority at George Mason as hiring a tax professor? Dean Manne responded that there are trade-offs implicit in any decision. While the school would continue to work hard to diversify the faculty, that issue was simply different from the need to teach a given subject matter."[66] Other members of the committee questioned whether the school's effort to increase the academic credentials of its students was consistent with substantial minority representation on the student body. In the end, this line of questioning fizzled out when supporters of GMU School of Law questioned where an affirmative action standard could be found in AALS rules.

The most daunting obstacle in building a first-rate law school at GMU was attracting resources for ambitious institution-building in a new university without a significant endowment, a deep pool of alumni, or an impressive university "brand name." This challenge hampered the law school's growth, damaged its early esprit de corps, and contributed to Manne's departure from the school's deanship. Despite George Johnson's commitments to the law school, these financial concerns emerged early on, as can be seen in a 1987 letter from Manne to the president of the Earhart Foundation.

> As I began to tell you at the AEI dinner, being dean at the George Mason University School of Law has been an exciting challenge. The pace has been quite hectic, but we have accomplished minor miracles. Quite frankly, however, the University, for all its support, has not been able to keep up with us. . . . In spite of their encouragement, the University administrators did not expect us to accomplish so much in so short a time. Consequently next year's budget does not provide the support services necessary for our new faculty to work to their full potential. . . . I am especially concerned that we not disappoint the new faculty, since their first reaction to the School will effectively determine our academic reputation with new recruits for years to come.[67]

Manne also faced challenges in obtaining corporate support for GMUSL. In a letter to one of his supporters, Manne complained, "As you undoubtedly know, many corporations, perhaps because of obsessive concern with 'competitiveness,' are substantially reducing or omitting contributions to educational institutions. . . . This is all particularly frustrating because I have finally reached the point where I can greatly leverage the influence of my programs."[68]

While financing was always a problem at GMUSL, Manne had some very important compensating assets. GMUSL was able to draw upon the local, Washington-based network of conservative-libertarian lawyers and jurists, in particular Robert Bork and Douglas Ginsburg, who quickly joined GMUSL's faculty. Jeffrey Parker, one of the earliest members of the faculty, recalls that Ginsburg "was extremely important, and it was all due to his long acquaintanceship with Henry. . . . There was a core of these really high-powered people who held the place in the zone of legitimacy while it was building itself out. . . . Doug had taught at Harvard, Bork had taught at Yale, these were people who could teach any place. But because of their relationship with Henry, and because of their intellectual interest in law and economics, they were here." Ginsburg, now the chief judge of the D.C. Circuit Court of Appeals has, in fact, taught at least one seminar a year since 1988. Manne recalls of Ginsburg that "while still at Harvard he attended the Economics Institute for Law Professors and became totally convinced (if he was not already) of the importance of law and economics. I knew him to be extremely bright, and I wanted him associated with the school as much as anything in order to help me out. Also I knew he would be a superb teacher. I don't think that any really important steps were taken without being vetted with Doug."

Other connections to the conservative movement have helped GMUSL, especially its support from the University's increasingly conservative board of trustees. Starting with the administration of Governor George Allen in 1994 and continuing into that of Governor James Gilmore, such conservative movement fixtures as William Kristol, Ed Feulner, and James Miller were chosen for the board, and Ed Meese was appointed the University's rector. These men were very familiar with law and economics and sensitive to the asset that a libertarian-tinged law school in the D.C.-area would represent for the conservative movement. The importance that the conservative movement attributed to GMUSL can also be seen in a 1993 grant report from the Olin Foundation, which had sharply reevaluated its judgment of Manne.

> Henry Manne has accomplished a great deal for the discipline of law and economics. Over forty percent of sitting federal judges have now attended one of his institutes, and the reliance on economic criteria to help make sense of legal problems is steadily winning acceptance in the courts after establishing a foothold in the law schools. George Mason is a law school with a growing reputation, and its serious commitment to law and economics gives it something unique to offer students. Staff believes that continued support for the Law and Economics Center at George Mason is warranted by these accomplishments. Furthermore, it is important to remember that Bill Clinton's election means that conservatives can no longer count on the changing composition of the federal judiciary to make judges concerned with the economic implications of their decisions. For twelve years the Reagan and Bush appointments to the federal bench created a judiciary that was steadily more inclined to consider market processes and economic effects in the decision-making. With Bill Clinton having the next three years to appoint liberals to the court, it is especially important that every sitting judge who is even slightly receptive to the law and economics approach be given every chance to become familiar with it.[69]

For a brief period in the late 1990s, the law school had fallen out of the *U.S. News* top 50 law schools, a list that is highly sensitive to faculty resources. William Kristol recalls that, recognizing the importance of the law school to the conservative movement, "under Meese's leadership, and I supported him, . . . we insisted on a reallocation of resources toward the law school. At the margin we wanted greater effort to go to the law school. It did happen, and subsequently the dean of the law school told me that it was useful. . . . This got them back onto the Top 50." While modest budget reallocations such as this may seem like a small matter, they are the sort of support at the margin that can make the difference between successful and unsuccessful organizational entrepreneurship. To the conservatives on the GMU Board of Visitors and the staff of the Olin Foundation, support for GMUSL was a way to shape the development of the law, even in periods like the late 1990s when their power over the courts was waning.

Henry Manne's original strategy for GMUSL was to take advantage of the path dependence of American legal education, which he thought was wasteful and ill suited to the character of contemporary legal practice. With a new curriculum made possible by of the lack of built-in constituencies for the status quo, Manne believed that GMUSL could attract high-quality students and place them with top firms. While GMU has been able to attract increasingly strong students over time, it does not appear that the school's pedagogy has given it the overwhelming competitive advantage Manne anticipated.

Instead, the market failure that GMU has exploited most successfully has been on the research side of legal education. Theorists since Becker have modeled discrimination as a "taste," believing that in a competitive market discriminators have to pay a price for satisfying this taste in the form of higher labor costs and consequently lower profits.[70] Conversely, firms that do not discriminate can take advantage of their rivals' taste for discrimination, by hiring the better quality (and cheaper) labor that they have spurned. Conservatives, including those at GMUSL, have long believed that conservatives are discriminated against in the academy. To the degree that this is true and entrance to the market is not artificially suppressed, institutions that do not discriminate on the basis of ideology should have a substantial competitive advantage.

What was bad for conservatives as a general matter, therefore, was good for GMUSL, allowing it to move up the ranking by exploiting a considerable market failure. Steve Eagle argues that

> people who were interested in law and economics and people who might have had a libertarian perspective on the world that was congenial to the rest of the faculty were typically not wanted elsewhere. So Mason was able to hire very high caliber people in its niche while its reputation was still comparatively tentative. We would never have been able to hire people of comparable quality who were seen as more mainstream by some, because they would have gravitated to law schools that were more established. So from a quality point of view we were able to get the cream of the crop in law and economics, whereas we would have been seen as an outlier and a new unproven school among the senior people we would have liked to have gotten in more established places.

The Becker theory of discrimination suggests that discrimination is not a stable competitive equilibrium, because the nondiscriminator will be able to take away market share from the discriminator. In the GMUSL case, this means that the law school's competitive advantage depends upon the continuing presence of ideological discrimination. As Daniel Polsby, the current dean of GMUSL, puts it, "Labor markets are sticky, and there are good reasons for that. We worry every day that what we do is going to get competed away. It's all public. There are no secrets, this is a public institution, everything we do is public unless it's in the bathroom. They know as much about it as we do. The problem is not a knowledge problem, it's an action problem. It is, 'Can you get your faculty to do what we can get our faculty to do in crucial personnel decisions?' The answer is usually no." It is not quite accurate to say that GMUSL is parasitic on discrimination against fellow legal conservatives. Most of the leaders of the school believe that the greatest intensity of discrimination in the market occurs at the initial hiring stage, when the objective merit of candidates is difficult to determine. GMUSL seeks to push a number of libertarian conservatives past this initial hiring stage, keeping these young lawyers in the academic pool until they are able to prove their objective merit. Polsby claims that

> what we want to do is to prepare people to overwhelm the prejudices and foolishness of the food chain. In the last analysis, it will be hard for schools further up in the food chain to prefer a plainly worse-qualified over a plainly better-qualified person. Somebody is out there with thirteen articles and one hundred citations, you know he or she is dominating somebody with three articles and twenty-nine citations. We are proponents of moneyball here, and we have a pretty simple predictive model of productivity here, and it very rarely fails us, and anybody can use it. Candidly, we're just smarter about these sorts of things. . . . We're not burdened by intolerance for people who have libertarian and conservative leanings, and we're not going to discriminate against them. It may be the case that we would discriminate against people on the left, with socialist inclination, but of equal talent, but that becomes very theoretical because our dear friends in the food chain snap those people up.

Given that GMUSL looks for scholars who have been undervalued in the academic marketplace, faculty attrition is built into the GMU model. Rather than focusing on retaining faculty, which is financially beyond GMU's means, the school supports the mobility aspirations of its faculty, operating as the minor league for conservative and libertarian law professors. According to Polsby, "We don't work on retention, we work on the opposite. Any time we can move somebody up the food chain, it adds credibility to the story we're telling the market about why you should come here rather than to our competitor to start your career. We've got now to a point where there's enough evidence for the proposition that skeptical people are entitled to believe it. . . . I don't want to hire anyone here who doesn't want to become the next Sterling Professor of Law at Yale." Another GMUSL professor makes a similar point, observing,

"What we really specialize in, in recent years, is people who aren't totally ripe for the market generally, and they come here two, three, four, five years and get seasoned and get a research agenda. We get a lot of those people here, and then they move on."[71] GMUSL seeks, quite openly, to perform a critical service to the larger conservative movement by increasing the market value of ideologically sympathetic young law professors. GMUSL's leaders believe that providing this public good to the conservative movement is wholly consistent with their institutional self-interest.

From the point of view of the larger conservative movement, how successful has GMUSL been? Unlike the Olin programs at elite law schools, GMU has not lost its ideological distinctiveness as it has grown in prestige. In addition, while retaining its libertarian character GMU has, by a number of different measures, improved more than any other law school in the last quarter-century. As Daniel Polsby suggests, "As a rule, the rank of schools as measured by the market test doesn't change. They are really stable. Our rank has changed; we are able to attract stronger faculty, and in comparison tests for student's picking law schools, there's movement. Interestingly, there's very little movement in the reputation numbers that *U.S. News* is using since the early 1990s. Those numbers we've moved a little bit in a favorable direction, but very little." GMUSL ranks considerably higher on objective measures of research output and student quality than in reputational surveys, reflecting the stickiness of academic distinction. For instance, three recent surveys of faculty quality, citations and scholarly productivity ranked it at number 22, number 23, and number 27 in the country,[72] while subjective surveys of faculty quality ranked GMU slightly lower, but not considerably.[73] Of particular interest, no school in the country showed as great a disparity between objective measures of faculty quality and *U.S. News* rankings as GMU.[74] This suggests that either GMUSL's connection to its parent university, or its libertarian reputation, has had a significant drag on its reputation in the legal academy. There is also insufficient evidence to conclude that GMU has been able to operate as a successful minor league for elite law schools. While GMU faculty have been hired by Vanderbilt, George Washington, Illinois, and William and Mary, the school has not yet made a dent in the law schools that bestow academic distinction. GMUSL's Todd Zywicki has visited at Georgetown, David Bernstein at Michigan, and Eugene Kontorovich at Chicago and Northwestern, but only Kontorovich has yet moved on to one of these elite law schools.[75]

This points to the limitations of GMUSL's original gamble. Because of the university's nonexistent national reputation, its administrators were willing to give Manne substantial leeway to create a law and economics law school with a clearly libertarian bent. The institutional weakness that facilitated innovation also limited the school's ability to compete in law school rankings. That said, there is evidence that the school has considerably improved the quality of its students. The most recent rankings of student quality put it at number 31, one spot above the older and better-endowed law school at Emory that Manne left twenty years ago.[76] This is an impressive achievement, but GMUSL still does not attract students who can compete for positions in top law firms, clerkships, or the legal academy.[77] GMUSL may influence America's legal culture in the next decade through the professional mobility of its young conservative law professors, but there are few indications that it will do so any time soon through its students.

Conclusion

Simply measured in terms of the penetration of its adherents in the legal academy, law and economics is the most successful intellectual movement in the law of the past thirty years, having rapidly moved from insurgency to hegemony. The commanding place of law and economics in the modern legal academy makes it tempting to conclude that this outcome was inevitable. While there were certainly structural forces that put the wind at the movement's back, there can be little question that organizational entrepreneurship and patronage played a critical role in allowing the law and economics movement to take advantage of the opportunity provided by these larger forces.

The law and economics movement went through a series of reasonably distinct stages on the way to its current status in the American legal academy, and at each stage patronage and entrepreneurial activity played important roles. In the beginning, law and economics (with the partial exception of its application to antitrust) was so far out of the legal academic mainstream as to be reasonably characterized as "off the wall." Limited almost exclusively to law professors who saw in the idea a powerful device for criticizing government intervention in the economy, the idea needed an institutional home to protect it until conditions changed. Without the nurturance of law and economics at Chicago Law School, therefore, the ground would not have been prepared for its rapid diffusion when environmental conditions changed.

Moving law and economics' status from "off the wall" to "controversial but respectable" required a combination of celebrity and organizational entrepreneurship. On the one hand, Richard Posner's sterling establishment credentials and powerful intellectual gifts meant that he could not be ignored. No matter how hard Posner's critics insisted that his arguments were off the wall, the fact that prestigious liberal legal academics were arguing with him suggested the opposite. In that sense, Posner played the classic role of the intellectual entrepreneur, demonstrating that the status quo is open to challenge and that an alternative is available.

Manne's organizational entrepreneurship worked hand in hand with Posner's intellectual entrepreneurship and celebrity in moving law and economics out of the legal academic periphery. A good deal of the resistance to law and economics came from two sources: unfamiliarity and ideological stigma. Manne's programs for law professors overcame unfamiliarity by equipping academics with the basic concepts of economics, eliminating the mystery associated with unfamiliar concepts. Those programs eroded the field's ideological stigma by creating personal bonds between the legal academy's mainstream and law and economics, and by convincing participants that economics was an ideologically neutral set of tools. Manne's programs for federal judges also helped erase law and economics' stigma, since if judges—the symbol of legal professional respectability—took the ideas seriously, they could not be crazy and irresponsible.

This account suggests the limitations of thinking about intellectual change through the metaphor of the "marketplace of ideas." In any market there are some things that participants simply will not buy and sell because they are considered immoral or inappropriate for exchange. Through most of the 1960s, for example, it could barely be said that law and economics was in the marketplace at all because the market's norm-setters refused to take it seriously. This points has two implications. First, the substance of an idea matters in the early development of an intellectual movement, but mainly through its ability to generate intense commitment from a small cadre of people willing to bear the disapprobation of the majority. Second, the early breakthrough of an idea into widespread discussion is more a function of its respectability than its truth content. Only after an idea has been treated as appropriate for discussion are its claims welcomed into the marketplace of ideas and its ideas discussed on the merits. This is a political and sociological process, rather than the playing out of the scientific method.

By the time this chapter opened in the early 1980s, law and economics had entered the marketplace of ideas but was still a distinctly niche player. The field's move out of this niche depended on a combination of environmental and entrepreneurial forces. Changes in the politics of the federal courts and regulatory agencies, the increasing prestige of market solutions, and the transformation of corporate law all increased the demand for law and economics. By the mid-1980s a "tipping point" was reached in which the prestige and relative position of elite law schools—the arbiters of distinction for legal education as a whole—became associated with the presence of a substantial law and economics program. Having become so associated, the law and economics trend filtered down to those lower in the legal education pecking order.

While these factors were certainly important in the rise of law and economics, the speed and depth of its absorption into legal education required agents capable of turning these opportunities into outcomes. Law and economics was given substantial financial support from corporations and foundations, in a way that no other conservative legal movement was. This was not because movement patrons, particularly foundations, were especially enthusiastic about law and economics, but because it seemed to have substantial momentum as well as the potential to be useful to the broader movement. Especially in elite legal education, these patrons provided strategic coordination and leadership as well as funding. Law and economics also attracted a handful of extremely able and enthusiastic organizational entrepreneurs. These entrepreneurs chose to invest their time in producing human capital in the form of their students, social capital in the networks that were a by-product of their intellectual activity, and cultural capital through their success in building a legitimate, respected place for conservatives in elite institutions. These entrepreneurs and their conservative patrons worked hand in hand, despite the fact that their goals were, in important ways, quite different.

In the process of moving law and economics from the periphery to the core of legal academia, however, the movement changed in important ways. The stigma attached to the idea in its early days ensured that its attraction was limited to legal scholars whose ideological commitments made them willing to bear a high degree of alienation. It was this very ideological commitment that attracted patrons like the Olin Foundation to the movement in the first place. As the stigma on law and economics disappeared and it moved to a position of considerable distinction in legal academia, its ideological base expanded accordingly. The movement took on the ideological and methodological coloration of its parent discipline of economics, as well as absorbing many of the qualities required for respectability in elite institutions. The law and economics that has attained such an impressive status in top law schools is not, in short, the aggressively free-market faith of the movement's early days. It might even be appropriate to say that law and economics is no longer a movement at all, but a discipline. Given the ideological distribution of the overall legal professorate, injecting that discipline into the law schools was a significant victory for conservative patrons like the Olin Foundation, but it is a victory that has come at a cost in ideological purity.

The GMU law school represents an illuminating alternative to the strategy of working through existing distinguished law schools. By avoiding the compromises—both methodological and ideological—that came with established institutions, Henry Manne was able to build a law school with a durable libertarian character. The ideological coloration of the school allowed it to actively seek to advance the interests of the larger conservative-libertarian movement, by providing an institutional space in which scholars out of the legal academic mainstream can develop a scholarly reputation and move on to higher-status institutions. The question going forward is whether GMUSL's place in the intensely status-conscious structure of legal academia will permit it to effectively serve its ambitious goals. In short, while the Olin programs' place in the legal academic establishment may have limited its ideological coherence, GMUSL's ideological coherence may limit its impact on the legal academic establishment.

7

Conservative Public Interest Law II: Lessons Learned

THE FIRST GENERATION of conservative public interest lawyers was hobbled by its failure to adapt to a transformed legal and political system, one in which the locus of political power had become firmly nationalized, and where agenda control, policy-specific knowledge, media savvy, appeals to idealism, and elite networks rivaled grassroots organization and business power. These early conservative lawyers also failed to learn from their liberal legal adversaries, instead replicating strategies that had been effective in other areas but were poorly adapted to the very different terrain of the law. As a consequence, the conservative public interest law movement failed in these years, with a few exceptions, to attract skilled, idealistic, creative young lawyers. Its reactive strategy made it difficult to set the political and legal agenda.

In contrast, it is impossible to deny the success of the second generation of conservative public interest law firms. Since their founding in 1991 and 1989, respectively, both the Institute for Justice and the Center for Individual Rights have established impressive track records of placing significant cases before the Supreme Court. IJ has successfully defended Ohio's school voucher plan before the Supreme Court (in *Simmons-Harris v. Zelman*) and challenged New York's ban on interstate shipment of wine (in *Swedenburg v. Kelly*). In spite of losing the argument before the Supreme Court in *Kelo v. New London*, IJ has effectively used the case to raise the salience of the issue and put eminent domain restrictions on the legislative agenda in statehouses across the country. CIR reached the Supreme Court with major, precedent-setting cases even earlier. CIR's challenges to the constitutionality of affirmative action in university admissions in *Gratz v. Bollinger* and *Grutter v. Bollinger* succeeded in limiting the use of preferences in undergraduate admissions, and came within one vote of eliminating them in law schools. Just as important were CIR's challenges to restrictions on academic speech and its victories in *Rosenberger v. Rector and Visitors of the University of Virginia*, a landmark religious liberty case, *Reno v. Bossier Parish School District*, which restricted the use of race in local redistricting, and *United States v. Morrison*, where CIR successfully argued that provisions of the Violence Against Women Act exceeded Congress's power under the commerce clause. Despite the millions of dollars that conservative patrons invested in first-generation firms, none of them came close to this record of winning important, precedent-setting cases.

While changes in the composition of the federal courts were certainly important in explaining this record of success, just as critical were the lessons that conservative organizational entrepreneurs drew from the failure of first-generation firms, and from the success of their liberal counterparts. The second-generation firms had clearer, more forthrightly libertarian principles than their first-generation predecessors. These principles gave CIR and IJ distance from traditional conservative interests like business and a willingness to draw on the rhetoric, strategies, legal precedents, and belief in an affirmative role for the courts created by legal liberals. In addition, CIR and IJ were led by authentic members of a conservative "new class": products of a new constellation of conservative institutions committed to a set of ideological principles rather than corporate interests. The changing profile of conservative public interest law's leaders went hand in hand with the growth of the Federalist Society and the rising number of conservatives in the legal academy. Conservatives were increasingly led not by representatives of the movement's core constituencies, but by those with the cultural, social, and human capital essential to the peculiarities of legal politics. This shift became possible as a result of the increasing prominence and sophistication of conservative foundations. The movement's patrons had been burned by the failure of the first-generation firms but were primed for alternatives by the Horowitz Report and by Chip Mellor's Center for Applied Jurisprudence project. When firms like IJ and CIR emerged that reflected what the movement had learned from its first, dispiriting fifteen years, foundation patrons were ready and willing to give them long-term support.

The second-generation firms were guided by a shared set of lessons about the conditions for effective legal change, in particular the importance of agenda control. Where the previous generation of conservatives had insisted on "judicial restraint," CIR and IJ had learned that conservative interests could only be protected by actively using courts to establish new or reinvigorate old rights, rather than simply standing in the way of the activism of the Left. Having established distance from business and shifted their strategy to initiating action in the courts, CIR and IJ had the freedom to choose an eclectic group of clients: small businessmen, local property-owners, consumers, students, professors, and racial minorities. This new, more strategic approach to client selection allowed CIR and IJ to pick cases with the potential to alter the nation's constitutional debate, transform the reputation of the conservative movement, and place significant opportunities for legal change before the courts.

Despite their substantial strategic similarity, CIR and IJ have widely divergent approaches to personnel, case selection, ground-level legal tactics, organizational ethos and presentation, and finances. Considered one by one, these differences may seem minor. Yet together, they constitute deep differences in organizational culture, which explain CIR and IJ's case selection, their relationship with the larger conservative movement, their willingness to invest in recruitment and training, and their capacity to sustain themselves over the long term.

Despite their impressive success, conservative public interest law firms face substantial constraints in their ability to reshape the law and American legal culture. Some of these constraints are rooted in the structure of American politics and society, while others are internal to the conservative movement itself. In particular, conservative public interest law continues to be dependent on the progress of the larger conservative program to transform the legal profession. Until conservatives, operating through organizations like the Federalist Society, have succeeded in fully integrating themselves into the legal profession—especially the nation's law schools—and integrated public interest practice more fully into their professional lives, the success of conservative public interest law firms will be limited.

Creating the Center for Individual Rights

Opening its doors in 1989, the Center for Individual Rights was the first conservative public interest law firm to emerge from the reevaluation of the field that began with Michael Horowitz's report a decade earlier. CIR's founders, Michael Greve and Michael McDonald, had worked in first-generation conservative law firms, and this experience, along with their close study of the liberals' legal strategies, shaped the design of CIR. The founding of CIR was not driven by a sudden change in the opportunity structure. Rather, a window of opportunity had been open for more than a decade, as the judiciary became more conservative, conservative lawyers populated the Justice Department, and the movement's organizational density increased. The creation of CIR is best understood as an "inside story," driven primarily by learning within the movement rather than stimuli in the political environment.

CIR's founders had been important players in the evolution of the conservative legal movement. Before coming to Washington, Greve received a PhD in political science at Cornell University, where he studied under Professor Jeremy Rabkin, an aggressive, take-no-prisoners conservative and a critic of the judiciary's role in the political process. Rabkin argued that special interest groups and the judiciary had cooperated to expand the meaning and force of statutes, achieving political outcomes that they no longer had the electoral power to legislate. Legal liberalism, Rabkin argued, had corrupted constitutional norms while claiming high constitutional principle.[1] Greve and Rabkin (who was a founding member of CIR's board of directors) believed that the high moral tone taken by special interests on the left was simply a cover for undemocratic, illiberal transfers of resources conducted through constitutionally illegitimate means. This overriding sense of liberal hypocrisy became powerfully stamped on CIR's organizational culture and communications style, and it gave the firm an edgy quality altogether lacking in most first-generation firms.

While much of CIR's edgy organizational style drew on Greve's and Rabkin's critiques of legal liberalism, its legal strategy drew primarily on McDonald's experience at the Washington Legal Foundation and its spin-off, the American Legal Foundation. For McDonald, WLF was a model for CIR's founders of how such a firm should *not* be run. McDonald recalls that, in his experience there,

> one day you'd be working on death penalty briefs, the next you'd be working on environmental law, the day after you'd be working on some qui tam action, the day after that you'd be working on separation of powers. There was no rhyme or reason. A lot of it was amicus work; a lot of it was driven by the perpetual need for fund-raising. . . . A lot of these organizations felt they had to develop large in-house staff, which is what elevated the fund-raising to such a key element. . . . They'd have three or four attorneys and four people doing fund-raising, so you'd have to have a million or two million just to run the place. You didn't have a lot of money left over to do actual litigation.

The lost opportunities were not more than theoretical, as the case of CIR's first client demonstrated.

> When I was at ALF . . . Tom Lamprecht came knocking on my door. He had been denied a radio license because—I kid you not—he was a man, and spent his life savings hiring a D.C. regulatory firm to litigate in front of the FCC. The case was great from every conceivable point of view—and it was a winner. But I was told we didn't have money to litigate it in court. I told Tom that if I ever started a law firm he should see us. He did, and we eventually won.[2] . . . [When CIR began] it was the only case we had, and it could have been WLF's. But, again, the thinking there was: it's just another affirmative action case and we're already "doing" those types of cases (i.e., filing amicus briefs in other people's cases) and getting as much bang for the buck from our donors as we can. . . . From the viewpoint of WLF, its overhead and expenses—it did vast amounts of direct mail in those days—it made no economic sense. You wouldn't reap any extra financial good from taking on Lamprecht, and it would have prevented

the attorney who took it from writing, I don't know, six amicus briefs for the same amount of time that could posture WLF as being in six other important areas of the law.[3]

Similar to Chip Mellor's experience at the Mountain States Legal Foundation, WLF frustrated McDonald's desire to engage in serious, strategically sophisticated public interest lawyering. This professional frustration, along with a desire to achieve conservative goals, spurred the search for a new kind of conservative public interest law firm.

Studies of movement investments in public interest law by Horowitz and CAJ had primed conservative patrons for the new approach that Greve and McDonald were proposing. Greve recalls that foundations were especially open to new forms of legal activism. "Foundations at the time were predisposed toward this. [We said,] 'Here's a better model . . . that reflects the insights of the Horowitz Report and the current thinking about this. There is significant start-up time on these things, so give us two or three years to try this out, this different model, and if it succeeds it's cool. If it doesn't, we'll be the first to tell you . . . and then we'll just shut our doors." In a conscious echo of the Horowitz Report, CIR's founders told their patrons, "Over the past fifteen years, foundations, corporations, and individuals have invested substantial sums of money in the conservative, free-market public interest law movement. On the whole, the return on that investment has not been great. Despite some notable success stories . . . the public interest law movement has, with few exceptions, failed to bring about meaningful and lasting legal change."[4] The cause of this failure was that "original litigation is the only effective way to change the direction of the law. With some exceptions, however, conservative, free-market law firms have initiated and litigated far fewer cases than liberal law firms of comparable size."[5] Drawing on the political science that Greve had cut his teeth on in graduate school and the experience of McDonald at WLF, CIR's founders traced conservative firms' reluctance to bring original litigation to the political economy of organizational maintenance.[6] CIR claimed that

> public interest law firms *can* successfully change the law, but only if they are of a certain size; they must be large enough to employ many attorneys, and they must maintain large enough administrative and support staffs to allow their attorneys to perform trial-level litigation. However, if a law firm reaches that size, Horowitz observed that it will also need to develop a budget in excess of one million dollars in order to cover its overhead costs. But since money is scarce, that firm will find itself in a constant struggle to avoid running a deficit. Many public interest groups are therefore driven into making either one of two choices: (1) to cut staff, avoid original litigation, and file cost-saving, but largely

ineffectual, amicus briefs; or (2) to maintain a large legal staff and reluctantly channel a sizeable portion of their budgets away from litigation and into non-stop fund-raising activities. Hence the increasing ineffectiveness of many litigation groups to effectuate meaningful legal reform.[7]

Part of the solution to this problem was specialization. This conclusion was based on the failures of the first-generation firms and a reevaluation of the strategies of their foes on the left. Greve recalls that the crucial flaw of first-generation firms was

> that they were general-purpose firms. It was based on the misperception that Ralph Nader had succeeded because he was a loud-mouth and had an opinion on everything. But that was actually not how he operated. It was actually a bunch of firms that are very highly specialized. Non-Nader funds on the left operated on the exact same principle—a very high degree of specialization and a lot of competition. . . . So our notion was that you have to have real live original litigation and you have to be specialized in certain areas . . . You don't win by funding amicus briefs and having an opinion on everything.

The founders of CIR recognized what political scientists have subsequently demonstrated, which is that, by becoming "repeat players" in specific areas of law, public interest law firms can spread their investment in developing expertise over a large number of cases. The returns on these specialized investments are a reputation for expertise, an appreciation for the strategies of opposing lawyers, a network of outside lawyers and supporting groups, and credibility with judges.[8]

The other advantage of small, focused firms is that they can rely on a handful of individuals and foundations, avoiding the loss of organizational focus that can come through from maintaining a base of large, low-dollar donors. In CIR's case, this strategy also made a virtue of necessity. "Our only source of money was foundations . . . and we knew that our natural source of money—the Olins, Scaifes, etc.—wouldn't give us that much, so we had to think small."[9] CIR's financial strategy was also driven by what Greve and McDonald (like the Capital Legal Foundation before them) had learned about the dangers of business patronage. The "constant quest for money has often resulted in a 'pro-business' strategy: case selection and litigation strategy have been driven by fund-raising needs. On occasion, conservative firms have also defended corporate positions in violations of free-market principles."[10] CIR's founders recognized that the power of public interest law comes from the perception that it is untainted by "private interests." Close financial connections to corporations preclude such a principled public face, creating "a reputation of conservative public interest law firms as a 'business front.' Ralph Nader's organizations or environmental groups are widely regarded as 'the public's' authentic representatives; conservative public interest law firms have been denounced as corporate America's hired guns."[11] Following Horowitz, CIR's founders also argued that conservative public interest law firms needed to demonstrate their public interest credentials by finding liberal "entrenched interests" to accuse of hypocrisy, secrecy, and conspiring against the public.

While they were critical of existing conservative firms, both Greve and McDonald were open to, and, because of their professional and academic background, fully capable of, learning from legal liberals. As McDonald remembers, "The ideas [behind CIR] came from rejecting what we'd seen on the right and imitating what we thought the Left was doing—whether it was [is] a different matter. I guess we thought that Alan Morrison of Public Citizen was a good model. You'd never hear from him for a while, and then he'd pop up with an *INS v. Chadha* or something at the Supreme Court. He didn't seem to have much of a staff either." Conservatives needed to go beyond standing in the way of lawyers like Morrison and instead mimic them by seizing control of the legal agenda to establish rights of their own that could be used against institutions controlled by liberals.[12] By initiating cases and thereby controlling the legal agenda, CIR could shape the facts and venue of cases, influence public perceptions, and force liberals onto the defensive by making them look like the defenders of an unaccountable status quo.

CIR believed that they could have a large impact despite their small size by leveraging the services of lawyers in private practice. The experience of liberal public interest firms had shown that "many small groups have been very effective in litigation because they make extensive use of existing 'free' resources—most prominently, the pro bono service of for-profit law firms. The Lawyers' Committee for Civil Rights, Trial Lawyers for Public Justice, and the—of course much larger—ACLU fit this description."[13] CIR would mimic these organizations by identifying cases and shaping strategy while farming out the heavy lifting (and costs) to pro bono litigators in wealthy private firms. This strategy depended on networks and resources that had not existed a decade before. McDonald recalls, "We thought that what with the influx of talented Reagan-era attorneys back into private practice, and through the Federalist Society, we had a great pool of talent to draw on to fit case to attorney." Federalist Society meetings would create opportunities to "solicit information and advice about cases and issues that fit the Center's agenda."[14] For an organization that, at least initially, would only have two full-time staff members, the ability to draw upon a large, geographically dispersed network to help find cases was essential. What is more, the Federalist Society network made it easier to identify lawyers ideologically attuned to CIR's mission and skilled in particular areas of law. The Federalist Society, in effect, reduced the trans-action costs of conservative public interest law. Just as important as the Federalist Society network was the existence of a pool of conservative lawyers with experience in government and a taste for doing policy-rele-vant legal work. CIR's hope was that once these lawyers went back into private practice, they would seize the opportunity to continue working on cases as interesting as those they had been responsible for in government. Inducing Reagan administration veterans to partner with CIR would allow the conservative movement to leverage the substantial resources of private firms for conservative legal activism. Over the years, CIR has in fact been able to draw very successfully on these Reagan alumni, including Theodore Olson and Douglas Cox of Gibson, Dunn and Crutcher, Mi-chael Carvin of Cooper, Carvin and Rosenthal, and Michael McConnell.[15]

This points to the important, and generally overlooked, mechanism of electoral success feeding back into the development of a legal support structure, through creating an "alumni" pool of former public servants whose work in government provides the skills, networks, and tempera-ment for legal activity outside government. But the creation of a cadre of experienced lawyers as a consequence of electoral success is only one-third of the equation. For this revolving door to spin effectively, the con-servative movement needed organizations like the Federalist Society to connect alumni to causes and groups like CIR to activate this "latent resource" for political action. These factors allowed CIR to maintain a lean, low-cost firm dependent primarily on foundation support and a small group of individual supporters, rather than mass mailings and cor-porate largesse.

The emergence of a new generation of wealthy libertarians in the tech-nology and finance sectors also helped CIR reconcile its funding needs with its strategic ambitions. Changes in the economy also helped CIR solve its organizational maintenance problems. First-generation firms depended heavily on funding from corporations (and their owners or senior management) in areas (such as ranching, extractive industries, and manufacturing) that were severely impacted by the new regulatory state and the Naderite firms who knew how to exploit it. By the late 1980s, entirely new sources of wealth had emerged, especially in high technology, and the result was a sizable number of very wealthy, rela-tively young, temperamentally libertarian donors.[16] As Greve argues, "The first generation played in the old economy, second generation in the new, with lots of rich, individual donors. I don't mean millionaires, I mean people who can write a six-figure check the way you or I buy bagels." These newly wealthy individuals were looking for opportunities to invest their money in organizations that shared the libertarian impulses that (at least in the late 1980s and early 1990s) characterized entrepreneurs in areas like software and the Internet. "The biggest contributors found us, sometimes based on news articles they'd seen, because they wanted to invest in this 'sector' and had asked around for worthwhile outfits. I did virtually no donor prospecting."[17] When combined with supportive foundations, a handful of very large individual donations from new economy millionaires were sufficient to fund CIR's lean organizational model. These new economy libertarians were unlikely to compromise CIR's legal strategy, since they were attracted to the firm primarily by its sharply defined ideological principles.

Finally, CIR aimed to mimic the Left in its relationship with the academy. An early planning document argued that

> liberal public interest law firms cooperate closely and in various ways with leading academic scholars. As a result, they have been able to gain access to legal and scientific expertise, to develop feasible litigation strategies; to secure a large amount of credibility in public policy forums and in court; and to draw upon a steady stream of talented law school graduates who will work for the firms. The conservative, free-market public interest law movement's connections to academic scholars have, on the whole, been rather tenuous. We are convinced that this is a serious weakness. Accordingly, the Center for Individual Rights maintains close contacts with legal scholars in the academic community. . . . Academic advisors are asked to identify potential litigation issues and to formulate a corresponding litigation strategy for the Center to pursue in court. They also give advice to the attorneys who litigate the Center's cases.[18]

CIR's intentions to disconnect conservative public interest law from business interests and to tie it to conservatives in the academy and the think tank community were two sides of the same coin. CIR's founders shared the growing sense of many libertarian conservatives that, with a few exceptions, businessmen could not be counted on to pursue the interests of a free market. Indeed, they were all too ready to cut deals with the activist state in the interest of their short-term bottom line.[19] Business was neither interested in the broader constitutional norms that protect free markets nor concerned about the social institutions that safeguard those markets. Conservative intellectuals, Federalist Society members, and conservative foundations—all based in or connected to the academy—shared the second-generation legal entrepreneurs' concern for the larger constitutional order, and could thus constitute the new "base" for conservative public interest law. This shift reflected the increasing autonomy of the conservative movement, a shift Horowitz had pointed to a decade earlier. This new cadre of Reagan-era conservative activists sought organizational forms in which they, not business, would hold the movement's strategic reins.

CIR's Strategic Opportunism

CIR's core commitments were to a method of organizing public interest law activism, a broad critique of the administrative state, and a set of roughly libertarian principles rather than to any particular area of law or public policy. While the Institute for Justice established very detailed litigation strategies even before the organization was founded (through the Center for Applied Jurisprudence), CIR adopted a market model of issue selection. Like the early NAACP, CIR's case selection was characterized by strategic opportunism: pursuing a range of theoretically attractive options and then throwing itself behind those that demonstrated traction in the courts and within their organizational network.[20] This opportunistic approach was itself opportunistic, in the sense that it was not the result of careful, advance planning, but was a response to feedback from the legal environment.

CIR attracted attention and developed a network early on, causing a stream of potential litigants to present themselves to the organization. The founders developed an ability to recognize cases with substantial legal potential (drawn from the cases they had induced to come through the door) that fit within the organization's general interests. That is, rather than planning, CIR emphasized case attraction and strategic sorting. As McDonald recalls,

> All—let me repeat—all of the CIR cases that made it to the Supreme Court had an element of pure fortuitousness to them. . . . Ron Rosenberger went to a number of other PILFs before he came to us. They turned him down. Maybe because of, let's call it, the WLF-*Lamprecht* problem.[21] We were clever enough to see the case's potential and wanted to litigate in that area, but it wasn't as though we designed the case through theory first and then "created" or found Ron Rosenberger. . . . We got into the VAWA [Violence Against Women Act] *Morrison* case because John Jeffries—the UVA law prof who argued *Rosenberger*—thought we were decent guys and when some local practitioner in Virginia called him for help in *Morrison*, because he didn't know about VAWA he said call CIR. Again, we didn't create *Morrison*. . . . And we got into the *Bossier* redistricting case because the attorney from Louisiana who had been handling it had heart problems. He consulted a federal judge who thought well of CIR and said why not call them. . . . [Our approach was to] be opportunistic—if a Lamprecht or a Rosenberger walks through the door and you see that their cases fit within one of your mission areas. *Bossier* fit within our mission area of race neutrality but was a bit more of a stretch perhaps, but you don't pass up an opportunity to argue before the Supreme Court. Doing that helps generate more potential cases. In the meantime, sure, we thought about what the next "logical" case would be to achieve x, y, or z in one area of another,

but . . . the only area where we could really design a strategy was in the area of race preferences. There we had our pick because no one else would litigate them for all sorts of reasons.

CIR embraced opportunism because, having tried both opportunism and planning as a mode of organizational agenda-setting, opportunism worked. McDonald recalls that "we thought of litigating against federal regulatory agencies . . . but it was next to impossible to find clients. We thought of doing environmental cases, but, again, [it was] difficult to find clients not already swept up in mega-Superfund litigation or some other kind of litigation. . . . Greve wrote a book on environmental law and could think up all sorts of cases, but none of them worked in practice."

This pattern of issue opportunism helps to explain the areas of legal activism CIR pursued as well as those it dropped. The fortunes of four issues illuminate CIR's evolving strategic focus. Despite strong initial interest, CIR dropped two of those issues—legal reform in institutions serving the disadvantaged and libel law—from its organizational agenda while aggressively pursuing two others, academic free speech and affirmative action (both of which are discussed in the next section).

While it was not part of its original grant proposals, CIR began designing a "Social Responsibility Project" shortly after it was created. This initiative was designed to use strategic litigation to "improve the functioning of schools and public housing agencies that serve the poor" and "support policies and institutions conducive to individual responsibility, self reliance, and a sense of social obligation"[22] The initiative dovetailed with then-Secretary of Housing and Urban Development Jack Kemp's emphasis on "empowerment" of the poor and the first Bush administration's interest in education reform.[23] The project focused on school discipline and safety in public housing, with CIR taking the side of local "empowerment-oriented" organizations who wanted the government to have more authority and discretion. As McDonald recalls, "We had a law clerk working on this full time to contact these types of groups—trolling for potential clients with legal problems to see if we could help with so-called empowerment." This was a far cry from the cases that would later make CIR's name, all of which attacked government discretion in the name of individual rights.

While the Olin Foundation funded the project for one year and CIR was able to enlist the help of organizations such as the National Association of Secondary School Principals and the National School Safety Center,[24] the firm ultimately abandoned the project. Greve recalls that the Social Responsibility Project "was in fact connected to Kemp's ownership initiatives, which also bombed, and for the same reason: lack of client competence. Plus, the distinction conservatives want to draw between 'law-abiding' public housing residents and 'lawbreakers' is illusory, since every law-abiding resident has a half-dozen lawbreaking relatives and doesn't want the book thrown at them. We spent a long time advising folks in HUD's flagship projects (e.g. Trenton) with little to show for it."[25] The Social Responsibility Project was a bad fit for CIR's organizational form, because of "the complexity and sheer mess of those types of situations. There really is no one target, but fifty different moving legal targets—nothing for you to get your arms around."[26] Practical experience and the firm's design impelled CIR to seek out relatively simple, potentially precedent-setting cases with a clear path to the Supreme Court rather than fighting rearguard efforts with geographically limited impact. The temperament of CIR's founders was also a poor fit with the slow, time-consuming demands of building credibility with representatives of the poor and racial minorities. While such cases might have made sense for an organization with a large staff, budget, and PR apparatus—as IJ would soon demonstrate—they made little sense for a firm with CIR's organizational commitments.

Despite McDonald's strong interest in libel law, rooted in his previous work at WLF and ALF, the issue was also dropped when it failed to bear fruit. CIR did develop a case in the area early on, *Krauser v. Consumer Reports*, which offered "an opportunity to test a 'no-fault' theory of libel, which would permit libel plaintiffs seeking solely a retraction (and no damages) to escape the overly demanding 'actual malice' standard of *New York Times v. Sullivan*."[27] CIR took on other libel cases over its first few years, representing conservative movement figures like S. Fred Singer and Dinesh D'Souza, but this line of work quickly fizzled out. The most important constraint, according to McDonald, was that, "unlike the area of racial discrimination, the playing field was woefully tilted toward the defense bar, and the Supreme Court wasn't going to budge." Even more important, by taking on the issue of "academic freedom" CIR found a new outlet for its interest in the First Amendment, but on the side of expanding the reach of constitutionally protected speech, rather than constricting it

The failure of the Social Responsibility Project and libel law reform helped to point CIR, both tactically and ideologically, toward a marked libertarianism in its caseload. Both libel law reform and the Project had more in common with traditional conservatism than they did with libertarianism, in that they sought to limit liberty in the name of a higher principle, such as individual reputation or school and neighborhood order. Current CIR president Terry Pell believes that traditional conservatives face systemic constraints in pursuing these objectives through public interest law, in a way that libertarians do not. "The courts [have] limited the ability of institutions to act in a deliberate and effective manner. . . .

Courts are most naturally used as a way to limit the executive branch, or institutions in general. And the laws are all set up as limits on the government. So if you're a public interest law firm using the courts, you're likely using laws that were designed to limit institutional authority in some way. That would all push you against any systematic effort to strengthen the prerogatives of institutions." The failure of the Social Responsibility Project and libel law reform provides an intriguing explanation for the greater success of CIR and IJ, which identified with opposition to, rather than defense of, government authority. Libertarians were able to work with the trend in American law initiated by liberals to strip executive institutions of discretion and force them to operate in accordance with clear, national rules or professional standards.[28] It is important to remember, however, that CIR's libertarian focus was an emergent, not a founding, commitment. Though McDonald and Greve were less committed libertarians than IJ's founders were, their interaction with the legal environment—combined with their temperamental instinct for going where the action was—gradually pushed CIR in a libertarian direction.[29] This is another example of how the conservative legal movement was shaped by the liberal legal system that it simultaneously sought to dislodge.

Issue Opportunism at CIR: Free Speech and Affirmative Action

Recognizing the futility of using conservative public interest law to support governmental authority, however, pointed to the solution—attacking institutions controlled by the Left on the basis of fundamental constitutional principles, such as the First Amendment's rights of free speech and religion and the Fourteenth Amendment's guarantee of the equal protection of the laws. "What we learned," Greve recalls, "is that public interest law works when you can wield a big constitutional club. On any other issue, the regulatory state will eat you alive." Universities provided a happy hunting ground for such cases, and also allowed CIR to adopt a posture of defending individuals against large, oppressive organizations, and to do so by using constitutional claims that liberals had pioneered. The opportunity for this new avenue for conservative litigation was the "political correctness" scare of the early 1990s, which provided a powerful cultural hook for CIR's litigation and alerted potential conservative donors to the importance of countering the campus Left.

CIR's founders knew from the start that specialization was vital, but lacked a clear sense of what their organization's specialty should be. The arrival of the "PC craze" solved its problem. McDonald recalls, "Initially, we only asked for two years of funding from foundations, on the assumption that we'd either find our 'niche' or not, in which case we'd close up shop. But then the PC craze hit and we'd found a niche. It hadn't been on our radar screen when we started CIR but it did fit within our core mission of protecting free speech and civil rights. We modified and adapted." CIR had no long-term litigation strategy in the area, but developed one in response to the cases that came in the door. "We had no idea that PC was going to be as big as it was. No idea whatsoever. When Tim McGuire walked into our office with the flap about admission records at Georgetown Law Center, we were floored when it ended up on the front pages of the *Washington Post* and the *New York Times*, and that was just the start of all sorts of other similar cases."[30] CIR had found a niche that matched the substantive interests and temperament of the organization's leaders, as well as their strong links with academia.

Sensing that attacking censorship on campus was both substantively important and appealing to donors and the larger conservative movement, CIR quickly formalized its work in the area into an Academic Freedom Defense Fund. An early planning paper for the AFDF makes clear that CIR had a clear sense that there was a need and a political opportunity in the area, as well as an issue likely to generate excitement from donors.

> Uniformly, our "advisors" argued that the establishment of an Academic Freedom Defense Fund (AFDF) is an idea whose time has come. We share this assessment for both substantive and, as it were, tactical reasons. As to substance, the "PC" movement is a genuine menace, and the protection afforded to conservative and middle-of-the-roadish students and academics by organizations such as the ACLU and the AAUP is insufficient and, shall we say, unreliable. As to tactics, Aaron Wildavsky has remarked that the "PC" movement is really the first issue that has split the Left on campus. This opportunity should be exploited: the more of a wedge we can drive between heretofore closely aligned leftist constituencies, the better.[31]

While the AFDF was clearly motivated by a genuine desire to defend the rights of (predominantly conservative) academics, Greve's comment shows that it was also seen as part of the "war of position" in the modern university between liberals and conservatives. The founders of CIR sincerely believed that efforts to limit the speech of those on the right were real and designed to shut off challenges to academic liberalism. For conservatives, campus politics was simply politics by other means in a different venue. Defending themselves required coalition-building strategies designed to split moderate liberals from those to their left, strategies that conservatives were deploying with increasing regularity in areas like school choice and welfare reform.[32] Attacking political correctness also had the advantage of attracting conservatives willing to donate their labor to the cause—a substantial advantage given CIR's dependence on outside counsel. The proposal for the AFDF noted that "CIR has received far more requests for cases in this than in any other area of activities."[33] Finally, the issue attracted substantial interest and consequently free public relations from the larger conservative movement. Conservative magazines loved stories about political correctness on campus, and publishers were recognizing that books on "liberal bias" in academia had a market.[34] Ever on the lookout for areas in which they could leverage free resources, academic free speech emerged as a clear winner.

Racial and gender preferences in education were not a focus of CIR's early strategy documents, and the firm shied away from the issue in its early years. In its original proposal for the AFDF, CIR made clear that affirmative action was freighted with danger, because of the intrinsic difficulty of winning cases in the area and because of the tensions it might produce with its potential allies.

> In our opinion, the AFDF should limit itself strictly to cases and controversies that have a bearing upon academic freedom and First Amendment rights. In particular, the AFDF should *not* get sidetracked into issues of related, but ultimately, quite different concern—most notably, race, including racial quotas in student admission and faculty hiring and promotion. When we discussed this with several of our "consultants," we received mixed reactions. Some advisors viewed race- and gender-based hiring, promotion, and admissions as *the* problem for conservative academics, and they urged that the envisioned AFDF provide legal assistance to victims of racial discrimination. Of course, racial and gender preferences do abound in higher education. Discriminatory policies are the source of many of the complaints and inquiries we receive (and would receive in larger numbers if the AFDF were established). Nonetheless, we believe that the AFDF should refrain from devoting its resources to reverse discrimination cases, at least as a general rule. First, "Title VI" and "Title VII" civil rights cases are exceedingly difficult and expensive. The proof problems are almost always daunting, and litigation costs run into hundreds of thousands of dollars for most cases. Second . . . the vigorous advocacy of First Amendment rights and academic freedom has the potential of driving a wedge between heretofore united political constituencies. This potential might be lost if the AFDF were perceived, not as a "civil libertarian" organization but, rightly or wrongly, as simply yet another conservative hobby horse.[35]

Appealing to nonconservatives was central to CIR's political strategy of splitting the Left, and explains why it went out of its way to explain to foundations its hesitation in pursuing affirmative action cases. "In order to attain their broader political and philosophical objectives, conservatives and moderates must seek to cooperate with non-radicalized liberals on issues on which both sides, for all their disagreements, happen to agree; and the defense of academic freedom is first and foremost among these issues. In this way, an Academic Freedom Defense Fund might contribute to a productive political 'realignment' on college campuses."[36]

Just a few years later CIR reversed itself and began filing the cases that led up to its Supreme Court challenges to affirmative action in *Gratz* and *Grutter*. What explains this rapid strategic shift? First, CIR had already nosed its way into the question of affirmative action in the *Lamprecht* challenge to FCC radio license policies and its free speech cases challenging university interpretations of their antidiscrimination duties. But the jump to a direct attack on affirmative action in university admissions threatened the support CIR sought to attract from centrists and liberals, might give the firm an unsavory racial stigma, and unquestionably required a large increase in funding. In its 1993 request for funding from the Olin Foundation, CIR addressed its previous concerns directly.

> When the AFDF was established two years ago, we decided to stay away from affirmative action and reverse discrimination cases. We believed that AFDF's success would depend on its reputation—and practice—as a (civil) libertarian organization dedicated to free speech and inquiry, and that a preoccupation with questions of race and gender might interfere with this strategy. In hindsight, this was the right approach. However, the time has come to revisit the original decision to stay away from quota cases. First, the AFDF (and CIR in general) now has developed a reputation as a principled civil libertarian organization. It can easily afford to take a few high-profile discrimination cases without blurring its central message. Second, the quotaization of the academy has continued apace. Unless and until hiring and admissions by numbers are arrested, all the other items on the agenda for higher education will, in the long run, be losing causes.[37]

McDonald believes that CIR's shift to enthusiasm for affirmative action litigation had a simpler motivation. The justification in 1993, in McDonald's telling, was "a retroactive highfalutin' attempt to justify the fact that a really good case involving racial preferences had come our way— namely *Hopwood*. . . . Here again, CIR didn't initiate the case, a local attorney by the name of Steve Smith did—but we got in touch with him and looked over the admissions policy and thought, '[There's] no way we cannot not do this.' " In 1991, when the firm was still quite young, a case like *Hopwood* would have stretched CIR's organizational capacity to its breaking point. "Take away our low (by comparison with what we could have been making at WLF, say) salaries and overhead and that doesn't leave you with much to do more than a few original cases each year, and, if you do, they'd better not be factually messy—fifty depositions and the like. We had to wait for the law to change, for the universities to become more brazen about their use of race . . . and for CIR to develop a good track record so that we could attract more and more good firms to our cause."[38] By 1993, CIR was convinced that it could handle one case like *Hopwood* without outstripping its fund-raising and organizational capacity.

Another factor that allowed CIR to consider a challenge to affirmative action was the increasing density of conservative organizations on campus, the most important of which was the National Association of Scholars. From the vantage point of its professorial constituency, NAS saw affirmative action as intimately connected to CIR's existing agenda of academic freedom. As Steve Balch, the president of NAS, told Greve in 1993,

> I realize the difficulty of attempting reverse discrimination cases. Nonetheless, they comprise the largest category of complaints we receive, and are, alas, likely to remain a growth industry. It's imperative that we deal with them for two reasons. First, they drive a lot of our people out of the business (not because they're all white males—we're not; but because reverse discrimination is most likely to be inflicted on white males who are also "politically incorrect"). Second, these policies comprise the linchpin of a whole regime of campus governance inimical to the ideals of liberal education. If, through some legal breakthrough, reverse discrimination was no longer permitted, university administrators would be compelled to configure an entirely new set of alliances to support themselves, drastically transforming the political equation on campus.[39]

Attacking affirmative action went hand in hand with defending the free speech rights of conservative professors. Attacking affirmative action would enhance the probability that conservatives would be hired, while CIR's existing free speech litigation would protect them once they made their way through the university's gates. As McDonald recalls, "Every time we'd do an academic case, the client or his colleagues would inevitably ask us to do race cases. . . . Dr. X would say, you should sue my school, too, because it has quotas." In affirmative action, conservatives had an issue with potentially large popular appeal, a newly vibrant infrastructure of conservative academics, support from conservative foundations, and a sense that, due to the hesitancy of Republican lawmakers, the courts were likely to be the only venue for policy change.[40]

The reason for the relative absence of effective challenges to affirmative action was not the dearth of attractive plaintiffs, but the absence of public interest lawyers interested in representing them. As McDonald recalls, this gave CIR the space to select clients and venues strategically.

> You had legitimately aggrieved plaintiffs a-plenty . . . it was a target-rich environment. You can't open any statute book, federal or state, without coming across some set-aside that has no sound predicate in law. But none of these groups were willing to touch them because it was very cost intensive and the

law was evolving. Once we got into this area of law and people found we were the only game in town, we had our choice of plaintiffs. There are economic reasons [for the absence of litigation]. For example, it might cost a couple of thousand dollars to file an amicus brief in the Supreme Court in the *Adarand* case, but then you can send out a fund-raising letter that says we filed a brief with the Supreme Court . . . and we're working on behalf of Mr. Adarand, even though they're not technically representing him.[41]

The success of CIR was as much a victory of organization as it was legal strategy or political opportunity. CIR's predecessors, with a few exceptions, had been caught in an organizational maintenance trap driven by dependence on business and unsophisticated direct mail donors. CIR, by contrast, had chosen an organizational design that limited its financial needs and allowed it to raise money primarily from a handful of sophisticated donors who understood its basic approach. This gave CIR the freedom to focus immediately on litigation and to spread their litigation bets until they hit on an issue—academic freedom—that worked.

The success of CIR's academic freedom cases won the firm a high public profile and enhanced its reputation within the conservative movement. Having developed a reputation as the scourge of political correctness, CIR attracted clients who believed their issues were akin to those the firm had already handled. This specialized reputation allowed CIR to sift through the "target-rich environment" of clients that came through its door, choose those with the greatest promise, rapidly test the litigation waters, and follow up on cases that bore fruit. This is the approach that allowed CIR to identify and successfully litigate such important, precedent-setting cases as *Morrison* and *Rosenberger*, and eventually led to its challenge to affirmative action in university admissions.

The Evolution of the Institute for Justice

Unlike CIR, the Institute for Justice's legal strategy and issue focus were designed through Mellor's Center for Applied Jurisprudence (described in chapter 3) before the organization was up and running. The books published by CAJ[42] provided IJ with an operational design, an approach to legal activism, and a set of thoroughly vetted legal strategies on specific issues. IJ's early planning documents identified economic liberty, educational choice, property rights, and the First Amendment as its key issues, and fifteen years later these remain its central commitments. IJ's history has been marked by the implementation of a well-established vision, in sharp contrast to CIR's opportunistic search for issues capable of providing legal and political traction.

From the moment it opened its doors, IJ was committed to pursuing libertarian goals by targeting groups typically associated with liberalism. For example, IJ's earliest proposals highlighted its pursuit of "economic liberty" through defending "low-capital entrepreneurs" like a "black Muslim entrepreneur whose African hairstyling salon is threatened with closure because Mr. Uqdah does not have a cosmetology license," as well as targeting licensing requirements in the taxicab business.[43] The same proposal identified its strategy of representing "low-income parents" in cases that "will place urban public schools on trial and clearly identify choice as a low-income empowerment solution."[44] These cases drew on the work that Bolick had done at the Landmark Legal Foundation, which built on the arguments of Stuart Butler, Walter Williams, Clarence Thomas (Bolick's mentor at the EEOC), and Robert Woodson that economic growth in the inner cities was being held back by government regulation, rather than insufficient spending.[45] These supporters of "empowerment" believed that "deregulating the inner city" would give conservatives political traction among traditional supporters of liberalism, African-Americans in particular.

The legal theory that accompanied empowerment was that attacking the impact of state regulation on the poor and racial minorities would help reinvigorate the property rights provisions of the Constitution. The line of cases that stood in IJ's way was, by its own admission, quite long.

> We believe it is timely and essential to begin a direct assault on the *Slaughter-House Cases*, which read the privileges or immunities clause out of the 14th Amendment. Such an assault must unfold as part of a carefully planned, long-term program to restore constitutional protection for economic liberty. It will be essential to identify licensing and permitting laws and other government-created barriers to entry that frame the economic liberty issue most compellingly. We have high confidence in our ability to do this since we have been very successful in all of our cases in identifying the best possible factual settings and the most sympathetic clients.[46]

These cases had ambitious long-term objectives but quite modest short-term aims, which made it difficult to persuade some of IJ's patrons that there was a high payoff to its activities, in comparison to those of CIR. The staff of the Olin Foundation responded to IJ's initial grant proposal by observing that "some of the litigation the Institute has started looks promising, while lawsuits to allow ghetto residents to start shoe shine or barber businesses are more quixotic."[47] Even today, Olin Foundation president James Piereson recalls, "I've had some mixed views on the other cases they've done, like the street vendors and the licensing stuff. It seems like small-bore sort of stuff; it's hard to find what the range and precedential value of it is. You get the beauticians freed up in Washington, D.C., but its not clear how far you can take it."

The founders of IJ did not share the Olin Foundation's skepticism. From the start, IJ judged that placing poor, black clients against large government institutions would improve their odds of success in the courts, magnify their public profile, and help change the reputation of conservatives and libertarians. By representing clients who were sympathetic by prevailing liberal standards, IJ could get around the usual assumptions of the media and courts that conservative lawyers were just fronts for big business. Representing traditionally liberal clients had the potential to transform the identification of civil rights with liberalism, and to remove the stigma of racism from conservatives. Once this identification had been broken, IJ's leaders calculated, it would be possible for conservatives to gain a hearing on a wide range of issues. "Once we make common cause on an issue like school choice, other pieces of the puzzle, such as economic liberty and private property rights, seem to follow logically. . . . Given that our goal is to give people greater control over their destinies, we should never cede either the moral high ground or the opportunity to put a human, compassionate face on our philosophy."[48]

The most daunting early challenge for IJ was financial, not strategic. Despite the substantial spadework that Mellor had done to show conservative patrons the need for an organization like IJ, fund-raising for the firm was more complex than Mellor anticipated. Mellor was hired by the Pacific Research Institute to resuscitate the think tank and was uncomfortable raising start-up funds for IJ from supporters. This meant that IJ had to solicit support from a single, large contributor to get the organization off the ground and develop its own funding base.

> I needed a seed funder, who was Charles Koch.[49] I'd known Charles for a long time and I thought, "This is just the sort of thing he should like." I never got to make a pitch directly to him; I went through some functionaries. [They said no.] I thought, what are we going to do, who else would give us enough money to be serious? And I had a really hard time thinking of somebody, when the call came and said, "We've been thinking about it again, and we'd like to listen to what you have to say." . . . He said, "Here's what I'm going to do. I'll give you up to $500,000 a year for three years, each year, but you have to come back each year and demonstrate that you've met these milestones that you've set out to accomplish and I will evaluate it on a yearly basis, and there's no guarantees."[50]

The universe of conservative patrons at the time was quite limited, and the number of those willing and able to make very large contributions was even smaller. On the other hand, the intimate nature of the conservative patronage network and their relatively flat organizational structure meant that Mellor could gain personal access to a deep-pocketed potential contributor based on his own reputation, produced through the network of conservative and libertarian organizations.

IJ's earliest grant proposals were of a piece with the strategies developed at the Center for Applied Jurisprudence. Given the "perilous state" of the rule of law in America, IJ argued, "It is not enough to depend on academic discourse or private lawyers to remedy this tragic situation." Instead,

> The inertia in the legal system and its dominance by special interests can be overcome only through skilled advocacy by individuals armed with philosophically and tactically consistent strategies based on natural rights and the Constitution. These advocates must pursue carefully selected cases having significant potential to set favorable precedent and to provide a compelling platform to argue the issue in the court of public opinion. Every case should be a building block in a progression of cases that relentlessly reshapes American jurisprudence.[51]

This emphasis on strategic litigation was familiar to the conservative patrons who had supported Mellor's work at the Pacific Research Institute. IJ's early grant applications made sure to recall foundations' previous support of CAJ: "Ultimate success depends upon our executing the program and talent you played such a key role in developing."[52] What was new was the recognition that conservative public interest law's problems went well beyond legal strategy to the underdeveloped state of conservative legal activism more broadly.

> While principled advocacy is essential, it is beyond the province of any one organization or group of individuals to accomplish all that needs to be done. Quite simply, there are not enough trained advocates who know how to make use of the unique tools that our type of public interest law has to offer. Consequently, a substantial effort must be made to train law students, lawyers, and policy activists how to apply their talent and idealism in the real world of litigation, media relations, and public debate. With such training, the talent pool of effective advocates will be increased dramatically and the chances of ultimate success will rise immeasurably.[53]

The solution was to conduct a series of seminars led by IJ staff and major conservative legal scholars (the grant proposal named Charles Fried of Harvard, Jonathan Macey of Cornell, and Michael Krauss of George Mason). The purpose was to overcome the problem that "lawyers, driven by the demands of private practice, rarely recognize opportunities to advance principles within the context of their practices."[54] The seminars would introduce conservative lawyers to the possibilities for pro bono legal activism and facilitate the "spontaneous, decentralized action" that libertarians have philosophical reasons to prefer to conscious, centralized planning. As we shall see later in this chapter, IJ's high hopes in this area have not, fifteen years later, been met.

In spite of its interest in looking beyond the courtroom, the primary activity of IJ has always been litigation, and unlike CIR it has been remarkably consistent in the kinds of cases it handles. For instance, IJ has litigated school choice cases since its founding. In 1992, it sued the Chicago and Los Angeles schools systems, arguing that their low quality of instruction violated state constitutional guarantees.[55] In these cases IJ accepted the idea that state constitutions established judiciable standards of government performance—a position usually associated with legal liberalism—but claimed that the failure of government argued for allowing parents to take their percentage of school funding to private schools. This case convinced the Olin Foundation to fund IJ, because "even if the courts do not issue injunctions mandating the equivalent of a voucher system, the publicity of putting urban public education 'on trial' would be very bad news for the defenders of the public education monopoly and its constant demands for still more money."[56] IJ lost both of these cases, however, and while it has occasionally used the courts to claim that school choice was an affirmative state duty, not simply a constitutional option,[57] this has ceased to be a major part of IJ's legal strategy.[58] The main purpose of these cases was to use the law to reinforce IJ's argument that the public school system is a source of unaccountable power, and that the interests of school providers should not be conflated with those of schoolchildren. Like their liberal predecessors, IJ sought to use the law to change the framing and salience of political issues.[59]

IJ's work in the area of Fifth Amendment takings jurisprudence is an even clearer instance of how it has used the law as a mobilizing tactic, to set the political agenda, and to transform public opinion. Mellor recalls that takings could easily have been seen as a libertarian issue of minor importance: "All the way along in *Kelo* [and in other litigation in the area], we had the challenge to take an issue that we thought was vitally important, but by its very nature conducted in such a way that it was not on the radar screen of most Americans. . . . We had to figure out ways to mobilize people and public outrage around the issue." For its first step in framing the issue, IJ could hardly have found a better enemy than Donald Trump, who had convinced the state of New Jersey to use its power of eminent domain to condemn a private home to make way for a casino parking lot.[60] IJ won and followed with a series of similar cases, including a challenge to Pittsburgh's plan to use eminent domain to make way for a downtown mall. In that case, IJ never filed a suit, helping instead to organize local community groups, staging protests, and launching a high-profile public relations campaign, the centerpiece of which were ten three-hundred-square-foot billboards. The city eventually promised not to use eminent domain. IJ followed up with a similar mix of legal and non-legal tactics in other states, as well as an ambitious program to train local activists. Mellor recalls that IJ "wanted to equip community activists with the tools to head off eminent domain even before it got to court. That is in fact what we did through on-line materials, but also through annual conferences, where we'd bring activists together for the weekend and teach them everything from organizing techniques, to media relations, to the legal procedures they could expect."

IJ finally reached the Supreme Court with a takings case in *Kelo v. New London*, where it took on the effort by the Pfizer Corporation and local government to use eminent domain to make room for the drug company's research facility. *Kelo* is a good example of the strange bedfellows coalitions that IJ hoped, from its founding, to put together: it was supported with an amicus brief signed by the NAACP, American Association of Retired Persons, and Southern Christian Leadership Conference. IJ lost the case in the Supreme Court, in a five-to-four decision, but was able to quickly transform legal failure into mobilization success.

> When we got the result, I came in the next day and announced that we were going to launch our "Hands Off Our Home" campaign, which was an evolution of the Castle Coalition, to take the *Kelo* decision to the state level, and fight it there. I said next week we're going to hold a news conference at the National Press Club to announce this new campaign, dedicate three million dollars to it. Fight the battle at the state level, whether it's through litigation, legislation, initiative, and try to create greater property rights against eminent domain.[61]

In addition to attracting large donations from existing donors, the failure in *Kelo* led to "several thousand new small dollar donations, and new activists to the Castle Coalition [IJ's property rights network]." While "winning the *Kelo* case with a resounding victory in the Supreme Court was the desired outcome" for IJ,[62] a narrow, divided or technical victory might have been worse than failure. As Mellor concludes, "A defeat with the kind of dissent that we got, is as good as it could possibly be. Not only has this ignited outrage across the country that will transform the debate for a long time to come, it will demonstrate the power of citizen activism on this issue. That's good for property rights and the democratic process, and it will leave IJ a much stronger organization as a result of the skills we've acquired doing this."[63] Polls taken after the decision show that it was resoundingly unpopular (although few respondents were likely to have substantial information on the issue). Politicians in over half of the states (as of June 2006) have passed legislation narrowing the use of eminent domain.[64] Legislation on the subject has even been debated in Congress. Using its newfound fund-raising power on the issue, IJ has hired staff to "mobilize across the nation in the states where eminent domain reform is being considered, and to be a catalyst to make sure that the best possible reform happens."[65]

IJ also used *Kelo* to expand the range of its organizational capacities. *Kelo* produced an outpouring of articles from libertarian law professors, demonstrating the impact that litigation can have on the scholarly agenda.[66] IJ has used the aftermath of *Kelo* to build its own research capacities, creating a Strategic Research Program designed to expand on the substantial research that it has already produced on eminent domain "abuse." IJ told its donors that

> the release of *Public Power, Private Gain*[67] gave the Institute for Justice great momentum moving forward, particularly with our case *Kelo v. City of New London*. Groups such as the NAACP have used strategic research for years, but there is no other group on our side of the ideological spectrum that has come close to conducting and using research as part of a focused litigation agenda, especially combined so potently with media relations and outreach components. Supplementing the work of traditional think tanks, we will produce and publish studies within our specific areas of concentration and move promptly to apply such research to our litigation agenda.[68]

IJ has given the program a $400,000 budget, hired an experienced PhD policy analyst as director of strategic research, and plans to run conferences, fund in-house research, and solicit academic articles and shorter papers that address specific issues that the firm has identified as critical in making its case before courts, with the public, and among experts. As far back as the Center for Applied Jurisprudence project, IJ's leaders have recognized the importance of coordinating litigation and research, but the experience of the very fact-intensive takings cases taught the firm that they needed to be much more deeply integrated. By attracting attention to these issues, *Kelo* had the further effect of increasing patrons' willingness to invest in IJ's organizational capacities, which will have an impact on all of its litigation in the coming years.

IJ's response to the *Kelo* decision shows that what Michael McCann has argued about the comparable worth movement also appears true of conservative litigation: it is possible to win, in the sense of encouraging popular mobilization and inducing action in venues other than the courts, by losing.[69] IJ's approach to the outcome in *Kelo* also casts doubt on the claim that legal activism is necessarily demobilizing.[70] In fact, IJ has typically used litigation to attract public attention by framing issues in stark, moralistic ways, helping reshape perceptions of the conservative movement's racial goodwill, build coalitions with traditionally liberal groups, and create emotionally charged events that help build more permanent forms of political mobilization. None of these are intrinsic to litigation as a political strategy, and it is certainly possible for law-heavy political strategies to sap energy from other approaches to political change. Law has the capacity to mobilize as well as demobilize, depending on the target of political change and the strategic approach of legal-organizational entrepreneurs.

Organizational Style and Legitimation in Conservative Public Interest Law

IJ and CIR came out of the same rethinking of conservative legal strategy, and extracted many of the same lessons from that experience: specialize; emphasize original, long-term litigation; appeal to idealism; and establish distance from business. Despite this common starting point, IJ and CIR have developed quite distinct organizational cultures, driven by the attitudes and preferences of their founders, the demands of organizational maintenance, and the mobilization of staff and patrons. These different organizational cultures have also influenced the firms' long-term prospects.

IJ's self-presentation is remarkably consistent, both physically and philosophically. Its Washington, D.C., office is laid out in an open plan with glass doors, an image that IJ consciously considered in its design.[71] The staff's attitude is strikingly upbeat, optimistic, and allergic to cynicism. In all my interviews with IJ staff, they combined an attitude of openness while staying on message, and seemed so motivated by their clients that the larger legal issues sometimes drifted into the background. This reflects the infusion of public relations throughout the entire organization: while IJ has two full-time public relations specialists to shape the firm's media strategy, all of its lawyers are expected to consider how its cases will play in the "court of public opinion."

IJ's cases are designed for maximum dramatic impact, typically through representing a racial minority or low-income person challenging a large institution, with a great deal of emphasis on the personal dimension of the case. John Kramer, IJ's vice president for communications, observes that its ideal case must have "compelling clients, very simple facts, and outrageous acts." IJ's press strategy reflects its case selection and its emphasis on the compelling personal stories of its clients. "We make it clear to reporters that our cases aren't just about increasing the number of cabs on the streets in a given city, or about improving the quality of education, or about sometimes obscure words on parchment that guarantee a right. Our cases demonstrate real-life human dramas. They are about real people and their dreams of a better life for themselves and their families."[72] Designing cases in this way allows them to work with the grain of modern television journalism, which is attracted to legal cases with a sympathetic individual plaintiff, a deliberate violation of individual rights, and a simple causal story.[73] One indication of IJ's success in this regard is that its school choice and eminent domain cases have been featured on *60 Minutes*. IJ's strategic judgment, in sharp contrast to CIR, is that judges need to sympathize with their clients and fear a public outcry if they fail to rule in their favor.[74] So, for example, in its school choice litigation IJ repeatedly brought large numbers of inner-city parents to the courthouse for important trials, a strategy that may have helped sway at least one judge in an early, critical trial in Wisconsin.[75] Bolick admits that IJ's emphasis on "helping the judge want to rule in our favor" through storytelling and social science evidence "is counterintuitive to many lawyers—indeed, offensive to some, especially government lawyers, who hate to hear about the equities—but it is an important part of the American legal tradition."[76] This approach reflects the lessons that IJ drew from its liberal predecessors in public interest law.

> We borrow heavily and consciously from the Left for our litigation strategies, mainly from the [NAACP] LDF in its campaign to overturn *Plessy*. A strategic, case-by-case, goal-oriented litigation strategy; sympathetic cases . . . and arguing in the court of public opinion. . . . In the 1980s, I devoured everything I could find on Thurgood Marshall, MLK, and the civil rights movement. From Marshall and MLK I derived the insights of setting the terms of the debate, pursuing a principled incremental, long-term agenda; expressing the cause in the most universal possible terms, and forging nontraditional alliances.[77]

In order to break through the public's instinctive suspicion of conservative and libertarian claims to speak for the public interest, IJ's founders thought it essential to generate sympathy for the organization's clients, typically with a simple, direct narrative whose fundamental injustice does not require a commitment to IJ's underlying principles.

Perhaps nothing reveals the stylistic differences between the CIR and IJ so well as the debate on affirmative action. Clint Bolick argues that "CIR would not think twice about representing a white male who had said something politically incorrect, in violation of a speech code. . . . We would. They are more aggressive about taking on political correctness. We're more focused on building a case in the court of public opinion."[78] CIR's current president accepts this distinction:

> [IJ] won't touch a case unless it will promote a certain kind of public debate. For example, my impression is they will never bring a reverse discrimination case on behalf of a white plaintiff. . . . It's an article of faith. . . . The reason for this is they don't want to be portrayed in the press as representing disgruntled white people. They want always to be representing racial minorities in these kinds of cases. That's a press strategy that drives their legal strategy, whereas we're just the reverse. We find the legal cases we want to bring, and then we

figure out how to promote them. We feel that it's very important in these very charged issues to speak from a consistent and principled point of view. . . . The reason they only want to bring these sorts of cases on behalf of African-Americans is . . . they want to blunt the argument that the other side makes that we're racially insensitive. . . . To our way of thinking, that's just playing racial politics that we're opposed to. We will not posture in these cases that way. We will bring a strong case that we believe represents the legal principle that we think ought to be strengthened. We'll go to great lengths to describe that principle in ways that we think will connect with people. We're not blind to racial politics. But we'd never construct a case around our desire to posture against the other side's mischaracterization of us, the way IJ would.[79]

While Pell's characterization of IJ may be harsh, it does reflect the very different self-images of the two organizations, and their relationship to the legacy of *Brown*. While both reject affirmative action, for instance, CIR has firmly associated itself with the more minimal "anticlassification" understanding of *Brown*, while IJ clearly identifies with the "antisubordination" tradition that interprets *Brown* as a call for undoing the legacy of slavery and segregation.[80] CIR legitimates its litigation by reference to the plain text of the Fourteenth Amendment and the Civil Rights Act of 1964, while IJ seeks to embody the broader aspirations of the civil rights movement. IJ is not simply playing "racial politics," as Pell suggests, although they certainly are trying to reshape the public reputation of conservatism. The leaders of IJ have actually internalized the loftier aspirations of the civil rights era, aspirations that the leaders of CIR claim have become a smokescreen to hide the old-fashioned politics of transfer-seeking.

Until its affirmative action litigation heated up, CIR did not employ any public relations staff, and, when it did, it hired a lawyer and government veteran, Terry Pell, rather than the public relations professionals employed by IJ.[81] CIR's public relations strategy is significantly constrained by its strategic choice to represent unpopular clients. As Greve argues, "It's a challenge if you have innocent but highly suspicious or suspect clients. It's a very different skill to handle those sorts of situations properly. You can't say, 'Here's the client. Isn't he an admirable person?' and we'll play the equities." Unable to draw on the attractiveness of their clients, as IJ has done so skillfully, CIR modeled itself instead on the ACLU. Jeremy Rabkin, a member of CIR's board since its founding, argues, "We liked harrumphing about *individual rights*, rather abstract claims where we could say, in the manner of the ACLU, 'The law is the law, no exceptions, you must live with it, you who wield authority.' " This was partially a matter of temperament—CIR's founders would have found drawing attention to the client's "story" insufferably sentimental. It was also a matter of principle, since they believed that policymaking through emotional appeals had led to the decline of constitutional formalities in the first place. As Terry Pell puts it, "We wanted to be what the ACLU should have been, and was at one point: an uncompromising defender of civil liberties and individual rights. We wanted to get rid of all the political litmus tests that the ACLU was beginning to apply to all their cases, [where there were] clear violations of individual rights that they wouldn't litigate because it didn't serve one of their favored constituencies or political causes." CIR's approach to public relations, according to Pell, is to develop a reputation for taking cases regardless of the client if an important principle is at stake, as it did in defending the free speech rights of Michael Levin, a professor of philosophy at CUNY with odious views on racial matters.[82] CIR gambled that observers of the organization would recognize that if the organization was willing to defend clients without IJ's marquee value, then the principle must *really* be important.

CIR has taken a more narrowly legalistic approach to strategic litigation than IJ, believing that the judges would be willing to accept uncomfortable outcomes when faced with a powerful claim rooted in constitutional principle. Emphasizing law, rather than the attractiveness of its client, draws on CIR's intellectual, academic organizational culture, as well as its darker, more sardonic mood. The highly intellectual background of the CIR's staff—both Greve and Pell have PhD's, and at least one of the organization's staff lawyers had hoped to go into teaching law before coming to CIR—led them to become frustrated in organizations where they were pressured to say things they knew were untrue and do things they thought were a waste of time. While McDonald and Greve were repelled by conservative public interest law, Pell found his way into conservative lawyering through his negative experience with corporate law.

> These firms defend big companies, and your job as an attorney is to think through every possible ambiguity or possibility that might cost the company money and get rid of it. Intellectually, it's quite stifling. Anything you might find interesting there's a good chance the client wouldn't find interesting. In fact your job is to keep interesting things from happening to your client. You just have to anticipate all the interest in these issues and wring it out. . . . So what they paid us a lot of money to do was essentially to figure the next and the next and the next logical step of these regulations so they could comply with those interpretations of the regulations. I found it to be a waste of time. I thought corporations were not particularly thoughtful about what they were doing; I'm not sure it made economic sense. I didn't find it reprehensible in a conventional moral sense, I just didn't want to be the one doing it. If they wanted someone to do it, fine, just not me.

CIR's organizational culture was attractive to lawyers like Pell, McDonald, and Michael Rosman, CIR's general counsel, because it allowed for a high standard of workmanship and professionalism, the kind of intellectually satisfying lawyering they found so lacking in their previous experiences. These men, in short, were looking for a way to be serious professionals, as well as effective ideological activists. In CIR they found it.

The founders' worldview was equally important in helping to structure the organizational culture of CIR. Greve recalls that, in contrast to the sunny optimism of IJ, "Mike [McDonald] and I always agreed that the world was going to pot." CIR's founders did not believe that history was on their side. McDonald and Greve believed that the hour was very late indeed, that liberalism had already corrupted the fundamental forms of law, politics, and society. The best that could be done was to use the law to point out the hypocrisy of the Left and to win enough battles to make liberals in government and universities hesitant in their use of power. CIR believed that, if a case was structured carefully enough, judges would conclude that they *had* to rule for their clients in order to preserve broader rules, often those created by legal liberals. Rabkin recalls that CIR thought that "we could do some good by showing that if courts were going to be activist policymakers, we could remind everyone that liberal constituencies wouldn't be the only beneficiaries."

This dark, sardonic mood of CIR comes out clearest in CIR's newsletter, the *Docket Report*, which summarizes the organization's cases while (especially before Greve left in 2000) simultaneously savaging its opponents in a casual, wisecracking, intensely personal way.[83] While the staff of CIR clearly believed in the merits of their cases, the newsletter shows that their mental energy was clearly directed at what they believed were hypocritical and intellectually mediocre opponents. Especially venomous was the opening essay in each issue, "The Last Line of Defense," which took its title from an Arnold Schwarzenegger movie, *True Lies*. For example, in reference to Title IX, the *Docket Report* mocked the feminist position. "For every female athletic slot that's been created over the past five years, five positions have been terminated. But that doesn't matter because we need equity and because without Title IX, women will again have their feet bound and because then what would that do to the WNBA."[84] Regarding the law firm of Harry Reasoner, the opposing counsel in *Hopwood*, CIR noted that "the [*National Journal*] ratings [of law firm minority participation] show, *inter alia*, the number of black partners at Mr. Reasoner's 539-lawyer firm, and wouldn't you know, the answer is *one*. Do let's hope Mr. Reasoner takes him to the country club."[85] Assessing the Violence Against Women Act, the *Report* cautioned that "in all the excitement over the discovery that there are constitutional limits to congressional power, it's easily overlooked that VAWA is not—repeat, not—a sensible law that, unfortunately, must give way to more important constitutional constraints. VAWA is a piece of feminist demagoguery—a 'conceptual breakthrough,' NOW calls it—that thoroughly deserves a short life and a brutal, violent death."[86] The common denominator in all of these comments is an unwillingness to accept, as IJ has, the purported goals of liberalism, which CIR consistently argued were a smokescreen for power and attempts to circumvent constitutional rights.

Limitations on the Conservative Public Interest Law Network

Though both organizations have succeeded in reorienting conservative public interest law, both CIR and IJ have faced important limits on their effectiveness. The most significant constraint is the limited number of conservative lawyers willing and able to provide their skills to pro bono work, especially in areas less glamorous than IJ and CIR's headline-grabbing cases. Attracting attorneys to participate in the conservative legal cause was a central part of the legal strategies mapped out by the second generation of conservative public interest law. This was especially true for the Center for Individual Rights, which sought to keep its staff and budget small by depending on outside pro bono counsel drawn from veterans of the Reagan administration and lawyers identified through the Federalist Society's recently developed lawyers chapters.

Inherent in the enterprise of public interest law—of any ideological coloration—is the challenge of attracting ambitious lawyers with enormous earning potential into poorly compensated, controversial, and time-consuming public interest work. As chapter 2 showed, this was one of the liberal legal networks' most vexing problems, but it has turned out to be even more difficult for conservatives than for their liberal predecessors. First, liberals have been able to draw upon the powerful cultural resonance between the pursuit of justice (defined in legal liberal terms) and a career in law, while there are relatively few such normative resources for conservative lawyers to draw upon.[87] Second, the suspicion among legal liberals that private, unregulated markets are a haven for injustice creates a target for activism in the millions of everyday transactions of a capitalist economy. Public interest lawyers doing even fairly mundane activities (such as bringing suits against landlords or poring through environmental impact statements) can easily imagine that they are part of a more sweeping attempt to civilize capitalism. Libertarian conservatives by contrast, want a less regulated society, and thus the environment for legal activism writ small is more circumscribed. Third, as chapter 2 documented, much of the infrastructure of modern public interest law, from law school clinics to pro bono activism in private law firms and service as government lawyers, has been organized by legal liberals and is encoded with the ideology of their designers. It should not be a surprise that these channels are not particularly open, or at the least attractive, to conservatives and libertarians. Fourth, and probably most important, conservatives rarely believe, as many liberals do, that large, corporate law firms are inherently morally polluting, and are consequently less willing to make the large financial sacrifices inherent in public interest law.

Conservative firms face the same competitive pressures as public interest law firms on the left. McDonald observes that

> the pay scale for good attorneys has gone off the [charts]. I think, in this respect, left or right, it's mostly the same. You're left with people whose heart is in the right (or left) place, and they may be competent, but what you really need are Supreme Court law clerk types who are really sharp. Otherwise you have attorneys of the type who run walk-in legal clinics and process cases. They learn their job, but it's just a job. They don't care. There are boutique constitutional firms in D.C. that pay really large salaries to get the people we wanted. We had a young woman who was excellent but since a firm like that offered her five times as much to work for them she couldn't "afford" the luxury of PI law.

CIR's original organizational design was, in part, a response to this competitive situation. "We couldn't afford to hire a Scalia or a Rehnquist clerk, but Jones Day or whomever could. Fine, let them hire the clerk, and then let CIR 'pitch' a good constitutional law case to them, and let them lobby their firm to take it."[88] While this model pushes much of the costs of litigation off CIR's books, it also puts extraordinary demands on its handful of in-house lawyers, who must be exceptionally skilled and creative, while also sufficiently malleable to fit the organization's peculiar structure. Given the still-limited resources of the larger conservative network, the constraints of public interest work, the temperament of conservative lawyers, and patrons' lack of interest in nurturing future staff members, CIR has faced a continuing problem of finding lawyers with the right temperament and skills. Pell recalls that

> we had this guy working for us for three years, the intake lawyer, a good guy, really smart. Compared to private sector salaries we were paying him a pittance. Well, it finally became clear when he left that he was independently wealthy. . . . [By contrast] Rosman and I, who are the permanent types around here now, just feel like we fell into this fantastic opportunity where we can do something that we really want to do. Both of us have decided that it's just worth paying the price, without any security. I don't know where you'd find people like us.

In addition to the problem of competing financially with private sector firms, the controversial nature of the firm's docket, the lack of job security, and the still imperfectly institutionalized nature of the organization create further challenges.

CIR is still a very ad hoc organization, and somebody who comes to work for CIR feels like they've walked off a cliff. It's partially the impermanence of the organization—who knows, it could be out of existence in a couple of years. It's partially the race question; it does not make it easy to go from CIR to academia or another law firm. IJ spends a lot of time cultivating all that institutional mystique and ethos, boot camps and weekends, clinic; they have all that junk. They're cultivating human assets. We don't spend ten seconds doing that and everybody knows it. Someone who comes to work for us basically knows they're on their own.[89]

CIR was able to do without a significant investment in recruitment and training for its first fifteen years because of the commitment of its founders and the draw that its caseload had on smart, ideologically committed young lawyers. Greve and McDonald have now moved on to other things, and the legal environment is no longer the "target-rich" environment that it once was. These changes may make CIR difficult to sustain as a major player in conservative public interest law in the coming years.

The Institute for Justice has gone much further than CIR in attempting to solve the supply problem, and it needs to, since its litigation strategy depends upon in-house lawyers and following up its high-profile cases with a large number of "copycat cases." From its earliest days, IJ put a substantial amount of time, energy, and money into training conservative legal activists. An early grant solicitation, which placed support for educating lawyers before IJ's litigation program,[90] noted that

> while principled advocacy is essential, it is beyond the province of any one organization or group of individuals to accomplish all that needs to be done. Quite simply, there are not enough trained advocates who know how to make use of the unique tools that our type of public interest law has to offer. Consequently, a substantial effort must be made to train law students, lawyers, and policy activists how to apply their talent and idealism in the real world of litigation, media relations, and public debate. With such training, the talent pool of effective advocates will be increased dramatically and the chances of ultimate success will rise immeasurably. . . . Law schools teach students how to be technicians manipulating an increasingly prescriptive system of laws and regulation, too often without regard for principle or philosophy. Lawyers, driven by the demands of private practice, rarely recognize opportunities to advance principles within the context of their practices. . . . Our seminars would thus fill an important niche and provide critically important training that would enhance the long term effectiveness of all who attend.[91]

IJ, unlike CIR, was deeply concerned in its early years that there were not enough skilled, experienced litigators to go around. While the Federalist Society would help identify interested lawyers, it could do little to increase the numbers of conservatives willing to devote themselves to full-time public interest litigation. IJ has tried to remedy the supply problem by encouraging young lawyers and law students to filter through conservative public interest law organizations, in the hopes that close contact with public interest law would lessen the draw of private law practice. IJ runs a three-day annual summer seminar at Georgetown University, and has substantial and well-developed clerkship and internship programs, including opportunities in its recently developed state chapters. According to John Kramer, these programs have played an important role in persuading young law students to consider a career in public interest law, and have identified a large number of IJ's hires over the last few years. "Historically, that is a real proving ground for us. The students come in through that, they've excelled before . . . and they've seen, from an inside perspective, how we operate and have an appreciation for that style of communication and litigation."

CIR, on the other hand, has always had a less fleshed-out educational and developmental program. Terry Pell attributes the difference between the two organizations in this area to the pressures of fund-raising.

> We have this summer clerk program, and it used to be this disorganized thing, and whoever showed up showed up and that was that. Well, one of the first things I did was to highlight this thing with a big article in the newsletter and a special letter to all of our donors introducing it. I even had these kids write letters. Then we sent out a questionnaire asking people to rank all the things CIR does and one of them was training young lawyers through the summer clerk program. Well, that was universally the lowest-ranked thing we did. Donors didn't care whether we did that at all. . . . Donors' basic message was, whatever you do, go win cases. Anything that's a distraction from winning cases we don't care about. So if we had a clinic, they would just say, you guys should be out winning cases, not running clinics. Somebody else should do that. IJ has different donors.

The training and development of lawyers has, at best, a second-order relationship to the issues that motivate CIR's patrons, who in most cases were attracted by the firm's reputation for high-profile litigation and naturally continue to be concerned with winning battles in the here and now. Identifying and nurturing talent is a reasonable fit with IJ's personal, human-scale organizational culture, its broader ambitions, and the image of itself that it projects to donors. CIR's abstract, intellectual, legalistic organizational culture and narrower focus on particular cases, by contrast, attracts different kinds of donors with, at least in Pell's view, different time horizons and willingness to accept diffuse outcomes that will be reaped by the conservative movement as a whole. While it would be very difficult to verify the qualitative difference in IJ and CIR's donor base, the following figures show significance convergence in CIR and IJ's foundation patrons, but considerable divergence in their individual donor base.[92]

A. Percentage of IJ $10,000-and-up donors who give anything to CIR:
   i. Foundations 16.7 percent
   ii. Individuals 8.1 percent
B. Percentage of IJ $10,000-and-up donors who gave at least $10,000 to CIR:
   i. Foundations 16.7 percent
   ii. Individuals 3.5 percent
C. Total number of $10,000-and-up donors to CIR vs. IJ:
   i. Foundations 8 vs. 37
   ii. Individuals 11 vs. 86
D. Percentage of all $10,000-and-up donors to CIR who also gave to IJ:
   i. Foundations 75 percent
   ii. Individuals 30 percent

Given IJ's substantially larger budget (three times larger than CIR),[93] it is not surprising that only a small percentage of its donors contribute to CIR. What is more surprising is that, despite its smaller budget, only 30 percent of CIR's larger donors gave to IJ. So it may be that the differences in the two organizations' ability to invest in human capital is, as Pell argues, driven by what can be sold to their patrons.

The leaders of CIR and IJ both agree that recruiting conservative lawyers into public interest law—either as a career or through pro bono work—has been the second generation's greatest organizational failure. Chip Mellor notes, "It's been one of our goals all along with our training program for lawyers, and I'll tell you, it hasn't been as successful as I'd like. It's had some success, but, boy, I would have hoped for much more. . . . I think every one we get is a plus, but I'm no longer thinking that there is this unmobilized army out there waiting to charge the ramparts." Rosman believes that much of the supply problem can be attributed to ideological bias. "It is very hard for conservative people in private practices in large firms to do pro bono work as easily as it is for those with liberal political views." In his experience, large private law firms are more likely to see public relations problems with conservative rather than liberal pro bono activities, even if they don't have a direct ideological bias against such activity. As chapter 5 shows, the Federalist Society has invested substantial resources in using publicity to change the behavior of large firms' pro bono committees and networking lawyers in private practice with public interest work, but it is too early to determine whether it will be successful.

The more fundamental source of the conservative legal movement's failure to match their liberal legal counterparts' commitment to public interest law work may be internal to the movement itself. Pell believes that the problem is traceable to the unwillingness of many conservative lawyers to play a supporting role in legal change:

> Conservatives have been trained with the idea that you can bring one blockbuster case that changes legal precedent forever, and you can do it without discovery by filing a few clever motions. . . . They are less likely to take cases where it's murky, complicated, involves lots of procedural hoops along the way and where you're playing the angles along the way through a lot of discovery. That is not the kind of case that appeals to conservative lawyers. The other kind of case that doesn't appeal to them is the run-of-the-mill "So-and-so didn't get tenure and it's a race preference. It's like every other one of these cases but it would be a good idea if someone took it, wouldn't you like to take it." The answer is invariably, "No, I would not." Let me litigate the Michigan case but I don't want to bother with some small employment discrimination case. There's no conservative who thinks they belong in the minor leagues, as a general matter. With liberals, if you go to any law firm pro bono committee, they just have dozens of moronic little cases where they're representing some tenant in a landlord-tenant dispute and it's the individual rather than the larger legal principle that attracts lawyers to those cases. . . . So somebody gets a sense that they are helping the cause when they bring one of these little cases. The conservative mission is not built around a lot of little cases, so people feel sidelined when you give them one.

Any legal movement needs to have an informal division of labor, with a substantial pool of lawyers willing to engage in fairly routine but often labor-intensive trial work that applies existing precedents. The conservative public interest law field, by contrast, is top-heavy, with a reasonable number of lawyers willing to volunteer for "A Team" work but few willing to participate at the lower ranks. This vice may be inseparable from the virtues of the more libertarian (as opposed to religious) side of conservatism: a belief system that does not celebrate an ethos of service, humility, or collective endeavor is likely to be hampered when movement activities call for just those attributes. Christian conservatives, by contrast, have been able to draw upon religious supports for these qualities, and seem to have been more successful in drawing a wide base of lawyers to bring non-precedent-setting cases.[94]

The lack of a "B Team" to support the CIR and IJ "A Team" has also meant that conservatives have been less able to avail themselves of the spontaneous, unplanned action that their Hayekian principles point to. The dearth of conservative and libertarian lawyers willing to engage in pro bono activity means that most conservative legal activism flows through firms like CIR and IJ, rather than bubbling up from below. As Mellor observes, "The biggest lack right now is dedicated pro bono work by a cadre of conservative and libertarian lawyers around the country.

I'm not even talking about finding them, because we don't use them. I'm talking about people who go out there and do it on their own voluntarily, and I just don't see it happening." This lack of unplanned, entrepreneurial litigation reduces the opportunity for unorthodox legal strategies or trial and error, and so conservatives are betting a great deal on the effectiveness of legal strategies developed at the top of the legal food chain.

Two of IJ's more recent projects, its entrepreneurship clinic at the University of Chicago and its state chapters, may have some effect on increasing supply in the long term. Started in 1997, IJ's Clinic on Entrepreneurship can be directly linked to its annual training program. University of Chicago law professor Richard Epstein recalls,

> We had two students, Mark Chenoweth, who is now at the Koch Foundation, and Tim Koh, who keeps bouncing around from one Senate committee to another and I think is now clerking for Justice Thomas. [They] went to an IJ conference where they talked about freedom of contract [and] limited government. . . . They came into my office and said, "You know Chip Mellor?" I said, "Yeah, I've been involved with Chip from the beginning." . . . They said, "We'd like to start a clinic here that would do some transactional work," and their attitude was that too many people who think about civil rights think about beating people over the head to hire them, and their attitude is rather than beat other people over the head, we want to beat the government over the head. . . . It will be a transactional clinic which will help people get through the regulatory maze. So they came to me and I was strongly in favor of it. The clinic people were originally very dubious about this. . . . IJ was known to be ideological, and what they didn't know is that . . . they have most stellar reputation of anyone I've every dealt with. . . . They have a terribly conciliatory style of doing business. There were hearings and objections. . . . He [Mellor] came here, and he never rose to the bait, which is more than you can say for me. The dean was Douglas Baird, and he was uneasy about doing this himself, so he set up a committee. In the end the committee realized it would be a great deal. In the first year there was some suspicion, but in the six or seven years it has been in place there has not been a peep of dissent or controversy on the part of anybody.

Given IJ's ideological reputation, opposition was almost inevitable. In the end, IJ's reputation for competence, its ability to fund the program itself, and the opportunity provided by the existing structure of clinical education at the Law School helped sweep away opposition. Epstein recalls that the clinic was

> in a sense . . . ideological, but in a way that appealed to both left and right. All of these clinics have an ideology. The mental health clinic trying to protect people who were thrown out in the street by the city, they would be appalled if they thought they were some sort of neutral [project]. . . . The program was

fully funded from the outside, which was a huge advantage when we needed to expand our capabilities. It was a transactional program when we had none before. . . . There was a long debate on whether they would have to take cases from needy clients that didn't fit their mission statement, like supporting quotas or affirmative action. After a while, people realized, hey, we don't tell any of our clinics what cases to take or how to run them. The questions were such things as who gets to control the appointments, and we decided that they [IJ] get to propose the appointments and we have to ratify.

The Law School was already supporting clinics with controversial cases, such as the MacArthur Justice Center, which specializes in challenges to the death penalty, prison conditions, and conditions at Guantánamo Bay. Consequently, it was difficult to challenge IJ's program on the basis of its ideology without raising problems for the existing programs. So far, the clinic has not produced any significant legal cases, and few if any of its alumni have gone into public interest law, which is not surprising given that most of its participants are specialists in business law, and its caseload is focused on transactions, not litigation. IJ hopes to replicate its clinic at other law schools when the right opportunity presents itself.[95]

IJ's other effort to extend its reach and attract new lawyers into libertarian public interest law work are its state chapters in Arizona, Minnesota, and Washington. Clint Bolick recalls the original impetus for the chapters:

We began noticing several years ago that in some areas, especially school choice and eminent domain, we were litigating mostly state constitutional issues. The Left discovered the utility of state constitutions decades ago. For all our talk about federalism, most conservative litigating groups have focused on federal constitutional issues. We began a two-year study of the potential for state chapters focusing on state constitutional issues. We also studied liberal groups, especially the ACLU, to examine their models.

So far, IJ's experience in state-level public interest law has been mixed. In Arizona, IJ had a number of advantages, not the least of which was Bolick's willingness to move to Phoenix when the chapter was created in 2001. In addition,

We chose Arizona because we had good contacts there, we had litigated there with success, it has an honest judiciary, there is a strong free-market policy organization (Goldwater Institute), and it has a libertarian tradition. Subsequently we opened chapters in North Carolina and Washington. North Carolina did not work out because we could not find the right director—we now recognize that human capital is the first prerequisite to success—and could not find sufficient core-mission cases. It is in transition to a North Carolina—based public interest law firm. Arizona and Washington are going great. We just won a wonderful eminent domain precedent in Arizona that will aid our efforts in other states. We are currently investigating potential in other states.[96]

Setting up state chapters is a natural outgrowth of IJ's emphasis on "grass-roots tyranny." Eminent domain, for example, has certain similarities to such popular liberal areas of litigation as housing and criminal law, in that there are thousands of opportunities to challenge administrative decisions, which allows individual lawyers to feel a part of something much more significant than their individual case. These cases, combined with IJ's increasing state-level organizational presence and additional libertarian-oriented clinics, may help to overcome the movement's continuing absence of a B Team. The effects of all of these activities are still unclear, and will be for some time to come.

Organizational Adaptation and Evolution

As we saw in the discussion of "boundary maintenance" in chapter 5, successful organizational entrepreneurs must avoid absorbing new functions that distract from or contradict their original mission while, at the same time, developing new areas of opportunity consistent with the organization's core functions. Failing at the first of these can lead to resource constraints, a loss of organizational focus, and a confused public image. Failing at the second can lead to a loss of organizational dynamism as rival organizations exploit new opportunities and staff become bored and move on to other opportunities. IJ began life with a clear and consistent legal strategy and issue focus, so the greatest threat to its organizational flourishing has been losing focus and being drawn into areas in tension with its original mission. Given that CIR was designed to be flexible and opportunistic, its greatest challenge has been to avoid being trapped in cases that limit its ability to discover and take advantage of unexploited prospects for legal change. While CIR maintained extraordinary dynamism in its early years, the demands of its affirmative action litigation have made it less effective than IJ in overcoming its fundamental challenge.

The issue of affirmative action has presented the most serious challenge to IJ's organizational focus. While IJ as an organization has never litigated the issues of affirmative action or race-based congressional districting, the topic was a priority for Clint Bolick, whose interest in it dated back to his service on the Equal Employment Opportunity Commission. Bolick's involvement with these issues reached its hottest point when President Clinton nominated Lani Guinier to be assistant attorney general for civil rights. Bolick famously penned an op-ed accusing both Guinier and Education Department nominee Norma Cantu of being "Clinton's Quota Queens,"[97] helping set off a controversial confirmation battle that ended with the withdrawal of Guinier's nomination. Bolick went on less than two years later to attack Deval Patrick, and then four years later Bill Lann Lee, for the same position as Guinier, and for the same reason.[98] Bolick capped off this involvement by publishing *The Affirmative Action Fraud* in 1996.[99]

This activity brought Bolick and IJ enormous public attention and a high profile in the conservative movement. Mellor recalls that "Clint was very good at being a media personality on [affirmative action]. He was the go-to guy whenever there was a contentious issue, and then he takes on Lani Guinier. To everyone's surprise, we win. And so he became a prominent national spokesperson on that issue, and with that came opportunities for more—litigation, money, publicity." Despite the enormous attention it attracted, affirmative action was an issue where opportunistically responding to attention ran counter to IJ's core mission. Mellor explains that

> there just came a point on it, after a couple of years, where it became clear that this was a distraction. We were really getting out into an issue that was not central to our mission, and furthermore it was [creating] conflict in the very [same] communities that were most directly active in our litigation and encumbering the organization and the other individuals in the organization with issues that were counterproductive. . . . So we said, let's not do that anymore. . . . Despite the fact that a lot of points were wonderfully well made and completely valid it just didn't complement our issues, and we had just gotten into it because of Clint's personal interest and the surprise success of the Lani Guinier issue and allowed that to be a target of opportunity that just pulled us further and further down this one path. . . . One of the keys to our success has been staying focused—seizing occasional targets of opportunity but staying focused and not getting distracted, and when we were distracted, getting rapidly out.

Affirmative action has always been a difficult issue for IJ. Despite Mellor and especially Bolick's intense disagreement with the policy, the issue runs counter to IJ's organizational culture, which is optimistic and oriented to pushing conservative "empowerment" approaches to the problems of the poor and racial minorities. Criticizing liberal policies like affirmative action was, by contrast, "more of a CIR thing."[100]

All of CIR's successes, by contrast, have come from being nimble and opportunistic, but the organization's responses to those opportunities have created commitments that now make it difficult to reorient it around new areas of litigation. This threatens to produce the kind of institutionalization its founders feared. Terry Pell recalls that "the Greve model was to blow up the institution, essentially. He never wanted the institution to get to the point where it couldn't be easily blown up." Greve's study of the environmental movements of the United States and Germany[101] had sensitized him to the risk that organizational maintenance imperatives could encourage public interest movements to stay committed to a particular line of cases or issues once the opportunity for a major impact had passed. This commitment to organizational nimbleness also reflected a strategic assessment of conservatives' position in modern American institutions.

> They [liberals] are much more concerned about permanently owning territory, so however the law changes, they just adapt them to the territory that they've already acquired. The Right does not own much institutional territory at all, so the only tool we've got is some big ideological or legal precedent that you can quickly get without having to run a lot of institutions. Whereas the Left owns every big university in the country because they control the personnel, the way we influence those institutions is to get their race preference policy struck down by the Supreme Court. Because we don't control those institutions, we have to do this from the outside.[102]

CIR believed that the most conservatives could achieve through the courts were formal legal victories that established a legal principle, rather than wholesale reform.

Staying nimble and remaining open to new areas of opportunity was, in part, a recognition of the limited potential of the law to transform institutions controlled by liberals. Avoiding excessive commitment to a particular issue was also connected to CIR's preference for a lean organizational form. Staying small required that CIR pursue reasonably clear precedents that would avoid the need for substantial, resource-intensive, follow-on litigation. This contrasted with what they viewed as the legal strategy of the Left, which was to obtain relatively diffuse, "balancing"-type rulings that could be used as a resource in subsequent waves of litigation and bureaucratic politics. Both CIR's size and the temperament and normative commitments of its staff made long-term commitment to an issue unappealing.

> Wanting to have clear laws drives the size of our organization and our desire to be nimble. People here do not find it interesting to file the same case over and over again . . . or to organize legions of lawyers to bring the same case over and over again. . . . Lawyers on the right, they always want to be involved in the biggest, baddest, most precedent-setting case around. They don't want to bring the follow-on cases. On the other hand, the Left has organized itself to bring hundred and thousands of follow-on cases. So if they get some little slight advantage in a legal precedent anywhere, they're organized to take advantage of it in all kinds of different contexts. That's one institutional advantage they have over us. We're just organized to do a different thing.[103]

The emphasis on "wholesale litigation" can be seen in the diminishing role of religious liberty and academic free speech in CIR's caseload. This was partially driven by the demands of CIR's affirmative action cases, which required a long-term commitment and attention to fund-raising that severely tested CIR's organizational design. The decline of the issue was also a matter of conscious design. As McDonald argues, "We did want to be first to make a big point and clear the way for other groups to do things wholesale." With its precedent in *Rosenberger*, for example, CIR created a powerful precedent that a wide range of other organizations, especially Christian conservatives like the American Center for Law and Justice, could use in their own litigation. By demonstrating that restrictions on campus free speech were vulnerable and would rarely be defended by the courts, CIR made it easy for groups like the Foundation for Individual Rights in Education and the Individual Rights Foundation to create an industry out of suing universities for violating the free speech rights of professors and students.

Paradoxically, CIR committed itself to both nimbleness and a willingness to stick with cases for as long as necessary. In its previous litigation, this latter commitment had not created any serious problems for CIR as the cases were not fact-intensive and were susceptible to relatively quick resolution. Terry Pell notes that the affirmative action cases, beginning with *Hopwood*, exposed this previously unimportant tension in CIR's strategy.

> The problem we ran into was the race preference cases. . . . If we say we're trying to change the law and set new precedent, we can't walk away from this. One of the things we tell our donors is that we pick the tough fights and stay in them for the long haul. . . . We're not dissuaded by this, that, or the other adverse opinion along the way. Well, that means that you can't just walk away from this stuff or your donors wonder what you're doing. In this case one of the big challenges we've had is that the race preference cases have swallowed up the ability of CIR to be flexible and take risks and move onto new areas. Our time is spent just keeping that thing alive and moving.

The difficulty that the affirmative action cases have presented is threefold. First, they absorbed an enormous amount of time and effort, which limited CIR's ability to develop new cases and areas of expertise. Second, the cases necessarily put a damper on CIR's freewheeling intellectual organizational culture. With a commitment as large and challenging as affirmative action, the scrutiny on CIR's utterances increased exponentially, and as a consequence there was pressure for staff to stay "on message." This meant, for example, avoiding saying in public what at least one staff member believed, which is that all of the civil rights laws reaching private conduct were unconstitutional. This created enormous stresses for an organization that prided itself on fearless truth-telling and an unwillingness to bend to political correctness. It also took some of the fun out of what, for its first few years, had been an incredibly exciting environment to operate in.

Finally, the fund-raising required by the affirmative action cases also had a profound effect on CIR's previously dynamic organizational structure. Affirmative action certainly fit CIR's strategy of attacking the discretion of liberal institutions and had the benefit of attracting a large number of new donors, many of whom were frustrated by the Republican Party's hesitancy in attacking the issue. After receiving a surprise gift of $1.5 million from a previously low-dollar donor, CIR hired a number of staff attorneys, moving the organization away from its original, lean structure, toward something that looked more like IJ. Michael McDonald recalls that

> the official rationale for hiring more attorneys was: we now know this stuff, affirmative action. So we don't need to continually look for cooperating counsel. We have the money to do the cases in-house, but we didn't really want to do run-of-the-mill AA cases. So we had one foot in the old model and one foot in the newer model. I saw it wasn't working and advocated returning to the older model, but we had the ACLU-envy problem. Certain people close to us or on our board would say, "Why can't you be like the ACLU and have a chapter in every state or do more wholesale litigation." I suppose that was one of the many things we never fully sorted out.

This influx of new money into the organization thus created two problems. First, it loosened the external constraints that made CIR's original organizational structure a necessity. Second, the presence of a substantial pool of new donors attracted by affirmative action and unfamiliar with CIR's organizational culture has made it difficult to reorient the firm around new issues. This has fed back into problems in attracting significant legal talent to the firm, since CIR can only compensate for its relatively low salaries and the stigma that attaches to its affirmative action cases by maintaining a reputation for intellectual excitement and challenge. It has become clear to CIR's leaders that what is necessary in order to attract entrepreneurial people—a constant stream of new cases—may run counter to what is necessary to hold onto a mature funding base.

> Donors are like students. They sign up for your class because they have an idea of what they're going to get, and you have to have an idea of what they think they're getting, so you can make them feel like they got that. We have a subset of our donors who are only interested in affirmative action, but I think that is only a subset. The larger group of donors is interested in affirmative action or other things like affirmative action. . . . So when you pick a new area you have

to take your donors as they are and kind of move them and explain to them why, given what they've already found interesting, they might also find this other thing interesting. So it's a game. . . . There is [also] an institutional fatigue factor. The people who started these things were very entrepreneurial; Mike Greve and Mike McDonald are examples of that. Well, you just get tired after a while. This institution has been around for ten years and it's just harder to get people excited about doing a new thing. So that pushes people in the direction of doing something that's predictable.[104]

Despite all the attention that *Hopwood*, *Gratz*, and *Grutter* brought to CIR, the issue also created a powerful, self-reinforcing dynamic rooted in its new donor base that has eaten away at the organization's opportunistic ethos. The choice to attack affirmative action was fateful, as once CIR took on affirmative action, its reputation within the conservative movement rested upon its ability to push these cases to a conclusion, no matter how long it took or the impact the cases had on its organizational culture.

IJ has effectively managed the challenges to its organizational focus, but CIR has found it difficult to move on from the affirmative action cases that have absorbed so much of its time and attention. IJ effectively extricated itself from the issue of affirmative action, thereby regaining its concentration on its core issues and eliminating a substantial obstacle to "strange bedfellows" coalitions with local minority groups. CIR has, in the last few years, begun to open up new litigation areas, such as its challenge to the authority of Child Protective Services agencies to order medical procedures opposed by parents or legal guardians.[105] While this issue may be genuinely important, it lacks the gut-level appeal to the conservative movement or the potential for establishing wide-ranging precedent of CIR's earlier cases. CIR, having thrived on opportunism in the past, may find it hard to regain the energy it once had as its involvement with affirmative action continues and the number of attractive targets for its style of litigation diminishes.

Conclusion

As the example of the first generation of conservative public interest law showed, opportunities, threats, and the availability of resources do not necessarily translate into effective social movement organizations. As a consequence, it is possible for social movements to miss opportunities when their organizations are not up to the task of exploiting changes in the political environment. The development of effective political organizations is a highly contingent process that unfolds over time, and to understand it requires probing deeply into social movements' internal reevaluation of past investments and innovations in political strategy and tactics. It is this internal rhythm of puzzling and problem solving, rather than changes in the political environment, that seems most important in explaining the emergence of conservative public interest law's second generation.

The second-generation conservative firms were the product of intra-movement learning: when combined with their continued interest in promoting legal change, patrons' post—Horowitz Report recognition that previous approaches to conservative public interest law had been failures provided an opening for new organizational entrepreneurs to approach patrons for support. Because first-generation firms faced strong incentives to maintain their approach, this learning process occurred through generational replacement rather than organizational evolution. It took ten years of missed litigation opportunities before this process of learning and generational replacement produced CIR and IJ. This points to a factor largely missing from studies of legal "backlash":[106] organizational entrepreneurs, and the patrons who support them, are the essential link between political opportunities and political outcomes. Explaining when and how backlash occurs thus requires that we recognize the considerable intellectual, organizational, and resource mobilization obstacles that countermobilizing agents face.

Overcoming the obstacles to effective countermobilization in public interest law depended upon the maturing of the broader conservative legal movement. Movement patrons had to wait for a new generation of leaders to emerge and for them to develop sufficient experience and strategic sophistication to be a reasonable outlet for sizable, long-term investment. In addition, second-generation strategies depended upon the growth of a broad network of conservative lawyers and the ripening of the movement's ideas. The Federalist Society was the conservative movement's core investment in the development of both of these resources, and so it is not an accident that the second-generation firms emerged after the Society had become a major, institutionalized presence in American legal culture.

The success of IJ and CIR also depended upon a shift in the character of conservative patrons, from business leaders to foundation directors. Leaders of the conservative legal movement had been repeatedly frustrated by the lack of imagination and principle of American businessmen and their willingness to cooperate with government despite their rhetorical attachment to antistatism. The emergence of forthrightly libertarian firms like IJ and CIR, therefore, had to await the decline of business's leadership of the conservative movement and its replacement with an alliance between intellectuals and charitable foundations. The leaders of these foundations shared with those they funded a primary locus of social-

ization and network in the world of ideas rather than the world of enterprise. Thus the public interest law firms capable of defending the free
market depended strongly on the emergence of a "new class" of conservative activists motivated by ideological and cultural goals rather than economic interests. This new class of conservative activists—both patrons
and organizational entrepreneurs—have found their inspiration in the empowerment of the inner-city poor, affirmative action, and academic freedom, rather than the interests of business.

The shift of conservative public interest law's "principals" from business to the new class of conservative patrons and entrepreneurs accompanied a transformation in the movement's ideological orientation. Whereas
most of the first-generation firms were traditionally conservative in orientation, Capital Legal Foundation, CIR, and IJ all flew the flag of libertarianism, and the most successful litigation by first-generation firms (such
as Pacific Legal Foundation's work in *Nollan*) had a libertarian spirit as
well. These firms were able to take advantage of a structural bias in the
American legal system orienting public interest law to challenging governmental discretion and power rather than (as many traditional conservatives preferred) defending it. When legal conservatives have sought to
limit the power of government, either through the use of the commerce
clause, the First Amendment, or the takings clause, their success has been
impressive. However, when they have attempted to use public interest law
to support the authority of government, they have found little success.[107]
This bias in the American legal system led CIR, for example, to converge
with the libertarianism of IJ, and has given the firm some unexpected
affinities with its liberal counterparts. Terry Pell observes that

> the norms [of most large institutions] are driven by the general principle of
> efficiency. That's what these managerial institutions are supposed to do, achieve
> a certain objective in the most efficient way possible without questioning
> whether that objective is a legitimate objective to pursue at all. . . . We, all of
> us, on the left and the right, are the ones saying, "No, we ought to be having a
> debate about whether efficiency in this area is such a good idea, and whether
> the ends being served here are appropriate in a free society."

The enterprise of public interest law gives firms like IJ and CIR other
interests in common with their liberal counterparts, especially where the
political economy of public interest lawyering is concerned. For instance, any measure that would reduce the financial lure of high-paying
corporate law work, or that increased the prestige of public interest law,
would solve both liberal and conservative firms' problems in attracting
high-quality legal talent. Firms like IJ and CIR are certainly a part of
the larger conservative-libertarian movement, but they are also public
interest lawyers, and this gives them a different view of the world than
their ideological allies.

Conclusion _____

THESE FINAL PAGES move beyond the case of the law, identifying directions for future research on large-scale political change and the lessons of the conservative experience for political entrepreneurs and patrons. Drawing on the cases in the preceding chapters, I present an approach to understanding the rhythms and mechanisms of large-scale political change, one that puts agency, contingency, and policy and institutional variability at its core. Second, I identify what the example of the law can teach us about the transformation of the conservative movement over the past forty years. In doing so, I place special emphasis on conservatism's shift from a movement dominated by business, grassroots organizations, and Republican elected officials to one increasingly directed by a conservative "new class" of ideologically motivated actors. Third, I conclude by asking what lessons the experience of conservatives in the law over the past forty years hold for political entrepreneurs and patrons, both in the law and beyond.

The Rhythms and Sources of Political Change

Social scientists have a long-standing fascination with modeling politics as a market with a natural tendency toward equilibrium. In the famous "Hotelling" model of political competition, losing political parties were modeled as adjusting their bids to the electorate by moving closer to the median voter.[1] The force of political competition, this model claimed, ruled out long-term political or policy advantage. American political history, however, has been marked by long periods in which one ideological "team" outcompetes the other, producing institutional and policy change in its preferred direction for decades. If politics is truly competitive, the losing side in political competition should rapidly compete away any advantages possessed by the winners.

The Hotelling model assumes that political markets are like markets for commodities, in that the demand is fixed, products are homogenous, technology of production is simple and transparent, start-up costs are low, and barriers to entry are nonexistent. These are very poor assumptions for modern politics, in which the agenda is up for grabs (demand is variable and products are differentiated), the technology of production is complex and nontransparent (expertise and political strategy are important), start-up costs are high (complex organizations are required that demand substantial trial and error to produce), and barriers to entry are significant (those created by policies and institutional design, and through the transfer of politically significant activity into civil society). The complexity of political competition means that actors do not limit themselves to the marginal advantages of median voter models, but seek to construct a "regime" that will generate supernormal profits over a span of decades. In that sense, politics is more like markets for technology than markets for potatoes.[2]

The foregoing chapters identified four sources of durable competitive advantage in politics: ideas and arguments, political strategies and institutional design, the reputations of political movements, and entrenchment in civil society. Of these, ideas are especially important. Political movements can attain a durable advantage by identifying their own ideas with common sense, intellectual seriousness, responsibility, professionalism, and ordinary decency, while claiming that their opponents' ideas are "off the wall"—eccentric, irresponsible, morally dubious, and outside the professional mainstream. A movement whose ideas have been effectively branded as off the wall will find it impossible to attract supporters who are, like most professionals, acutely concerned with being seen as responsible, serious, and mainstream.

Ideational entrenchment was an especially acute challenge for conservatives, and overcoming it was the object of some of the movement's longest-term projects. In its early years the organizational entrepreneurs of the law and economics movement devoted enormous effort to overcoming the widespread belief that the approach was nothing more than thinly veiled ideology, properly dismissed rather than argued with. The Federalist Society was founded by conservative students in elite law schools to force the legal establishment to seriously consider ideas that were typically dismissed as strange or reactionary. Public interest law firms faced the challenge of ideational entrenchment as well, and were forced to devote significant resources to convincing courts that resurrecting the commerce and takings clauses of the Constitution was something more than a far-out attempt to take the nation back to the era of Lochnerism. It was only after they broke through the powerful ideological insulation of legal liberalism that conservatives were able to compete on a reasonably even playing field.

Political strategies and institutional design are a second source of durable competitive advantage in politics. For example, chapter 2 described how liberals developed a network of public interest groups, tied to congressional subcommittees, the regulatory bureaucracy, and the legal profession that were able to maximize the potential of regulatory statutes despite the significant costs this imposed on business and local governments. While conservatives tried to overcome this organizational-institutional alignment through efforts to "defund the Left" and by creating a network of conservative firms to provide the "other side," chapter 3 showed that, well into the 1980s, neither strategy was effective in eroding this source of legal liberals' competitive advantage. It took more than two decades before conservatives were able to effectively use legislation to erode many of the accomplishments of public interest law, and a decade and a half before they had public interest law firms of their own vying for the agenda of the federal courts.[3]

A third source of competitive political advantage can be found in the reputations of political movements. A common device that ordinary citizens and potential recruits use to decide whether to support movements is reliance on the moral reputation of advocates on particular issues. These reputations are sticky because people readily attend to information that reinforces their preexisting evaluations, and so once a movement has developed a reputation, it can be hard to shake. By the 1960s, legal liberalism had come to be associated, especially among the young, with idealism, the individual, civil rights, and a concern with justice, while conservatism was tarred with the brush of self-interest, unseemly ties to business and other large concentrations of power, and a lack of concern for racial justice. These reputations were so powerful that for almost twenty years conservative public interest law was treated as an oxymoron, and with it the belief that the highest ideals of the legal profession could be reconciled with ideological conservatism. The programming of the conservative movement over the last twenty-five years was, to a considerable degree, aimed at transforming this reputation. The Federalist Society organized its conferences and campus speakers to convince young lawyers that conservatism was the movement of serious intellectual thought and legal liberals the defenders of a stale status quo. Following the argument that Michael Horowitz made in 1980, the Institute for Justice's caseload was designed to use high-profile litigation to make liberals look like the defenders of irresponsible, self-interested, concentrated power, while conservatives were the protectors of the public interest, the little guy, and the cause of racial equality. These nonlegal goals meant that IJ could win, in the sense of helping to alter the reputation of conservatism, even when it lost in court.

The final source of durable competitive advantage is political entrenchment in civil society, in our case the legal profession and the nation's law schools. Law schools are especially important to the construction of durable advantage because they are one of the main arbiters of distinction in the legal profession. Competition over control of law schools was, therefore, a battle for who would determine standards of professional honor and prestige and control the boundaries on the kinds of ideas that are held by respectable lawyers. By the early 1970s, the ideological assumptions of law professors, their construction of the profession of legal education, and the movements and interest groups that were institutionally connected to law schools had developed a significant bias toward legal liberalism. Given the self-reproducing character of the professoriate, the perception (if not the reality) that legal education was hostile to conservatives, and the greater attractions of private practice for those on the right, conservatives faced a strategic problem without an obvious solution. While law and economics was a reasonably rapid response to liberal dominance in legal education, in other areas (especially constitutional law), change has been slow. One response, the Olin Fellows program administered by the Federalist Society, appears to have had some success in encouraging the hiring of non–law and economics faculty in elite law schools, but this is still work at the margins.

In all four of these areas, conservatives invested significant time and engaged in widespread experimentation before they figured out how to erode the competitive advantage of legal liberalism. The lag between the emergence of liberals' initial advantage and the development of an effective conservative response was a matter of decades. What can explain this persistence of durable advantage? How can we make sense of when these advantages erode or disappear? To develop an answer, we must begin by reframing the concept of "regime." As I use it, a regime can be said to exist when there are multiple, reinforcing sources of durable advantage present in any particular policy or institutional domain (or, more broadly, when such advantages exist across an entire polity). So, for example, we can say that there was a "liberal legal regime" because of the interacting sources of durable advantage in the realm of ideas, institutions and political strategy, movement reputations, and civil society. The deeper the durable advantage, the more we can say that a particular regime is "entrenched." Put in economic terms, an entrenched regime can be said to allow its supporters to extract monopoly rents or "supernormal" profits.

Thinking of regimes in terms of competition helps us to endogenize the process of political change, because few if any of the sources of durable change are so entrenched as to be immune from challenge. Rather than being noncompetitive, it is better to think about entrenched regimes as being "contestable markets."[4] If regimes really were pure monopolies, then the losers in politics would have no option but to sit back and wait for some exogenous shock to bring them salvation.[5] Like incumbents in contestable markets, however, political regimes almost always have vulnerabilities. Resistance is almost never futile. In most cases, the regime's advantage comes because it has created a "technology" that the other side finds hard to replicate. This is one way to think about the explosion of public interest law in the late 1960s and early 1970s: liberals had created a tool that took conservatives a very long time to make sense of and master, and it was embedded in a social network that conservatives could not match. There was nothing in the liberal advantage in the area that could not be competed away, but it required intellectual, strategic, and organizational creativity that emerged only with a very significant lag.

When these durable competitive advantages are eroded depends upon the character of entrenchment and the quality of agent response. To understand entrenchment and how agents maneuver around it, let us start with two examples from technology. Microsoft was able to derive supernormal profits for a sustained period of time because of barriers to entry created by its intellectual property and the network effects that attracted users and software producers to its dominant standard in operating systems. Dell Computer quickly developed a commanding position in the market for personal computers by combining a just-in-time production process with direct sales to consumers. In the first instance, Microsoft's powerful position on the desktop made it almost impossible to mount a "symmetrical" challenge in the form of an alternative operating system. Instead, Microsoft's competitive position has been threatened by an "asymmetric" challenge from competitors such as Google seeking to move software off the desktop entirely, through web-based applications. In Dell's case, there was never any mystery as to what it was doing, but competitors had substantial investments in preexisting ways of organizing production and sales or failed to reengineer their organizations to execute with Dell's efficiency. Eventually competitors eroded this competitive advantage by a symmetric strategy of mimicry: they simply got better, over time, in doing the things that Dell had done for years. For a decade, however, Dell was able to sustain very high profits and sales, despite its completely transparent strategy. In the first case, change happened when competitors hit upon a rival strategy that exposed a previously unseen or unexploited angle of attack. In the second case, change happened when rivals developed organizational forms that rivaled those of their competitors. In both cases, change came from the skill of rival agents at discovering weaknesses in the dominant actor and developing strategies or organizational forms capable of exploiting it.

The metaphor of technological change can help us understand the endogenous sources of large-scale policy and institutional change, and the cases of IJ and the Center for Individual Rights are a useful place to start. The first source of endogenous change is learning. Previous generations of conservative public interest lawyers simply did not understand the sources of liberal public interest lawyers' success and missed out on significant opportunities to learn from them. It took a new generation of firms, with lawyers who had studied their liberal predecessors closely, to draw appropriate lessons. The second source of endogenous change is organizational structure. The first generation of public interest lawyers was organized along geographic lines in an increasingly centralized polity that rewarded D.C.-based networks and the opportunistic selection of venue. This organizational form was exceptionally sticky, but when conservatives developed new, D.C.-based firms with weak or nonexistent ties to business, they were able to rapidly produce significant victories in the courts and in public opinion. A final source of endogenous change can be found in relationships with patrons. The first generation of public interest lawyers failed to recognize the strategic importance of idealism, and as a consequence their close ties to business hurt their reputation for "public interestedness" and their ability to attract high-quality lawyers. Large-scale change happened when competitors to legal liberalism developed ties to new patrons, leading to a shift in their reputation and ability to attract young lawyers comparable to those of their competitors.

In none of these cases were opportunities for effective political competition unavailable in the decades before they were effectively exploited. That is, the regime of public interest law had *always* been vulnerable. Thinking of entrenchment in terms of unexploited vulnerability moves our attention away from the incumbent to the challenger. If there are almost always vulnerabilities in the incumbent's position, why then are they not taken advantage of? The answer is that entrenchment is the joint product of the structure of the incumbent regime and the failures of rival agents. The rhythm of political change is produced by the interaction of the problems and puzzles generated by the dominant regime with the problem-solving and adaptation of their opponents.

Theorists of path dependence made a significant breakthrough in understanding large-scale political change when they observed that macro-structural stimuli like changing world economic conditions or electoral shocks did not influence countries, or policy areas within countries, equally.[6] The structure of inherited policy commitments or national institutional forms, they argued, substantially mediated the impact of these structural forces. While this was a major step forward in political analysis, it only added one deterministic variable on top of another: instead of electoral power or macroeconomic conditions determining policy outcomes, the structure of inherited commitments did. The losers in this model simply disappear from view, but as the examples in this book show, losers have substantial room for effective action, even when faced with seemingly imposing constraints on change. Strategically sophisticated losers in one period can invest resources in such a way that they are able to erode the disadvantages they will face in the future.[7]

In Paul Pierson's work, special attention is put on the phenomenon of myopia: much of the cause of entrenchment is the focus actors place on the short term, since in the short term it almost always makes sense to pursue marginal gains within an existing regime rather than challenging it. Myopia, however, is a variable rather than a constant, as the examples of long-range behavior in this book make clear. For example, intellectual entrepreneurs at Chicago like Simons and Director made the University into a safe space—an "abeyance structure"—for free market thought at a time when most academic institutions were either hostile or uninterested. In other words, they invested their time and sought out resources for activities designed in the hope that the opportunity structure in the future would be more open than it was in the present. The patrons of the first generation of conservative public interest law, by contrast, invested in activities closely tied to their own firms' short-term bottom line. The returns on their myopic political investments were correspondingly meager.

The patrons of the second generation, by contrast, were willing to wait much longer for their returns. They invested in law and economics in the hopes that it would provide ammunition to defend free markets at some indefinite time in the future and that it would help—in a way that was not entirely clear to them—to shift the balance in law schools. They invested in the Federalist Society, despite the fact that the organization's main outputs, such as networks and idea development, were difficult to measure or trace back to their source and would only bear fruit decades later, when generations of law students matured into senior, practicing lawyers and law professors. They invested in Chip Mellor's Center for Applied Jurisprudence, despite the fact that it was a planning exercise for a firm that did not yet exist and that did not open up shop for another six years. There was nothing dramatically new about the opportunity structure in the 1980s and 1990s where any of these activities were concerned. Instead, change happened because, by that point, a new network of entrepreneurial agents recognized previously ignored strategic opportunities, had plausible plans for how to take advantage of them, and identified long-term oriented patrons willing to bankroll their ideas.

In short, there are always more opportunities floating around a political system than there are actors with the acuity to recognize them or the capacity to effectively exploit them. It is this surplus of opportunities that provides a tempting playing field for organizational entrepreneurs. Skill matters in exploiting these opportunities, but skillful agents are a very scarce commodity, which means there will often be very significant "big bills left on the sidewalk" of political competition.[8] The first generation of public interest law shows what can happen when abundant resources chase too few effective agents, or when those agents are embedded in organizational structures in which creative activity is impossible.

One final point about the sources of long-term change emerges from the examples of the previous chapters: the importance of networks and information. An effective process of learning is vital for political movements seeking to erode entrenched regimes, but learning happens most productively through carefully nurtured networks that facilitate multiple, ongoing interactions by movement actors. Understanding learning, therefore, means understanding the structures in which it occurs. Learning depends on the free flow of information, since the consequences of past experiences need to be quickly conveyed to other agents, compared, and lessons drawn and disseminated. For this to occur, agents need abundant, credible, and reliable information. Where information flow is slow, unreliable, or poorly structured, lesson-drawing will be hampered and experiences will not flow back into subsequent decision-making.

The key to the diffusion of information and the drawing of effective lessons is the development of networks and structured processes for feedback. Networks are often described as emerging through a spontaneous, evolutionary process, but some of the most important networks are the result of conscious design and construction by network entrepreneurs. For example, chapter 5 showed how the debates, meetings, and conventions of the Federalist Society produce powerful networks of conservative lawyers because they create the opportunity for repeated interactions over time and because the ethos of the organization encourages trust. A number of the professors I interviewed for chapter 4 insisted that, in the 1970s, Henry Manne's seminars for law professors and Liberty Fund conferences helped produce networks among the otherwise thinly scattered group of scholars in the field. These meetings allowed for the development, among other things, of personal reputations. For example, the Liberty Fund conferences helped George Priest, then at the obscure University of Puget Sound Law School, to get on the elite legal academy's radar screen, eventually helping him land at Yale Law School.

Information and lesson-drawing also occur through formal processes of feedback, processes that are of special interest to foundation patrons because of their keen interest in evaluating their political investments. The Horowitz Report was solicited by the Scaife Foundation to provide an unvarnished look at conservative public interest law, and the report's lessons deeply impressed themselves on the major conservative patrons. Building on Horowitz's arguments, Mellor's Center for Applied Jurisprudence (funded by the Koch, Bradley, Olin, and Smith Richardson foundations) brought together a wide range of figures in law and other disciplines to consciously think through the experience of conservative public interest law and to identify opportunities and organizational forms that might make it more successful in the future. IJ's emphasis on black empowerment instead of race neutrality, for example, can be traced to these sessions.

Conservative foundations were well suited to acquiring information and feeding it back into movement programming. The conservative patronage strategy of "spread betting"—supporting a wide range of projects and then reinvesting in those that worked—required leaders with the experience to effectively evaluate the success of movement ventures. The continuity of foundation leadership—Michael Joyce, James Piereson, and Richard Larry each served for a quarter-century—meant that there were people in critical positions with long, personal experience with the movement's political entrepreneurs. The networks they built increased their access to reliable information, and their position far up on the learning curve meant that they were in a strong position to draw lessons and, through their disbursement of money, to make those lessons stick.

The key claim of this section is that the durability of a policy or institutional regime is determined in large part by the ability of its rivals to discover or implement an effective response. Through the 1970s and well into the 1980s, the liberal legal regime thrived, despite its weakening electoral support, because conservatives found it difficult to develop organizational capacity in the academy, the legal profession, and public interest law. Since that time, conservatives have dramatically improved their effectiveness in elite organizational mobilization. As a consequence, they have rendered competitive areas of the law that were once effectively monopolistic.

What conservatives have not been able to do is move beyond competition to actually displace the liberal legal network and construct a dominant regime of their own. Movement investments like the Olin programs in law and economics helped increase the number of conservatives on elite law school faculties, but they still remain a relatively small minority. Conservatives' one significant effort to create a noteworthy law school of their own, at George Mason University, has been remarkably successful given its modest founding but is nowhere close to challenging the legal academic elite. Conservatives have a deeper bench of public interest law firms than twenty years ago, but few of their rivals—the NAACP LDF, ACLU, Environmental Defense Fund, Mexican American Legal Defense and Educational Fund, and Natural Resources Defense Council—have disappeared or even been markedly weakened. The Federalist Society has taken on many of the functions of the organized bar, but conservatives have not attained significant power within the ABA or AALS, and both organizations continue to draw conservatives' ire. This same pattern of competition rather than hegemony can be seen in a variety of other areas outside the law, such as Social Security, education, and the environment.[9] At the same time, legal liberals have captured little, if any, new institutional or ideational turf since the early 1970s. Largely as a consequence of the increasing effectiveness of conservative organizational mobilization, their energies have been devoted increasingly to holding on to what they already have.

What this pattern of effective conservative mobilization without significant displacement of liberalism may point to are the diminishing possibilities for regime construction in modern American politics. Partisans of realignment theory once believed that American politics always featured a dominant "sun" party and a reactive "moon" party.[10] This metaphor no longer accurately describes American politics, which is increasingly characterized by two equally competitive parties, each capable of deploying resources in civil society as well as in Washington, D.C. This heightened level of organizational mobilization means that any competitive advantage possessed by one party—whether it be electoral, social, or even religious—will lead to the rapid development of organizational infrastructure to challenge it.[11] While political agents continue to try to create durable regimes in institutions and policy domains, competitive pressures have become sufficiently robust that the returns on investing in regime status are lower than in the past. The failed attempt by Karl Rove to create a durable Republican Party regime of the kind built by Mark Hanna and William McKinley in the late nineteenth century is just the most visible example of the difficulty faced by regime builders in an organizationally competitive political system. Increasingly, therefore, our politics is characterized by the absence of a dominant party, an era without a regime, in which political time has dramatically sped up: what, in another context, Stephen Skowronek called a "politics of permanent preemption."[12] If anything, this condition is even more profound than Skowronek's argument would lead us to believe, because the tight competition that produces the reactive, preemptive modern style of politics now characterizes civil society and organizational mobilization as well as elections.

Understanding Modern Conservatism

In the late 1960s, conservatism was still a movement tightly linked to, and governed by, the interests of business, grassroots activists, and Republican elected officials. These interests are still vital parts of modern conservatism, but they have been increasingly joined by, and in some cases rendered subordinate to, a network of conservative organizations whose members are primarily motivated by ideological principle rather than coalitional affiliations. In the process of adding this ideologically motivated stratum to the conservative movement, and in responding to the challenge of liberal entrenchment, conservatism was transformed philosophically and strategically as well as organizationally. This section briefly sums up the book's findings on this transformation and lays the groundwork for the discussion of the larger lessons of the conservative experience with elite mobilization, the subject of the third and final section.

In the early 1970s, conservative ideas and political strategy were animated by the belief that the genie of legal liberalism could be put back in the bottle. This hope led to conservative support for "judicial restraint" or "strict constructionism," concepts borrowed from an earlier generation of liberal thought. These ideas argued for a strictly limited role for federal courts in public policy, claiming that the activist judiciary of the Warren Court was inconsistent with democratic rule. Decades earlier, conservatives had been attracted to quite a different judicial philosophy, which saw the courts as a bulwark against a democratic mob that, if given free rein, would destroy private property and centralize power in a strong national state. Judicial restraint was a fundamentally negative idea, a theory about what courts should not do, rather than what they ought to do. This philosophy became increasingly unattractive to conservatives as the federal courts and the legal profession became increasingly influenced by liberalism, and as conservatism became a more populist movement. The political strategy that accompanied judicial restraint was placing believers in "strict construction" on the federal bench and creating conservative public interest groups to present the "other side" when liberals sought to use the courts to advance their policy goals. Together, the idea of judicial restraint, a reconfigured federal judiciary, and public interest lawyers capable of balancing out the information available to judges, would resurrect the constitutional status quo ante, before the disruptions of *Brown*, *Griswold*, *Goldberg*, and the like.

The professional and ideational entrenchment of legal liberalism made it impossible to turn the clock back, and so conservatives were forced to adapt to the structure of the regime they sought to displace. First, conservatives learned that they needed to adapt many of their rivals' organizational forms. Whereas conservatives' strength was in grassroots and business mobilization at the state and local level, they were forced to build up their elite infrastructure in Washington, D.C. Ironically, to counter centralization, conservatives had to centralize their own organizational apparatus. Second, conservatives learned that they could not simply create alternatives to institutions controlled by liberals, but would have to organize within them. The reputations of academic institutions, for example, are highly sticky, and their role in conveying distinction very difficult, if not impossible, to replicate. As a result, conservatives sought out ways to operate inside of institutions where they were unwelcome. In the process, however, they had to play by the rules created by their rivals. Third, while most conservatives were suspicious of the central place of civil rights and an activist judiciary in American legal culture, these had become so deeply entrenched that conservatives had to find ways to adapt them for their own purposes. The symbolic stature of *Brown* meant that conservatives needed to adjust to its standard of justification, by arguing that their goals—like school choice—were truer to *Brown*'s egalitarian aspirations than those of their liberal counterparts. This strategic necessity provided an opening for conservatives who genuinely believed in a vigorous role for the courts and the moral idea of civil rights—like the founders of IJ— to drag the conservative legal movement in their direction. This philosophical shift went hand in hand with the discovery that the tools of public interest law were more suited to challenging government authority than defending it. The shift of conservative public interest law to libertarianism, therefore, can be understood as an endogenous adaptation to legal liberalism's transformation of American law.

These adaptations were accompanied by a shift of power within the conservative legal movement, from grassroots activists, Republican politicians, and business to a "new class" of legal professionals and academics. Where the first generation of conservative public interest law was dominated by business, second-generation firms were led by lawyers and intellectuals whose primary commitment was to ideological principle and a standard of legal professionalism. The Federalist Society was rooted in law schools, not party politics, fired by a mission of creating a conservative legal establishment with distinguished credentials, and armed with ideas that the legal academy could not ignore.

The coming to power of the conservative new class was a necessary— albeit not uncontested—adaptation to the character of the American legal profession and the competitive demands of responding to legal liberalism. The technical and intellectual character of modern law and the importance of prestige and distinction in the legal profession meant that, in order to be taken seriously by the profession, conservatives had to develop a network of experts with command over a wide range of issues and processes, the respect of mainstream lawyers and academics, and markers of professional distinction. In addition, countering the liberal legal network required a deep familiarity with its strategy, organizations, and ideas that could only come from a cadre of leaders drawn from the same professional background as their adversaries. Finally, the development of a conservative new class was necessary to convince potential elite recruits to the cause that legal professionalism was consistent with conservative ideas.

However functional we might think these changes in conservatism were, none were obvious or automatic, and most emerged only very gradually and after a great deal of trial and error. Too often, the story of modern conservatism has been told through the "myth of diabolical competence." Oddly enough, this myth has characterized accounts of conservatism written on the left *and* the right. Focusing primarily on conservatives' successes, this myth tells a tale of conservative movement actors who carefully and strategically planned out an assault on liberalism, an assault that was almost always successful. This approach, by focusing on the programs that succeeded while ignoring those that failed, is guilty of survivor bias. It is true that conservatives have, in many cases, showed significant strategic acumen. But the lessons of the first generation of conservative public interest law show that the movement went through a very long period of almost complete organizational failure. Conservative philanthropists invested very substantial sums in Henry Manne's entrepreneurial activities on behalf of law and economics, only to pull back sharply just as he was at the cusp of creating a major new piece of the conservative organizational infrastructure. CIR's strategy of attacking affirmative action and defending free speech on college campuses may seem far-sighted and strategic now, but it was nowhere to be found in its original plans. While the conservative movement has had its very considerable strengths, it was never a monolith, often made serious errors, and succeeded by shrewd adaptation rather than by the far-sighted pursuit of a grand plan.

Lessons from Conservatives

What lessons, if any, does the history of conservative legal mobilization hold for political entrepreneurs and patrons in the future? This question has, of late, been a matter of some urgency for liberals in particular. Liberal donors have pored over studies of how conservatives built their policy infrastructure in the hopes of replicating their accomplishments.[13] Most of these analyses, unfortunately, have been based on publicly available information and thus lacked a nuanced sense of the challenges actually faced by conservative patrons and entrepreneurs or the way that they responded to them. Serious political learning, by contrast, requires a view from the inside, and with it an effort to empathize with the challenges faced by the actors from whom one wishes to learn. This final section sums up the lessons for political activists that I have drawn from the development of the conservative legal movement, as well as suggesting some limits on lesson-drawing.

The most serious mistake those seeking to learn from legal conservatives could make would be to create carbon copies of conservatives' organizational apparatus, mimicking rather than learning. The most successful conservative projects, such as the Federalist Society, were adaptations to specific weaknesses of the conservative movement and responses to the character of liberal entrenchment. By the late 1970s and early 1980s, conservatives were strong at the grass roots, but lacked dense networks in Washington and representation in the elite strata of the legal profession. Their ideas were taken very seriously in the everyday world of electoral politics, but lacked legitimacy in the highest ranks of the legal academy.

While they were increasingly integrated into American culture and politics, conservatives felt like strangers in the elite ranks of the legal academy and organized bar. The structure of the Federalist Society made unquestionably good sense as a response to these specific problems and as a way to maneuver through institutions that were controlled by their rivals. The success of the Federalist Society, however, does not mean that it can be cloned, for actors today face a very different set of challenges than conservatives did. So, for example, legal liberals remain very strong in the elite circles of the legal profession and continue to be well networked in Washington, but they are weak in grassroots mobilization, and their elite organizations have few thick connections to mass organizations.[14] Their ideas continue to possess unquestioned legitimacy in elite circles, even as they have lost their grip on the public imagination and become in some cases the object of ridicule. Legal liberals can still call law schools their home, even as they have become more and more isolated in American culture. To the degree that liberals invest resources replicating conservative organizations designed for problems different from the ones they face today, they will waste money, time, and human capital.

That does not mean that there are no lessons of general applicability from the conservative organizational mobilization in the law. The first is the need for honesty. Conservatives were willing to face, at times brutally, the ideational and organizational weaknesses of the movement. The Horowitz Report, for example, was a major turning point for conservatives because it laid bare the manifest inadequacies of the movement, criticizing almost the entirety of the conservative infrastructure in the law, and did so directly to the holders of the movement's purse strings. As painful as they were, these sharp criticisms primed conservative patrons for new kinds of organizations, led by new kinds of leaders. Those seeking to learn from conservatives would be well served, therefore, by being open to the possibility of failure.

The conservative experience also suggests that little significant change is likely to come from existing organizations or leaders. Mellor and Bolick at IJ and Greve and McDonald at CIR had been miserable at MSLF and the Washington Legal Foundation because cases that represented real opportunities for legal conservatism, such as the Denver cable case and the cause of Thomas Lamprecht, could not be effectively pursued within their organizational confines. Change came instead from new organizations, and their predecessors only changed much later, if at all.[15] This suggests that political movements need to anticipate, and, in fact, encourage, a significant degree of creative destruction in their own organizational apparatus if they are to quickly and effectively develop more effective responses.

The history of the conservative legal movement suggests that successful political patrons engage in spread betting combined with feedback and learning, rather than expecting too much from grand planning.[16] Conservatives' learning and feedback did not, however, involve using narrow, technical forms of evaluation. Conservative patrons were willing to accept fairly diffuse, hard-to-measure goals with long-term payoffs when they had faith in the individuals behind the projects. This goes against the grain of much of contemporary philanthropy, which emphasizes rigorous, usually quantitative, evaluative measurement. Conservative patrons were typically quite close to the entrepreneurs they funded and depended on their own subjective evaluation of both a given entrepreneur's effectiveness and the information that flowed through trusted movement networks—rather than on "objective" measures of outcomes. Where goals such as transforming the climate of opinion are concerned, this form of subjective evaluation may be more effective than seemingly precise measures that often leave out the most important, albeit difficult-to-measure, outcomes.

Legal conservatives did not achieve as much as they have simply by more effectively packaging or marketing their ideas. Instead, conservatives became more effective by challenging, and ultimately changing, their ideas. Decades of debate in Federalist Society conferences and within the network of conservative scholars led to jettisoning the concepts of judicial restraint and strict constructionism, and then original intent, before finally settling (at least provisionally) on "original meaning." Where legal conservatives in the early 1970s were focused on limiting the implications of *Brown*, the new generation of legal conservatives such as Clint Bolick of IJ openly embraced the more radical "antisubordination" interpretation of *Brown*, while disagreeing vigorously with liberals about its implications.[17] The conservative legal movement took ideas very seriously, and its patrons invested significant resources in serious, first-order discussion of fundamental commitments with little if any short-term payoffs. While many contemporary liberals seem obsessed with creating their own think tanks to allow for "instant response," conservatives recognized the need to go back to "first things." This was reflected, for instance, in the Federalist Society's convention norms that panels should include debates among conservatives, as well as with liberals.

Conservatives, therefore, were willing to carve out enough space from the movement's old categories, commitments, and constituencies to allow serious intellectual discussion and argumentation, leading to a reconsideration of ideas, strategies, and alliances. This suggests that political movements need organizations and norms of deliberation that allow members to argue fervently among one another on matters of fundamental principle. Going back to first things also meant that conservatives were willing to distance themselves from their existing constituencies, even when this meant challenging their allies' short-term interests. Conservatives went out of their way to find cases that put them on the other side of business or that appealed to constituencies, such as inner-city blacks, who were outside of the conservative coalition. The willingness of intellectuals to reconsider fundamental principles went hand in hand with using litigation to reach out to new groups as part of a strategy of reshaping the movement's reputation. Conservatives used strategic litigation to reshape perceptions that they were greedy, callous, captured by big business, and uninterested in the cause of racial justice. In the process, they reached out to new constituents by organizing around new issues. The willingness to experiment with new organizational approaches that is essential to organizational entrepreneurship, therefore, is most likely to come out of an environment of intellectual openness.

Perhaps one of the most common mistakes that have been made by those who have attempted to learn from the conservative legal movement has been the tendency to confuse direct organizational goals and the desired by-products of activities with other ends. The Manne programs in the 1970s and 1980s and the lectures and conventions of the Federalist Society, for example, contributed mightily to the development of academic and professional networks. These networks spurred intellectual productivity, improved the information that conservatives could access in government, and assisted in identifying ideological sympathizers when staffing the federal judiciary and administrative agencies. As important as these outputs were, however, they were by-products, or external benefits, of activities and organizations that worked because they were *not* aimed directly at these goals. Professors and judges attended Manne's seminars because they were deeply intellectually stimulating, and, despite the unquestioned presence of opportunists within its ranks, such stimulation remains the main force drawing lawyers and law students to Federalist Society meetings. Strong networks of the kind that came from these programs developed because of the emotional and intellectual intensity that comes from an activity that knits people together and not because the organizations serve instrumental goals for their members. Even when the objective of organizational mobilization is narrowly political, therefore, it may be more effectively pursued through means that are broader and more indirect.

The final lesson to be drawn from the conservative legal experience concerns the relationship between structure and agency and is relevant to both social scientists and political activists. At any one time, the constraints of an existing regime can seem crushing and inescapable, frustrating the ability of individuals to create change of any consequence in the world. The constraints and structures of any particular period are, however, often the creation of a previous generation's political agents. In the short term, politics is, in fact, a world of constraints, but to agents willing to wait for effects that may not emerge for decades, the world is rich with opportunity. Activists would do well to learn from, and act upon, these examples of long-term effects. So, too, political scientists would serve their discipline well by taking the time to study them.

Appendix

Interviews

Douglas Baird. Dean (1994–99), University of Chicago Law School; currently Harry A. Bigelow Distinguished Service Professor of Law. October 2005.

Derek Bok. President Emeritus and current Interim President, Harvard University; Dean (1968–71), Harvard Law School. October 2005.

Clint Bolick. Cofounder and Counsel for Strategic Litigation, Institute for Justice; currently President and General Counsel, Alliance for School Choice. October 2003.

Steven Calabresi. George C. Dix Professor of Constitutional Law, Northwestern University School of Law; Cofounder, Federalist Society. October 2001.

Laurence Claus. Professor of Law, University of San Diego School of Law; former John. M. Olin Fellow at Northwestern University School of Law. December 2005.

Robert Cooter. Herman F. Selvin Professor of Law and Director of the Program in Law and Economics, University of California, Berkeley Boalt Hall. May 2006.

Roger Crampton. Dean (1973–80), Cornell University Law School. November 2005.

Kenneth Cribb. Assistant to the President for Domestic Policy, Reagan administration. April 2004.

Steven Eagle. Professor of Law, George Mason University School of Law. July 2005.

Richard Epstein. James Parker Hall Distinguished Service Professor of Law, University of Chicago Law School. October 2005.

George Gillespie. Director of the Washington Post Company and partner at Cravath, Swaine; at the Olin Foundation's closing in 2005, President and Treasurer of its Board; formerly John M. Olin's personal lawyer. October 2005.

Michael Graetz. Justus S. Hotchkiss Professor of Law, Yale Law School. April 2006.

Michael Greve. Cofounder, Center for Individual Rights; currently Director of the Federalism Project, American Enterprise Institute. July 2001; May 2004; August 2004.

Ernest Hueter. President, National Legal Center for the Public Interest. June 2004.

Sanford Jaffe. Program Officer (1968–83), Government and Law Program, Ford Foundation. October 2006.

David Kennedy. President of the Earhart Foundation and Chairman of the Board of the Institute for Justice. March 2004.

Duncan Kennedy. Carter Professor of General Jurisprudence, Harvard Law School. October 2005.

John Kramer. Vice President of Communications, Institute for Justice. October 2004.

William Kristol. Editor, *Weekly Standard*; Chief of Staff (1989–93) for vice president of the United States; Board of Visitors (1997–2001), George Mason University. September 2005.

Gary Lawson. Abraham & Lillian Benton Scholar, Boston University School of Law. July 2005.

Leslie Lenkowsky. CEO (2001–3), Corporation for National; and Community Service; President (1990–97), Hudson Institute. May 2004.

Henry Manne. Dean Emeritus, George Mason University School of Law; former Director of the Law and Economics Center (University of Miami, 1974–80; Emory, 1980–86). November 2004; July 2005; August 2005.

Jerry Mashaw. Sterling Professor of Law, Yale Law School. May 2006.

Fred McChesney. Class of 1967 James B. Haddad Professor of Law, Northwestern University School of Law; formerly Associate Director for Policy and Evaluation, Federal Trade Commission; 1986–87 John M. Olin Fellow in Law & Economics at the University of Chicago Law School. October 2005.

Michael McDonald. Acting Assistant Chairman for Programs, National Endowment for the Humanities; Cofounder, Center for Individual Rights. July 2001; August 2004.

David McIntosh. Partner, Meyer Brown and Platt; member of Congress (1995–2001), Indiana 2nd; head of George H. W. Bush's Council on Competitiveness. July 2005.

William H. (Chip) Mellor. President and General Counsel, Institute for Justice, which he founded in 1991; President (1986–91), Pacific Research Institute for Public Policy. July 2001; October 2003; July 2004; October 2004; May 2006.

Eugene Meyer. President, Federalist Society. June 2004; October 2005; July 2006; November 2006.

Jim Moody. Capital Legal Foundation. June 2004.

Lee Liberman Otis. Office of Legal Counsel, George H. W. Bush administration; General Counsel (2001–5), Department of Energy. July 2005.

Jeffrey Parker. Professor of Law, George Mason University School of Law. July 2005.

Terry Pell. President, Center for Individual Rights. November 2003; June 2004.

James Piereson. Executive Director, Olin Foundation, 1985–2005. April 2004; August 2005; July 2006.

Daniel Polsby. Dean and Foundation Professor of Law, George Mason University School of Law; formerly Kirkland & Ellis Professor of Law, Northwestern University School of Law. July 2005.

Richard Posner. Judge, United States Court of Appeals for the Seventh Circuit; Senior Lecturer in Law, University of Chicago Law School. October 2005.

George Priest. John M. Olin Professor of Law & Economics and Codirector of the John M. Olin Center for Studies in Law, Economics, and Public Policy, Yale Law School. May 2005; July 2005.

Jeremy Rabkin. Professor of Government, Cornell University; founding member of Board of Directors, Center for Individual Rights. August 2004.

Richard Rosett. Dean (1990–95), Rochester Institute of Technology College of Business; Dean (1974 to 1983), University of Chicago Business School. September 2005.

Michael Rosman. General Counsel, Center for Individual Rights, 1993–present. November 2003.

Warren Schwartz. Professor of Law and Director of the John M. Olin Program in Law and Economics, Georgetown Law School. July 2006.

Robert Scott. Professor (1974–2006) and Dean (1991–2001), University of Virginia School of Law. Currently Alfred McCormack Professor of Law, Columbia University. May 2006.

Steven Shavell. Samuel R. Rosenthal Professor of Law and Economics and Director of the John M. Olin Center for Law, Economics, and Business, Harvard Law School. October 2006.

Todd Zywicki. Professor of Law, George Mason University School of Law. July 2005; July 2006.

Notes

Introduction

1. Patrick J. Buchanan to Richard Nixon, Washington, November 10, 1972, in *From the President: Richard Nixon's Secret Files*, ed. Bruce Oudes (New York: Harper and Row, 1989), 558–68. David Yalof observes that Nixon made changing the behavior of the courts a central plank of his 1968 campaign, and explicitly directed his attorney general that he was looking for "young conservative nominees." David Yalof, *Pursuit of Justices: Presidential Politics and the Selection of Supreme Court Nominees* (Chicago: University of Chicago Press, 1999), 100.

2. Vincent Blasi, ed., *The Burger Court: The Counter-Revolution That Wasn't* (New Haven: Yale University Press, 1983).

3. William Kristol, "Disappointed, Depressed and Demoralized," *Weekly Standard*, October 3, 2005.

4. Todd Zywicki, "A Great Mind?" *Legal Times*, October 10, 2005, http://mason.gmu.edu/~tzywick2/Legal%20Times%20Mier%20Op%20Ed.pdf.

5. Donald Critchlow, *Phyllis Schlafly and Grassroots Conservatism: A Woman's Crusade* (Princeton: Princeton University Press, 2005); Jane Mansbridge, *Why We Lost the ERA* (Chicago: University of Chicago Press, 1986).

6. Theda Skocpol, *Diminished Democracy: From Membership to Management in American Civic Life* (Norman: University of Oklahoma Press, 2003).

7. Steven Teles, *Whose Welfare? AFDC and Elite Politics* (Lawrence: University Press of Kansas, 1996); Steven Teles, "Conservative Mobilization Against the Activist State," in *The Transformation of American Politics*, ed. Paul Pierson and Theda Skocpol (Princeton: Princeton University Press, 2007); Jeffrey Henig, "Conservatives and Education, 1980–2005" and Judith Layzer, "Conservatives and the Environment, 1980–2005," in *Conservatism and American Political Development*, ed. Brian Glenn and Steven Teles (forthcoming).

8. There is one significant segment of the conservative countermobilization in the law that I do not examine directly in this book, and that is religious conservatives. The reasons for this are more practical than theoretical. First, there is already an excellent study of the subject, Steven Brown's *Trumping Religion: The Christian Right, the Free Speech Clause, and the Courts* (Tuscaloosa: University of Alabama Press, 2003). Second, I do not believe that I could have obtained access to the kind of "inside" materials on religious conservatives that I have obtained on the rest of the conservative movement. Third, I lack the intellectual background, especially on the substance of American religious thought and organization, to do the subject justice. That said, I do believe that substantial work remains to be done on the subject, and that my emphasis on strategic choice and organizational development would add considerably to the foundation laid by Brown.

Chapter 1
Political Competition, Legal Change, and the New American State

1. Robert Kagan, *Adversarial Legalism: The American Way of Law* (Cambridge: Harvard University Press, 2001).

2. Martha Derthick, *The Influence of Federal Grants* (Cambridge: Harvard University Press, 1970).

3. Skocpol, *Diminished Democracy*; Matthew Crenson and Benjamin Ginsberg, *Downsizing Democracy: How America Sidelined Its Citizens and Privatized Its Public* (Baltimore: Johns Hopkins University Press, 2002).

4. An analysis of the connection between a diffuse policy process and the rise of networked forms of coordination can be found in Chris Ansell, "The Networked Polity: Regional Development in Western Europe," *Governance*, July 2000, 303–33.

5. Jack Walker, *Mobilizing Interest Groups in America: Patrons, Professions, and Social Movements* (Ann Arbor: University of Michigan Press, 1991).

6. See, for example, Shep Melnick's *Regulation and the Courts: The Case of the Clean Air Act* (Washington, D.C.: Brookings, 1983) and *Between the Lines: Welfare Rights in Court* (Washington, D.C.: Brookings, 1994).

7. Skocpol, *Diminished Democracy*; Crenson and Ginsberg, *Downsizing Democracy*; Sidney Milkis, *The President and the Parties* (Oxford: Oxford University Press, 1993).

8. See in particular Mark Landy and Martin Levin, eds., *The New Politics of Public Policy* (Baltimore: Johns Hopkins University Press, 1995).

9. John Skrentny, *The Minority Rights Revolution* (Cambridge: Harvard University Press, 2002); Benjamin Ginsberg and Martin Shefter, *Politics by Other Means* (New York: Norton, 2002); Martha Derthick, *Policymaking for Social Security* (Washington, D.C.: Brookings, 1979).

10. Bryan Jones and Frank Baumgartner, *The Politics of Attention: How Government Prioritizes Problems* (Chicago: University of Chicago Press, 2005).

11. Jeffrey Berry, *The New Liberalism* (Washington, D.C.: Brookings, 1999).

12. Jo Freeman, "The Political Culture of the Democratic and Republican Party," *Political Science Quarterly* 101 (1986): 327–56.

13. Alvin Ward Gouldner, *The Future of Intellectuals and the Rise of the New Class: A Frame of Reference, Theses, Conjectures, Arguments, and an Historical Perspective on the Role of Intellectuals and Intelligentsia in the International Class Contest of the Modern Era* (London: Macmillan, 1979). Neoconservatives also became attracted to the concept of the new class: one expression of their understanding of this phenomenon can be found in B. Bruce-Briggs, ed., *The New Class?* (New Brunswick, N.J.: Transaction, 1979).

14. Geoffrey Kabaservice, *The Guardians: Kingman Brewster, His Circle, and the Rise of the Liberal Establishment* (New York: Henry Holt, 2004).

15. Jacob Hacker has persuasively argued that this strategy of "drift" has reduced the risk reduction functions of the American welfare state. Jacob Hacker, "Privatizing Risk without Privatizing the Welfare State: The Hidden Politics of Social Policy Retrenchment in the United States," *American Political Science Review* 98, no. 2 (2004): 243–60.

16. John Skrentny observes, for example, that when the Bilingual American Education Act was passed in 1967, "No one spoke out against bilingual education, either as a violation of American assimilationist ideals or as a pedagogy that would not or may not work." Skrentny, *The Minority Rights Revolution*, 204.

17. This broader understanding of party actors has similarities to the concept of the "political block" used by David Plotke in *Building a Democratic Political Order: Reshaping American Liberalism in the 1930s and 1940s* (Cambridge: Cambridge University Press, 1996). An account that makes activists a central component of the modern political party, and that attributes a significant degree of contemporary party polarization to them, is John Aldrich, in *Why Parties?: The Origin and Transformation of Political Parties in America* (Chicago: University of Chicago Press, 1995), chapter 6.

18. The most concrete example of this incorporation of interest groups into the party system in contemporary politics is the Republican Party's "K Street project," and Grover Norquist's "Wednesday Meeting" of conservative activists, but this coordination of interest group and party activity has now become an institutionalized feature of American politics across the political spectrum. See Nicholas Confessore, "Welcome to the Machine," *Washington Monthly*, July–August 2003.

19. David Horowitz, *The Professors: The 101 Most Dangerous Academics in America* (Washington, D.C.: Regnery 2006); Dinesh D'Souza, *Illiberal Education: The Politics of Race and Sex on Campus* (New York: Free Press, 1991); Charles Sykes, *Profscam: Professors and the Demise of Higher Education* (Washington, D.C.: Regnery, 1988); Eric Alterman, *What Liberal Media? The Truth About Bias and News* (New York: Basic Books, 2004); Bernard Goldberg, *Bias: A CBS Insider Exposes How the Media Distort the News* (Washington, D.C.: Regnery, 2001); Robert Lichter, *The Media Elite: America's New Power Brokers* (Bethesda, Md.: Adler and Adler, 1990); Sally Satel, *PC, M.D.: How Political Correctness is Corrupting Medicine* (New York: Basic Books, 2000).

20. Robert Dahl, "Decision-Making in a Democracy: The Supreme Court as National Policy-Maker," *Journal of Public Law* 6, no. 2 (1957): 279.

21. Gerald Rosenberg, *The Hollow Hope* (Chicago: University of Chicago Press, 1991), 15.

22. Keith Whittington, " 'Interpose Your Friendly Hand': Political Supports for the Exercise of Judicial Review by the United States Supreme Court," *American Political Science Review* 99, no. 4 (2005): 583–96; J. Mitchell Pickerill and Cornell Clayton, "The Rehnquist Court and the Political Dynamics of Federalism," *Perspectives on Politics* 2, no. 2 (2004): 233–48; Howard Gillman, "How Political Parties Can Use the Courts to Advance Their Agendas: Federal Courts in the United States, 1875–1891," *American Political Science Review* 96, no. 3 (2002): 511–24.

23. Bruce Ackerman, *We the People: Foundations* (Cambridge: Harvard University Press, 1993).

24. Roy B. Flemming and B. Dan Wood, "The Public and the Supreme Court: Individual Justice Responsiveness to American Policy Moods," *American Journal of Political Science* 41, no. 2 (1997): 468–98; William Mishler and Reginald S. Sheehan, "The Supreme Court as a Countermajoritarian Institution? The Impact

of Public Opinion on Supreme Court Decisions," *American Political Science Review* 87, no. 1 (1993): 87–101; James A. Stimson, Michael B. Mackuen, and Robert S. Erikson, "Dynamic Representation," *American Political Science Review* 89, no. 3 (1995): 543–65.

25. Jack Balkin and Sanford Levinson, "Understanding the Constitutional Revolution," *Virginia Law Review* 87, no. 6 (2001): 1045–1104. A similar argument is made by David Adamany, who emphasizes that the Supreme Court is most likely to come into conflict with rising partisan coalitions at precisely the moment when their legitimacy is most in doubt—in their early years. Thus, far from serving the legitimating function that Dahl pointed to, the Supreme Court tends to erode the legitimacy of rising political orders. David Adamany, "Legitimacy, Realigning Elections, and the Supreme Court," *Wisconsin Law Review* 73:790–846.

26. Pickerill and Clayton, "Rehnquist Court," 236.

27. Stephen Skowronek, *The Politics Presidents Make* (Cambridge: Harvard University Press, 1997).

28. Balkin and Levinson, "Understanding the Constitutional Revolution," 1088.

29. Charles Epp, *The Rights Revolution* (Chicago: University of Chicago Press, 1998), 3.

30. Epp's concept of the support structure is quite similar to Skowronek's "alternative governing coalition," described in *Building a New American State* (New York: Cambridge University Press, 1982). Because I believe the concepts to be roughly similar, I will use the terms interchangeably.

31. Marc Galantner, "Why the 'Haves' Come Out Ahead: Speculations on the Limits of Legal Change," *Law and Society Review* 9, no. 1 (1974): 95–160; Kevin T. McGuire, "Repeat Players in the Supreme Court: The Role of Experienced Lawyers in Litigation Success," *Journal of Politics* 57, no. 1 (1995): 187–96; Lee Epstein and Joseph Kobylka, *The Supreme Court and Legal Change* (Chapel Hill: University of North Carolina Press, 1992).

32. H. W. Perry, Jr., *Deciding to Decide* (Cambridge: Harvard University Press, 1991).

33. Jack Balkin, "*Bush v. Gore* and the Boundary Between Law and Politics," *Yale Law Journal* 110, no. 8 (2001): 1444–45.

34. Owen Fiss, "Objectivity and Interpretation," *Stanford Law Review* 34, no. 4 (1982): 739–63.

35. Epstein and Kobylka, *Supreme Court.*

36. Michael Klarman, *From Jim Crow to Civil Rights* (Oxford: Oxford University Press, 2004). Recent evidence of this can be found in the Supreme Court's decision in *Gratz v. Bollinger,* 539 U.S. 244 (2003) at 18–20.

37. Artemus Ward and David Weiden, *Sorcerers' Apprentices: 100 Years of Law Clerks At the United States Supreme Court* (New York: NYU Press, 2006), 73. Under Burger, Warren and Vinson, the percentage drawn from these seven schools was only slightly lower, 69 percent.

38. David Yalof provides persuasive evidence that President Nixon found it very difficult to identify potential Supreme Court nominees, because of the shallow pool of viable conservative nominees and the weakness of the network that his attorney general could draw upon in identifying them. David Yalof, *Pursuit*

of Justices: Presidential Politics and the Selection of Supreme Court Nominees (Chicago: University of Chicago Press, 1999), 97–132. The nomination of Sandra Day O'Connor, at the height of Ronald Reagan's political power, can also be seen as an example of the consequences of a president being forced to make an ideologically uncertain nomination because of the thin pool of judicial candidates from which to draw. A strong network will also enhance the ability of the president to make "stealth" nominations to the bench when his own coalition has "private" information not accessible to opponents.

39. This reproductive process will be limited by competitive pressures from rival law schools (which are, for the top law schools, somewhat muted because of the force of reputation and financial endowment) and the desire to hire former Supreme Court clerks as professors (which will be influenced by the partisan makeup of the Court). The latter pressure may have declined with the increasing importance of publications and joint degrees in initial legal academic hiring.

40. Peter Eisinger, *The Conditions of Protest Behavior in American Cities* (Madison, Wisc.: Institute for Poverty Research, 1973); Hanspeter Kriesi, "Political Context and Opportunity," in *The Blackwell Companion to Social Movements*, ed. David Snow, Sarah Soule, and Hanspeter Kriesi (Oxford: Blackwell, 2004), 67–90; H. P. Kitschelt, "Political Opportunity Structures and Political Protest: Anti-Nuclear Movements in Four Democracies," *British Journal of Political Science* 16, no. 1 (1986): 57–86.

41. John McCarthy and Mayer Zald, "Resource Mobilization and Social Movements: A Partial Theory," *American Journal of Sociology* 82, no. 6 (1977): 1212–41.

42. Marshall Ganz, *Five Smooth Stones: Strategy, Leadership, and the California Agriculture Movement* (Oxford: Oxford University Press, forthcoming).

43. While Paul Pierson has urged us to think of structures as the consequence of actions earlier in a temporal sequence, he has, to my mind, underplayed the importance that conscious agent action can play in producing structures in future periods. The difference here is one of emphasis—Pierson sees structures as largely the result of accidents, while my approach emphasizes those that are the product of conscious political investment, defined as the expenditure of resources in one period designed to produce returns in future periods. Put another way, path dependence can be the product of agents oriented to the long term. Paul Pierson, *Thinking in Time* (Princeton: Princeton University Press, 2004).

44. Derthick, *Policymaking for Social Security*; Marc Landy, Marc Roberts, and Steven Thomas, *The Environmental Protection Agency: Asking the Wrong Questions* (Oxford: Oxford University Press, 1994); Richard Harris and Sidney Milkis, *The Politics of Regulatory Change: A Tale of Two Agencies* (Oxford: Oxford University Press, 1996), Skrentny, *The Minority Rights Revolution*.

45. Critchlow, *Phyllis Schlafly*; Lisa McGirr, *Suburban Warriors: The Origins of the New Right* (Princeton: Princeton University Press, 2001).

46. Thomas Burke has made a similar argument in "On the Resilience of Rights," in *Seeking the Center: Politics and Policymaking at the New Century*, ed. Martin Levin, Marc Landy, and Martin Shapiro (Washington, D.C.: Georgetown University Press, 2001).

47. Antonio Gramsci, *Selections from the Prison Notebooks*, trans. Quentin Hoare and Geoffrey Nowell Smith (London: Lawrence and Wishart, 1971), 182. David Plotke refers to this as the "common sense" produced by a dominant political party. Plotke, *Democratic Political Order*.

48. For examples of Bourdieu's application of the "field" concept see his *Homo Academicus*, trans. Peter Collier (Stanford: Stanford University Press, 1988) and *The Rules of Art: Genesis and Structure of the Literary Field*, trans. Susan Emanuel (Stanford: Stanford University Press, 1996). Bourdieu's concept of "fields" has similarities with the concept of "realms" in Daniel Bell's *Cultural Contradictions of Capitalism* (New York: Free Press, 1976).

49. Peter Bachrach and Morton Baratz, "Two Faces of Power," *American Political Science Review* 56, no. 4 (1962): 947–52. Similar arguments are made in Deborah Stone, "Causal Stories and the Formation of Policy Agendas," *Political Science Quarterly* 104, no. 2 (1989): 281–300; Roger Cobb and Marc Howard Ross, *Cultural Strategies of Agenda Denial* (Lawrence: University Press of Kansas, 1997); Frank Baumgartner and Bryan Jones, *Agendas and Instability in American Politics* (Chicago: University of Chicago Press, 1993); Steven Lukes, *Power: A Radical View* (London: Macmillan, 1974).

50. The following argument draws heavily on Mark Blyth, *Great Transformations* (Cambridge: Cambridge University Press, 2002), as well as Frank Knight's classic *Risk, Uncertainty and Profit* (New York: Harper and Row, 1965).

51. A similar point was made by Lee Ann Banaszak in her comparison of American and Swiss suffrage movements, *Why Movements Succeed or Fail: Opportunity, Culture and the Struggle of Women's Suffrage* (Princeton: Princeton University Press, 1996).

52. Traci Sawyers and David Meyer emphasize that existing opportunities may simply be "missed" due to lack of sufficient mobilization. "Missed Opportunities: Social Movement Abeyance and Public Policy," *Social Problems* 46, no. 2 (1999): 187–206.

53. Pierre Bourdieu, "The Forms of Capital," in *Handbook for Theory and Research for the Sociology of Education*, ed. J. G. Richardson (Westport, Conn.: Greenwood Press, 1986), 241–58; Pierre Bourdieu, *The State Nobility: Elite Schools in the Field of Power*, trans. Lauretta C. Clough (Stanford: Stanford University Press, 1996).

54. Insurgent intellectuals constantly struggle to legitimate their academic endeavors. See Scott Frickel and Neil Gross, "A General Theory of Scientific/Intellectual Movements," *American Sociological Review* 70, no. 22 (2005): 204–32.

55. Mark A. Smith, *The Right Talk: How Conservatives Transformed the Great Society into the Economic Society* (Princeton: Princeton University Press, 2007).

56. Erik Bleich, *Race Politics in Britain and France* (Cambridge: Cambridge University Press, 2003), 26–27. For a classic article on framing and social movements, see David A. Snow, E. Burke Rochford, Jr., Steven K. Worden, and Robert D. Benford, "Frame Alignment Processes, Micromobilization, and Movement Participation," *American Sociological Review* 51, no. 4 (1986): 464–81.

57. Jane Mansbridge, "The Making of Oppositional Consciousness," in *Oppositional Consciousness: The Subjective Roots of Social Protest*, ed. Jane Mans-

bridge and Aldon Morris (Chicago: University of Chicago Press, 2001), 7. The concept of oppositional consciousness is connected to what Doug McAdam has called "cognitive liberation." See Doug McAdam, *Political Process and the Development of the Black Insurgency, 1930–1970* (Chicago: University of Chicago Press, 1982), 48–51.

58. Baumgartner and Jones, *Agendas and Instability*.

59. An example of how shared ideas can provide coordination in the absence of hierarchical oversight can be found in Herbert Kaufman, *The Forest Ranger: A Study in Administrative Behavior* (Washington, D.C.: RFF Press, 1967), chapter 6.

60. Chris Ansell, "Symbolic Networks: The Realignment of the French Working Class, 1887–1894," *American Journal of Sociology* 103, no. 2 (1997): 359–90.

61. Kevin Smart, *Principles and Heresies: Frank S. Meyer and the Shaping of the American Conservative Movement* (Wilmington, Del.: ISI, 2002). See also George Nash, *The Conservative Intellectual Movement in America Since 1945* (New York: Basic Books, 1976); and Jeffrey Hart, *The Making of the American Conservative Mind: National Review and Its Times* (Wilmington, Del.: ISI Press, 2005).

62. James Coleman, "Social Capital in the Creation of Human Capital," *American Journal of Sociology* 94, Supplement (1988): 118.

63. Gerald Marwell and Pamela Oliver, *The Critical Mass in Collective Action: A Micro-Social Theory* (Cambridge: Cambridge University Press, 1993).

64. Marc Granovetter, "The Strength of Weak Ties," *American Journal of Sociology* 78, no. 6 (1973): 1360–80.

65. Marc Granovetter, "Economic Action and Social Structure: The Problem of Embeddedness," *American Journal of Sociology* 91, no. 3 (1985): 481–510.

66. Joel Podolny and Karen Page, "Network Forms of Organization," *Annual Review of Sociology* 24 (1998): 62–64.

67. Randall Collins, *The Sociology of Philosophies: A Global Theory of Intellectual Change* (Cambridge: Harvard University Press, 1998).

68. Teles, "Conservative Mobilization."

69. This may explain why so many of the early leaders of the conservative organizational network were neoconservatives (that is, former leftists or liberals). See in particular Irving Kristol, *Reflections of a Neo-Conservative* (New York: Basic Books, 1983).

70. For a description of this long-term strategy of change, see Martha Derthick and Steven Teles, "From Third Rail to Presidential Commitment—And Back? The Conservative Campaign for Social Security Privatization and the Limits of Long-Term Political Strategy," in Glenn and Teles, *Conservatism and American Political Development*; Teles, "Conservative Mobilization."

71. James Q. Wilson, *Political Organizations* (Princeton: Princeton University Press, 1995); Charles Perrow, "The Analysis of Goals in Complex Organizations," *American Sociological Review* 26, no. 6 (1961): 854–66.

72. The classic discussion of the role of patrons in solving the collective action problem is Walker, *Mobilizing Interest Groups*. Walker was responding in this work primarily to Mancur Olson, whose *The Logic of Collective Action* (Cambridge: Harvard University Press, 1971) predicted that while concentrated inter-

ests would form groups with relative ease, it would be almost impossible for more diffuse interests to do so (with the exception of groups capable of providing selective incentives for membership).

73. Edwards and McCarthy, for example, found that MADD chapters that received support from patrons were more than two and a half times as likely to survive as those that did not. Bob Edwards and John McCarthy, "Strategy Matters: The Contingent Value of Social Capital in the Survival of Local Social Movement Organizations," *Social Forces* 83, no. 2 (2004): 621–51.

74. This was a significant challenge for the NAACP LDF in its early years, when conflicts between the organization's vision of civil rights led to conflict—and ultimately the withdrawal of support—with its major donor, the Garland Fund. Mark Tushnet, *The NAACP's Legal Strategy Against Segregated Education* (Chapel Hill: University of North Carolina Press, 2005).

75. Alan Jacobs, "The Politics of Investment: Theorizing Governments' Policy Choices for the Long Term," paper delivered to the American Political Science Association Meeting, September 2006; Teles, "Conservative Mobilization."

Chapter 2
The Rise of the Liberal Legal Network

1. Epp, *The Rights Revolution*.

2. Skrentny, *The Minority Rights Revolution*.

3. Spencer Weber Waller, *Thurman Arnold* (New York: NYU Press, 2005), 126–27, 151–52. The most important of these was Coca-Cola. Thurman Arnold had built a close relationship with Coke's president, Robert Woodruff, when he was assistant attorney general in the Antitrust Division, and leveraged this contact to sign up the company as Arnold, Fortas and Porter's first major client.

4. Peter Irons, *The New Deal Lawyers* (Princeton: Princeton University Press, 1982), 298.

5. Laura Kalman, *Abe Fortas: A Biography* (New Haven: Yale University Press, 1992), 133.

6. Robert Stevens, *Law School: Legal Education in America from the 1850s to the 1980s* (Union, N.J.: Lawbook Exchange, 2001), 207.

7. Ibid., 213.

8. Elizabeth Gaspar Brown, *Legal Education at Michigan, 1859–1959* (Ann Arbor: University of Michigan Law School, 1959), 85–87.

9. Sandra Epstein, *Law at Berkeley: The History of Boalt Hall* (Berkeley, Calif.: IGS Press, 1997), 203, 224, 225.

10. Robert Gordon, "Professors and Policymakers: Yale Law School Faculty in the New Deal and After," in *History of the Yale Law School: The Triennial Lectures*, ed. Anthony Kronman (New Haven: Yale University Press, 2004), 84–91.

11. Stevens, *Law School*, 157.

12. Student Association of the School of Law, Yale University, *The Yale Reporter: 1948 Supplement*.

13. Arthur Sutherland, *The Law at Harvard: A History of Ideas and Men, 1817–1967* (Cambridge: Harvard University Press, 1967), 311.

14. Irons, *The New Deal Lawyers*, 299.

15. Quoted in Jenna Rae McNeil, *Groundwork: Charles Hamilton Houston and the Struggle for Civil Rights* (Philadelphia: University of Pennsylvania Press, 1983), 71.

16. Tushnet, *NAACP's Legal Strategy*, 30.

17. Risa Golubuff, *The Lost Promise of Civil Rights* (Cambridge: Harvard University Press, 2007); Kenneth Mack, "Rethinking Civil Rights Lawyering and Politics in the Era Before Brown," *Yale Law Journal* 115, no. 2 (2005): 256.

18. Tushnet, *NAACP's Legal Strategy*, 145.

19. Ibid., 157.

20. The NAACP LDF was not, even after the formalization of its national staff, a wholly hierarchical organization. Its network of lawyers often initiated litigation at cross-purposes to its larger strategic objectives, a point noted in Tushnet and explored in greater detail in Risa Golubuff, " 'Let Economic Equality Take Care of Itself': The NAACP, Labor Litigation, and the Making of Civil Rights in the 1940s," *UCLA Law Review* 52, no. 5 (2005): 1393.

21. Samuel Walker, *In Defense of American Liberties: A History of the ACLU* (New York: Oxford University Press, 1990), 86.

22. Ibid., 168.

23. Ibid., 206.

24. Ibid., 267.

25. Jerold Auerbach, *Unequal Justice: Lawyers and Social Change in Modern America* (Oxford: Oxford University Press, 1977), 192.

26. Ibid., 193.

27. *Annual Report of the American Bar Association* (Chicago: Headquarters Office, 1950), 339.

28. President's Annual Address, "The Lawyer's Responsibility to America," in *Annual Report of the American Bar Association* (Chicago: Headquarters Office, 1951), 443.

29. Critchlow, *Phyllis Schlafly*, 79–80.

30. Auerbach, *Unequal Justice*, 199.

31. Ibid., 236; Percival Roberts Bailey, "Progressive Lawyers: A History of the National Lawyers Guild, 1936–1958," PhD diss., Rutgers University, 1979.

32. *Annual Report of the American Bar Association* (1950), 222.

33. *Annual Report of the American Bar Association* (1951), 218.

34. Richard Abel, *American Lawyers* (Oxford: Oxford University Press, 1991), 132.

35. *Ford Foundation Annual Report 1953* (New York: Ford Foundation, 1953), 43; *Annual Report of the American Bar Association* (Chicago: Headquarters Office, 1953), 119.

36. These grants included $300,000 to the NLAA to work with the ABA in developing permanent legal aid offices in large cities, and to expand the availability of legal aid in underserved areas. *Ford Foundation Annual Report 1957* (New York: Ford Foundation, 1957), 31.

37. Ibid., 68.

38. *Ford Foundation Annual Report 1958* (New York: Ford Foundation, 1958), 40.

39. *Gideon v. Wainwright*, 372 U.S. 344 (1963).

40. *Annual Report of the American Bar Association* (Chicago: Headquarters Office, 1963), 440–41.

41. Earl Johnson, *Justice and Reform: The Formative Years of the OEO Legal Services Program* (New York: Russell Sage, 1974), 23.

42. Martha Davis, *Brutal Need: Lawyers and the Welfare Rights Movement, 1960–1973* (New Haven: Yale University Press, 1993), chapter 3; Dorothy J. Samuels, "Expanding Justice: A Review of the Ford Foundation's Legal Services Program," Ford Foundation Archives, January 1984, 18.

43. Robert Gordon, "The Legal Profession," in *Looking Back at Law's Century*, ed. Austin Sarat, Bryant Garth, and Robert Kagan (Ithaca, N.Y.: Cornell University Press, 2002), 32.

44. Susan Lawrence, *The Poor in Court* (Princeton: Princeton University Press, 1990), appendix C.

45. Teles, *Whose Welfare?*, chapter 6.

46. *Annual Report of the American Bar Association* (Chicago: Headquarters Office, 1961), 527.

47. Johnson, *Justice and Reform*, 54.

48. *Annual Report of the American Bar Association* (Chicago: Headquarters Office, 1965), 392–93.

49. Ibid., 395. An internal Ford Foundation report from 1984 attributes the ABA's shift to the "education spadework" done by the ABA's committee on legal aid headed by Whitney North Seymour, and funded by the Ford Foundation. Samuels, "Expanding Justice," 14.

50. *Annual Report of the American Bar Association* (Chicago: Headquarters Office, 1966), 426.

51. Ibid., 429.

52. *Annual Report of the American Bar Association* (Chicago: Headquarters Office, 1967), 470.

53. *Annual Report of the American Bar Association* (Chicago: Headquarters Office, 1970), 709.

54. Ibid., 659, 661. Similar statements suggesting legal reform and activism as an alternative to violence in the streets can be found in the presidential addresses of Orison Marsden—*Annual Report of the American Bar Association* (1967), 402–and William Gossett—*Annual Report of the American Bar Association* (Chicago: Headquarters Office, 1969), 435, 437.

55. *Annual Report of the American Bar Association* (1969), 439; *Annual Report of the American Bar Association* (1970), 664–65.

56. Stephen Botein, " 'What We Shall Meet Afterwards in Heaven': Judgeship as a Symbol for Modern American Lawyers," in *Professions and Professional Ideologies in America*, ed. Charles Geison (Chapel Hill: University of North Carolina Press, 1983), 49–69.

57. This shift in the American elite's attitudes toward liberalism is captured wonderfully in Kabaservice, *The Guardians*.

58. Edward Kuhn, "The ABA's Number One Issue," *Time*, August 20, 1965, http://www.time.com/time/magazine/article/0,9171,841981,00.html.

59. Johnson, *Justice and Reform*, 22.

60. *Ford Foundation Annual Report 1963* (New York: Ford Foundation, 1963), 25.

61. *Ford Foundation Annual Report 1964* (New York: Ford Foundation, 1964), 23.

62. *Ford Foundation Annual Report 1966* (New York: Ford Foundation, 1966), 6.

63. Charles Epp makes this point convincingly in *The Rights Revolution* by pointing to the failure of the Ford Foundation's substantial investment in Indian legal reform.

64. McGeorge Bundy, *Action for Equal Opportunity* (New York: Ford Foundation, 1966), 3, http://www.fordfound.org/elibrary/documents/0325/toc.cfm. The text was delivered as a speech to the Urban League, August 2, 1966.

65. Ibid., 5.

66. Ibid., 7.

67. Ibid., 9.

68. Among the members of the board were the senior leadership of Bechtel, Polaroid, Royal Dutch Petrol, Cummins Engine, the *Minneapolis Star and Tribune*, and, of course, Henry Ford II.

69. For example, grants for "minority rights" increased from 2.5 percent to 40 percent of Ford Foundation giving between 1960 and 1970. Samuels, "Expanding Justice," 22.

70. Washington Legal Foundation, *In Whose Interest? Public Law Activism in the Law Schools* (Washington, D.C.: WLF, 1990).

71. Heather MacDonald, "*This* Is the Legal Mainstream?" *City Journal*, Winter 2006, http://www.city-journal.org/html/16_1_law_schools.html.

72. Ibid.

73. "Enhancing Theory with Practice: Evaluation of Four Years of Work by the Council on Legal Education for Professional Responsibility (CLEPR)—a Foundation-supported Institution to Promote the Use of Clinical Education in Law Schools," Project Evaluation, Division of National Affairs, Ford Foundation Archives (#002165), November 1972, 1.

74. Samuels, "Expanding Justice," 3.

75. Ford Foundation, "Enhancing Theory with Practice," 90.

76. Ibid., 89.

77. Ibid., 90.

78. Ibid., 96–97.

79. Quoted in Laura Kalman, "Professing Law: Elite Law School Professors in the Twentieth Century," in Sarat, Garth, and Kagan, *Looking Back*, 351.

80. John Randall, Presidential Address, ABA National Meeting, Washington, D.C., August 1960, *Annual Report of the American Bar Association* (Chicago: Headquarters Office, 1960), 480.

81. See, for example, Orison Marsden's ABA presidential address in 1969, when he advocated federal government support for clinical education to train

lawyers to conduct criminal cases. *Annual Report of the American Bar Association* (1969), 662.

82. Ralph Brown, David Cavers, Harry Kalvern, and Murray Schwartz, "Evaluation of the Professional Responsibility Program of the National Council of Legal Clinics," Ford Foundation Archives (#000417), May 1965.

83. Ibid.

84. "Docket Excerpt—Board of Trustees Meeting, 3/28–29/68. National Affairs (Government and Law) 68-894. Establishment of a Council on Legal Education in Professional Responsibility," Ford Foundation Archives, March 1968, 2.

85. Robert Stevens, "Law Schools and Law Students," *Virginia Law Review* 59, no. 4 (1973): 579–80.

86. "Between 1957 and 1970, entering students at each school we studied became increasingly liberal or radical. Combining percentages of 'far left' and 'liberal' students the Yale aggregate rose from 56 percent in the class of 1960 to 80 percent in the Class of 1972. By 1972, no less than 32 percent of the Yale entering class described themselves as 'far left,' a percentage at least twice as large as that at any other school. By 1972 'moderates' and 'conservatives' could muster only 13 percent of the entering Yale class; in the Class of 1960, 40 percent of the Yale respondents had put themselves in those categories. At the remaining schools, the percentage of 'far left' and 'liberal' students had risen dramatically, but about half of the 1970 and 1972 classes still thought of themselves as 'moderate' or 'conservative.'. . . Legal education and liberal or radical political views appear to be related. While the great majority of students tended to retain the same political outlook they had on entering law school, among those whose political philosophies shifted, 65 percent moved leftward. The liberalizing tendency was most perceptible in two instances. First, over a fifth of those who entered law school with a moderate political outlook characterized themselves as 'liberals' on graduation. Second, almost as large a percentage with a conservative political perspective on entering law school emerged viewing themselves as 'moderates.' " Stevens, "Law Schools and Law Students," 583–84.

87. George Hicks, "The Conservative Influence of the Federalist Society on the Harvard Law School Student Body," *Harvard Journal of Law and Public Policy* 29, no. 2 (2006): 634.

88. *Ford Foundation Annual Report 1972* (New York: Ford Foundation, 1972), 6.

89. Between 1974–75 and 1984–85, the number of electives in "discrimination in the law" in American law schools increased by 92.9 percent, while electives in natural resources and the environment increased by 20 percent, on top of what appears to have been very substantial growth in the years just before. That said, electives in patent, copyright, and trademark leaped 115.6 percent. William Powers, *A Study of Contemporary Law School Curricula* (Indianapolis: Office of the consultant on Legal Education to the American Bar Association, 1987), 36. The new classes that reflected more liberal priorities were, in effect, layered onto the old law school curricula, rather than fundamentally altering it.

90. Laura Holland, "Invading the Ivory Tower: The History of Clinical Education at Yale Law School," *Journal of Legal Education* 49, no. 4 (1999): 504–34.

91. Ibid., 520.

92. See, for example, J. Peter Byrne, "Academic Freedom and Political Neutrality in Law Schools: An Essay on Structure and Ideology in Professional Education," *Journal of Legal Education* 43 (1993): 315.

93. Auerbach, *Unequal Justice*, 278–79.

94. Donna Fossum, "Law Professors: A Profile of the Teaching Branch of the Legal Profession," *American Bar Foundation Research Journal* 5, no. 3 (1980): 505.

95. Ibid., 505.

96. Laura Kalman, *The Strange Career of Legal Liberalism* (New Haven: Yale University Press, 1996), 60.

97. Everett Carl Ladd and Seymour Martin Lipset, *The Divided American Academy* (New York: McGraw Hill, 1975).

98. Ibid., 60.

99. John McGinnis, Matthew Schwartz, and Benjamin Tisdell, "The Patterns and Implications of Political Contributions by Elite Law School Faculty," *Georgetown Law Journal* 93, no. 4 (2005): 1175, 1184.

100. Charles Reich, "Midnight Welfare Searches and the Social Security Act," *Yale Law Journal* 72, no. 7 (1963): 1347–60; "The New Property," *Yale Law Journal* 73, no. 5 (1964): 733–87; "The Law of the Planned Society," *Yale Law Journal* 75, no. 8 (1966): 1227–70; "Mr. Justice Black and the Living Constitution," *Harvard Law Review* 76, no. 4 (1963): 673–754.

101. Davis, *Brutal Need*, 82.

102. Reich, "Mr. Justice Black," 745.

103. Davis, *Brutal Need*, 84.

104. Reich, "The New Property," 782–83.

105. Ibid., 779.

106. Ibid., 783–85.

107. Elizabeth Bussiere, "The New Property Theory of Welfare Rights: Promises and Pitfalls," *Good Society* 13, no. 2 (2004): 6.

108. Lawrence, *The Poor in Court*, 32–33.

109. One example of the impact of these law professors–activists is Richard Daynard's Tobacco Control Research Center at Northeastern University Law School, which nurtured the antismoking movement's legal network in its early days. Start-up funding for the Center was provided by the Rockefeller Foundation, and it "received a grant of more than $1 million from the National Cancer Institute to do 'the legal research and analysis needed to support states, municipalities, health insurers and public interest groups as they pursue innovative legal interventions to reduce tobacco use." Martha Derthick, *Up in Smoke* (Washington, D.C.: CQ Press, 2004), 100–101.

110. Alexander Bickel, *The Least Dangerous Branch: The Supreme Court at the Bar of Politics* (Indianapolis: Bobbs-Merrill, 1962), 16ff.

111. Kalman, *The Strange Career*, 50.

112. Ibid., 51.

113. Fiss, "Objectivity and Interpretation," 741.

114. For instance, Frank Michelman's foreword to the *Harvard Law Review*'s issue on the 1968 term began, "In the end, no doubt, a victorious War on Poverty will have somehow attacked and conquered relative deprivation." Frank Michel-

man, "The Supreme Court, 1968 Term," *Harvard Law Review* 83, no. 1 (1969): 7–282.

115. See also Ronald Dworkin, *Taking Rights Seriously* (Cambridge: Harvard University Press, 1977); Laurence Tribe, *American Constitutional Law* (Mineola, N.Y.: Foundation Press, 1978); Bruce Ackerman, *Social Justice in the Liberal State* (New Haven: Yale University Press, 1980); Owen Fiss, "Groups and the Equal Protection Clause," *Philosophy and Public Affairs* 5, no 2 (1976): 107–77.

116. Martin Shapiro, "Interest Groups and Supreme Court Appointments," *Northwestern University Law Review* 84 (1990): 955. There is still not, as of 2006, a significant constitutional law casebook written by a conservative or libertarian, although a few are being prepared.

117. Kalman, *The Strange Career*, 52.

118. Mark Tushnet, "Truth, Justice and the American Way: An Interpretation of Public Law Scholarship in the Seventies," *Texas Law Review* 57 (1979): 1319.

119. A good example of this skepticism can be seen in Duncan Kennedy, "American Constitutionalism as Civil Religion: Notes of an Atheist," *Nova Law Review* 19 (1995): 909. Among the most prominent of the attacks on CLS were Duke Law School dean Paul Carrington, "Of Law and the River," *Journal of Legal Education* 34 (1984): 222 and Owen Fiss, "The Death of the Law," *Cornell Law Review* 72 (1986): 245.

120. Walker, *Mobilizing Interest Groups*.

121. Works whose arguments were in the air at the time included Theodore Lowi, *The End of Liberalism* (New York: Norton, 1969); Grant McConnell, *Private Power and American Democracy* (New York: Vintage 1966); Olson, *Logic of Collective Action*.

122. Interview with McGeorge Bundy, Ford Foundation Archives, 25–26.

123. "Advocacy, Law and the Public Interest" (Confidential Information Paper), Ford Foundation Archives, March 1970, 3.

124. Interview with Sanford Jaffe, conducted by Thomas Hilbink, University of Massachusetts-Amherst, Ford Foundation Archives, October–November 2001, 19, 20, 23, 24.

125. Ibid., 20.

126. Ford Foundation, "Advocacy, Law and the Public Interest," 14. Donald Rumsfeld's defense of legal services, and of OEO more generally, are discussed in James Mann, "Up Close: Young Rumsfeld," *Atlantic*, November 2003.

127. Jaffe, interview by Hilbink, 24.

128. Ibid., 18.

129. Jaffe interview.

130. Ford Foundation, "Advocacy, Law and the Public Interest," 9.

131. Ibid., 10.

132. Ibid., 13.

133. Jeffrey Berry, *Lobbying for the People* (Princeton: Princeton University Press, 1977), 51.

134. Jaffe, interview by Hilbink, 25.

135. Berry, *Lobbying for the People*, 52. Interestingly, Ruckleshaus would later go on to be a significant figure in supporting public interest law, serving as cochair-

man of the Council for Public Interest Law, which was directed by none other than Charles Halpern, the cofounder of the Center for Law and Social Policy. See for example the major report, Council for Public Interest Law, *Balancing the Scales of Justice: Financing Public Interest Law in America* (Washington, D.C.: Council for Public Interest Law, 1976).

136. Jaffe, interview by Hilbink, 25–26.

137. Robert Rabin, "Lawyers for Social Change: Perspectives on Public Interest Law," *Stanford Law Review* 28 (January 1976): 236.

138. Jaffe interview.

139. Jaffe, interview by Hilbink, 35.

140. Anthony King, ed., *The New American Political System*, 2nd ed. (Washington, D.C.: American Enterprise Institute, 1990); Marc Landy and Martin Levin, *The New Politics of Public Policy* (Baltimore: Johns Hopkins University Press, 1995).

141. Daniel Patrick Moynihan, "The Professionalization of Reform," *Public Interest*, Fall 1965.

142. Julian Zelizer, *On Capitol Hill* (Oxford: Oxford University Press, 2004).

143. Richard Stewart, "The Reformation of American Administrative Law," *Harvard Law Review* 88, no. 8 (1975): 1667–1813.

144. Joseph Smith, "Judicial Procedures as Instruments of Political Control: Congress' Strategic Use of Citizen Suits," *Legislative Studies Quarterly*: forthcoming; Joseph Smith, "Congress Opens the Courthouse Doors: Statutory Changes to Judicial Review Under the Clean Air Act," *Political Research Quarterly* 58 (March 2005): 139–49; Michael McCann, *Taking Reform Seriously* (Ithaca, N.Y.: Cornell University Press, 1986), 61–67; Thomas Burke, *Lawyers, Lawsuits and Legal Rights: The Battle over Litigation in American Society* (Berkeley and Los Angeles: University of California Press, 2002).

145. On the concept of legislative "high demanders" and its implications for congressional organization, see Barry R. Weingast and William J. Marshall, "The Industrial Organization of Congress; or, Why Legislatures, Like Firms, Are Not Organized as Markets," *Journal of Political Economy* 96, no. 1 (1988): 132–63. On traceability, see Douglas Arnold, *The Logic of Congressional Action* (New Haven: Yale University Press, 1992).

146. William Lunch, *The Nationalization of American Politics* (Berkeley and Los Angeles: University of California Press, 1987).

147. Skocpol, *Diminished Democracy*.

148. McCann, *Taking Reform Seriously*, 33.

149. Teles, *Whose Welfare?*; Melnick, *Between the Lines*.

150. Epstein and Kobylka, *Supreme Court*.

151. On the role of judges as instigators of this movement, see Malcolm Feeley and Edward Rubin, *Judicial Policymaking and the Modern State* (Cambridge: Cambridge University Press, 1998). On the role of public interest litigants in prison reform, see Margo Schlanger, "Beyond the Hero Judge: Institution Reform Litigation as Litigation," *Michigan Law Review* 97 (1999): 1994–2036.

152. Epstein and Kobylka, *Supreme Court*.

153. Jane Sherron de Hart, *Litigating Equality: Ruth Bader Ginsburg, Feminist Lawyers and the Court* (Chicago: University of Chicago Press, forthcoming); Reva Siegel, "Constitutional Culture, Social Movement Conflict and Constitutional Change: The Case of the de facto ERA," *California Law Review* 94 (2006): 1323.

154. Sid Milkis and Richard Harris, *The Politics of Regulatory Change: A Tale of Two Agencies* (Oxford: Oxford University Press, 1996).

155. Skrentny, *The Minority Rights Revolution*.

156. David Kirp and Donald Jensen, eds., *School Days, Rule Days* (Philadelphia: Falmer Press, 1986).

157. Ronald Formisano, *Boston Against Busing* (Chapel Hill: University of North Carolina Press, 2003); Jennifer Hochschild, *The New American Dilemma: Liberal Democracy and School Desegregation* (New Haven: Yale University Press, 1984). Hochschild is quite clear that school desegregation could not be accomplished through normal, participatory political processes.

158. Epstein and Kobylka, *The Supreme Court*.

159. Melnick, *Regulation and the Courts*.

160. Melnick, *Between the Lines*, 236.

161. This suggests that the "non-median policy outcomes" that Jacob Hacker and Paul Pierson have identified with the contemporary Republican regime may not be an anomaly of the last decade, but a persistent feature of our constitutional system. Jacob Hacker and Paul Pierson, *Off Center: The Republic Revolution and the Erosion of American Democracy* (New Haven: Yale University Press, 2005).

162. This is discussed in greater detail in chapter 3.

163. Carlyle Hall, "CLIPI's 30 Most Important Cases," August 1997, http://www.clipi.org/pdf/importantmatters.pdf; see also *New York Times*, February 8, 1975.

164. Michael Greve, "Why Defunding the Left Failed," *Public Interest*, Fall 1987, 91–106.

Chapter 3
Conservative Public Interest Law I: Mistakes Made

1. Chapters 3 through 7 are based to a considerable degree on materials obtained from privately available files. Unless otherwise noted, all sources were acquired under a condition of nontransferability and are on file with the author.

2. Peter Swenson, *Capitalists Against Markets* (Oxford: Oxford University Press, 2002).

3. David Vogel, "Why Businessmen Distrust Their State: The Political Consciousness of American Corporate Executives," *British Journal of Political Science* 8, no. 1 (1978): 45–78.

4. The classic study of asymmetric information is George Akerlof, "The Market for 'Lemons': Quality Uncertainty and the Market Mechanism," *Quarterly Journal of Economics* 84, no. 3 (1970): 488–500.

5. For a detailed discussion of these changes, see Lucas Powe, *The Warren Court and American Politics* (Cambridge: Belknap Press of Harvard University Press, 2001).

6. David Yalof, *Pursuit of Justices* (Chicago: University of Chicago Press, 2001), 97–132.

7. George Bisharat, "Right Lawyers for the Right Time: The Rise of the Pacific Legal Foundation," unpublished manuscript.

8. Hueter interview. Also see James Singer, "Liberal Public Interest Law Firms Face Budgetary, Ideological Challenges," *National Journal*, December 8, 1979, 2055.

9. Jefferson Decker, "The Conservative Non-Profit Movement and the Rights Revolution," paper delivered to the American Society of Legal Historians, Baltimore, November 18, 2006, 2–3.

10. As Jefferson Decker notes, the election of Jerry Brown as governor of California in 1975 made it obvious to PLF that assistance from the state was unlikely to be forthcoming. As a consequence of this, PLF moved away from the welfare and social services cases that Zumbrun had brought with him from government service to the environmental issues that agitated his business supporters. Ibid., 4.

11. Lee Epstein, *Conservatives in Court* (Knoxville: University of Tennessee Press, 1985), 133.

12. Lewis Powell, "Attack on the American Free Enterprise System," confidential memorandum to the United States Chamber of Commerce, August 23, 1971, 2, www.pbs.org/wnet/supremecourt/personality/sources_document13.html.

13. Ibid., 6.

14. Hueter interview.

15. For example, Theberge was the founding director of the Media Institute, one of the conservative movement's first responses to "liberal media bias." John Salmoa, *Ominous Politics* (New York: Hill and Wang, 1984), 112.

16. Ibid., 125.

17. Hueter interview.

18. Unless otherwise documented, quotations derive from the interviews listed in the appendix.

19. Hueter interview.

20. R. McGreggor Cawley, *Federal Land, Western Anger: The Sagebrush Rebellion and Environmental Politics* (Lawrence: University Press of Kansas, 1996).

21. Kennedy would ultimately become the chairman of the board of the Institute for Justice, as well as the president of the Earhart Foundation.

22. As discussed later in this chapter, Mellor would go on to be the president of the Pacific Research Institute and then the president of the Institute for Justice.

23. Mellor interview.

24. Decker, "Conservative Non-Profit Movement," 3.

25. William E. Schmidt, "Denver Suit Looming as Threat to Way Cities Award Cable TV Franchises," *New York Times*, December 2, 1982. See also *Mountain States Legal Foundation v. City of Denver*, 567 F.Supp. 476 (D.Colo 1983), appeal dismissed 751 F.2d 1151 (1983).

26. Vogel, "Why Businessmen Distrust Their State."

27. Kennedy interview.

28. Chip Mellor, "Free Market Comes Full Circle," *Carry The Torch*, May 1995, http://www.ij.org/publications/torch/ctt_5_95.html.

29. Horowitz was appointed chief counsel of the Office of Management and Budget in the first term of the Reagan administration, and is now a senior fellow at the Hudson Institute.

30. I am indebted to Oliver Houck of Tulane Law School, who generously provided me with a copy of the Horowitz Report after I had done months of futile searching.

31. Michael Horowitz, "In Defense of Public Interest Law," in Institute for Educational Affairs, *Perspectives on Public Interest Law*, Foundation Officers Forum Occasional Papers, no. 2 (1981): 7–8.

32. Michael Horowitz, "The Public Interest Law Movement: An Analysis with Special Reference to the Role and Practices of Conservative Public Interest Law Firms," unpublished manuscript prepared for the Scaife Foundation, 1980, 24.

33. Ibid., 3.

34. Ibid., 73.

35. Ibid.

36. Ibid., 58.

37. This same point was made, from a standpoint hostile to the conservative movement, in Oliver Houck, "With Charity For All," *Yale Law Journal* 93, no. 8 (1984): 1415–1563.

38. Horowitz, "Public Interest Law Movement," 26.

39. Ibid., 28.

40. Ibid., 30.

41. Ibid.

42. Ibid., 63.

43. Ibid., 72.

44. Ibid., 54.

45. Ibid.

46. Ibid.

47. Amicus curiae participation can have an impact on judicial outcomes, but only when it is strategically focused and combined with actual control over litigation, in particular the choice of client and venue. Furthermore, Paul Collins has convincingly shown that it is not the sheer fact of participation, but the information that amici provide to the court, that leads to their (fairly small) impact. Paul Collins, "Friends of the Court: Examining the Influence of Amicus Curiae Participation in U.S. Supreme Court Litigation," *Law and Society Review* 38, no. 4 (2004): 807–32.

48. Horowitz, "Public Interest Law Movement," 83.

49. McCann, *Taking Reform Seriously*. John Patrick Diggins makes the point in *Up From Communism* (New York: Columbia University Press, 1993) that many of the former communists among the early leaders of the conservative movement shared the temperament—if not the ideology—of their former comrades. It was specifically this nonconservative temperament that Horowitz sought to deploy for conservative ends.

50. Cases that pitted conservatives against business interests would be, not problematic, but especially attractive, as they would help the movement "divest

itself of the label and reality of being 'business oriented' " and help it "establish the moral high ground." Horowitz, "Public Interest Law Movement," 87.

51. Ibid., 85–86.

52. Among the works that Horowitz may have had in mind were Thomas Sowell, *Black Education: Myths and Tragedies* (New York: McKay, 1972); Nathan Glazer, "The Limits of Social Policy," *Commentary* 52, no. 3 (1971); Martin Anderson, *Welfare: The Political Economy of Welfare Reform in the United States* (Palo Alto: Hoover Institution, 1978); James Q. Wilson, *Thinking About Crime* (New York: Basic Books, 1975).

53. The best examples of this were two books by Stuart Butler: *Enterprise Zones: Greenlining the Inner Cities* (New York: Universe Books, 1981) and, with Anna Kondratas, *Out of the Poverty Trap* (New York: Free Press, 1987).

54. Olin Grant Proposal Record (for Southeastern Law Foundation), December 12, 1980. All dates on Olin Foundation reports are the date that the grantee was notified, which is consistent across the foundation's history.

55. Olin Grant Proposal Record (for Southeastern Law Foundation), January 25, 1982.

56. Olin Grant Proposal Record (for New England Legal Foundation), September 29, 1982.

57. Olin Grant Proposal Record (for Washington Legal Foundation), February 9, 1982.

58. Olin Grant Proposal Report (for Institute for Justice), June 16, 1992. Despite this skepticism, Olin provided the first foundation support to IJ beyond its original seed funders.

59. Ibid.

60. Dan Burt, *Abuse of Trust: A Report on Ralph Nader's Network* (Chicago: Regnery Gateway, 1982).

61. Ibid.

62. Olin Grant Proposal Record, September 25, 1980.

63. Olin Grant Proposal Record, June 23, 1982.

64. Among the lawyers who rejected Westmoreland's case were Clark Clifford of Clifford and Warnke, Edward Bennett Williams of Williams and Connolly, and Stanley Resor of Debevoise and Plimpton. Connie Bruck, "How Dan Burt Deserted the General," *American Lawyer*, April 1985, 118.

65. Sally Bedell and Dan Kower, "Anatomy of a Smear: How CBS News Broke the Rules and 'Got' Gen. Westmoreland," *TV Guide*, May 24, 1982.

66. Lenkowsky interview.

67. Karen Donovan, *V. Goliath: The Trials of David Boies* (New York: Knopf, 2005), 46.

68. Although he was assisted by David Dorsen, an experienced libel lawyer, Burt actually tried the case.

69. Donovan, *V. Goliath*, 48.

70. Bruck, "Burt Deserted the General," 118.

71. Nancy Blodgett, "Ralph Naders of the Right," *American Bar Association Journal* 70 (May 1984): 71. Here Burt is listed in the profiles of major conservative players.

72. For instance, the Federalist Society's journalists' guide to legal experts lists seven experts in libel law, mainly professors of law, http://fedsoc.eresources.ws/doclib/20070326_JournalistGuide.pdf.

73. Dan Burt to Michael Joyce, October 25, 1985.

74. Described in detail in chapter 7.

75. Capital Legal Foundation, Proposal for Funding, "Barriers to Entry Project," appended to a letter from Dan Burt to James Piereson, August 8, 1986, 5–6.

76. Ibid., 6.

77. Ibid., 7–8.

78. "The Center for Constitutional Litigation," 1985, 1 (no author on document, but authored jointly by Chip Mellor and Clint Bolick).

79. Ibid.

80. Ibid., 4.

81. Ibid., 3.

82. Mellor interview.

83. Pacific Research Institute, "Proposal for The Center for Applied Jurisprudence," 1987, 2.

84. Ibid.

85. Among the "possible task force participants or leaders" mentioned were Richard Epstein (professor of law, University of Chicago), Bernard Siegan (professor of law, University of San Diego), Fred McChesney (then professor at Emory University, now at Northwestern University School of Law), Randy Barnett (then professor of law at Chicago-Kent School of Law, now Georgetown University Law Center), Henry Manne, Rex Lee (former solicitor general of the United States), Clint Bolick, and Michael Horowitz. Ibid., 2–3.

86. Pacific Research Institute, "Proposal for Center," 3–4.

87. Center for Individual Rights, "A Brief Description of Program Activities," 1989, 11.

88. Clint Bolick, *Unfinished Business* (San Francisco: Pacific Research Institute for Public Policy, 1991).

89. Ibid., 4.

90. Ibid.

91. Ibid., 137.

92. Clint Bolick, "Clinton's Quota Queen," *Wall Street Journal*, April 30, 1993.

93. Bolick, *Unfinished Business*, 141.

94. Ibid., 136.

95. Ibid., 140.

96. Ibid., 141.

97. On the idea of "counterrights," see Thomas Burke, "On The Resilience of Rights," in Levin, Landy, and Shapiro, *Seeking the Center.*

98. *Nollan v. California Coastal Commission*, 483 U.S. 825 (1987).

99. Bolick, *Unfinished Business*, 142–43.

100. This is a lesson that recent scholars have framed as the "constitution beyond the courts." See Reva Siegel and Robert Post, "Legislative Constitutionalism and Section Five Power: Policentric Interpretation of the Family and Medical Leave Act," *Yale Law Journal* 112 (2003): 1943–2059.

Chapter 4
Law and Economics I: Out of the Wilderness

1. In the terms of the social movement literature, the University of Chicago served as an "abeyance structure" for the movement. Taylor defines the term *abeyance* as a "holding process by which movements sustain themselves in nonreceptive political environments and provide continuity from one state of mobilization to another." For classical economics, that "nonreceptive" period lasted from the 1930s to the 1960s, and the existence of the University allowed classical economic ideas to develop despite their unpopularity, so that they were available when the political tides changed. Verta Taylor, "Social Movement Continuity: The Women's Movement in Abeyance," *American Sociological Review* 54, no. 5 (1989): 761–75.

2. Ronald Coase, "Law and Economics at Chicago," *Journal of Law and Economics* 36, no. 1 (1993): 243.

3. Aaron Director, in "The Fire of Truth: A Remembrance of Law and Economics at Chicago, 1932–1970," ed. Edmund Kitch, *Journal of Law and Economics* 26, no. 1 (1983): 176.

4. Barbara Fried, *The Progressive Assault on Laissez-Faire: Robert Hale and the First Law and Economics Movement* (Cambridge: Harvard University Press, 1998).

5. Director, in "The Fire of Truth," 179.

6. Henry Simons, "Some Comments on University Policy," Henry Simons Papers, University of Chicago Special Collections, Box 8, Folder 8, pp. 23, 25.

7. Henry Simons, *Personal Income Taxation: The Definition of Income as a Problem of Fiscal Policy* (Chicago: University of Chicago Press, 1938).

8. Henry Simons, *A Positive Plan for Laissez-Faire: Some Proposals for a Liberal Economic Policy* (Chicago: University of Chicago Press, 1936).

9. George Stigler, in "The Fire Of Truth," 178.

10. Juan Gabriel Valdes, *Pinochet's Economists: The Chicago School in Chile* (Cambridge: Cambridge University Press, 1995).

11. Henry Simons, "Memorandum I On a Proposed Institute of Political Economy," Henry Simons Papers, University of Chicago Special Collections, Box 8, Folders 8–9.

12. R. M. Hartwell, *A History of the Mont Pelerin Society* (Indianapolis: Liberty Fund, 1995), 90.

13. A detailed examination of the history of this project can be found in Steven Teles and Daniel Kenney, "Spreading the Word," in *Growing Apart?: America and Europe in the 21st Century*, ed. Jeffrey Kopstein and Sven Steinmo (Cambridge: Cambridge University Press, 2007).

14. The idea of "remnantism" is most typically associated with Albert Jay Nock, *Memoirs of a Superfluous Man* (New York: Harper and Brothers, 1943), but it can also be seen in the conclusion of Alisdair McIntyre's *After Virtue: A Study in Moral Theory* (Notre Dame, Ind.: University of Notre Dame Press, 1984).

15. Coase, "Law and Economics at Chicago," 246.

16. Simons, "Memorandum I," 1.

17. Ibid., 2–3.

18. Ibid., 8–9.

19. Ibid., 12.

20. Henry Simons to Friedrich Hayek, May 18, 1945, Henry Simons Papers, University of Chicago Special Collections, Box 8, Folder 9.

21. Director, in "The Fire of Truth," 181.

22. Wesley Liebeler, in "The Fire of Truth," 183.

23. Robert Bork, in "The Fire of Truth," 183.

24. While it is possible to overstate this point, consider also Ronald Coase's comment, quoted later in this section, that he was Saint Paul to Director's Christ.

25. A similar account appears in Kitch, "The Fire of Truth," 184.

26. Among the important figures who were a part of the Anti-Trust Project were John McGee, John Jewkes, William Letwin, David Sawers, Richard Stillerman, Robert Bork, and Ward Bowman.

27. Coase, "Law and Economics at Chicago," 247–48.

28. Harold Demsetz, in "The Fire of Truth," 189.

29. Kitch, "The Fire of Truth," 290.

30. Coase, in "The Fire of Truth," 192.

31. This was largely due to student editing, a cause of persistent annoyance among law and economics scholars. See in particular Richard Posner, "The Future of the Student-Edited Law Review," *Stanford Law Review* 47 (Summer 1995): 1131.

32. An intellectual history of law and economics, or one less focused on its place within the conservative movement, might emphasize the work of Guido Calabresi and the "Yale School" as much as I emphasize Posner and Chicago.

33. See for example Guido Calabresi, "The Decision for Accidents: An Approach to Nonfault Allocation of Costs," *Harvard Law Review* 78, no. 4 (1965): 713–45.

34. Gary Becker, "Crime and Punishment: An Economic Approach," *Journal of Political Economy* 76, no. 2 (1968): 169–217.

35. A shrewd analysis of the Chicago "style" can be found in Jedediah Purdy, "The Chicago Acid Bath," *American Prospect* 9, no. 36 (1998), www.prospect .org/print/V9/36/purdy-j.html.

36. George Priest, "Henry Manne and the Market Measure of Intellectual Influence," *Case Western Reserve University Law Review* 50 (Winter 1999): 325. It is generally accepted today that while *Economic Analysis of Law* was a powerful intellectual statement, Posner's grasp on economic concepts was, at times, uneven.

37. Interview with Henry Manne, conducted by Fred McChesney, Liberty Fund, 2006.

38. Roberta Romano, "After The Revolution in Corporate Law," *Journal of Legal Education* 55 (September 2005): 342.

39. Baird interview.

40. Dennis Carlton from the business school joined Lexecon's leadership in 1978.

41. Romano, "After the Revolution."

42. Michael Mandel, "Going for the Gold: Economists as Expert Witnesses," *Journal of Economic Perspectives* 13, no. 2 (1999): 115–16.

43. Ibid., 115.

44. Amy Bach and Matt Siegel, "Midas Touch in the Ivory Tower: Selling Law and Economics," *American Lawyer,* April 1994, 61.

45. The original writing of this chapter and chapter 6 was completed before the publication of Henry Manne, "How Law and Economics Was Marketed in a Hostile World: A Very Personal History," in *The Origins of Law and Economics: Essays by the Founding Fathers,* ed. Francesco Parisi and Charles Rowley (Cheltenham: Edward Elgar, 2005). Some of the quotations from my interviews with Manne closely track his discussion of similar matters in this essay.

46. Henry Manne, "Mergers and the Market for Corporate Control," *Journal of Political Economy* 73, no. 2 (April 1965). Manne's direct target was Adolph Berle and Gardiner Means's classic of old-style, liberal law and economics, *The Modern Corporation and Private Property* (New York: McMillan, 1936).

47. Henry Manne, *Insider Trading and the Stock Market* (New York: Free Press, 1966).

48. S. M. Amadae and Bruce Bueno de Mesquita, "The Rochester School: The Origins of Positive Political Theory," *Annual Review of Political Science* 2, no. 1 (1999): 269–95; the term *mother ship* is Kenneth Shepsle's, quoted in Jonathan Cohn, "When Did Political Science Forget about Politics?" *New Republic,* October 25, 1999, http://www.nuff.ox.ac.uk/users/Kayser/TNR%20Cohn.pdf.

49. Henry Manne to President W. Allen Wallis, "Report on Law Schools," January 1968, 3–4.

50. Ibid., 5.

51. Ibid., 18.

52. Ibid., 31–32.

53. Ibid., 24–25.

54. Ibid., 30.

55. Ibid., 7.

56. Letter from Henry Manne to Pierre Goodrich, October 5, 1970.

57. Ibid.

58. Letter from Henry Manne to Pierre Goodrich, December 15, 1972.

59. Ibid.

60. Ibid.

61. Rosett interview.

62. Henry Manne, "An Intellectual History of the George Mason University School of Law," 1993, http://www.law.gmu.edu/econ/history.html. The Rochester bar seemed to believe that a new law school at Rochester would lead to a glut of lawyers in the area. The school's heavy dependence on the stock price of Xerox and Eastman Kodak may have played a role after Manne left, but during the time he was there the price of both companies increased considerably.

63. Ibid.

64. See, for example, Ralph Winter, "State Law, Shareholder Protection, and the Theory of the Corporation," *Journal of Legal Studies* 6, no. 2 (1997): 251–92 and Douglas Ginsburg, "Making Automobile Regulation Work: Policy Options and a Proposal," *Harvard Journal of Law and Public Policy* 2 (1979): 74–102. Ginsburg also taught, in 1979, in an LEC advanced course for law professors, and became a close friend and advisor to Manne.

65. Henry Manne to George Pearson, Fred C. Koch Foundation, December 20, 1973.

66. Ibid.

67. Confidential Memorandum from Henry G. Manne on The Center for Studies in Law and Economics at the University of Miami Law School, April 16, 1974.

68. Henry Manne to Richard A. Ware, President, Earhart Foundation, February 21, 1975.

69. Ultimately published as Kitch, "The Fire of Truth."

70. Priest, "Henry Manne."

71. Priest was never made an offer at Virginia because, as Goetz recalls, "he was dinged by his classmate Ron Cass, who said, "George didn't even make law review!"

72. Randall Collins, *The Sociology of Philosophies* (Cambridge: Harvard University Press, 1998).

73. Henry Butler, "The Manne Programs in Economics for Federal Judges," *Case Western Reserve Law Review* 50, no. 2 (1999): 355.

74. Ibid., 357.

75. Ibid., 359; Manne, "How Law and Economics Was Marketed," 320.

76. Butler, "The Manne Programs," 370.

77. Ibid., 376.

78. Ibid., 366.

79. Alliance for Justice, *Justice for Sale: Shortchanging the Public Interest for Private Gain* (Washington, D.C.: Alliance for Justice, 1993); Community Rights Counsel, *Nothing for Free: How Judicial Seminars Are Undermining Environmental Protections and Breaking the Public's Trust* (Washington, D.C.: Community Rights Counsel, 2000).

80. Legislation has been proposed that would, in effect, ban privately funded programs for judges, and transfer all such programming to the Federal Judicial Center. *Federal Judiciary Ethics Reform Act of 2006*, S2202, 109th Cong., 2nd sess. FREE notes that its seminars, like those of the LEC, are funded solely by charitable foundations, not corporations, and that legal challenges to its conferences in the federal courts have been firmly rejected. See FREE, "Info for Journalists," http://www.free-eco.org/funding.php.

81. Manne, "How Law and Economics Was Marketed," 319. The propriety of the LEC seminars has been defended by a frequent participant, James Q. Wilson, in "Junket Science?" *Wall Street Journal*, July 10, 2006.

82. This strategy was later followed by other conservative organizations inside the university, including Robert George's James Madison Program at Princeton University. Timothy Webster, "A New Birth of Civic Education on Campus," *Philanthropy* 16, no. 2 (2002): 17–23.

83. Manne, memorandum.

84. Manne interview.

85. Ibid.

86. Ibid.

87. Manne to Ware.

88. Henry Manne to Henry King Stanford, March 18, 1980.

89. Memorandum from Dennis Lynch, Associate Dean, University of Miami Law School, "Subject: Report of the Dean Search Committee to the Faculty," October 30, 1979. This memo reported that "Henry Manne informed the Com-

mittee that he regularly is contacted about his interest in being a Dean at other law schools. He has told all the schools that he has no interest unless they wish to bid for the Law and Economics Center. His asking price is $1,000,000 and two schools are interested, but he expects they will not make a firm offer. In any case, if a Dean who is committed to building a law and economics program is appointed at Miami, it would take a good deal more to attract him to another school." It should be noted that this memo was written at a time when Manne was in substantial conflict with the administrators writing the minutes, so at the very least the tone may have been overstated. Manne in fact specifically challenged most of its claims, including that the LEC had an "asking price" of $1 million in a letter to the dean on November 9, 1979. Among the schools that had shown some interest in Manne was Cornell, an incident that is discussed in detail in chapter 6.

90. "Chronology of Events with Supporting Documents, Re: Law and Economics Center Shift to Emory University," November 22, 1980, 5.

91. The impact of UVA and USC on the penetration of law and economics into elite institutions can be seen, for example, at Yale, NYU, and Chicago. Six of their most prestigious professors—Robert Ellickson (USC, 1970–81), Michael Graetz (UVA, 1972–79, USC, 1979–83); Jerry Mashaw (UVA, 1968–76), Allen Schwartz (USC, 1976–87), Richard Epstein (USC, 1968–73), and Michael Levine (USC, 1968–87)—spent a significant part of their early careers at UVA or USC. UVA has done better at retaining its top figures in law and economics from this period, such as Lillian BeVier, Michael Dooley, and Charles Goetz. This list could also include Warren Schwartz of Georgetown and Robert Scott of Columbia, both of whom were at UVA in the 1970s (Scott left for Columbia in 2006). Early adoption of law and economics appears to have had a bottom-line effect on the status of the respective law schools. In the most recent US News rankings, UVA ranked 10 and USC 16, considerably above the level of their undergraduate counterparts (24 and 27, respectively).

92. Sanford Kadish and Monrad Paulsen, Criminal Law and Its Processes: Cases and Materials (Boston: Little, Brown, 1969).

93. Michael Graetz and Charles Whitebreak, "Monrad Paulsen and the Idea of a University Law School," Virginia Law Review 67, no. 3 (1981): 445.

94. Scott interview.

95. Michael Levine, " 'Law and . . .' in Theory and Practice: The USC Style and Its Influence," USC Law Review 74 (November 2000): 225.

96. In the words of Michael Levine, "[Robert] Ellickson, like me, had had difficulty interesting other law faculties in his style of analysis." Levine, "Law and . . ." The term moneyball was popularized by Michael Lewis, Moneyball: The Art of Winning an Unfair Game (New York: Norton, 2003).

97. Scott interview.

98. While there are innumerable examples of these traditions, a few early works that focused on explaining political failure were: James Buchanan and Richard Wagner, Democracy in Deficit: The Political Legacy of Lord Keynes (New York: Academic Press, 1977); William Niskanen, Bureaucracy and Representative Government (Chicago: Aldine, Atherton, 1971); Roger Noll, "The Nature and Causes of Regulatory Failure," Administrative Law Review 23, no. 4 (1971): 424–37; Olson, Logic of Collective Action.

99. Among the most important Caltech public choice scholars were John Ferejohn, Morris Fiorina, Charles Plott, Lance Davis, and Roger Noll; its faculty also included important non-public-choice scholars Morgan Kousser and Bruce Cain.

100. Levine, "Law and . . ." A good example of the outcome of this relationship with Caltech is Michael Levine and Charles Plott, "Agenda Influence and Its Implications," *Virginia Law Review* 63, no. 4 (1977): 561–604. At UVA, an early example of economist-lawyer collaboration using public choice is Jerry Mashaw, Charles Goetz, F. Goodman, Warren Schwartz, et. al., *Social Security Hearings and Appeals: A study of the Social Security Administration Hearing System* (Lexington, Mass.: Lexington Books, 1978).

101. Mashaw begins his book *Greed, Chaos and Governance: Using Public Choice to Improve Public Law* (New Haven: Yale University Press, 1997) by recalling that "our monthly meetings in the early 1970s alternated between Charlottesville and Blacksburg. Papers were read. Wine was drunk. Argument lasted deep into the night" (vii).

102. Ehrlich became famous in the mid-1970s for his work on the economics of crime, especially "The Deterrent Effect of Capital Punishment—A Question of Life and Death," *American Economic Review* 65, no. 3 (1975): 397–417.

103. Liquidated damages are a mechanism to encourage contractual compliance, whereby the damages to be paid if one or the other party violates contractual conditions are specified in the contract. The article was Charles Goetz and Robert Scott, "Liquidated Damages, Penalties, and the Just Compensation Principle: A Theory of Efficient Breach," *Columbia Law Review* 77 (1977): 554.

104. This connection between clustering and increasing returns has been observed in economic geography, as in Masahisa Fujita, Paul Krugman, and Anthony Venables, *The Spatial Economy* (Cambridge: MIT Press, 2001), and in the sociology of ideas, as in Randall Collins, *The Sociology of Philosophies* (Cambridge: Harvard University Press, 1998).

105. While admitting that the Manne programs had an important impact on others, Scott recalls that "Graetz, Jeffries and I, looking back on it, behaved a little badly. We didn't take it quite as seriously as Henry wanted us to. . . . It was the collection of very smart, productive scholars at Virginia at that time, the young Turk, ambitious part of the faculty, that had the greatest influence on me, especially in private law." Scott interview.

106. Olin Grant Proposal Record, Olin Foundation Archives, September 19, 2001.

107. Thomas D. Morgan, "Status Report on the School of Law, Emory University," July 15, 1981, 30–31.

108. Olin Grant Proposal Record (for Olin Fellowship Program), Olin Foundation Archives, September 25, 1980.

109. Olin Foundation, "A Report on the Law and Economics Program at Emory University," Olin Foundation Archives, 1983, 1.

110. Manne interview.

111. Olin Foundation, "Report on the Law and Economics Program," 1.

112. Manne interview.

113. James T. Laney to Henry Manne, May 3, 1982.

114. Henry Manne to John M. Olin, May 17, 1982.

115. Ibid.

116. F. Stuart Gulley, *The Academic President as Moral Leader: James T. Laney at Emory University, 1977–1993* (Macon, Ga.: Mercer University Press, 2001), 174.

117. Ibid., 42.

118. Lewis Rockwell to Henry Manne, March 31, 1982.

119. Memo from Roger Miller, "Re: Location of LEC Building," no date, attached to March 31, 1982 letter from Lewis Rockwell.

120. Henry Manne to Michael Joyce, May 5, 1982.

121. Olin Foundation, "Report on the Law and Economics Program," 2.

122. Ibid., 2.

123. Ibid., 2–3.

124. Piereson interview.

125. Olin Foundation, "Report on the Law and Economics Program," 3.

126. Michael Joyce to Henry Manne, December 1, 1982.

127. James Laney to Henry Manne, December 10, 1982.

128. Minutes of the Meeting of the Executive Committee of the John M. Olin Foundation, Olin Foundation Archives, March 31, 1983.

129. "Statement of Purpose: Chattahoochee Institute," attached to letter from Manne to Jim Cowart, May 17, 1983.

130. Expanded activities come from document titled "New Institute," attached to letter of April 25, 1983.

131. William Rosett to Henry Manne, May 24, 1983.

132. John Miller, *A Gift of Freedom: How the John M. Olin Foundation Changed America* (New York: Encounter, 2005), chapter 3.

133. Olin Grant Proposal Record (for Economics Institute for Federal Judges), Olin Foundation Archives, November 1, 1985.

134. Manne interview.

Chapter 5
The Federalist Society: Counter-Networking

1. See, for example, People for the American Way, *The Federalist Society: From Obscurity to Power*, http://www.pfaw.org/pfaw/dfiles/file_4.pdf, August 2001; Institute for Democracy Studies, *The Federalist Society and the Challenge to a Democratic Jurisprudence*, January 2001.

2. The Society typically presents itself as an organization of "conservatives and libertarians," which describes their programs and membership accurately. For the sake of felicity of expression, I will simply use the term *conservative* to describe the Society's ideas, except where the distinction is relevant.

3. David Brock, *Blinded by the Right: The Conscience of an Ex-Conservative* (New York: Crown, 2002).

4. "Proposal for a Symposium on the Legal Ramifications of the New Federalism," Federalist Society Archives, 1982, 1.

5. Ibid., 5

6. Ibid., 2.

7. Lee S. Liberman to Richard Larry, August 29, 1982.

8. "Proposal To Form a National Conservative Legal Organization," Federalist Society Archives, October 15, 1982.

9. Ibid.

10. Ibid.

11. Eugene Meyer to Richard Larry (Scaife Family Charitable Trusts), October 25, 1983. It would be a mistake to assume that the prominence of these placement activities reflects their importance to the Society's leaders. Rather, they were emphasized because the impact of the majority of the Society's activities were, as the letter notes, "difficult to measure accurately."

12. Eugene Meyer is the son of Frank Meyer, who, as an editor at *National Review*, took the lead in meshing tradition and liberty into conservative "fusionism."

13. Hicks, "Conservative Influence," 650; Otis interview.

14. Otis interview. The Institute for Educational Affairs was started by Irving Kristol to funnel corporate money into conservative organizations. While IEA was not an overwhelming success, its support for the Federalist Society was a notable exception.

15. Michael Horowitz was general counsel to the Office of Management and Budget between 1981 and 1985. Today, he is a senior fellow at the Hudson Institute.

16. McIntosh had founded the Chicago chapter of the Society along with Lee Liberman Otis.

17. Cribb interview.

18. An excellent study of the Reagan administration's view of the permanent bureaucracy, especially in the Department of Justice, is Marissa Martino Golden, *What Motivates Bureaucrats? Politics and Administration During the Reagan Administration* (New York: Columbia University Press, 2000).

19. I am indebted to Todd Zywicki for this insight.

20. Sidney Blumenthal, "Quest for Lasting Power: A New Generation is Being Nurtured To Carry the Banner for the Right," *Washington Post*, September 25, 1985.

21. "How To Form a Conservative Law Student Group," Chicago Federalist Society, Harvard Society for Law and Public Policy, Stanford Foundation for Law and Economic Policy, Yale Federalist Society, and the Leadership Institute, 1982, 3.

22. Ibid., 4.

23. Ibid., 7.

24. As we shall see later, the Society created institutional mechanisms, such as the absence of elections for national leadership, that also helped to dampen factional conflict.

25. "How to Form a Conservative Law Student Group," 4.

26. McIntosh interview.

27. The debate between original intent and original meaning focuses on whether fidelity to the Constitution requires judges to deduce the intention of the framers of a particular provision, or whether attention should be focused solely on the meaning of the terms at the time that it was passed.

28. Recall that *Nollan* was the breakthrough takings case of the Pacific Legal Foundation, discussed in chapter 3.

29. Hugh Heclo, *A Government of Strangers: Executive Politics in Washington* (Washington, D.C.: Brookings, 1977).

30. Federalist Society for Law and Public Policy Studies, Form 990, 1983–2000.

31. The source for the Student and Lawyer Chapters, 1996–2001 is the "Federalist Society Annual Reports, 1995–2001." The 1993 data is taken from "December 7, 1993 Trustee Meeting Briefing Materials," Federalist Society. Data for 1988, 1991, 1994, and 1995 are rough estimates taken from the same document.

32. Meyer interview.

33. Figures taken from "Campaign for the Federalist Society," Federalist Society Archives, 1997, 14.

34. The decline in the Society's membership in 2002 was driven by a sharp drop in its programming in law schools (which are its primary mechanism of campus recruitment) due to speakers' reluctance to fly in the wake of the 9/11 attacks.

35. A number of one-half travel stipends are available for travel to the annual student conference of the Society, chapter heads have their expenses covered for an annual training meeting in Washington, and fairly small honoraria are provided to speakers.

36. Otis interview.

37. Eugene Meyer to Michael Joyce, August 20, 1984.

38. Meyer interview.

39. Eugene Meyer to James Capua, Institute for Educational Affairs, October 21, 1983. The specific figures were $30,000 from IEA, $36,000 from the Olin Foundation, $2,500 from the Intercollegiate Studies Institute, $15,000 from the JM Foundation, and $15,000 from the Sarah Scaife Foundation.

40. Miller, *A Gift of Freedom*.

41. Lee Liberman Otis to E. Spencer Abraham, March 6, 1985.

42. "Development Board for Federalist Society," Federalist Society Archives, February 1988. Hatch's name comes up repeatedly in fund-raising memos, as well as in fund-raising letters sent out by the Society under his name. Along with Robert Bork, he appears to be the figure with the strongest and most consistent support for the Society's fund-raising activities. For example, the five-year plan indicates that Bork and Hatch were the cochairmen of the development push that helped bring the Society's budget to over a million dollars per annum. Federalist Society Board of Directors, "Five Year Plan and Development Activities, Revised and Annotated" (submitted to the Development Board), Federalist Society Archives, 1989, 7.

43. Federalist Society Board of Directors, "Five Year Plan," 5.

44. Ibid.

45. A powerful critique of the public choice approach to interest groups and social movements is Wilson, *Political Organizations*.

46. "Confirmation Hearing on the Nominations of Michael Chertoff and Viet D. Dinh to be Assistant Attorneys General," Hearing before the committee

on the Judiciary, United States Senate, 107th Cong., 1st sess., May 9, 2001, Senate Hearing 107–298.

47. Ibid., written questions submitted by Senator Patrick Leahy (D-Vt.).

48. Senator Orrin Hatch, "In Defense of the Federalist Society," 108th Cong., 1st sess., *Congressional Record* (January 9, 2003). S120-3.

49. For the distinction between civil and enterprise association, see Michael Oakeshott, *On Human Conduct* (Oxford: Oxford University Press, 1975). For the need to find a balance between these poles, see Michael Oakeshott, *The Politics of Faith and the Politics of Skepticism* (New Haven: Yale University Press, 1996).

50. "Proposal to Form a National Conservative Legal Organization."

51. Irving Kristol to Eugene Meyer, October 3, 1985. Just a few months earlier the idea was referred to in a letter from Eugene Meyer to Mr. Tom Bell, Simpson, Thatcher and Bartlett, July 19, 1985.

52. "The Federalist Society Litigation Center," Federalist Society Archives, summer 1985.

53. "Federalist Society Litigation Center: Status Report," Federalist Society Archives, May 5, 1986.

54. "Federalist Society Litigation Task Force," Federalist Society Archives, date uncertain, 1985–86.

55. Confidential letter to Eugene Meyer, name and date redacted.

56. Meyer interview.

57. Federalist Society, Grant Proposal to the Brady Foundation, Pro Bono Populi Center, Executive Summary, 3.

58. Federalist Society, "Pro-Bono Activity at the AmLaw100," 2003, http://www.fed-soc.org/resources/id.45/default.asp.

59. Federalist Society, Pro Bono Populi Center proposal.

60. Ibid., 2.

61. Eugene Meyer estimates that it was from 1983 or 1984.

62. "Federalist Society Recommendation and Evaluation of Judges," Federalist Society Archives, 1983–84.

63. Confidential interview.

64. Sekulow is chief counsel at the American Center for Law and Justice.

65. David D. Kirkpatrick, "In Alito, GOP Reaps Harvest Planted in 1982," *New York Times*, January 30, 2006.

66. Meyer interview.

67. Jeanne Cummings, "Point Man For Miers Juggles Allegiances," *Wall Street Journal*, October 26, 2005, A4.

68. Minutes, Federalist Society for Law and Public Policy Studies, Organizational Meeting, July 31, 1982, Westpark Hotel, Rosslyn, Va., Item 3.

69. Theda Skocpol, "Associations Without Members," *American Prospect* 10, no. 45 (1999), www.prospect.org/print/V10//45/skocpol-t.html.

70. Francesca Polletta, *Freedom Is an Endless Meeting: Democracy in American Social Movements* (Chicago: University of Chicago Press, 2002).

71. Jo Freeman, "Crises and Conflicts in Social Movement Organizations," *Chrysalis* 5 (1978): 43–51.

72. Meyer interview.

73. The remarkable density of the Federalist Society's networks is demonstrated in Anthony Paik, Ann Southworth, and John Heinz, "Lawyers of the Right: Networks and Organization," Case Western Reserve University School of Law Legal Studies Research Paper No. 06-10, May 2006, http://papers.ssrn.com/sol3/papers.cfm?abstract_id=903326.

74. Dinesh D'Souza, *Letters to a Young Conservative* (New York: Basic Books, 2002), 33–34.

75. On this point, consider a very early (August 20, 1984) letter from Eugene Meyer to Michael Joyce of the Bradley Foundation, where he notes that, despite the critical need to engage practicing lawyers for financial purposes, "we are convinced that it is best to direct our efforts to involve the legal community as a whole more toward the educational rather than the networking aspects."

76. Society networks also increase the probability that conservatives can identify other conservatives in the employment process, through the increasing the number of "weak ties" within the movement. On the importance of weak ties in employment, see Granovetter, "Strength of Weak Ties."

77. Behavioral research has shown that discussions in groups organized on ideological lines tends to produce greater polarization. See, for example, Cass R. Sunstein, "Deliberative Trouble: Why Groups Go to Extremes," *Yale Law Journal* 110, no. 1 (2000): 92–94. This suggests that the Society and its liberal sister, the American Constitution Society, do not simply reflect ideological polarization, but may help to accelerate it by increasing the frequency of personal interactions in ideologically homogeneous settings.

78. One way of thinking about stigma is that it is the opposite of what Bourdieu has called "distinction." Reducing stigma is, consequently, a critical contribution to building up the cultural capital of the movement. This concept is discussed in greater detail in chapter 1.

79. This was true in the Society's early years, one example of which is Russell Van Patten, then-head of the Yale Federalist Society, who noted back in 1986 that "there are a lot of closet Federalists." Jill Abramson, "Right Place at the Right Time," *American Lawyer*, June 1986, 99.

80. See chapter 6.

81. "Three Year Expansion Plan for the Development of the Federalist Society Into An Effective National Conservative Legal Organization," Federalist Society Archives, 1984.

82. On the idea of preference falsification, see Timur Kuran, *Private Truths, Public Lies: The Social Consequences of Preference Falsification* (Cambridge: Harvard University Press, 1995).

83. IJ's state chapters are discussed in greater detail in chapter 7.

84. Where the Society has been less effective has been in convincing conservative lawyers that ideologically informed pro bono activity is a professional obligation. The consequences of this are discussed in greater detail in chapter 7.

85. "Federalist Society General Proposal, 1983–1984," Federalist Society Archives, 6.

86. "Three Year Expansion Plan," 2.

87. Ibid., 4.

88. Thomas P. Main to Eugene Meyer, January 3, 1984. Meyer responded to this letter by noting that "it is very likely that a majority of the ABA's membership is to the right of the leadership and staff which are primarily responsible for the organization's public opinions. This also explains why the ABA's political bias is not as well known as it should be. I think this subject is worth a small monograph . . ." Eugene Meyer to Thomas Main, January 23, 1984. After the defeat of the Bork nomination, the Society would begin to increase its watchdog role vis-à-vis the ABA well beyond a "small monograph."

89. "Federalist Society General Proposal, 1984–1985," Federalist Society Archives, 6.

90. "From the Editors," *ABA Watch* 1, no. 1 (August 1996): 2. http://www.fed-soc.org/Publications/ABAwatch/August1996/editors.htm.

91. Calabresi clerked for Bork on the D.C. Circuit and helped him write *The Tempting of America* (New York: Free Press, 1997).

92. "Development Planning Meeting, October 4, 1990," attached document entitled, "Trustee Action Status (as of 10/03/90)," Federalist Society Archives.

93. For example, "1991 Development Projects Discussion and Timetable" in the Federalist Society Archives mentions the effectiveness of Judge Bork in the area of direct mail, signifying Bork's usefulness in rallying support for the Society among the broader conservative movement.

94. The full list of practice groups includes administrative law, civil rights, corporations, criminal law and procedure, environmental law and property rights, federalism and separation of powers, financial services and e-commerce, free speech and election law, intellectual property, international and national security law, labor and employment law, litigation, professional responsibility, religious liberties, and telecommunications.

95. Eugene Meyer to Kristen Avansino, E. L. Wiegand Foundation, July 28, 1995, 1–2.

96. Ibid.

97. Federalist Society, "Interim Report on the E.L. Wiegand Practice Groups," Federalist Society Archives. This report was submitted to Kristen Avansino by Eugene Meyer.

98. Ibid.

99. There is also a program of Olin Fellows in Law and Economics, which is administered directly by the Olin programs in law and economics at individual law schools.

100. "Proposal to the John M. Olin Foundation Inc. for the John M. Olin Fellows in Law for the 2000–2001 Academic Year," Federalist Society Archives, March 15, 1999, 3.

101. Ibid.

102. This is discussed in greater detail, in the case of law and economics, in chapter 6.

103. Anne Schneider-Mayerson, "Harvard Law on a Heterodox Spree, Listing to the Right," *New York Observer*, December 5, 2005, http://www.observer.com/printpage.asp?iid=11980&ic=News+Story+3, accessed December 17, 2005.

104. Confidential interview.

105. Confidential interview.

106. Moore interview.

107. See Steven Teles, "Conservative Counter-Mobilization and the Modern Administrative State," in *Transformations of American Politics*, ed. Paul Pierson and Theda Skocpol (Princeton: Princeton University Press, 2007).

108. For a concise study of this success, see Steven Teles and Timothy Prinz, "The Politics of Rights Retraction: Welfare Reform From Entitlement to Block Grants," in Levin, Landy, and Shapiro, *Seeking the Center.*

109. An insightful argument for the benign influence of this movement is John Judis, *The Paradox of American Democracy: Elites, Special Interests and the Betrayal of the Public Trust* (New York: Pantheon, 2000), while a useful history of this establishment is Kabaservice, *The Guardians.*

Chapter 6
Law and Economics II: Institutionalization

1. Morton Horwitz, "Law and Economics: Science or Politics?" *Hofstra Law Review* 8, no. 4 (1980): 905.

2. As noted in chapter 1, the concept of an idea being "on" or "off the wall" comes from Jack Balkin, "*Bush v. Gore* and the Boundary Between Law and Politics," *Yale Law Journal* 110, no. 8 (2001): 1407–58.

3. Survey evidence shows that economists are not, in any simple way, more "conservative" than the general public—there are about as many questions where economists are more liberal than the public than where they are more conservative. The distinctions come in the composition of economists' attitudes. Caplan finds that, compared to the general public, economists "are even less worried about high profits, executive pay, and downsizing, and are more likely to see both downsizing and current economic disturbances as good on the whole. Economists are also much more likely to accept a supply-and-demand explanation for the gas price rise, and have more optimistic views of the quality of new jobs, and the growth of real incomes and wages over the past 20 years. . . . [On the other hand, they] worry even less about foreign aid, immigration, welfare, affirmative action, and the work ethic. . . . Economists also have left-leaning perspectives on high taxes, tax cuts, and female labor force participation, and right-leaning perspectives on tax breaks, business investment in the workforce, and families' need for two incomes." Bryan Caplan, "What Makes People Think Like Economists? Evidence on Economic Cognition from the 'Survey of Americans and Economists on the Economy,' " *Journal of Law and Economics* 44, no. 2 (2001): 414. To the degree that "lawyer-economists" share the preferences of disciplinary economics, they will tend to share the social—and even redistributive—liberalism of their colleagues in the legal academy, but will differ from the markedly in their preference for market arrangement in the economy.

4. Miller, *A Gift of Freedom*, 21.

5. Donald Downs, *Cornell '69: Liberalism and the Crisis of the American University* (Ithaca, N.Y.: Cornell University Press, 1999).

6. Minutes, Board of Trustees Meeting, Olin Foundation Archives, July 5, 1979, 4.

7. Crampton interview.

8. John M. Olin to Thomas Rhodes, 1980.

9. Miller, *A Gift of Freedom*, 67.

10. Ibid.

11. Minutes of the John M. Olin Foundation Steering Committee Meeting, Olin Foundation Archives, November 25, 1981.

12. Minutes of the John M. Olin Foundation Steering Committee Meeting, Olin Foundation Archives, March 15, 1983.

13. Minutes, John M. Olin Foundation Board of Trustees Meeting, Olin Foundation Archives, March 31, 1983, 2.

14. Minutes, John M. Olin Foundation Board of Trustees Meeting, Olin Foundation Archives, January 22, 1981, 1.

15. "Report to the Trustees on the Future Direction of the Grants Program" (prepared by the Foundation Staff and reviewed by the Steering Committee), Olin Foundation Archives, November 23, 1982, 6.

16. Ibid., 24.

17. It should also be noted that in the twenty years after this report was written, the S&P 500 would increase tenfold (and this ignores the impact of dividends). In combination with the additional funds that were put into the foundation at Olin's death, his direction that all of the funds be spent in a relatively short period of time, and the relatively few existing commitments of the foundation, the resources for aggressive grant-making were substantial.

18. Olin Grant Proposal Record (for Yale Law School), Olin Foundation Archives, May 16, 2000.

19. Harvard and Yale law schools have placed more graduates in top teaching positions than all other law schools combined. Leiter Reports, "The Best Law Schools for the 'Best' Jobs in Law Teaching," http://www.leiterrankings.com/jobs/2006job_teaching.shtml.

20. Mark Tushnet, "Critical Legal Studies: A Political History," *Yale Law Journal* 100, no. 5 (1991): 1515–44.

21. David Kairys, "Law and Politics," *George Washington Law Review* 52 (1984): 243–62; Clare Dalton, "An Essay in the Deconstruction of Contract Doctrine," *Yale Law Journal* 95, no 5 (1985): 997–1114.

22. Morton Horwitz, *The Transformation of American Law, 1780–1860* (Cambridge: Harvard University Press, 1977).

23. Duncan Kennedy, "Legal Education as Training for Hierarchy," in *The Politics of Law*, ed. David Kairys (New York: Basic Books, 1982; 2nd ed., 1990; 3d ed., 1998).

24. Horwitz's PhD from Harvard was, in fact, in government.

25. Duncan Kennedy, "First Year Law Teaching as Political Action," *Law and Social Problems* 1 (1980): 47.

26. Duncan Kennedy, "Rebels from Principle: Changing the Corporate Law Firm From Within," *Harvard Law School Bulletin*, Fall 1981, 39.

27. Calvin Trillin, "A Reporter at Large: Harvard Law," *New Yorker*, March 26, 1984, 53. George Gillespie confirms that the Trillin article was very important in spurring the interest of both himself and fellow board member Richard Furlaud.

28. Minutes, John M. Olin Board of Trustees Meeting, Olin Foundation Archives, May 22, 1984.

29. Minutes, John M. Olin Board of Trustees Meeting, Olin Foundation Archives, May 31, 1984.

30. Piereson interview.

31. See, for example, his defense of the Socratic method of law teaching in Philip Areeda, "The Socratic Method," *Harvard Law Review* 109, no. 5 (1996): 911–22.

32. Minutes, John M. Olin Board of Trustees Meeting, Olin Foundation Archives, December 13, 1984.

33. Minutes, John M. Olin Board of Trustees Meeting, Olin Foundation Archives, January 17, 1985.

34. My account draws heavily on Hicks, "Conservative Influence."

35. Ibid., 674. The letter was so inflammatory that Morton Horwitz, who was originally on the CLS side of the panel with Kennedy, withdrew.

36. Ibid., 676.

37. Ibid., 684.

38. Bok is alluding in this passage to the tenure denials of Clare Dalton and David Trubek, which are considered by many to be the turning point in the fortunes of CLS at Harvard.

39. Arthur Schlesinger, *The Vital Center: The Politics of Freedom* (Boston: Houghton, Mifflin, 1949). A more recent version of the same argument can be found in Peter Beinart, *The Good Fight: Why Liberals—And Only Liberals—Can Win the War on Terror* (New York: HarperCollins, 2006).

40. Olin Grant Proposal Record, Olin Foundation Archives, October 10, 1973.

41. Robert C. Clark to William E. Simon, November 28, 1994; emphasis added.

42. Robert Cooter, "What is Law and Economics? Why Did it Succeed," lecture, Vanderbilt University, Nashville, April 28, 2006.

43. Figure 6.1 is based on data on grants to law and economics compiled by Media Transparency, and accessed at http://www.mediatransparency.org. It understates some of these sources, such as the Earhart Foundation, for which data was only available from 1995 onward. It also fails to include donations from individuals to law and economics programs.

44. They were William Baxter, Kenneth Scott, John Barton, Marc Franklin, Paul Goldstein, Mitch Polinsky, Tom Campbell, Robert Ellickson, Ronald Gilson, and Robert Mnookin, as well as the future Nobel Prize–winning economist Myron Scholes, who held a joint appointment in the school.

45. Paul Brest to James Piereson, May 26, 1987.

46. Olin Grant Proposal Record (for Stanford Law School), Olin Foundation Archives, May 23, 1996.

47. Ibid.

48. Overview of John M. Olin Grants in Law (Academic), Olin Foundation Archives, spring 2002.

49. Olin Grant Proposal Record (for Stanford Law School), Olin Foundation Archives, April 12, 2004. The Olin Foundation's terminal grant to Stanford's Law and Economics Program was $3 million.

50. Olin Grant Proposal Record (for Boalt Hall School of Law), Olin Foundation Archives, June 18, 1987.

51. Olin Grant Proposal Record (for Boalt Hall School of Law), Olin Foundation Archives, March 29, 1994.

52. See discussion of this incident in chapter 7.

53. Olin Grant Proposal Record (for Georgetown University), Olin Foundation Archives, December 21, 1993.

54. Olin Grant Proposal Record (for Columbia University School of Law), Olin Foundation Archives, March 29, 1994.

55. Williamson, who also held positions in the business school and economics department, moved to Berkeley from Penn in 1988.

56. Olin Grant Proposal Record (for Boalt Hall School of Law), Olin Foundation Archives, September 15, 1998.

57. Ibid.

58. Cooter interview.

59. One study showed that there were six Republicans as compared to thirty-six Democrats on the Boalt Hall faculty. See Daniel Klein and Andrew Western, "How Many Democrats per Republican at UC-Berkeley and Stanford? Voter Registration Data Across 23 Academic Departments," *Academic Questions*, 2004, http://www.ratio.se/pdf/wp/dk_aw_voter.pdf.

60. This point is made in greater detail in Richard Posner, "A Review of Steven Shavell's Foundations of Economic Analysis of Law," *Journal of Economic Literature* 44, no. 2 (2006): 405–14.

61. Letter from [name redacted] to James Piereson, October 31, 1990.

62. Manne interview.

63. Henry Manne, "An Intellectual History of the George Mason University School of Law," Law and Economics Center, GMU School of Law, 1993, www.law.gmu.edu/econ/history.html.

64. Admission to AALS is effectively mandatory for law schools that aspire to a national reputation. Affirmative action continues to be a major bone of contention between the GMU law school and its credentialing authorities. David Bernstein, "Affirmative Blackmail," *Wall Street Journal*, February 15, 2006.

65. Thomas Morgan, "Admission of George Mason to Membership in the Association of American Law Schools," *Case Western Reserve Law Review* 50, no. 2 (1999): 447–48.

66. Morgan, "Admission of George Mason," 450.

67. Manne to David Kennedy, Earhart Foundation, May 13, 1987.

68. Manne to Robert J. Hurley, VP and General Counsel, NL Industries, June 18, 1987.

69. Olin Grant Proposal Record (request for LEC, federal judges workshop, faculty workshops, research projects and Supreme Court Economic Review), Olin Foundation Archives, December 21, 1993.

70. Gary Becker, *The Economics of Discrimination*, 2nd ed. (Chicago: University of Chicago Press, 1971).

71. Zwycki interview.

72. Leiter's Law School Rankings, http://www.utexas.edu/law/faculty/bleiter/rankings02/faculty_quality.html; http://www.utexas.edu/law/faculty/bleiter/rankings02/citations.html; http://www.utexas.edu/law/faculty/bleiter/rankings02/books.html.

73. Ibid., http://www.utexas.edu/law/faculty/bleiter/rankings/rankings03.html.

74. Ibid., http://www.utexas.edu/law/faculty/bleiter/rankings/differences_from_USNews.html.

75. As of fall 2006.

76. Ibid., http://www.leiterrankings.com/students/2006student_quality.shtml.

77. GMU is unranked in placing law teachers, is not in the top 25 in placing students in top law firms, and did not place any clerks on the Supreme Court until the 2008 term. http://www.leiterrankings.com/jobs/2006job_teaching.shtml; http://www.calvin.edu/admin/csr/students/sullivan/law/; http://www.leiterrankings.com/jobs/1991scotus_clerks.shtml.

Chapter 7
Conservative Public Interest Law II: Lessons Learned

1. Jeremy Rabkin, *Judicial Compulsions* (New York: Basic Books, 1989).

2. *Lamprecht v. Federal Communications Commission*, 958 F.2d 382 (D.C. Cir. 1992).

3. McDonald interview.

4. Center for Individual Rights, "A Brief Description of Program Activities," 1.

5. Ibid., 2.

6. As noted earlier, Greve had studied at Cornell with Jeremy Rabkin, a student of James Q. Wilson at Havard, whose *Political Organizations* put the question of organizational maintenance at the forefront in explaining the behavior of interest groups and social movements. This same focus on organizational maintenance is present in Michael Greve, "Environmentalism and the Rule of Law: Administrative Law and Movement Politics in West Germany and the United States," PhD diss., Cornell University Department of Government, 1987.

7. CIR, "A Brief Description."

8. For a systematic study of the benefits of repeat play, see Kevin McGuire, "Repeat Players in the Supreme Court: The Role of Experienced Lawyers in Litigation Success," *Journal of Politics* 57, no. 1 (1995): 187–96.

9. McDonald interview.

10. CIR, "A Brief Description," 3.

11. Ibid., 2.

12. This strategy of "counterrights" is described in Burke, "On the Resilience of Rights."

13. CIR, "A Brief Description," 4.

14. Ibid., 5–6.

15. The Reagan administration did not just produce conservative lawyers, but also helped in the creation of conservative law firms. Both Cooper, Carvin and

Rosenthal and Wiley, Rein and Fielding were founded in the 1980s by veterans of the Reagan administration, and along with the older Gibson, Dunn and Crutcher provided a welcoming environment for lawyers interested in conservative public interest law.

16. A highly critical assessment of the libertarianism of Internet millionaires can be found in Paulina Borsook, *Cyberselfish: A Critical Romp Through the Terribly Libertarian Culture of High Tech* (New York: Public Affairs, 2000).

17. Greve interview.

18. CIR, "A Brief Description," 10–11.

19. Paul Weaver's *The Suicidal Corporation* (New York: Simon and Schuster, 1988) is a powerful statement of how some thinkers of libertarian sympathies were recognizing this insight.

20. Tushnet, *NAACP's Legal Strategy.*

21. By the "WLF–*Lamprecht* problem," McDonald is referring to the first generation's unfavorable organizational economics of taking on major, original litigation.

22. Center for Individual Rights, "Social Responsibility Project," n.d., probably late 1989.

23. Robert Kuttner, "Bleeding Heart Conservative: Jack Kemp, Caring Republican," *New Republic*, June 11, 1990.

24. "A partnership of Pepperdine University and the United States Departments of Justice and Education," Ronald Stephens, Executive Director, to Michael S. Greve, October 20, 1989.

25. While this point may seem harsh, it is not without scholarly support, such as Tracey Meares and Jeffrey Fagan, "Punishment, Deterrence and Social Control: The Paradox of Punishment in Minority Communities," March 2000, Columbia Law School, Public Working Paper No. 010. Available at http://papers.ssrn.com/sol3/papers.cfm?abstract_id=223148.

26. McDonald interview.

27. Center for Individual Rights, "A Proposal and Request for Funding" (submitted to the John M. Olin Foundation), February 1990, 3.

28. See, for example, Malcolm Feely and Edward Rubin, *Judicial Policymaking and the Modern State* (Cambridge: Cambridge University Press, 1998).

29. Further evidence that the move toward libertarianism was driven by the imperatives of American law, rather than the preferences of conservative activists, can be seen in the shifting emphasis of religious conservative public interest lawyers. Where they once focused on reviving older understandings of the establishment clause, religious conservative PILFs have shifted their energies to the free speech provisions of the First Amendment. In practice, this has led those firms to move from defending to circumscribing the authority of local governments. In the process, religious conservatives have increasingly drawn lessons from—and in many cases drawn on the precedents created by—civil libertarians. This shift is shrewdly described in Stephen Brown, *Trumping Religion: The New Christian Right, The First Amendment, and the Courts* (Tuscaloosa: University of Alabama Press, 2004).

30. McDonald interview. McGuire had been employed by the Georgetown Law Center admissions department in an administrative capacity. While working

there, he examined the files of admitted applicants, and found a substantial gap between the GPAs and LSAT scores of black and white students. He subsequently published an article in the law school paper reporting his findings, which touched off a ferocious debate, including demands for his expulsion. Ultimately, McGuire and the law school settled on a reprimand for violating a duty of nondisclosure. McGuire's account of the issue can be found in Timothy McGuire, "My Bout with Affirmative Action," *Commentary* 93 (April 1992): 50–52.

31. Michael Greve to James Piereson, April 5, 1991, 1.

32. See, for example, Jeffrey Henig, "Education Policy and the Politics of Privatization Since 1980," in Glenn and Teles, *Conservatism and American Political Development.*

33. Greve to Piereson, 2.

34. Dinesh D'Souza's bestselling *Illiberal Education* came out at the same time that CIR threw itself into the area of campus free speech.

35. Greve to Piereson, 3–4.

36. Center for Individual Rights, "A Proposal and Request For Funding" (submitted to the John M. Olin Foundation), May 6, 1991, 3.

37. Center for Individual Rights Academic Freedom Defense Fund, "Report on Activities, 1992–1993 and Request for Continued Funding," (submitted to the John M. Olin Foundation), May 18, 1993, 2–3.

38. McDonald interview.

39. Steven Balch, President, NAS, to Michael Greve, May 12, 1993, 2.

40. This legislative hesitancy is documented in John Skrentny, "Republican Efforts to End Affirmative Action: Walking a Fine Line," in *Seeking the Center,* 132–71, as well as Gary McDowell, "Affirmative Inaction: The Brock-Meese Standoff on Federal Racial Quotas," *Policy Review* 48 (Spring 1989): 32–37.

41. The case he refers to is *Adarand Constructors v. Pena,* 200 U.S. 321, 337.

42. Bolick, *Unfinished Business*; Mark Pollot, *Grand Theft and Petit Larceny: Property Rights in America* (San Francisco: PRI, 1993); Jonathan Emord, *Freedom, Technology and the First Amendment* (San Francisco: PRI, 1991). Mark Pollot's book was originally designed to be written by Gail Norton, then at the Mountain States Legal Foundation. Her participation was cut short when she was elected attorney general of Colorado, a position that served as a stepping-stone to her recent position as U.S. secretary of the interior.

43. Institute for Justice, Grant Application Letter (recipient redacted) February 10, 1992, 4.

44. Ibid.

45. Stuart Butler, *Enterprise Zones: Greenlining the Inner Cities* (New York: University Books, 1981); Walter Williams, *The State Against Blacks* (New York: McGraw Hill, 1982); Nina Easton, *Gang of Five: Leader at the Center of the Conservative Crusade* (New York: Simon and Schuster, 2000), 196.

46. Chip Mellor to James Piereson, September 2, 1994, 4.

47. Olin Grant Report on the Institute for Justice, June 16, 1992.

48. Clint Bolick, *Voucher Wars* (Washington, D.C.: Cato, 2003), 218, 219.

49. Charles Koch is the CEO and owner of Koch Industries, the largest privately held corporation in the United States. He was also a founder of the Cato

Institute in 1977, and has been the largest supporter of libertarian causes over the last thirty years.

50. Mellor interview.

51. Institute for Justice, Grant Application Letter, 1–2.

52. Ibid., 6.

53. Ibid., 2.

54. Ibid., 3.

55 *Jenkins v. Leininger* (filed in the Cook County, Ill., Circuit Court, County Department, Chancery Division, on June 10, 1992) and *Arviso v. Honig* (filed in the Los Angeles County Superior Court on June 11, 1992). IJ's detailed description of the cases can be found at http://www.ij.org/schoolchoice/chicago/backgrounder.html.

56. Olin Grant Report, June 16, 1992.

57. For example, in 2002 IJ filed suit in Arizona along the lines of its earlier suits in Chicago and Los Angeles. http://www.ij.org/schoolchoice/az_voucher_remedy/3_7_02pr.html. In this case, IJ attempted to intervene in an existing school funding case, arguing that the remedy for state constitutional violations should be vouchers rather than additional funding for the public school system.

58. Mellor interview.

59. Michael McCann, *Rights at Work* (Chicago: University of Chicago Press, 1994).

60. *Casino Reinvestment Development Authority v. Coking* (filed in Atlantic County, NJ Superior Court on December 10, 1996).

61. Mellor interview.

62. Ibid.

63. O'Connor's dissent claimed starkly, "Any property may now be taken for the benefit of another private party, but the fallout from this decision will not be random. The beneficiaries are likely to be those citizens with disproportionate influence and power in the political process, including large corporations and development firms. As for the victims, the government now has license to transfer property from those with fewer resources to those with more." 454 U.S. 469 (2005).

64. This figure is taken from Institute for Justice, "Legislative Action Since Kelo," http://www.castlecoalition.org/pdf/publications/State-Summary-Publication.pdf. Excellent studies of the post-*Kelo* backlash, and its effects on the planning process, can be found in David Cole, "Why Kelo is Not Good News for Local Planners and Developers," *Georgia State University Law Review* 22, no. 4 (2006): 803–56; Timothy Sandefur, "The 'Backlash' So Far: Will Americans Get Meaningful Eminent Domain Reform," *Michigan State Law Review* 2006, http://ssrn.com/abstract=868539; Ilya Somin, "Controlling the Grasping Hand: Economic Development Takings After *Kelo,*" *Supreme Court Economic Review* 15 (2007), http://ssrn.com/abtract=874865.

65. Mellor interview.

66. McCann, *Rights at Work,* 51. See, for example, Somin, "Controlling the Grasping Hand," Sandefur, "The 'Backlash' So Far," Ilya Somin and Jonathan Adler, "The Green Costs of Kelo: Economic Development Takings and Environ-

mental Protection," *Washington University Law Review* (forthcoming); and the symposium "The Death of Poletown: The Future of Eminent Domain and Urban Development: After County of Wayne v. Hathcock," *Michigan State Law Review* 2004, no. 4.

67. Dana Berliner, *Public Power, Private Gain: A Five-Year, State-by-State Report Examining the Abuse of Eminent Domain* (Washington, D.C.: Institute for Justice, 2003).

68. Institute for Justice, "Proposal: Strategic Research Program," October 2006.

69. McCann, *Rights at Work*.

70. This is one of the most important claims of Gerald Rosenberg, *The Hollow Hope* (Chicago: University of Chicago Press, 1993).

71. Chip Mellor, "The IJ Way," *Carry the Torch*, August 2000, http://www.ij.org/publications/torch/. IJ has since moved to new offices in Arlington, Virginia.

72. John Kramer, "A Vision to Communicate," *Liberty and Law* 5, no. 4 (1996), http://www.ij.org/publications/liberty/.

73. William Haltom and Michael McCann, *Distorting the Law: Politics, Media and the Litigation Crisis* (Chicago: University of Chicago Press, 2004).

74. Bolick, *Voucher Wars* , 110–11.

75. Ibid., 90.

76. Bolick, quoted in ibid., 110–11.

77. Bolick interview.

78. Diana Schemo, "Group Vows to Monitor Academia's Responses," *New York Times*, June 25, 2003, A2.

79. Pell interview.

80. The distinction comes from Jack Balkin and Reva Siegel, "The American Civil Rights Tradition: Anti-Classification or Anti-Subordination?" *Miami Law Review* 58 (2003): 9–33.

81. Pell was deputy assistant secretary of education from 1985 to 1988, then general counsel and chief of staff in the Office of Drug Control Policy in the George H. W. Bush administration.

82. Levin was infamous for his views on the relationship between race, IQ, and criminality, and defended the use of "statistical discrimination." For a discussion of the case, see Nathan Glazer, "Levin, Jeffries and the Fate of Academic Autonomy," *Public Interest*, Summer 1995, 14–40.

83. Ann Coulter, for example, was on the staff of CIR before carving out a career attacking liberalism.

84. Center for Individual Rights, *Docket Report*, October 1998, 8.

85. Center for Individual Rights, *Docket Report*, August 1996, 3.

86. Ibid., 7.

87. Among the many movies that place liberal lawyering at their center are *To Kill a Mockingbird, And Justice for All, A Civil Action, North Country,* and *Erin Brockovich*. It would be difficult to come up with a single film that places a lawyer for a conservative issue in the same light.

88. McDonald interview.

89. Pell interview.

90. This ordering may have been due to IJ's expectation of donor interest, rather its own sense of priorities.

91. Chip Mellor, Foundation Funding Request (specific foundation redacted), February 3, 1992, 2–3.

92. While IJ's list of those who have given $10,000 or more to the organization is publicly available, CIR's is not. In order to get a rough sense of the overlap between the two organizations' funding base while keeping CIR's donors anonymous, I presented Terry Pell of CIR with IJ's $10,000-plus list and asked him to calculate these figures.

93. http://www.ij.org/pdf_folder/financials/financial_snapshot.pdf; http://www .cir-usa.org/articles/cir_ar_2004_new.pdf.

94. Brown, *Trumping Religion*. Brown also observes that the Alliance Defense Fund has invested considerable resources in training Christian conservative lawyers, and has demanded that those who attend its programs donate a specific number of hours to public interest litigation.

95. Bolick interview.

96. Ibid.

97. Clint Bolick, "Clinton's Quota Queens," *Wall Street Journal*, April 30, 1993, A12.

98. Clint Bolick, "Civil Rights Nominee, Quota Clone," *Wall Street Journal*, February 2, 1994; Clint Bolick, "A Vote for Lee is a Vote For Preferences," *Wall Street Journal*, October 27, 1997. See also Bolick's follow-up on Patrick, Clint Bolick, "Coronation of a Quota King at Justice," *Wall Street Journal*, August 31, 1994.

99. Clint Bolick, *The Affirmative Action Fraud* (Washington, D.C.: Cato Institute, 1996).

100. Mellor interview.

101. Greve, "Environmentalism and the Rule of Law."

102. Pell interview.

103. Ibid.

104. Ibid.

105. *Mueller v. City of Boise, St. Luke's Medical Center, et al.* was a class-action suit filed against alleged violations of parents' right to direct the medical treatment of their children.

106. The classic backlash argument is Rosenberg, *The Hollow Hope*. A more recent version of the argument can be found in Michael Klarman, "Brown, Lawrence (and Goodridge)," *Michigan Law Review* 104, no. 3 (2005): 431.

107. The exception, of course, is IJ's school choice litigation, but even that defended the government authority to enact a libertarian policy.

Conclusion

1. Harold Hotelling, "Stability in Competition," *Economic Journal* 39, no. 153 (1929): 41–57; Anthony Downs, *An Economic Theory of Democracy* (New York: Harper and Row, 1957). There are other mechanisms for the production of equilibrium. For example, Reva Siegel has argued, "If the constitutional law that officials pronounce diverges too far from understandings to which American

citizens subscribed, a mobilized citizenry knows how to hold judges and the elected officials who appoint them to account." Reva Siegel, "Constitutional Culture, Social Movement Conflict and Constitutional Change: The Case of the de facto ERA," *California Law Review* 94, no. 5 (2006): 1419. In Siegel's model, mobilization and countermobilization ultimately move constitutional law back to something like the equilibrium position of public values. This assumes, however, that the challenges for the first movers and the countermobilizers are symmetric: the key point of my argument is that they are not, and it is this asymmetry that produces constitutional regimes.

2. Paul Pierson, *Politics in Time: History, Institutions and Social Analysis* (Princeton: Princeton University Press, 2004).

3. Three examples of legislative erosion are the Personal Responsibility and Work Opportunity Act of 1995, the Antiterrorism and Effective Death Penalty Act of 1996, and the Prison Litigation Reform Act of 1995.

4. Mine is an imprecise adaptation of the concept described at greatest detail in William Baumol, John Panzar, and Robert Willig, *Contestable Markets and the Theory of Industry Structure*, rev. ed. (New York: Harcourt, 1988). Baumol's account builds on, among others, Harold Demsetz, "Why Regulate Utilities?" *Journal of Law and Economics* 11, no. 1 (1968): 55–65. The most important part of these works, for my purposes, is that monopoly status is consistent with vulnerability to competition.

5. Kathleen Thelen, "Historical Institutionalism in Comparative Politics," *Annual Review of Political Science* 2 (1999): 369–404.

6. Peter Hall and David Soskice, eds., *Varieties of Capitalism: The Institutional Foundations of Comparative Advantage* (Oxford: Oxford University Press, 2001); Paul Pierson, *Dismantling the Welfare State?* (Cambridge: Cambridge University Press, 1994).

7. Teles, "Conservative Mobilization"; Teles and Prinz, "Politics of Rights Retraction"; Teles, *Whose Welfare?*, chapter 7.

8. The phrase, and the concept behind it, come from Mancur Olson, "Distinguished Lecture on Economics in Government: Big Bills Left on the Sidewalk: Why Some Nations are Rich, and Others Poor," *Journal of Economic Perspectives* 10, no. 2 (1996): 3–24. On the importance of skill in political entrepreneurship, see Adam Sheingate, "The Terrain of the Political Entrepreneur," in *Formative Acts: Reckoning with Agency in American Politics*, ed. Stephen Skowronek and Matthew Glassman (Philadelphia: University of Pennsylvania Press, 2007).

9. The achievements, and limitations, of conservatives in these areas are discussed in detail in Glenn and Teles, *Conservatism and American Political Development*.

10. Samuel Lubell, *The Future of American Politics* (New York: Harper and Row, 1952).

11. The Democratic Party's attempt to reverse Republican's competitive advantage among the religious can be seen in the enormous efforts that have been devoted to creating a recognizable "religious Left." See, for example, Cayle Murphy and Alan Cooperman, "Religious Liberals Gain New Visibility," *Washington Post*, May 20, 2006, A1.

12. Skowronek, *The Politics Presidents Make*, chapter 8.

13. Matt Bai, "Wiring the Giant Left-Wing Conspiracy," *New York Times Magazine*, July 25, 2004. Some of the mistakes that have come from this effort to learn from conservatives are described in Ari Berman, "Big $$ for Progressive Politics," *The Nation*, October 16, 2006.

14. Skocpol, *Diminished Democracy*.

15. Clayton Christensen shows a similar pattern in the introduction of new technologies, in which "disruptive innovations" are almost always adopted by new firms, rather than by existing market leaders. Clayton Christensen, *The Innovator's Dilemma* (New York: HarperCollins, 2003).

16. The importance of learning from failure in philanthropy is discussed in depth in Peter Frumkin, *Strategic Philanthropy: The Art and Science of Philanthropy* (Chicago: University of Chicago Press, 2006).

17. The distinction between "anticlassification" and "antisubordination" is laid out in Balkin and Siegel, "American Civil Rights Tradition."

Index

PRINCETON STUDIES IN AMERICAN POLITICS

Historical, International, and Comparative Perspectives

Ira Katznelson, Martin Shefter, and Theda Skocpol, Series Editors

Prisoners of Myth: The Leadership of the Tennessee Valley Authority, 1933–1990 *by Erwin C. Hargrove*

Political Parties and the State: The American Historical Experience *by Martin Shefter*

Politics and Industrialization: Early Railroads in the United States and Prussia *by Colleen A. Dunlavy*

The Lincoln Persuasion: Remaking American Liberalism *by J. David Greenstone*

Labor Visions and State Power: The Origins of Business Unionism in the United States *by Victoria C. Hattam*